WOMAN'S VOICE,
WOMAN'S PLACE

Lucy Stone, ca. 1856 (Library of Congress, Manuscript Division, Blackwell Family Papers)

WOMAN'S VOICE, WOMAN'S PLACE

Lucy Stone and the Birth of the Woman's Rights Movement

Joelle Million

Westport, Connecticut
London

Library of Congress Cataloging-in-Publication Data

Million, Joelle
   Woman's voice, woman's place : Lucy Stone and the birth of the woman's rights
movement / by Joelle Million.
     p. cm.
   Includes bibliographical references and index.
   ISBN 0–275–97877–X (alk. paper)
     1. Stone, Lucy, 1818–1893.   2. Suffragists—United States—Biography.
   3. Women's rights—United States—History—19th century.   I. Title.
   JK1899.S8M545   2003
   324.6'23'092—dc21
   [B]   2002044981

British Library Cataloguing in Publication Data is available.

Library of Congress Catalog Card Number: 2002044981
ISBN: 0-275-97877-X (alk. paper)

First published in 2003

Praeger Publishers, 88 Post Road West, Westport, CT 06881
An imprint of Greenwood Publishing Group, Inc.
www.praeger.com

Printed in the United States of America

∞™

The paper used in this book complies with the
Permanent Paper Standard issued by the National
Information Standards Organization (Z39.48–1984).

10 9 8 7 6 5 4 3 2 1

Contents

Acknowledgments

During the many years I worked on this project, I was aided by family, friends, colleagues, acquaintances, and strangers, and I thank them all. I am especially grateful to Peter Jarnstrom, director of interlibrary loan at Minnesota State University, Mankato, who tirelessly helped me secure materials, and to my mother, Katherine Million, who accompanied me on my first research trip and served as scribe when fragile documents could not be photocopied. Roberta Zonghi and Giuseppe Bisaccia of the Boston Public Library and Gertrude Jacob and Emily Epstein of the Oberlin College Special Collections were especially helpful. I am indebted to the staffs of other libraries for their help in securing documents and facilitating my research: Vassar College Library, the Massachusetts Historical Society, the Arthur and Elizabeth Schlesinger Library at Radcliffe Institute, the Houghton Library at Harvard University, the American Antiquarian Society, the Worcester Historical Museum, Smith College Library, the Illinois Historical Society, and the Vernon County Historical Society in Viroqua, Wisconsin. And heartfelt thanks go to the dozens of librarians and archivists across the country, too numerous to name, who generously answered mail inquiries and provided photocopies of requested materials.

The late Arthur B. Jay introduced me to West Brookfield and provided much information about Lucy Stone's hometown. Thomas Sturrock provided material about his great-great-grandmother, Hannah Tracy Cutler. John Blackwell, Stone's great-grandnephew, was a much-appreciated source of support and encouragement. Marlene Merrill, coeditor of the correspondence between Stone and Antoinette Brown Blackwell, offered much helpful advice, served as a sounding board for hunches and interpretations, and read both an early draft and the final version of the manuscript. She also led me to the 1853 travel book account of Stone's "pay strike" at Oberlin College. Leslie Wheeler, editor of the correspondence between Stone and her husband, helped me clarify their financial dealings and evaluate the nature of their relationship. Melodie Andrews, associate professor of history at Minnesota State University, Mankato, edited another version of this material. W. J. Woodin Jr. and Margaret Hallowell Titus gave permission to publish the photograph of their great-grandfather, Thomas Wentworth Higginson. To all of these, my most heartfelt thanks.

I am grateful for the support of my children, Tad and Sara Runkle, who shared their mother with Lucy Stone for many of their growing-up years, and of my husband and best friend, Johannes Postma, whose encouragement helped bring this project to completion.

Introduction: "Shall Woman's Voice Be Hushed?"

During the decade before America's Civil War, Lucy Stone was one of the nation's best-known orators. In a day when public speaking was a primary medium of entertainment and instruction and the spoken word rivaled the written word in spreading ideas and shaping public opinion, she was famous for an eloquence and persuasive power reputed to "win all who once hear[d] the sound of her voice."[1] More than any other individual, she opened the world of public speaking to women and secured their access to the public ear.

Presenting Stone to a national gathering of abolitionists in 1856, William Lloyd Garrison quoted lines he had used twenty-four years earlier when he asked women to help abolish American slavery and sparked a nationwide controversy about woman's place in society:

Shall we behold unheeding,
Life's holiest feelings crushed,
When woman's heart is bleeding,
Shall woman's voice be hushed?[2]

Less about female oratory than female involvement in public affairs, the question challenged a prevailing social ethic that decreed separate spheres of action and influence for the sexes and limited woman's sphere to home and private life. The controversy led Stone to undertake a deliberate crusade to change attitudes, customs, and laws concerning women. By 1856, when Garrison alluded to her as "woman's voice," she had been waging her campaign for ten years, lecturing to vast crowds across the country and inspiring women to knock on doors closed against them. She had helped create a formal woman's rights movement embodied in the National Woman's Rights Convention, spearheaded petitioning for women's equal legal and political rights, and become the first person to appeal for those rights before a body of lawmakers. When she married Henry Blackwell in 1855, they made a public protest against laws that gave a husband superior rights over his wife's property and person and Blackwell pledged never to avail himself of those rights. Labeled a "woman's rights marriage," the Stone-Blackwell ceremony became a model for other reform couples. And Stone claimed her right to individuality and autonomy by rejecting the custom of taking her husband's name and retaining her birth name instead.

In the spring of 1856, when Garrison asked again, "Shall woman's voice be hushed?" and presented Lucy Stone as an answer, she embodied all the levels of meaning that question suggested. As an orator, she symbolized the right, ability, and desire of women to exercise a public voice. As an organizer of suffrage petition drives, she represented the demand that women be given a voice in their government. And as the principal spokesperson of the woman's rights movement, she was the voice of American women demanding equal rights with men.

Part One
The Making of a Reformer

2

Learning Woman's Lot

Through both her father and her mother, Lucy Stone came from families that had been in Massachusetts since the mid-seventeenth century.[1] Francis Stone and Hannah Matthews, both born in New Braintree in 1779, were heirs to the religious beliefs and social values of their Puritan forebears, but having grown up during America's post-Revolutionary decades, they reflected two distinctly different sides of the New England culture into which Lucy was born.

Although Enlightenment ideas from Europe fueled the egalitarian fervor of America's Revolutionary War, they also spread a rationalism that undermined traditional religious beliefs and weakened allegiance to organized religion. The religious mood after the war was one not merely of apathy, but of active contempt. Rowdy gangs broke up worship services and jeered clergymen, previously the nation's most revered leaders. Accompanying a decline in church membership and attendance was a loosening of church-enforced social mores, nowhere more evident than in attitudes toward drunkenness. Although colonial New Englanders had frowned on excessive drinking and public intoxication, their post-Revolutionary descendants not only tolerated it, but condoned and expected it. Social visits began and ended with drink, marriages and funerals became occasions of public drunkenness, and workers took their wages partly in whiskey or rum. Between 1792 and 1810 registered distilleries increased from twenty-five hundred to over fourteen thousand and consumption of alcohol tripled. With the increase in drinking came an increase in vagrancy, prostitution, and neglect and abuse of families.[2]

Hannah Matthews was a faithful adherent to their religious heritage, while Francis Stone rejected it. She was a member of the Brookfield Congregational Church; he was one of the vast majority of America's "unchurched." Pious and serious, Hannah attended faithfully to her prayers and Scripture reading and earnestly cultivated her spiritual life, while Francis, an outgoing, gregarious man, spent his leisure time socializing with friends. He paid his hired hands with rum, several of his close friends were habitual drunkards, and he himself

frequently overindulged. A practical man who abhorred pretenses, a prankster
with a lively sense of humor, he was popular in the community and affection-
ately called "Captain Frank" by those who had known his father, a captain in
the Revolutionary War and a local hero for his role in Shays's Rebellion.[3]

Along with his older brother, Calvin, Francis had inherited a farm and tannery in New Braintree when their father died in 1802, and he married Hannah
Matthews, daughter of Solomon Matthews and Lydia Bowman, the following
year. In addition to their growing families, the brothers supported their mother
until her death in 1808 and two half sisters, Sarah Barr, who had been abandoned by her husband, and Amy, who had never married. When the tannery
could not support both families, Francis bought a farm ten miles away on the
eastern slope of Coy's Hill, in an area that would later become West Brookfield.
He moved his family into its large two-and-one-half-story farmhouse in the
spring of 1817. There, on August 13, 1818, Hannah gave birth to a daughter
she named Lucy. Although the eighth of nine children, Lucy joined only five
siblings, for her parents had already buried two sons. Greeting her birth were
eleven-year-old Frank, third in the line of Francis Stones; Elizabeth Matthews,
nine; seven-year-old William Bowman, whom the family called Bo; four-year-
old Rhoda; and Luther, not yet two. Also present was Sarah Barr, "Aunt Sally"
to the children, who had moved with Francis while Amy stayed with Calvin.
When Lucy was three she was joined by another sister, Sarah.

Although farm life was hard work for the entire family, it provided a life
that Lucy recalled years later as "opulent." The Stones lived simply, with no
rugs or curtains, but with all the food they wanted. Their cheese room stored
up to two hundred cheeses at a time, their cellar was always filled with barrels
of meat and fruit, and they had more honey, fresh eggs, milk, cream, and butter
than they could use. They traded produce for the few store-bought goods they
needed and often drove to Worcester, thirty miles away, to sell wool and surplus
goods for cash.

In Lucy's eyes, the family was wealthy, and that wealth belonged to each
member of the family, for each helped produce it. While Francis worked the
fields and Hannah tended house, Aunt Sally did the family's knitting and the
children helped according to their ability. One of Lucy's earliest jobs was sitting
on the floor beneath her mother's loom, handing up threads as they were
needed. When she was about five or six, she dropped corn and pumpkin seed
into holes dug by Frank and Bo. Because Lucy and Luther were near in age,
they often shared chores. Together they filled the wood boxes beside the fire-
places and drove cattle to pasture before sunrise. When a little older, Lucy
joined her sisters doing piecework for the regional shoe industry, and their
income helped pay for goods the family bought at the village store.[4]

Despite their many chores, the children were free to do as they pleased most
of the day, and Lucy was forever on the go, jumping rope with her pet lamb,
roaming through the pastures and woods, and climbing trees. Luther was her
companion and cohort, but Lucy usually took the lead. She was spunky and

high-spirited, adventurous and bold, and he rather timid and easily frightened. When they came upon a snake during their rambling, it was Lucy who seized a rock and killed it. When a neighbor's bull threatened the herd of cattle they drove to pasture, Luther cowered while Lucy defiantly set their dog after it.[5]

On long winter evenings, the children popped corn or roasted apples before the hearth while their father told stories and passed a quart mug of cider for all to sip. In the corner next to the brick oven sat Aunt Sally, then in her sixties, her head bobbing over her knitting. Often present was one or more of three former schoolmates of Lucy's father: Darius Dodge, Jim Clark, and "old Smith." These men were habitual drunkards, with no regular employment and few friends. They showed up when down on their luck, and because Francis never turned them away, their frequent and prolonged stays made them almost part of the family. The circle included hired hands as well, and often a neighbor or two, such as the blacksmith Lamberton.[6]

Lucy was lulled to sleep by her mother's voice rising in prayer from the parlor below. Like many New England women of her day, Hannah Stone was her family's religious leader. Although in colonial times the father usually served as the family's spiritual head, by the early 1800s this role had passed to women, mainly by default. During the decades of religious decline, it was primarily the women who remained faithful and comprised the bulk of church membership. And during the religious revival historians call the Second Great Awakening, which reached New England in the 1810s, female converts out-numbered male converts three to two. Traveling in the United States in the 1830s, English novelist Frances Trollope said she had never seen a land "where religion had so strong a hold upon the women, or a slighter hold upon the men." Ministers looked to women to preserve religion in their families and to help redeem their menfolk. "We look to you, ladies, to raise the standard of character in our own sex," appealed one Massachusetts clergyman in 1810. "We look to you for the continuance of domestick purity, for the revival of domestick religion, for the increase of our charities, and the support of what remains of religion in our private habits and publick institutions."[7]

During the early 1800s, New England's Congregational ministers waged a vigorous campaign to restore religion in the lives of the people, and they en-listed women like Hannah Stone to support and assist their efforts. Theirs was a two-pronged effort: reclaiming those who had strayed and stopping the spread of Unitarianism. This movement—which advocated the use of reason over unquestioning faith and rejected many traditional doctrines—had gained so much influence within the Congregational Church that when it broke off and formally organized the Unitarian Association, it took 125 churches with it. To counter the growing threat, orthodox ministers mounted an intense out-reach program that took religion to people out of touch with the church instead of ministering only to those who came to it. Having lost Harvard to Unitarians, they established orthodox theological seminaries at Andover, Massachusetts, and Bangor, Maine, and a network of local societies to help subsidize the faculty

and students. They established new churches to replace those lost in Boston
and other Unitarian strongholds, and mission boards to provide ministers for
churchless parishes. Joining with other denominations intent on rekindling
religious interest, they established tract societies to print low-cost, popularly
written pamphlets and a network of local auxiliaries to purchase and distribute
them. They founded religious newspapers and Bible societies to spread and
sustain religion where churches and ministers were scarce, and to compensate
for the neglect of religious training in the home, they established Sunday
schools to provide weekly religious instruction to children.[8] In all of this work,
the clergy looked to the women of their congregations for support and assistance. They urged women to form auxiliaries to the various ministerial associations and to raise funds for the printing and distribution of Bibles and tracts
and for the support of missionaries, faculty, and theological students. Across
New England, women met in prayer and sewing circles to advance the work
of their ministers. And in their homes, they used their influence "for the revival
of domestick religion" and "to raise the standard of character" in the male sex.

So it was Hannah Stone who provided the religious training and example of
piety for her family. She oversaw the children's Bible study and prayer and
trained them to search for God's truth in their own consciences. Through her
domestic influence, she tried to redeem her husband and his wayward friends.
Hannah had known her husband's friends in their youth and was pained by
the course their lives had taken. Once Lucy overheard her talking to Dodge,
reminding him of what a good scholar he had been and what promise he had
shown, and urging him to reform and be a man equal to his potential. But with
tears running down his cheeks, he stammered despairingly that he was worth
no more than a pig in her barnyard. Alcoholism was not then recognized as
addiction or illness; it was behavior willfully chosen. Congregational ministers
taught that those who had God's grace within them strove to live according to
his truths out of a sense of moral duty and a genuine desire to do his will. Sin
was not so much wrong conduct as the alienation from God from which wrong
conduct sprang. So Hannah believed Dodge could become a responsible man
simply by accepting God's grace and deciding to reform. But to Dodge, his
inability to do this was evidence of his innate depravity and worthlessness.[9]

With her children, too, Hannah was more concerned with developing an
inner sense of right and wrong than with instilling compliance to a set of rules,
believing that if the soul and conscience were right, behavior would be, too.
Although both she and her husband spanked their children, their primary
method of discipline was appealing to conscience. One of Lucy's earliest lessons
from her mother had to do with stewardship of nature. To console Lucy after
a particular disappointment, Aunt Sally took her to the swamp, gathered bird
eggs from the brush, blew out their insides, and threaded the empty shells into
a necklace. When they got home, though, Hannah would not let Lucy wear
the necklace, but hung it above the parlor mirror to serve as a reminder of
senseless destruction wrought for the sake of vanity.[10]

By example and precept, Hannah and Francis Stone sought to instill in their children the values of hard work, frugality, simplicity, honesty, compassion, and generosity. Lucy worked hard at being a child of God and could not bear to have her integrity doubted. While playing in trees alongside the road, she found a pair of horseshoes and took them to her father, who paid the children six cents for every good shoe they brought him. Francis doubted that shoes in perfect condition, still tied together, could have been found as his daughter claimed and accused her of stealing. He took them to blacksmith Lamberton to try to determine who their owner might be, but Lamberton said they had probably been found just as Lucy claimed. When Francis returned and held out twelve cents for Lucy, she refused the coins and stomped away deeply hurt by his distrust.[11]

Lucy was a willful and proud child, and these traits caused one of the harshest spankings she ever received. Although her partner in work and play, Luther was also her rival. When they were little and their mother taught them hymns as they carried wood, Luther received more praise and encouragement even though Lucy learned faster and better. As they grew older, it seemed to her that Luther always received preference. Feeling slighted, she tried to win her parents' approval by being and doing better than he, and became contemptuous of what she considered his major character flaw—cowardice. One evening their father told Luther to get more cider from the cellar, and Luther asked Lucy to accompany him to hold the candle. Lucy said she was not needed, but their father ordered her to go along. Once outside, however, she refused to go further. There was no need of it at all, she told Luther, for he could perfectly well set the candle on the floor while drawing the cider. Luther complained to their father, who put Lucy over his knees and spanked her soundly. Angry and obstinate, she accompanied Luther to the cellar but set the candle on the floor, proving her point that only his fear of the dark required her presence.[12]

Lucy's age at the time of this spanking—around ten or twelve, too old to be turned over her father's knees—and the fact that he used "his whole strength" made this incident unusual and memorable. Years later when Lucy and Bowman reminisced about their childhoods, Bowman recalled how "indignant" he had felt about the spanking. One of Stone's biographers, maintaining that both Lucy and her sister Sarah had "bitter memories" of their father's "harsh or abusive behavior," called this spanking a "beating" and said Bowman recalled its "brutality" and "his own shame and frustration at being unable to help." But neither Lucy, Sarah, nor Bowman ever used the term *beating* in reference to childhood punishments or described their father as abusive or mean. Sarah specifically said he was "not very harsh" and described his contrite tenderness toward her after a spanking his wife considered too severe. Corporal punishment was also used in the schools, and Lucy said one of the hardest blows she ever received—a strike to the ear with a ruler that made her head ring—was administered by a teacher.[13]

When Lucy was very young, Sarah had been the object of her jealousy. As

Lucy watched her father playing with baby Sarah on his knee, she felt robbed of his affection and resented her little sister. When they were older, Sarah became a tattletale and pest, and often goaded Lucy into losing her temper. But as Lucy matured, she began to see that her own faults—jealousy, pride, temper, "natural combativeness"—were as indicative of sin as dishonesty, drunkenness, or cowardice. Once as she angrily chased Sarah through the house, she caught a glimpse of herself in the mirror and was horrified by the reflection. This was the face of a murderer! she thought; it surely did not belong to a child of God. Contemplating her spiritual state, she resolved to subdue her pride and combative spirit and hold her tongue when angry. It was a resolution difficult to keep in a family of teasers, and she often fled to the woods to seek solace in nature.[14]

Lucy tried to emulate her older sisters, whom she greatly admired. Rhoda, just four years older than she, was an excellent scholar, her trailblazer, confidant, and support. Eliza, although not as bright as the others, was kind and selfless. Her schooling had ended shortly after Lucy's birth, and she worked with their mother in the house. When Lucy was about ten, she came home from school with a long rip in her dress, made while climbing a fence row to reach hazelnuts. She was afraid she would get a spanking, but Eliza stayed up late to mend the rip before their mother could see it. One year when the girls' shoe income exceeded expenditures at the store and their father gave them the profit, Lucy and Rhoda gave their shares to Eliza, agreeing that her hard work entitled her to it.[15]

Bowman and Frank, too, were sympathetic, kind, and protective. Frank was a tease and prankster like his father, and even though he often pinched and tormented Lucy, he was her favorite. Frank kept a watchful eye over his young sister, and whenever he saw her falling into some undesirable habit, he gently steered her aright. A pint mug of hard cider always stood at their father's place at breakfast, and young Lucy took frequent sips, growing quite fond of it, until Frank drew her aside and warned that that was how people became drunkards. Another time he heard her imitate their father's language, using the term *strumpet* in calling to a straying cow, without the slightest idea of what the word meant. Again he took her aside and explained that was not proper language, and although their father used it, she should not.[16]

As Lucy learned to trust her conscience, sometimes her inner arbiter of right condoned action others might consider wrong. She did not think it fair that the burden of her father's generosity to his shiftless friends fell on her mother. Hannah did the men's laundry and mending, fixed their meals, and cleaned up after them. Although she was always kind and solicitous of their well-being, Lucy resented the arrangement, and when the opportunity came to mete a measure of justice as she saw it, she acted. Jim Clark had come with a jug of rum, planning to stay a few days and "have a good drunk." Luther saw the jug sitting beside a stone wall where Clark had left it, and together he and Lucy plotted to break it in such a way that they could, without speaking falsehood, deny having done it. When Clark discovered the dashed jug and reported the mishap, Francis summoned the suspects before him. Luther admitted he had seen the jug and picked it up to see how much was in it. But he had set it down unharmed and not touched it since. Lucy, who, guided by Luther, had knocked a stone onto the jug from the other side of the fence, said truthfully she had not seen the jug at all and pointed out that sheep often jumped over the wall and knocked off loose stones. Although Clark insisted the children were responsible, Francis said that they were truthful and that he believed them innocent.[17]

Lucy also thought it not at all fair that her mother had no control of money. Francis refused her money of her own and usually denied requests for purchases. As a result, Hannah had resorted to taking coins from the purse under his pillow or secretly selling a cheese. It might seem like stealing, she told Lucy, but she believed she had a right to it. Once she wanted a new table cloth for company but decided not to bother asking, for she knew it would be denied. Lucy asked instead, and as Hannah expected, Francis angrily refused, declaring that a cloth good enough for family was good enough for company. Another time when Francis denied requested money, Lucy herself took a twenty-pound cheese to sell in Ware, concealing it under her cloak as she mounted a horse in full view of her father. The deception caused Lucy to feel neither guilt nor shame, but rather, a deep resentment toward her father for driving her mother to stealth to use what was rightfully hers.[18]

When Stone said, "There was only one will in our family, and that was my father's," she described family government characteristic of her day. Francis Stone ruled his family according to what he considered his duty and right. A frugal and practical manager, he spent only for what he judged worthwhile. Although as a child Lucy resented his control of family resources, she later realized that custom, rather than he himself, was to blame. When Sarah complained that his will left all the property to the boys and only $200 apiece to the girls, Lucy replied that although it was blatantly unfair, their father followed custom and did what he thought was right. It only demonstrated "the necessity of making custom right, if it must rule."[19] But this realization, which she expressed at age twenty-seven, was the result of a gradual accumulation of evidence that her father's attitudes and treatment of her mother were part of a larger, more general system of male dominance over women.

The Stones' neighbor, Lamberton, often went on drinking binges for days or weeks at a time, leaving his wife and children alone. After one prolonged absence, his pregnant wife sent word to her father to bring a wagon so she and the children could go to his home in nearby Ware. But Lamberton heard of the move, hurried to Ware, and ordered his father-in-law to turn the wagon around and return his belongings. Lucy Lamberton's father had no choice but to comply, for law upheld the husband's rights.

When Lucy Stone heard the story, she was shocked. "Can't her own father take care of her?" she asked incredulously. This incident, Stone said years later, was her first realization of the legal subjugation of women.[20] But she soon discovered that women had very few legal rights. In the early nineteenth century, a married woman had no right to property, earnings, or even control over her body. Her husband had the right to collect, use, and give away as he might choose any money or property she brought to the marriage, earned, or received by gift or bequest. Children belonged to the father, who might apprentice them or will them away from their mother without her knowledge or consent. A woman's husband had the right to physically discipline and restrain her. Over his wife, her property, and their children, the law gave a husband complete authority.

This was a revelation to Stone, but it fit the picture that was becoming increasingly apparent to her. As a young child she had been sensitive to the praise and encouragement for scholarly achievement proffered Luther but denied her. She had taken it personally, not realizing then that learning was expected of boys but not of girls. Although a common-school education was just preparation for Frank and Bo, who went on to academies and colleges, it was the sum total for Eliza and Rhoda. The boys could choose any of numerous trades or professions, but although New England's mills and homes of the wealthy provided jobs for women, they did not offer remuneration enough for self-support. Lucy and her sisters had no real choice in life except to marry and become the dependents of their husbands.

But even in marriage a woman had no control over her destiny, as Aunt Sally's life aptly demonstrated. For many years Sarah Barr had worked alongside her husband, contributing to family production while rearing two sons. But when her husband left, she had nothing. With no legal claim to any property or possessions and stripped of her function and status as a wife, she was forced to become a dependent of her brothers. Among Lucy's memories of Aunt Sally were the image of her crying as she roamed over the meadows and her oft sobbed lament: "It was the cruelest thing in the world for Hugh Barr to go off and leave me."[21]

The lives of Aunt Sally, Lucy Lamberton, and her own mother, and the prospects for her sisters and herself, demonstrated how law robbed women of control over their lives and made them dependent upon the goodwill and generosity of men. Although it was law, Lucy's inner sense of justice told her it was not right. Then one day as she studied her Bible, she came upon Genesis 3:16: "Unto the woman he said, I will greatly multiply thy sorrow and thy conception; in sorrow thou shalt bring forth children; and thy desire shall be to thy husband, and he shall rule over thee." The verse, Stone later said, stabbed into her heart with such force she never forgot the pain.[22] Here, it seemed, was God's own sanction for women's subjugation. She wrestled with the meaning of the verse a long time, trying to fit it into what she had been taught about individual accountability to God. Unable to make sense of it, she asked her mother for an explanation. But Hannah knew only that, because woman had sinned first and tempted man, it was woman's duty to submit. When Lucy was born, Hannah had regretted that the baby was a girl, for she did not want it to experience the sorrow of woman's lot. Submission was not easy, Hannah assured her. But this was, indeed, her fortune, and Lucy must seek God's help, as she herself did, to maintain a submissive spirit.

As an old woman Stone still recalled the heartbreak she had felt as a young girl thinking of how God had "put women down." Feeling robbed of a birthright, she repeatedly turned to the Bible verse, trying to understand. Then a revelation came to her. "Thy desire shall be to thy *husband*, and he shall rule over thee." The verse did not apply to all women, Lucy concluded, only to wives. Women did have control over their lives, just as men did, but upon marrying, they surrendered it to their husbands. The great pain in her heart subsided as she resolved never to marry. "I will call no man my master," she vowed.[23]

Separate Spheres and Female Education

As a child of New England, Lucy Stone enjoyed educational advantages not available to girls in other parts of the country. Considering it essential that every child be able to read Scripture, her Puritan ancestors had required parents to educate their children, and towns to establish common schools. The educational system deteriorated after the Revolution, but Horace Mann's push for universal education revived and strengthened it, so that around the time of Stone's childhood, over 75 percent of New England's children attended school, compared with only 38 percent in the South.[1]

When Lucy was about twelve years old, however, her father announced that it was time she left school. Children were free to attend the common schools until they completed the primary course or reached age sixteen, whichever came first, but there was no requirement that they go that far, and girls generally did not. But after much pleading, Lucy persuaded her father to let her stay. Demonstrating that schooling would not interfere with household duties, she took over the family laundry, one of the most strenuous household tasks. In order to wash one load of clothes, fifty gallons of water had to be heated over an open fire and then poured into washtubs. Clothes were scrubbed on a washboard, rinsed, wrung, and rinsed and wrung again before being spread on bushes or wooden racks to dry in the sun. Hauling pails of water and lifting heavy, soaked garments was a backbreaking job even for grown women. For a petite twelve-year-old, it was especially hard, but Lucy did it willingly.[2]

When Lucy completed the primary course at age fourteen, her formal schooling came to a halt despite a proliferation of secondary schools in New England. A generation earlier, only the wealthy had access to education beyond the primary level. Latin grammar schools prepared their sons for college and the professions, while finishing schools prepared their daughters for attracting husbands. With the industrial revolution, however, a new middle class demanded schools that prepared young men for careers in industry and commerce rather than for college. In response, dozens of new academies offered a practical "English" course of modern languages, geography, history, and the natural sciences that attracted the daughters as well as the sons of the middle class. Then, as part of the state's drive for universal education, the Massachusetts legislature required large towns to establish public high schools for those who could not afford private academies. Because officials could not justify the expenditure of public funds on educating girls, the high schools were for boys only. Nevertheless, when Lucy Stone left the common school in 1832, enough academies admitted girls that it could be said with a measure of accuracy that there were "few branches, if any, in which boys are instructed, which are not now equally open to girls."[3]

Academies were beyond Lucy's reach, however, at least for the time being. Even if her father had been inclined to send her, he could not afford to do so. Frank and Bowman earned academy tuition by teaching in district schools, which Lucy could also do once she turned sixteen. Until then, she stayed at home and learned housekeeping. The family's mending became her responsibility, and she became an excellent seamstress.

Shortly after Lucy's sixteenth birthday, her sister Eliza married and Francis Stone began thinking of Lucy as a prospective bride. Although rather plain, she was an attractive girl, small and thin but healthy and energetic, with a glowing, rosy complexion and joyful countenance. She wore her dark brown hair short, in the style for girls of her day. Her eyes were gray and expressive, her nose was rather broad and slightly upturned, and she had a mole on her upper lip. When her father teased about her looks not attracting suitors, Lucy responded that she wished she were plainer still, for she did not wish to marry, would not have a husband for anything, and wished the mole on her lip were an inch long so as to hang down![4]

Lucy had taught at least one term in district schools by the summer of 1836 when Mary Lyon, traveling the region to raise funds for a female seminary in western Massachusetts, visited Lucy's sewing circle and introduced her to the movement for "female education." Among books promoting education for women, the most popular and widely quoted, like Thomas Gisborne's 1796 *Enquiry into the Duties of the Female Sex* and Hannah More's 1799 *Strictures on Female Education*, argued that girls needed education to enable them to better fulfill their duties as wives and mothers. Explaining that a wise Provider placed women in a different sphere from men, where their function was to contribute to the comfort of family and mold the human mind and character during early stages of development, Gisborne urged that girls be trained for these functions.[5] Although the idea that a girl needed formal schooling for her adult roles had been around at least since the Revolution, during the years of Stone's childhood it was fueled by growing popularity of a "separate spheres" ideology.

In addition to creating a middle class that demanded and could afford to pay for secondary education, industrialization removed men from the home and eliminated middle-class women's role as producer and economic partner with their husbands. Searching for purpose and meaning in their new circumstances, women seized on Gisborne's idea of separate spheres and developed a social philosophy based on the idea that God had ordained different spheres of action and influence for the sexes. The private realm of home and family were "woman's sphere," as her maternal capacities and reticent nature attested, while the public world of business and politics belonged to man, as his physical strength and competitive nature attested.[6]

Although separate spheres ideology was developed and promulgated primarily in New England, a rapidly expanding publishing industry spread it across the country with a flood of novels, magazines, and marriage, child-rearing, and housekeeping manuals. Women constituted not only the bulk of the industry's audience (about four-fifths of the reading public at mid-century) but also a large segment of its authors and editors. As a variety of writers embellished the doctrine, they developed the theory that the sexes were not only different, but opposite and complementary. Men were daring, aggressive, ambitious, and individualistic. Women were passive, submissive, dependent, and cooperative. Men were ruled by mind and reason; women, by heart and emotion. As selflessness, innocence, charity, and forbearance were ascribed to women, an interesting reversal of pre-Revolutionary attitudes occurred. Once viewed as the moral inferiors of men, their lustful and insatiable temptresses, now women were held to be more spiritual and morally pure.[7]

The new philosophy drew lines between what was masculine and feminine, imposing standards that had not existed before. Because money and money-making belonged to the masculine sphere, a womanly woman was interested in neither. She gave no thought to finances, but trusted her men to provide for her. "The love of money in a lady is calculated to destroy all that is feminine, tender, and benevolent," explained Mary Lyon. "Our men are sufficiently money-making. Let us keep our women and children from the contagion," pleaded Sarah Josepha Hale, editor of *Godey's Lady's Book*, which served for decades as an arbiter of feminine standards and conduct. Because the sex drive was now defined as a masculine trait, it could not be a feminine one, so a womanly woman cared nothing for sexual intercourse and submitted only out of wifely duty and a desire for children. Because higher education and learning were male prerogatives, intelligence and scholarly accomplishment were un-feminine. Any proper woman would recoil in shame to be considered a "strong-minded woman."[8]

Separate spheres writers denigrated politics as an arena of selfishness, competitiveness, and ambition. Because government belonged to the masculine sphere, womanly women were not interested in civic affairs or political voice, but relied on male family members to represent their interests. Because labor and employment belonged to the masculine sphere, womanly women worked only when fate robbed them of a masculine provider. Because physical exertion and strength were characteristic of men, languor, frailty, delicacy, and pallor were prized feminine traits. The nation's womanly women took to fainting en

masse and became bedridden invalids, and this was considered part of the natural order of things.

Although separate spheres ideology rationalized women's exclusion from
most areas of employment, it helped them gain access to public school teaching.
Advocates of hiring women as teachers pointed out that women were designed
for the job by God himself, divinely given the characteristics needed to superintend the development of mind and character. Advocates of educating women
used similar arguments. In promoting her seminary, Mary Lyon explained that
because "future statesmen and rulers, ministers and missionaries must come
inevitably under the molding hand of the female," she must be specially trained
to influence them in the right way. Seeking funding from the New York legislature for her female academy, Emma Willard said that just as women's character and duties differed from men's, so must their education.[9] The movement
for female education sought not to open high schools and colleges to women,
but to establish a new type of education for them alone, to prepare women for
their distinct role in society.

When Mary Lyon came to Stone's sewing circle with plans for a female
seminary in western Massachusetts, several existed in the eastern part of the
state, including Ipswitch Female Seminary, with which she had been associated
for several years. But Lyon's Mount Holyoke Female Seminary was to have
its own physical plant instead of being housed in the home of its principal, and
it was to be publicly endowed, making it financially secure and permanent
rather than dependent upon the woman who ran it. A circular sent to churches
soliciting students and funds said the seminary would be "a school for the
daughters of the church, the object of which shall be to fit them for the highest
degree of usefulness." It would be "designed to cultivate the missionary spirit
among its pupils; the feeling that they should live for God, and do something
as teachers or in such other ways as Providence may direct."[10]

Perhaps Lucy Stone had heard or read the ministers' appeal before going to
the meeting addressed by Lyon in the summer of 1836. But as she listened,
both the messenger and the message stirred her soul. Lyon was a country girl
whose father had died when she was young and whose mother had been unable
to provide for her. She had taught in district schools and worked her way
through Ashfield and Amherst academies by age twenty-seven. She was now
thirty-nine, an unmarried woman leading a noble and independent life. She
was a worthy model for Stone to emulate.

Lyon's description of the proposed seminary excited Stone. Unlike other
women's schools, which taught embroidery, drawing, dancing, French, and
manners—the ornamentals considered essential for the wives of men of wealth
and influence—Mount Holyoke would teach religion and moral philosophy,
the study of ethics and duty. And it would prepare women for teaching, their
highest and noblest calling. To keep costs low, its teachers would receive small
salaries, no more than sustenance, and its students would perform all necessary
domestic labor.

Stone resolved to attend Mount Holyoke Female Seminary and, like Lyon, become an educator of women. But she knew she must earn her way. Frank had returned from Marietta College in Ohio and was now enrolled at Bangor College in Maine. Bowman was attending Amherst College, and Luther was also continuing his schooling. They paid their expenses by teaching at district schools, supplemented by loans from their father. Lucy would have to finance her education in the same way, but with the lower compensation paid to women teachers, it would take her longer to earn or repay needed funds. Her beginning pay had been $1.00 a week at a time when male teachers got $2.75. When she substituted for Bowman the previous winter, the school committee reduced the pay, explaining that they could not give a her a man's pay. All this she contemplated as she stitched a shirt for a theological student, and suddenly the irony struck her. Besides having to work longer for an education than the young man for whom she sewed, she would have no circle of sympathizers easing her way. Setting the unfinished garment aside, she resolved that hereafter all her energy would go toward helping women.[11]

When Lucy announced her intention of attending Mount Holyoke, her father was astonished. "Is the child crazy?" he asked his wife. But Hannah Stone encouraged her daughter's desire to remain single and supported her quest for more education. And Rhoda, who was teaching in a neighboring district, urged her to get all the education she could.[12]

Mount Holyoke Female Seminary was to open in the fall of 1837. For the next year, Lucy tried to raise the sixty dollars needed for one year's tuition and board, teaching in New Braintree that fall and in North Brookfield the following spring. She also prepared for Mount Holyoke's entrance examinations. Applicants were expected to have mastered certain required texts, most of which Frank and Bowman had used and were available to her. But when she needed a particular book they did not have and asked for money to buy it, her father refused. Undaunted, she went to the woods and gathered chestnuts enough to buy the book herself. Twenty years later, at the height of her fame, she looked back on that accomplishment with "a prouder sense of triumph" than she had known since.[13]

But when Mount Holyoke opened its doors in November 1837, Stone's teaching had not given her enough money to enroll. Those who promoted the hiring of women as teachers, such as Mary Lyon, Emma Willard, and Sarah Hale, always cited low cost as a benefit to the community. "To make education universal," explained Catharine Beecher, another pioneer educator of women, "it must be at a moderate expense, and women can afford to teach for one-half, or even less, the salary which men would ask, because the female teacher has only to sustain herself; she does not look forward to the duty of supporting a family, should she marry, nor has she the ambition to amass a fortune."[14] Thus, low pay was built into women's teaching from the very beginning. Under this system, it would be some time before female pay would permit Lucy Stone the luxury of a female education.

Description: Recounting the story of America's antebellum woman's rights movement through the efforts of Lucy Stone (1818-1893), this important account differs dramatically from those that focus almost exclusively on Susan B. Anthony or Elizabeth Cady Stanton. Million examines the social forces of the 1830s and 1840s that led Stone to become a woman's reformer and her early agitation as a student at Oberlin College, including what may well be the nation's first "strike" for equal pay for women. Million chronicles not only the public side of Stone, but her personal battles as well. Considering a woman's right to self-sovereignty as the central issue of the movement, Stone tried to prove that marriage need not rob a woman of her autonomy. With Henry B. Blackwell, Stone attempted to establish a marriage of truly equal partners, in which she maintained her personal and financial independence. She worked tirelessly during the 1850s, not only as the movement's "silver-tongued" orator, but also as the organizer and manager of the National Woman's Rights Conventions, champion of coeducation, instigator of nation-wide petitioning efforts, and first person to plead for women's equal legal rights before a body of lawmakers.

The contributions of several prominent male leaders are presented, along with coverage of agitation in New England and the western states. Million also details the trials of motherhood that eventually led Stone to pass leadership of the movement to Anthony and Stanton on the eve of the Civil War.

4

Rousing Woman's Voice

Shortly before her encounter with Mary Lyon, Lucy Stone's attention had been drawn to the reform movements then exciting New England. She and Rhoda had begun taking the *New England Spectator*, a religious journal published in Boston that carried reports of various benevolent and reform organizations and promoted women's involvement in them. Although separate spheres ideology reserved public affairs for men, it also justified women's religious and benevolent labor, and many clergymen entreated women to help "redeem the sin-ruined world" by aiding reform movements.[1]

By the 1830s, women's participation in religious and charitable enterprises was a well-established tradition in New England and New York. As ministers expanded their evangelism from reviving religion to reforming society, they pulled their feminine support system with them into the larger arena. Women now bolstered not only the ministers' Bible, tract, mission, and Sunday school associations but also their education, peace, and temperance movements. Religious journals such as the *New England Spectator* urged women to serve these "holy" causes not only through maternal influence and private efforts like shunning military parades and boycotting merchants who sold alcohol but by joining reform societies, distributing tracts, and writing for reform journals. To any who questioned the propriety of women engaging in such work, ministers rejoined that if there was nothing inappropriate in a woman's joining a church and openly renouncing evil, then there was nothing inappropriate in her joining a temperance society either. In fact, the moral obligation for her to do so was the same in both cases.[2]

So it was with clerical encouragement, under the prodding and direction of their ministers, that churchwomen stretched the bounds of woman's sphere. By the 1830s, ministers and their feminine coadjutors were well on their way to restoring religion and the clergy to their former position of social authority and influence. Protestant clergymen, whose numbers nearly tripled during the next two decades, led the nation's humanitarian movements, founded and su-

perintended schools and colleges, and edited magazines and journals with immense circulations. The arbiters of society's morals, their influence exceeded
even that of the press, so although the increasingly public nature of women's
reform work raised not a few eyebrows, clerical sanction was all that was needed
to make it respectable.[3]

But women's prominent role in the movement to abolish slavery became the
straw that broke the back of society's tolerance. As opposition to antislavery
agitation mounted during the early thirties, so too did opposition to women's
public labors. By the time the Stone sisters began taking the *Spectator*, woman's
duty and right to labor publicly had become as obtrusive and controversial an
issue as the abolition question itself. At the center of both controversies was
William Lloyd Garrison, the young newspaper editor who had launched the
movement for "immediate emancipation" five years earlier.

The antislavery sentiment prevalent at the time of the American Revolution
had waned during the first decades of the nineteenth century as the nation's
economy became increasingly dependent on cotton agriculture and processing.
Unable to propose any program that would not upset the new economic order,
the few remaining antislavery societies grew disheartened and weak. Then in
1816 the American Colonization Society offered a "gradual" approach to ending slavery by purchasing slaves for resettlement in Africa. Colonization, promoted as the only practical program for freeing slaves, was embraced by
religious leaders whose churches had become increasingly lenient toward slavery. The Society of Friends (Quakers) was one of few religious sects that continued active, although modified, antislavery agitation, with Benjamin Lundy
waging a solitary campaign to persuade slaveholders to voluntarily manumit
their slaves.[4]

This was the status of antislavery activity in 1830 when Garrison, a twenty-
five-year-old journalist writing for Lundy's *Genius of Emancipation*, was con-
victed of libel for denouncing a shipper involved in the domestic slave trade.
He emerged from a Baltimore jail radicalized by efforts to silence him and on
January 1, 1831, began publishing a new antislavery journal, the *Liberator*,
based on the principle of immediate emancipation. He preached that slavery
was sin, no more excusable or tolerable than murder or theft, and that all
involved in the system were guilty of that sin: the slaveholder, to be sure, but
also the shipper, the manufacturer, the merchant, the banker, the consumer—
all who created demand for slave labor or benefited from it. And once convinced
of their sin, Garrison insisted, it was the duty of professed Christians to stop
sinning at once rather than looking for painless ways to gradually withdraw
from it. Immediate emancipation was the right of the slave and the duty of the
slaveholder. But although Garrison urged immediate action on the personal
level, he recognized it would translate to gradual abolition on the national level.
Immediate emancipation was a principle, not a strategy.[5]

Like other evangelical reformers, Garrison believed in the necessity of
"moral suasion." He maintained that slaveholders, like all sinners, must be

convinced of their sin and persuaded to renounce it, because although coercion might destroy the physical structure of slavery, it could not touch the beliefs and attitudes, the greed and prejudices that were slavery's roots. Garrison rejected physical force as a means for ending slavery, but his critics took the demand for immediate emancipation literally, believed he advocated the sudden and total freeing of all slaves, and branded him a dangerous fanatic. A bloody slave insurrection in Virginia just seven months after the *Liberator's* appearance fueled the outcry against him. A North Carolina grand jury indicted him for distributing incendiary matter, and the Georgia Legislature offered a $5,000 reward for his capture and conveyance to the state for trial.[6]

At first, Garrison did not attract a large following. Not until January 1, 1832, did twelve disciples organize the New England Anti-Slavery Society, the first group committed to the principles of immediate emancipation. Expecting protestant churches to become the motive force of the movement, Garrison tried to enlist the support of religious leaders such as Lyman Beecher, leader of the Congregational campaign against Unitarianism, who would soon take charge of a new theological seminary in Cincinnati. But Beecher considered colonization a more practical solution to the problem of slavery. Convinced that colonization distracted those who should be leading the attack on slavery, Garrison published a pamphlet accusing the American Colonization Society of serving and reinforcing the institution of slavery. Although the society's assumed aim was the gradual reduction of slavery, Garrison pointed out that it freed fewer slaves in a year than were born in America each day, and it freed only those willing to go to Africa. Pledged not to oppose or interfere with the institution of slavery, the colonization society recognized human beings as legitimate property and, in purchasing them, increased their value. The New England Anti-Slavery Society, on the other hand, recognized the common humanity of all persons, recognized blacks as fellow countrymen, and repudiated the program of expatriation. It sought not only to abolish slavery but "to improve the character and condition of the free people of color, to inform and correct public opinion in relation to their situation and rights, and obtain for them equal civil and political rights and privileges with the whites."[7]

Garrison's *Thoughts on Colonization* startled men across the nation. Campus debates contrasting colonization with the principle of immediate emancipation resulted in the formation of scores of antislavery societies. A three-week debate at Cincinnati's Lane Seminary converted almost all of the student body, southerners as well as northerners, from whom would come thirty-two of the new movement's lecturing and organizing agents. By the summer of 1833, the New England Anti-Slavery Society had dozens of affiliates and several thousand members across the country. Parliament's abolition of slavery in the British West Indies on August 1 gave the crusade a new aura of respectability and possibility. Two months later, New York City's evangelical circle headed by wealthy businessmen Lewis and Arthur Tappan, which had hesitated in forming an antislavery society because of public sentiment against the movement, organized. And two months after that, in December 1833, abolitionists from ten states met in Philadelphia and formed the American Anti-Slavery Society.

Slave interests responded to the antislavery societies' appeals and petitions with a spate of books and pamphlets defending slavery as a legitimate, historical institution. Quoting the Bible to sustain their positions, church conferences in slave states appealed to northern churches not to countenance the new movement. Swayed by these appeals, many free-state clerics actively opposed the abolition movement and its leaders. Southerners became boldly aggressive in seeking to suppress antislavery agitation. When the American Anti-Slavery Society mailed pamphlets to public leaders across the country, a mob broke into a South Carolina post office and burned the sacks containing them. Slave-state legislatures asked free-state legislatures to prohibit the printing of publications that might make slaves "discontented." Slave-state governors asked free-state governors to "crush the traitorous designs of abolitionists," and southern planters prevailed upon their northern contacts to put down abolition activity. Their sympathizers formed vigilance committees to break up antislavery meetings, assaulted antislavery lecturers, ransacked the offices of antislavery societies, destroyed antislavery presses, and vandalized the homes of abolitionist leaders. In October 1835, a mob dragged Garrison through the streets of Boston and only the mayor's intervention—hauling him off to jail—saved him from being lynched. Ministers, editors, and public officials denounced the rising tide of violence but blamed abolitionists for inciting it.[8]

As criticism of the abolition movement mounted, so too did criticism of women's involvement in it. Garrison had lit the spark for this controversy in December 1831 when he urged women to join the abolition crusade and circulate petitions for the abolition of slavery in the District of Columbia. In asking women to participate in mass petitioning, Garrison urged them to exercise a public and political voice that most Americans believed women should not have. Less than two years earlier, he himself had considered women's petitioning "an uncalled for interference, though made with the holiest of intentions." Writing for Lundy's *Genius* in February 1830, he noted that seven hundred Pennsylvania women had petitioned Congress on behalf of Indian rights. They were probably Quakers who were more or less immune to the proscriptions of separate spheres ideology. But Garrison had absorbed the social mores of his native New England and complained that if the practice became general, no question could be agitated in Congress "without eliciting the informal and contrarient opinions of the softer sex."[9]

However, by December 1831 Garrison's ideas on the duties and rights of women had changed, influenced perhaps by Quaker poet Elizabeth Margaret Chandler, with whom he had worked at the *Genius*. Now he commended another group of Pennsylvania women for petitioning Congress to ban slavery in the nation's capital and urged other women to follow their example. Reversing his previous position, he said it was proper for women not only to feel but also to "express in the most public manner" their sympathy in behalf of their enslaved sisters. In the following weeks, he established a "ladies' depart-ment" in the *Liberator*, printed the Pennsylvania women's petition for others to copy, and continued appealing for women to take an active part in the ab-olition cause. Garrison told his readers that women's tendency to "undervalue their own power, or, through a misconception of duty, to excuse themselves from engaging in the enterprise" impeded the cause of abolition. "The cause of bleeding humanity is always, legitimately, the cause of Woman," he insisted. "Without her powerful assistance, its progress must be slow, difficult, imperfect. . . . When woman's heart is bleeding, Shall woman's voice be hushed?"[10]

Among the first to respond to Garrison's call were the free black women of Salem, Massachusetts, who organized a female antislavery society in February 1832. Women formed societies in several Massachusetts and Rhode Island towns the following summer and in October established the New England Female Anti-Slavery Society, later renamed the Boston Female Anti-Slavery Society. Although women had previously joined reform societies along with their husbands and brothers, they had done so as passive members, lending support by their presence alone because custom dictated that they not speak in assemblies of men. By forming their own societies, women abolitionists became active participants in the antislavery movement, formulating and executing their own strategies.[11]

Among the leading individuals who answered Garrison's call was Lydia Ma-ria Child, whose housekeeping and child-rearing manuals were national best-sellers. Her *Appeal in Favor of That Class of Americans Called Africans*, a lengthy essay against slavery and racial discrimination, won many prominent and influential men to Garrisonian principles. Prudence Crandall converted her Connecticut school for white girls to a school for black girls, inciting a com-munity uproar but also setting an example for other women abolitionists to make educating blacks one of their special endeavors. Inspired by Garrison's remarks on the power of female influence, Maria W. Miller Stewart, an African American who had already authored a tract on the responsibility of free blacks, ventured onto the lecture platform.[12] Although a powerful advocate for the rights of her race and an effective example of the ability of her sex, as a pioneer woman orator she was doomed. Only one woman before her had attempted oratory in America, and that woman had only reinforced strictures against it. As a black woman attempting to lecture at a time when even male black lec-turers were unknown, Maria Stewart was in no position to challenge the stigma that the dread Fanny Wright had bequeathed to female oratory.

Frances Wright was a wealthy Scotswoman who in the late 1820s founded an experimental plantation in Tennessee aimed at demonstrating how slaves could earn their freedom while learning skills and knowledge needed to support themselves. But two years after its founding, the plantation became the center of scandal when a trustee revealed that some residents lived together without benefit of marriage. Wright's attempts to defend her ideas only fueled the scandal. In the journal she coedited and in lectures given across the country, she proclaimed her goal to be to "overthrow priestcraft, to hasten the downfall of the clergy, . . . and render the odiousness of their profession apparent to all eyes." She demanded woman's right to love whomever she pleased without marital sanction, and she advocated a guardianship system of education that would place children in government-run boarding schools where they would be free of parental influence. At a time when America was experiencing a powerful reawakening of religion and morals, celebrating motherhood, and extolling woman as molder of the human character, Wright's ideas were deemed so evil that both the speaker and the act of public speaking by woman were branded as perverted and dangerous. Although Wright left the United States in 1830, the controversy she created was still fresh in the public mind when Maria Stewart appeared at the public rostrum in Boston two years later to plead the unpopular causes of emancipation and racial equality. Boston's black community feared her lecturing would taint the abolition movement with the odium of "Fanny Wrightism" and prevailed upon her to stop.[13]

In addition to circulating petitions, New England's female antislavery societies purchased and distributed tracts, raised funds to support the *Liberator* and antislavery lecturers, and encouraged the boycotting of products of slave labor. When abolitionists formed the American Anti-Slavery Society in December 1833, they praised the women's activism and urged others to organize. Women in Philadelphia and New York City formed female antislavery societies in the following year, and state conventions, declaring the cooperation of women essential to the overthrow of slavery, continued to urge upon them the duty of antislavery labor.[14]

Emboldened by appeals for their active involvement in the antislavery movement, women associated with the Tappans' evangelical circle took a larger role in the antiprostitution movement, too. Started by Boston women as mission work to convert prostitutes, the enterprise was carried to New York by a missionary who established a paper devoted to the new reform, organized a network of support among churchwomen, and expanded the focus from combating female depravity to combating masculine lust. However, his exposés of brothel patronage incited such opposition that male supporters retreated and his paper foundered. In 1834, his female supporters assumed responsibility for employing him, purchased his paper, and, identifying woman's economic oppression as the major cause of prostitution, began calling for wider employment opportunities and fairer pay for women workers. Within a year, women were the motive force behind this movement, known as "moral reform."[15]

But by then, backlash against abolition agitation had erupted and, with it, criticism of women's public labors. Both pulpit and press accused antislavery women of neglecting their domestic responsibilities to attend meetings and circulate petitions. Their meddling in public affairs, critics charged, exhibited an unfeminine lack of delicacy and desire for notice, and incited social unrest and turmoil. The opposition to women's public labor aroused by their involvement in the abolition movement spread to other reforms. Early in 1835, Boston women organized a Ladies' Peace Society in response to an appeal from their ministers, but a few months later when they sought clerical assistance in forming a moral reform society, ministers refused to give support or publicity to any "society of ladies." The women proceeded on their own, but their organizing meeting was broken up by a mob who mistook it for an antislavery meeting.[16]

It was at this point in the developing controversy that Lucy and Rhoda Stone began following it through both the *New England Spectator* and copies of Garrison's *Liberator* that Bowman sent from Amherst. The *Spectator* championed many aspects of woman's cause. It promoted the employment of women as teachers in the common schools, gave favorable notice to magazines edited by women, and published the proceedings of women's reform societies. And in the developing debate on woman's duties and rights, it sided with abolitionists. The *Spectator* was especially supportive of women's involvement in the moral reform movement. Agreeing that oppression, rather than depravity, was at the root of female licentiousness, it denounced the restricted employment opportunities of women, the "miserable pittance" paid them, and the "impossibility of procuring the necessities of life by honest industry" that pushed desperate women into prostitution. It published the movement's calls for an end to the double standard of morality and for society to demand male chastity as it did female chastity.[17]

In the spring of 1836, shortly after the Stone sisters began reading the *Spectator*, Congress passed its first of several annual resolutions refusing to receive antislavery petitions. Some congressmen saw the rules as a way to silence those whom they thought should not have political voice in the first place. "If the ladies and Sunday school children would let us alone," complained a Mississippi senator, "there would be but few abolition petitions." The attempt to nullify women's political voice turned the debate over their duty to labor publicly into a debate over their political rights. Opponents argued that because women were ruled by emotion rather than reason, they should not be allowed to influence public policy. Catharine Beecher, daughter of Lyman Beecher, denounced abolitionists' assertion that women should become involved in public affairs. Insisting that petitioning was man's duty, not woman's, she said women should conform to the divine order that appointed man the superior sex. But abolitionists rejected such views. "We hold no sympathy with such sentiments . . . that woman has no duties of a public nature," James Thome told antislavery women a month after Congress passed the gag rule. Abolitionists, he said, held that it was woman's duty "to contribute [to] and be active in the common welfare. . . . Here is Woman's Sphere!" When a legislator asserted that Congress had no obligation to heed women's petitions because women had no right to vote, Massachusetts Representative John Quincy Adams countered that he was not convinced women did not possess the right. The debate stretched all the way to Illinois, where a young state legislator named Abraham Lincoln declared: "I go for all sharing the privileges of the government who assist in bearing its burdens. Consequently, I go for admitting all whites to the right of suffrage who pay taxes and bear arms, by no means excluding females."[18]

Ignoring Congress's refusal to receive their petitions, Maria Weston Chapman, guiding force of the Boston Female Anti-Slavery Society, urged New England women to intensify their work. "We are bound to the constant exercise of the only [political] right we ourselves enjoy . . . the right of petition." That right, she said, had been bestowed by the first Congress through constitutional amendment and could not be nullified by a simple resolution of the last Congress. Bracing themselves against criticism and rejection, women carried petitions door-to-door in nearly every county of Massachusetts. If Congress had been upset by petitions bearing 34,000 names in 1836, it could only have been thoroughly dismayed when its attempt to stop the flow swelled it to 112,000 signatures the next year.[19]

Hoping to stave off retreat by women abolitionists in other states and expand their petitioning, leaders of the Boston Female Anti-Slavery Society proposed a convention to organize a nationwide effort. In May 1837, women from seven states met in New York during "anniversary week," when thousands of men from across the country convened for annual meetings of various benevolent associations. As a national assembly of women, the Anti-Slavery Convention of American Women was a radical first. A letter from Maria Chapman, unable to attend because of pregnancy, urged a national petitioning effort and praised women's defiance of custom and public opinion that would keep them silent: "Are we free, it is because we have burst our manacles in the effort to undo those that weigh so heavily on [the slave]." The convention declared antislavery petitioning the duty of every American woman and adopted a plan to collect one million signatures to their petitions before the next session of Congress. It also adopted, although not unanimously, a resolution declaring that "as certain rights and duties are common to all moral beings," woman should "no longer remain satisfied in the circumscribed limits which corrupt custom and a perverted application of Scripture have encircled her." Repudiating separate spheres ideology, it urged each woman to do all she could, by her example, her purse, her pen, and her voice, to overthrow American slavery.[20]

The women's convention sparked interest in the issue of woman's rights. Within weeks of its close, an Ohio newspaper drew the judicial movement for married women's property rights into the debate. Noting the introduction of a bill in New York designed to expand married women's property rights, the *Cleveland Messenger* asked: "By what principle of justice does the law wrest from a woman, the moment she is married, all the patrimony of her father and all her own hard earned wages and place them at the entire disposal of her husband? We admit that in an important sense the husband and wife 'are one flesh,' but certainly not in any sense as to destroy the personal identity of each." The article, which Garrison reprinted in the *Liberator*, asked why women did not rise up en masse and petition state legislatures for the restoration of property rights "so unjustly wrested from them."[21] Here was a suggestion that women petition for their own rights, an activity not easily rationalized as moral duty or benevolence.

The national convention of women abolitionists was not the primary impetus for the woman's rights debate that engulfed Massachusetts the following summer. It sprang, instead, from an attempt by the state association of Congregational ministers to suppress women's public work just as abolitionists were trying to expand it. Although the main purpose of the association's pastoral letter was to close churches against all abolition lecturers, it took special aim at two women who had just begun speaking in public.

Angelina and Sarah Grimké were daughters of a prominent South Carolina slaveholding family who had moved to Philadelphia, become involved in antislavery activity, and heard British abolitionist George Thompson appeal for women's petitioning. Angelina responded with *An Appeal to the Christian Women of the South*, urging them to petition their state legislatures, and Sarah with *An Epistle to the Clergy of the South*, refuting Biblical arguments used to support slavery. When the American Anti-Slavery Society held a two-week conference to train a corps of lecturing agents in the fall of 1836, the sisters were invited to attend. Although separate spheres ideology barred women from public speaking, custom allowed them to address private gatherings of other women, and it was for this role that the Grimkés were commissioned—to speak to small groups of women and organize women's antislavery societies. Their work in New York and New Jersey during the following winter, however, proved that they were effective witnesses against the institution they had grown up with, and they were invited to New England to help counteract charges that abolitionists distorted and exaggerated the realities of slavery.[22] But if their testimony was to be effective in Massachusetts, it had to be heard by men as well as women.

The ability to persuade others through public speaking had for centuries been a revered accomplishment and a political power exercised by the elite only. America's laboring class had begun to share that power after gaining the franchise in the 1820s, but oratory was still a political tool reserved for public leaders. For women to presume they had the right and ability to influence public thought through public address was to challenge a long tradition of masculine exclusivity. Later, in the controversy roused by the Grimkés addressing public audiences, defenders claimed that the Grimkés opened their meetings to men not by deliberate design, but only because men insisted on coming. But the sisters' correspondence suggests otherwise. At a meeting with other abolitionists after their arrival in Massachusetts, Angelina reported, "the brethren" suggested it was time women's "fetters were broken" and "a new order of things" established. In preparation for their speaking tour, Maria Chapman asked antislavery women to assist the sisters and thereby help refute the idea that God had ordained different spheres for men and women. It was of paramount importance to the antislavery cause, she said, for men and women to understand that in spiritual matters the responsibilities of the sexes were identical, and that in temporal pursuits, all individuals were "bound to the strenuous exercise of such faculties as God has given them." She issued a potent invitation to the Grimkés' meetings: "Let there be no exclusive system adopted in our societies . . . . Whosoever will, let them come." Less than a week after they began speaking, Sarah reported to Theodore Weld, general agent of the lecturing corps, that their meeting at Roxbury would be open to men. A few days later when asked if men were barred from their lecture in Lynn, she answered no. And shortly thereafter, she reported to friends that their meetings were held "irrespective of sex . . . Whoever will come and hear our testimony may come."[23]

The Congregational ministers who met at North Brookfield on June 27–29 had learned of this assault on masculine prerogative. While adopting resolutions against itinerant lecturers speaking in Congregational churches without their pastors' consent, they also denounced those men who encouraged women to assume "an obtrusive and ostentatious part in measures of reform" or to "itinerate in the character of public lecturers and teachers." The clerics said they appreciated woman's private prayers in advancing religion but warned that when she assumed "the place of man as a public reformer," she violated her feminine nature. "If the vine, whose strength and beauty is to lean upon the trellis . . . thinks to assume the independence and the overshadowing nature of the elm," they warned, "it will not only cease to bear fruit, but will fall in shame and dishonor into the dust."[24]

Lucy Stone was among the first persons to hear the pastoral letter. Teaching in North Brookfield and boarding with an aunt and uncle at the time of the convention, she and a cousin attended as observers. As the letter was read aloud, each of its offending sentiments provoked an elbow nudge from Stone, and there were so many her cousin complained afterwards that her ribs were black and blue. Stone recalled that as one minister read the letter, another "walked up and down the aisle, turning his head from side to side and looking at the women in the gallery as if to say, 'Now! Now we have silenced you!'" She was so infuriated that she resolved if ever she had anything to say in public, she would say it—and all the more because of that pastoral letter. "If I had ever felt bound to silence by misrepresentation of Scripture texts or believed equal rights did not belong to women," she said years later, "that pastoral letter broke my bonds."[25]

Stone was not the only person upon whom the ministers' admonitions had an effect opposite from that intended. From Massachusetts' earliest days, Congregational meetinghouses had served as open forums for all public matters. New Englanders valued their freedom of conscience, and many objected to the idea of surrendering it to their pastors. Comparing the letter to a papal edict, poet John Greenleaf Whittier called it the "Brookfield Bull" and denounced the attempt of "priestly power" to fetter parishioners' minds. So while the pastoral letter succeeded in causing some to retreat, it spurred others out of complacency. Two weeks after the ministers' convention, West Brookfield organized its first antislavery society. Among its founding members were two deacons of the Congregational church, whose minister was a staunch colonizationist and vehemently opposed the abolition movement.[26]

The pastoral letter carried the question of woman's rights to people who had not given it much thought. At the time of the ministers' convention, the *Liberator*, which ran weekly reports of the Grimkés' work, had not yet revealed that the sisters were addressing mixed audiences, and the fact was not generally known. Ironically, it was the pastoral letter itself, as it was disseminated in July and August, that drew attention and audiences to the Grimkés' lectures. And following Chapman's urging that antislavery women help the sisters refute separate spheres ideology, local women joined them at the rostrum, opening their meetings, introducing the speakers, leading prayer, and offering supporting remarks.[27]

The pastoral letter fueled discussion about woman's rights among antislavery women, too. Some, including Mary Parker, president of the Boston Female Anti-Slavery Society, agreed with its authors and advocated retreat. Sarah Grimké responded in a series of "Letters on the Province of Woman," which the *New England Spectator* began publishing the third week of July. Just as she had earlier refuted biblical arguments used to support slavery, she now refuted biblical arguments used to restrict female activity and defend male authority. Simultaneous with Sarah's letters in the *Spectator*, the *Liberator* published letters from Angelina responding to Catharine Beecher's criticism of women's petitioning. Both sisters insisted that "whatever is morally right for a man to do, is morally right for a woman to do."[28]

Through Sarah's letters in the *Spectator* and Angelina's in the *Liberator*, Lucy Stone and other New Englanders were offered a double portion of woman's rights nearly every week throughout the summer and fall. Suddenly the spark kindled by Garrison six years earlier burst into a raging fire. Some clergymen preached sermons against the women, others preached in their favor. Some newspapers charged antislavery women with Fanny Wrightism, others encouraged them to exercise their rights. The *New England Spectator*, which kept the Stone sisters up-to-date on the controversy, was one of the latter: "Women must fulfill their duties according to the talents God has given them, and are responsible to Him alone," it said. With so many arguing about the duties and rights of women, Stone told her brother Bowman she wished she had not been born until fifty years later so she could "see the result and reap the fruit of the present contest." Bowman said she ought to be thankful she lived at a time when she could "help it on." Recalling the exchange a few years later, Stone said his reply made her feel rebuked and ashamed, and she never again entertained such a wish but, "glad to live in such an age and at such a time," resolved to devote her life to the cause of woman's rights.[29]

"The Confounded Woman Question"

Lacking sufficient funds to enroll at Mount Holyoke Female Seminary when the school opened its doors in November 1837, Lucy Stone taught again the following winter and watched with great interest as agitation for woman's rights began to divide the very movement from which it had sprung. To many abolitionists, the principle of human rights upon which they based their movement applied equally to women as to the Negro race. Theodore Weld noted in August 1837 that antislavery discussions during the previous four years had "wrought wonders for woman's rights . . . by lodging in the public mind a principle that involves woman's rights and leads to them, and gives eyes to see them and prepares the heart to welcome them." Although few people had given much thought to the question before abolitionists began agitating it, now, he said, four out of five people who believed in the equality of the races also believed in the equality of the sexes, or were "so far on the road that they [would] get there soon."[1] But Weld's assessment of support for woman's rights among abolitionists was optimistic. The pastoral letter and the Grimkés' lecturing sharpened opposition to Garrison's leadership among a faction who blamed him for the lack of antislavery support from religious bodies. Already upset by his harsh criticism of churches that did not oppose slavery and his call for abolitionists to follow the biblical injunction to "come out from the unclean thing" by withdrawing from them, a group of ministers on the periphery of the movement began to distance themselves from positions and actions that could be viewed as antireligion. Issuing an "Appeal of Clerical Abolitionists on Anti-Slavery Measures," they protested Garrison's stand on several issues having to do with the church. Although previous attempts to discredit him had had little effect, this indictment from clergymen among his followers commanded more attention. Foes outside the movement hailed the ministers' protest and urged them to overthrow Garrisonian leadership or form a new organization more respectful of the church.[2]

Encouraged in their criticism, these self-termed clerical abolitionists issued additional appeals accusing Garrison of weakening the antislavery cause by weighing it down with dangerous side issues. The woman question, as the controversy over woman's rights had become known, was just one of these objectionable side issues. Nonresistance, the idea that defensive force was as wrong as aggressive force, was another. The justification of defensive war had been a controversial issue in the peace movement since 1815 when both Massachusetts and New York formed state peace societies and took opposing positions on the question. The New York society denounced all war, but the Massachusetts society maintained that Scripture sanctioned defensive wars. The Massachusetts view had prevailed in the national organization until 1828, when a leadership change tilted it toward the New York position. Then, at its anniversary meeting in May 1837, the American Peace Society adopted a declaration against defensive war in its new constitution. Most Massachusetts peace activists, many of whom were colonizationists, resented the fact that New England abolitionists—Garrison and followers—had strengthened the New York position. Shortly thereafter, Garrison extended nonresistance principles to government. Refuting a statement that abolitionists, as Christians, were bound to obey all civil laws and authorities, he said that Christians owed no allegiance to civil governments or human laws that conflicted with God's "higher law." Furthermore, he said that participating in a government bound to protect slavery was collusion with slavery, and therefore abolitionists should not vote or serve in public office. So simultaneous with the woman question, another controversy erupted over Garrison's so-called no-government views. The clerical remonstrants seized upon these ideas to bolster their view of Garrison as antiscriptural, for the Bible clearly directed Christians to "Render unto Caesar that which is Caesar's." Adding to his opponents' arsenal was Garrison's defense in the *Liberator* of Henry C. Wright, a member of the antislavery lecturing corps who was working that summer in eastern Massachusetts and mixing nonresistance with his antislavery lectures. The fact that the Grimké sisters, too, spoke on nonresistance contributed to the clerical ire against them.[3]

The perception that the abolition movement was unchristian and anticlerical, and that this was so because of Garrison's influence, gained credence as national officers in New York offered no rebuttal to the criticism. Although some of the measures that offended the Massachusetts clergy had originated with the New York evangelicals who comprised the executive committee of the national organization, and although strong religious censure had been adopted with great unanimity by the national convention, New York leaders offered no help in fending off the clerical attack. Activists in New England interpreted this silence as agreement with Garrison's critics, and when the executive committee pulled Wright out of Massachusetts and disclaimed any connection with the Grimkés, their action implied agreement on the matter of "side issues" as well. And in fact, Arthur and Lewis Tappan, president and secretary of the national association as well as its principle benefactors, did sympathize with the Massachusetts remonstrants. Whereas many abolitionists were ready to wage the battle without the church's aid, the Tappans still believed emancipation could not be achieved without it and did not want to further alienate holdouts.

In the face of the clerical uproar, therefore, Massachusetts abolitionists came under increasing pressure to retreat on these "lesser" issues. But Garrison refused to drop his discussion of woman's rights in the *Liberator*. When he issued his annual prospectus in December 1837, he told his subscribers that although the abolition of slavery and the enfranchisement of the Negro race remained the object of his labors, the *Liberator* would continue to discuss other topics "intimately connected with the great doctrine of inalienable rights." For good measure he added, "As our object is universal emancipation, to redeem woman as well as man from a servile to an equal condition, we go for the rights of woman to their utmost extent."[4]

Now an avowed woman's rights paper, the *Liberator* became the special target of Garrison's critics. Although it was Garrison's personal enterprise, it had always received financial support from local and state societies, and the Massachusetts Anti-Slavery Society, which had been the New England Anti-Slavery Society prior to the founding of the national society, had just voted to assume total financial responsibility for it. This the clerical abolitionists wanted to change. They urged New Englanders to drop the *Liberator* in favor of an antislavery paper more respectful of religion, and the paper they had in mind was the *New England Spectator*. Since publishing the clerical protests, the *Spectator* had increasingly sided with the dissidents. It still promoted woman's rights but warned against Garrison's influence. "Women must be elevated. They must have intelligence, dignity, influence, property, and character before society shall become what the reign of Christ will make it." But, it cautioned, those "who undermine the authority of the Bible as the word of God, divinely inspired, will prove the enemies, not the friends, of women."[5]

The clerical abolitionists blamed Garrison's unchristian spirit and harsh language, his unscriptural views on woman's rights, the Sabbath, and nonresistance, and his anticlericalism for keeping the nation's religious leaders from embracing abolition. Believing the movement would not succeed unless led by the clergy, they wanted to take control of the state society and manage it in a manner acceptable to the nation's religious leaders. To ensure representation in the state organization, they formed their own society, the Evangelical Anti-Slavery Society of Boston, which, the *Spectator* explained, was for those who wanted to act on behalf of the slave but could not "conscientiously cooperate with the present antislavery movements because they think they see in them principles of radicalism which threaten to subvert the foundations of society." A month later, the remonstrants' hope for a rival paper was dashed when the *Spectator* folded. It had never been on firm financial ground, and positioning itself against Garrison and the Massachusetts Anti-Slavery Society had only hastened its decline.[6]

The *Spectator's* demise in April 1838 removed one of Lucy and Rhoda Stone's windows onto the woman's rights debate, but they had already come to rely on the *Liberator* for their coveted news. In January and February the *Liberator* had reprinted from the *Spectator* Sarah Grimké's "Letters on the Province of Women," which greatly influenced Stone's thinking and became a primary reference for her later essays and lectures. Perhaps it was Grimké's letter on the legal disabilities of women that first called Stone's attention to the fact that single women who paid taxes were subjected to "taxation without representation." It may also have been the first discussion she saw concerning married women's rights, or lack thereof, under various state legal codes. And it was probably her introduction to the famous quotation from William Blackstone's *Commentaries on the Laws of England* that in marriage, "the very being or legal existence of a woman is suspended, or at least it is incorporated or consolidated into that of the husband." Grimké's letter titled "Relation of Husband and Wife" charged that marriage robbed women of their individuality and independent being, and thus lowered women instead of elevating them.[7]

Stone discussed the Grimké letters with her brother Frank, who had graduated from Bangor's collegiate department and was to about to begin studies in its theological institute. Removed from the influence of Massachusetts abolition, he was still a colonizationist and sided with Garrison's critics on the woman question as well. Lucy insisted that Sarah Grimké said nothing in her letters on the equality of the sexes that she did not prove, and Lucy was confident that if Frank read them he would agree. At any rate, she told him, Grimké's writing only reinforced her resolution not to marry.[8]

In addition to reprinting Sarah Grimké's letters, the *Liberator* told the Stone sisters about a Boston Lyceum debate at which abolitionists argued not only for the right of women to petition and vote but, more broadly, for woman's "intellectual, moral, and social equality" with man. The *Liberator* reported the historic appearance of Angelina Grimké before the Massachusetts legislature in February. Becoming the first woman to address a legislative body in America, Grimké testified on behalf of women's antislavery petitions and defended women's petitioning not only as a moral and religious duty but also as a political right. The previous summer she had written in her reply to Catharine Beecher that she believed it was woman's right "to have a voice in all laws and regulations by which she is governed, whether in Church or State." She contended that woman had "just as much right to sit in solemn counsel in conventions, conferences, associations, and general assemblies as man—just as much right to sit upon the throne of England or in the presidential chair of the United States." Clearly defending woman's political equality, Grimké did not specifically mention the right to vote because she saw no point in naming a right that she, like Garrison, believed abolitionists should not use.[9]

Now moral reform women joined antislavery women in petitioning. They had already hired women agents to speak to women and organize auxiliaries— two years before the American Anti-Slavery Society asked the Grimkés to do the same. And they had initiated a campaign to make seduction a criminal offense, writing letters to legislators, urging victims to sue their seducers, and asking ministers to preach on the seventh commandment. But not until 1838, after publishing an article by Sarah Grimké urging women to interpret the Bible for themselves and reevaluate their role in society, did moral reform women begin circulating petitions. They based their political action not on the premise of woman's equal rights, however, but on woman's moral superiority and power to influence male behavior. Leaders of the moral reform movement were connected with the Tappans' New York evangelical circle, and as these men began to hold aloof from Garrison's movement, so too did their female coadjutors.[10]

The division widened when Massachusetts abolitionists challenged the custom of men and women working in separate organizations. This practice, which ran counter to egalitarian principles, also seemed to some abolitionists "like a pair of scissors" cutting their efforts in two. So when women abolitionists met in May 1838 for their second national convention, some proposed that they suspend separate gatherings and attend the American Anti-Slavery Convention instead. Although the majority voted to continue meeting separately, two weeks later a group of women led by Maria Chapman and Abby Kelley attended the New England Anti-Slavery Convention, where they spoke and voted on matters before the assembly and Kelley was appointed to a committee. Shortly thereafter, women also joined the Massachusetts Anti-Slavery Society. That fall, a Boston peace convention dominated by Garrisonians not only appointed women to committees but also elected them to officer positions and to the executive committee of the organization it established—the New England Non-Resistance Society. Women abolitionists in Rhode Island and Pennsylvania also began joining state societies.[11]

These actions fueled the assault against Garrison and the board of the Massachusetts Anti-Slavery Society. After the New England convention accepted women, several clergymen withdrew in protest and the religious bodies to whom the convention sent a memorial refused to receive it on the ground that a woman, Kelley, had helped draft it. Critics launched a new round of charges that Garrisonians flouted St. Paul's clear injunction against women's preaching, while defenders insisted that a person's sex was of no relevance in the fight against slavery.

As the debate raged around her, Lucy Stone put away money for Mount Holyoke. In March 1838, just after Lucy finished teaching a winter term, her sister Eliza Barlow died at age twenty-nine, leaving two small daughters. After taking time to care for her nieces awhile, Lucy taught again in the summer and then, with other friends wanting a tutor, hired one of Bowman's Amherst friends, a Mr. Bartlett, to help her complete required studies for Mount Holyoke. Bartlett brought Sarah Grimké's *Letters on the Equality of the Sexes*, which Garrison had just published in pamphlet form, and Lucy was thrilled to find him a believer in woman's rights. She was attracted to him, and he to her, and before long they fell in love. Bartlett was an intensely religious young man preparing for the ministry. Lucy was now twenty years old and possessed the qualities befitting a clergyman's helpmate—intelligence, devotion, and a clear sense of purpose. Together they accomplished, at long last, the conversion of Francis Stone, and when Lucy and Sarah Stone joined the West Brookfield Congregational Church in March 1839, their father joined with them. Although Bartlett helped win Francis Stone, he could not shake Lucy's resolve to remain single.[12]

Lucy's studies were interrupted by the necessity of filling in for Rhoda, who became ill and unable to finish teaching the fall term at Paxton. She taught again that winter at another school in the same town, whose teacher had quit. In recruiting Lucy for that school, officials did not mention trouble with the students, but when she approached the schoolhouse on her first day, threatening remarks from one of the larger boys revealed that her predecessor had been thrown into a snowdrift. Lucy used the day to get to know her students, talking with them individually and winning their approval and cooperation. She finished the term without mishap and, indeed, said she had had no problem with discipline at all. Lucy possessed what her sister Sarah called a "peculiar power over the minds of children" with which she "could turn them whithersoever [she] would." But there was no mystery to Lucy's "peculiar power." She had learned that in order to influence people, one must first win their trust and goodwill.[13]

Lucy entered Mount Holyoke Female Seminary at the beginning of its spring term in April 1839. The school's curriculum was intended to be the feminine counterpart of a college education. Where it differed was in its omission of the classics, its teaching of homemaking skills, and its particular indoctrination of students. Stone soon learned that Lyon had no sympathy with the agitation for woman's rights. Like moral reformers, her support for woman's cause—improving women's educational and employment opportunities and wives' and widows' legal rights—was based on the idea of woman's moral superiority and the desire to purify and elevate marriage. She never failed to state her strongly rooted belief in the domestic character of woman's true interests and no doubt agreed with the sentiment expressed in *Godey's Lady's Book* earlier that year: "When a married woman talks excessively of women's rights, then you can guess that woman is less than conscientious about performing her wifely duties." Disapproving of female leadership roles, Lyon's goal was to train each Mount Holyoke graduate to be "an efficient auxiliary in the great task of renovating the world"—man's helper, not his equal.[14]

If this vision of "female education" had been acceptable to Stone in 1836, by 1839 it was not. Too much had happened in the intervening years to develop and bolster her egalitarian views. While Lyon and other pioneers in female education argued that women should be educated to influence men, Stone believed they should be educated for their own sake. "We read in the newspapers, we are taught at the fireside and at the female seminary," she said years later, "that we must seek to obtain the graces and accomplishments which will make us better pleasing to the men. My soul loathes such meanness with perfect loathing! If there were no being in the world for her to influence, I would, for the sake of her own deathless nature, insist that for herself alone, woman should receive the highest mental cultivation of which she is capable." Stone also disapproved of making domestic training part of women's education. "I should never think of making a course of special study for those who may be mothers, any more than for men who may be fathers," she told a college president many years later. She believed the purpose of higher education was to fit students for whatever profession they chose, and therefore it should offer men and women the same course of study.[15]

Stone was disgusted not only with Mount Holyoke's female education but also with its refusal to let students think for themselves. As an orthodox Congregationalist, Lyon discouraged any inclination among her students toward abolition and woman's rights. If student sympathies leaned toward antislavery, the teachers tried to redirect them toward home and foreign missions. Stone held her own against such influences. Instead of putting her spare pennies into the missionary boxes kept by most students, she put hers into a collection box of the antislavery society, and after finishing issues of the *Liberator* that Bowman sent her, she placed them in the seminary's reading room. But the *Liberator*'s attacks on the church and its leaders, as well as its "unscriptural views" and "unchristian language," made it, in Lyon's view, unacceptable reading material for Mount Holyoke women. In addition to these long-standing criticisms against the *Liberator*, at the time Stone began leaving it in the reading room, the feud between Garrison and his clerical rivals had become so acrimonious that it seemed to infect everyone involved.[16] Lyon certainly did not want the contagion spread to her school.

The failure of clerical abolitionists to discredit Garrison on the basis of his woman's rights, nonresistance, and religious views had demonstrated that there was little support among Massachusetts abolitionists for their positions. But in the fall of 1838, another basis on which to ground an assault had been suggested to them—political abolitionism. Even though antislavery conventions consistently rejected the idea of uniting abolitionists into a political force, some abolitionists had become convinced that legislative coercion might be the only peaceful way to achieve emancipation. Meanwhile, slave interests' efforts to suppress antislavery agitation by violating constitutionally guaranteed freedoms of speech, petition, and press had created a public sympathy with the antislavery movement and, more importantly, an antisouthern sentiment totally separate and apart from that sympathy.[17] The November 1837 murder of abolitionist editor Elijah Lovejoy in Alton, Illinois, fed this sentiment and increased hope among some abolitionists that they might become a political force that could reach into the slave states and compel planters to emancipate their slaves. In western New York, a group of abolitionists developed a theory of federal authority over slavery and began advocating the formation of an antislavery party to work for federal action.

Although political abolitionism had a strong following in western New York, it attracted little interest in New York City, where the Tappan evangelical circle predominated, or in Quaker Pennsylvania or Garrisonian New England. But when one of its young enthusiasts returned to Massachusetts in the fall of 1838, he quickly saw how the conflict there could advance the third-party movement. Henry B. Stanton, a Lane convert hired by the American Anti-Slavery Society as one of its field agents, had worked in Massachusetts the previous year and had supported the Grimké sisters' lecturing. He was now the national society's financial secretary and assigned to Massachusetts to raise funds for the national treasury, which had been severely diminished by the panic of 1837. Because Garrison's position against voting and holding office counteracted efforts to organize an antislavery political party, Stanton readily joined the clericals' anti-Garrison movement and helped it formulate a new strategy.

Stanton helped draft a set of resolutions arguing the need for political organization and, therefore, a new paper to advance antislavery politics in Massachusetts. Hoping to send enough people committed to these aims to the annual meeting of the state society so they could gain control of the board of managers, the clericals sent the resolutions, along with someone to lobby for them, to every local and county antislavery meeting held before the convention. They also sent letters to ministers throughout the state asking them to send full, *male* delegations pledged to vote for the new paper.[18]

Garrison learned of the scheme and exposed it in the *Liberator,* and his followers successfully repelled the clericals' attempt to take over the January 1839 annual meeting of the Massachusetts Anti-Slavery Society. On all three fronts—woman's rights, political organization, and a new newspaper—the challengers were defeated. Nevertheless, they established their rival paper the next month and appointed Stanton temporary editor. In April they packed the annual meeting of the Boston Female Anti-Slavery Society with women from their congregations, who helped the society's proclerical members pass a resolution diverting the proceeds of its annual fair from the *Liberator* and state society to the national society. The society's board of managers, however, refused to capitulate and organized a rival fair.[19]

Thus, in the spring of 1839 when Stone began leaving issues of the *Liberator* in Mount Holyoke's reading room, all of Massachusetts was caught up in the abolitionists' internecine warfare. And it just got worse. Backed by Lewis Tappan's newly formed Evangelical Anti-Slavery Society of New York City and ministers from other parts of the country, Massachusetts' dissidents tried to take control of the national society at its May anniversary. The question of women's membership was, as expected, the test of strength. The American Anti-Slavery Society's constitution specified that all "persons" who agreed with the society's principles were eligible for membership, and a number of women representing local women's societies and three state societies sought admission. For three whole sessions the convention debated whether these women were *persons* under the terms of its constitution. Although Stanton promoted the clericals' antiwoman position, other political abolitionists, such as Gerrit Smith, who presided, supported the women. "If some prefer to send up here as their delegates your Chapmans, your Kelleys, and your Barneys, have we the right to object?" he asked in their defense. "If a woman can do my work best, I wish to be at liberty to select a woman." The convention voted to admit the women and, defeating opponents' efforts to restrict their membership rights, appointed both Abby Kelley and Eliza Barney to committees. Three weeks later, the dissidents tried to get the New England Anti-Slavery Convention to rescind its acceptance of women. When they failed, they withdrew and organized a rival Massachusetts Abolition Society.[20]

With the formation of this society, the Massachusetts abolition movement was formally split into two camps, one "clerical" and anti–woman's rights and the other "Garrisonian" and pro–woman's rights. Although the defectors had accepted help from Stanton and his band of political enthusiasts, and even installed one of them, Elizur Wright Jr., as permanent editor of their *Massachusetts Abolitionist,* the political question really had nothing to do with the new organization. In their "Address to the Abolitionists of Massachusetts" explaining why they had formed a second state society, its founders said their only object was to disconnect abolition from the encumbrances that had been forced upon it, mainly woman's rights. The old society, they said, "upheld a change in the sphere of woman's action that was a moral wrong, a thing forbidden alike by the word of God, the dictates of right reason, the voice of wisdom, and the modesty of unperverted nature." Thus, the new organization provided no base from which to launch a third-party campaign. In a private letter that soon became public, Elizur Wright told Stanton that unless an antislavery convention meeting in Cleveland under the auspices of the national society moved toward nominating presidential candidates, their work in Massachusetts was in vain. The new organization, he said, was "shockingly mismanaged. Everything has been made to turn on the Woman Question." If the Cleveland convention started the move toward national politics, "and not by our movements, then we can take hold with all our might; . . . the confounded Woman Question will be forgotten—and we shall take a living position."[21]

So it was finally out in the open. The clerical defectors had not been genuinely interested in politics, and their young political supporters did not really sympathize with their antiwoman aims. Each faction had entered the alliance merely to increase its own strength. Nevertheless, the internecine warfare continued, with both the "new organizationists" and the Garrisonians accusing each other of being unprincipled and dishonest. Those who assumed one reason for the clerical defection had been objection to Garrison's "unchristian" spirit and language were surprised to find the new organization every bit as personal and caustic. Theodore Weld marveled that Wright exhibited "personal hostility which inflicts pain with a relish" and that nearly everyone in Massachusetts was "poisoned by this fierce feud."[22]

With the *Liberator* full of the infighting, Mary Lyon did not want it in her students' reading room. She confiscated every copy she discovered and for the longest time could not discover who was placing it there. But finally she summoned Stone before her. Lyon explained that even the wisest and best people were divided on the question of abolition. Because it bred such unchristian and uncharitable feeling even among those united in purpose, she thought it best not to inflict the controversy upon Mount Holyoke and directed Stone not to leave the *Liberator* in the reading room again.[23]

Mount Holyoke's spring term ended on July 24, 1839. The speaker at its closing ceremonies said that although he agreed women deserved more education, he knew of nothing else that women were due. "Not till you change the laws of nature and the whole framework and structure of society," he declared, "can the female sex be thrust upon the sphere of action designed for men." Her one term at Mount Holyoke completed, Stone left with no intention of returning. She was determined to get the best education she could and was convinced it would not come from a female seminary. Stone's experience at Mount Holyoke made her a lifelong foe of sex-segregated education. "We don't want women's schools or colleges," she told her later audiences. "I abhor woman schools and Negro pews, and for the same reason." She believed that, in order to develop their full potential, women needed not only more education but the same education that society found desirable for men. "Only let females be educated in the same manner and with equal advantages that males have," she wrote Bowman a few months after leaving Mount Holyoke, "and, as everything seeks its level, I would risk but we would find our 'appropriate sphere.'"[24]

A Hand to Be Counted

Just days after Lucy Stone returned from Mount Holyoke, twenty-five-year-old Rhoda died following a long illness on July 31, 1839. The next month, Lucy enrolled at Wesleyan Academy at Wilbraham with her one surviving sister. She had enough money remaining from her Mount Holyoke funds to see her through only two terms, so, to stretch their money, she and Sarah stayed in a private home and prepared their meals in their room. Sarah left after the winter term, but Lucy borrowed money from her father to complete the year. Despite the customary division of the students into the Young Ladies' Literary Society and the Young Men's Debating Club, Stone found the school much more tolerant of ideas on woman's rights than Mount Holyoke had been. "It was decided by a large majority in our literary society the other day," she reported to Bowman, "that ladies ought to mingle in politics, go to Congress, etc. etc."[1]

At Wesleyan Academy, Stone read widely from the school's books and periodicals, keeping up with current topics of interest and exploring new ideas. She contemplated the theological doctrine of Christian perfection, the idea that because sin was a human invention, the result of alienation from God, human beings who accepted God's grace could restore their souls to a state of moral perfection. "I have been examining the doctrine of Christian Perfection," Lucy wrote to Bowman, "and I cannot avoid the conclusion that it is attainable in this life." Bowman had graduated from Amherst College, enrolled in Andover Theological Seminary, withdrawn because the faculty did not allow students to organize an antislavery society, and now studied under the Reverend George Trask of Warren. Lucy wrote to him for religious advice and aid: "I often think that I have never been a Christian, for how can one who has ever known the love of God go so far away? Will brother sometimes pray for me?"[2]

An idea attracting wide attention during Stone's year at Wesleyan was physiological reform, or the "Graham system," a popular health movement launched by temperance lecturer Sylvester Graham in 1832. His ideas, a selective synthesis of the medical literature of the day together with his own peculiar philosophical underpinning that emphasized preventing disease through healthful living, found eager reception among a population anxiously awaiting the arrival of the cholera epidemic then ravaging Asia and Europe. Graham taught that physical health was as much a matter of moral duty as spiritual health, that Christians should strive for physical perfection as they did spiritual perfection, and that by observing natural laws they could attain it. Holding that disease and debility were caused by stimulation and exhaustion, Graham advocated restraint in diet and in physical and intellectual exercise. He advocated a minimal diet of whole-grain bread, raw or nearly raw vegetables, little or no meat, and no spices. He discouraged the use of alcohol, coffee, tea, tobacco, and sweets. He advocated moderate physical exercise not just for its physical benefits but as a diversion from intellectual exercise, which, he said, could also be carried to unhealthy excess. He also advocated frequent bathing, ventilating sleeping rooms, exercising outdoors, and wearing loose, unrestrictive clothing. Opposing practices of the regular medical profession such as bleeding and the use of drugs, he also promoted individual responsibility for health, self-treatment, and health education.[3]

Because Graham viewed stimulation and exhaustion as unhealthy, he advocated moderation and deliberation in sexual activity. Orthodox physicians of his time denounced masturbation and adultery because of the wasteful expenditure of the male's "vital force," but Graham said sexual excess within marriage was just as harmful. Warning also against the effect of sexual excess on women's health, he taught that sexual intercourse should be engaged in only for procreation and only when conditions for conception were optimal—when both spouses were in good health and were physically and economically capable of providing for any child conceived.[4]

Amid growing dissatisfaction with orthodox medicine, Graham's focus on prevention and self-determination found a receptive audience. Thousands flocked to his lectures and read his books. Disciples established Graham boarding houses, physiological societies, and, in 1837, the American Physiological Society, with its organ, the *Graham Journal of Health and Longevity*, to promote his teachings. Stone adopted Graham's principles to some extent and when she heard that Frank was allowing himself to become "fleshy," urged him to leave his studies once in a while to take a walk. Although woman's sphere ideology dictated that physical exertion was unfeminine and harmful to the delicate female constitution, Stone liked Graham's view of feminine exercise. "Miss Adams and I walked out to Springfield last Saturday, and back again, the whole distance being nearly twenty-five miles," she reported to Bowman. "We do not feel any inconvenience from it."[5]

The Graham movement gave birth to another advance for women—scientific lectures to female audiences. Because the general populace considered it inappropriate for a man to lecture to women about their bodies, Graham could not address female audiences about applying his principles to their particular health concerns. To fill the void, Mary Gove lectured on physiology and health to her students in Lynn, Massachusetts. Boston women invited her to lecture there, and soon she was in such demand she gave up her school to lecture full time.[6] Ironically, Grahamism created a demand for and legitimized female lecturing at the very time women abolitionists were denounced for speaking in public. But Gove lectured only to women on topics too personal to be addressed by a male lecturer, so her work, like that of moral reform women, who also spoke only to female audiences, was considered more appropriate than that of antislavery women, who insisted on addressing general audiences.

During Stone's year at Wesleyan, the schism between the leadership of the Massachusetts Anti-Slavery Society and the clerical and political factions of the national movement widened. Because women who pressed for inclusion were generally Garrisonians who opposed political organization, their voting at antislavery meetings could be expected to work against the third-party movement. Therefore, some politicos cooperated with the clericals in trying to restrict women's involvement. In the summer of 1839, a group political abolitionists invited the nation's "freemen" to an antislavery convention at Albany that it hoped would be the first step toward political organization. Reminding the convention that it was held under the auspices of the American Anti-Slavery Society, which had ruled that women were members in equal standing with men, Garrison tried to persuade the convention to override the organizing committee's exclusion of women, but it refused. Nevertheless, the convention rejected proposals for political organization. It was after this defeat that Elizur Wright urged Henry Stanton to seek a foothold at the Cleveland convention. But western abolitionists admitted women and spurned the politicos. Giving up hope of securing the cooperation of existing organizations, political abolitionists met in Albany the following spring and, without support from any state society, formed the Liberty Party and nominated James G. Birney for president of the United States.[7]

Following this example, clerical abolitionists prepared to secede from the American Anti-Slavery Society. While lining up forces to outvote Garrisonians at the May anniversary, the national executive committee transferred ownership of the national organ, the *Emancipator,* to one of its members, where it would remain under their management no matter what happened. With confrontation fully expected, more than one thousand people enrolled as delegates when the American Anti-Slavery Society met in New York City on May 12, 1840. One hundred fifty of these were women. Because the previous convention had already settled the question of their membership, the test of power was their rights as members. When the presiding officer appointed Abby Kelley to the business committee, opponents objected and launched another debate of the woman question. But a vote of 557 to 451 upheld the women's right to serve on committees. The next day, those opposed to women's participation withdrew and formed the American and Foreign Anti-Slavery Society.[8]

The woman question had already killed the Boston Female Anti-Slavery Society. After taking control of its April meeting, the proclerical faction declared the society dissolved and then organized a Female Emancipation Society auxiliary to the clericals' state society. Garrisonian women quickly reconstituted the society, but because they had already begun meeting with the men, the Boston Female Anti-Slavery Society soon ceased to exist.[9]

Stone followed these developments with much interest. "You ask me if I am a friend of such a New Organization," she wrote to Bowman. "No, brother, I am not. If that is the spirit of N.O., I am *far enough* from being its friend. There seems to be no feeling of Liberty about it. Its great object seems to be (if I mistake not) to crush Garrison and the women. While it *pretends* to endeavor to remove the yoke of bondage on account of color, it is *actually* summoning all its energies to rivet more and more firmly the chains that have always been fastened upon the neck of woman."[10]

Stone read an account of the Connecticut State Anti-Slavery Convention held later that month, where clerical abolitionists tried to amend the society's constitution to specifically prohibit women from speaking and voting in its meetings. Abby Kelley, whom the Massachusetts Anti-Slavery Society had hired as a field agent to work in Connecticut, attended the meeting, and when she rose to address the question, the chairperson ruled her out of order. The convention overruled his decision, and Kelley spoke briefly, defending woman's right to deliberate and communicate on the platform of common humanity. But the presiding officer, the Reverend Henry C. Ludlow, protested this "outrage on decency" and insisted that no woman would speak where he presided. "I will not consent to have woman lord it over men in public assemblies. . . . Where woman's enticing eloquence is heard, men are incapable of right and efficient action. . . . I had enough of woman's control in the nursery. Now I am a man, I will not submit to it." He vacated the chair, grabbed his hat, and stormed out of the hall. The meeting proceeded with a new chairperson, but Ludlow returned and resumed his protest: "Mr. Chairman, I can assure this meeting we will not go with the men who are going to compel us to submit to the rule of women . . . we will not sail under the Garrison flag." In the debate that followed, Kelley and the other women were not permitted to speak. In the end, the convention voted to keep the constitutional provision granting membership rights to all "persons" but passed a resolution saying it should not be interpreted as granting equal membership rights to women. The convention disavowed any endorsement of "the so-called question of woman's rights" or authorization for women "speaking, voting, and acting on committees, in public bodies, or in the public meetings of the society." Although forbidden to vote, Kelley and other women defiantly raised their hands against the resolution, eliciting hisses and cries of disapproval: "Put down that hand! Her hand shall not be counted if she raises it." Nevertheless, the women persisted in raising their hands every time a vote was taken.[11]

"Look at the ridiculous conduct of H. G. Ludlow at the anniversary of the Anti-Slavery Society of New Haven," Stone commented after reading the account in the *Liberator*. Complaining to Bowman that "the talent, or if you please, half talent" God gave to woman was wrested from her, she said that Ludlow had made himself the keeper of woman's conscience and must answer for her at Judgment Day. "Hear him answer to 'Where is the half talent I gave her?' 'Lord, thinking I knew better than thou didst, and believing that might gave right, I violently took it from her, though she strove hard to maintain it.'" Stone said she admired "the calm and noble bearing" of Abby Kelley throughout the ordeal and wished there were more kindred spirits.[12]

Henry C. Wright, who reported these proceedings to the *Liberator*, stated the crux of the woman question and predicted its continued agitation. "The subject of human rights as it relates to woman will now go through the state, into every district, town, and society, into every family and church and pulpit. Nothing can prevent it," he said. "The issue is fairly made. Do human beings, regardless of sex as well as of color, stand on the same platform of equal and inalienable rights? Have men, because they are men, a right to dictate to woman, because she is a woman, where and when she may speak and vote? Church and state will be agitated with this. The more the better—till it shall be received as a practical truth 'that all men (human beings) are created equal.'"[13]

The woman question did spread, even across the Atlantic. With the calling of a World's Anti-Slavery Convention to meet in London in June, it was inevitable that it should. But new organization clerics ensured that its introduction would not be on Garrisonian terms. The call for the international meeting, received in America the preceding fall, had invited "friends of the slave," and both the Massachusetts and Pennsylvania state societies had appointed women to their delegations. But after Garrison's foes alerted organizers that women were to be sent, subsequent directives indicated that only "gentlemen" would be received. Not wanting to cause discord, the Pennsylvania Society revoked its appointment of women. The Massachusetts society, however, let its appointments stand, and ignoring the new directive, the Boston and Philadelphia female societies appointed delegates and the American Anti-Slavery Society added Lucretia Mott to its delegation.[14]

The World's Anti-Slavery Convention opened in London on June 12, 1840, with five hundred delegates from more than ten countries present. Ann Greene Phillips and Emily Winslow from the Massachusetts Society, Abby Southwick from the Boston society, and the Philadelphia delegates—Lucretia Mott, Mary Grew, Sarah Pugh, Abby Kimber, and Elizabeth Neall—presented their credentials but were denied admission. Unwilling to accept the committee's decision, Wendell Phillips, head of the Massachusetts delegation, took the matter to the convention floor and asked that all persons delegated by any antislavery body be admitted. Debate raged for most of the opening session, until James Birney charged that women's intrusion had caused dissension among American abolitionists and split both the Massachusetts and national societies. Despite an eloquent rejoinder from Phillips, the convention rejected the women delegates.[15]

Phillips reported that Garrison adversary Henry B. Stanton, newly appointed secretary of the American and Foreign Anti-Slavery Society, voted in favor of the women in the unrecorded tally. Although he insisted that Stanton himself told him this, Stanton denied it and both James Birney and one of the women delegates said he voted "emphatically" not to seat the women. Garrison was not present for the vote. Having remained in America for the national convention and then delayed at sea by a storm, he arrived on the convention's fifth day. Although he had anticipated the confrontation and probable result, he nevertheless decided to protest the women's exclusion. The women's antislavery societies held that it was the duty of abolitionists to fight racial segregation by sitting with blacks in the areas set apart for them in churches and public meetings. Acting upon that principle, Garrison and the three delegates who arrived with him—including Charles Lenox Remond, an African American—sat with the rejected delegates and refused to participate in the convention. Their action stunned the assembly and imbedded the woman question in the minds of British reformers. Sir John Bowring, one of the women's supporters, regretted that Massachusetts abolitionists had attempted the "novel experiment" without enlisting the aid of British reformers, who knew very little about the controversy. Nevertheless, Bowring told Garrison, the arguments for woman's rights made a deep impression and won apostles in England.[16]

They also roused Lucretia Mott. Having grown up within the Society of Friends, which accorded women equality in church affairs but separated men and women in various meetings, Mott had not objected to dividing the sexes in reform work. She attended the founding meeting of the American Anti-Slavery Society in 1833 as an observer, with no thought of participating in the meeting or joining the society. Although she offered a suggestion during the drafting of the society's founding statement, it never occurred to her, she explained years later, to ask to sign the document, just as it never occurred to the men to invite her to do so. Not until Massachusetts women proposed that women abolitionists attend the American Anti-Slavery Society convention instead of holding their own was her attention drawn to the inconsistency of abolitionists segregating the sexes. When Abby Kelley criticized the national convention of antislavery women for voting to continue meeting separately, Mott advised her to "yield . . . to the conscientious objections" of those not ready to breach the custom. But efforts to persuade her not to press for admission to the London convention, along with the debate on the convention floor, ended Mott's patience with "conscientious objections." Sending a message to the Grimké sisters, who had quit public work after Angelina's marriage to Theodore Weld in 1838, Mott urged them to come out of retirement and speak out for oppressed woman. "[A] great struggle is at hand," she said, and "all the friends of freedom for woman must rally round the Garrison standard."[17]

Reports from London filled the *Liberator's* pages as Stone completed her year at Wesleyan Academy. After replenishing her education funds, she enrolled at Monson Academy, with Sarah again accompanying her.[18] Her term there ended in August 1841, the same month Oberlin Collegiate Institute in far-off Ohio graduated three women from its collegiate course. For the first time in the nation's history, women had studied the same courses as men, right alongside them, and had been awarded collegiate degrees. Although the remarkable event was not hailed by a cheering world as a long-awaited advance for humanity, it was so received by Stone.

Oberlin was a colony-church-college that had been carved out of the Ohio wilderness in 1833 by Congregational missionaries as an institute to prepare ministers for serving the western frontiers. Reflecting the progressive attitude toward female education, its founders had established a ladies' course alongside the men's collegiate and theological departments. But in the fall of 1837, following the eruption of the woman question, four young women applied for admission to the collegiate program and, this being before abolitionists divided into pro- and anti-woman's rights camps, they were admitted. Four years later, three of them became the first women in the nation to graduate from a regular college.[19]

When Stone learned that such an opportunity existed, she announced to her family that she would go. Francis Stone received this latest of his daughter's schemes with no less consternation than he had her previous ones. But now even her mother objected. A college education was not needed to teach in female academies and seminaries, and an Oberlin education, Hannah feared, might even hinder such a career. For Oberlin was a center of controversy. Presbyteries refused to license graduates of its theological seminary, and orthodox churches and missionary boards refused to appoint them. A deacon in West Brookfield took the *Oberlin Evangelist*, but his wife refused to touch it and handed it to him with a pair of tongs.[20] The primary cause of the prejudice against Oberlin was its professor of theology, Charles Grandison Finney, the evangelist whose revivals had set New York ablaze with religious fervor in the 1820s and early 1830s. To his admirers, Finney was a second Apostle Paul; but to his critics, he was a dangerous wild man, leading poor souls down the wrong path and creating havoc in the religious life of the nation. Oberlin was also criticized for the "extreme" position it took on most reforms—including its admission of Negroes and its "joint education" of the sexes. But Stone was in complete agreement with Oberlin's reforms. Once again she began preparing for an entrance examination and saving money for tuition.

In the winter of 1841–42, while Stone was home between teaching jobs, Abby Kelley came to West Brookfield. Stone had followed Kelley's work for two years and greatly admired the thirty-one-year-old woman who personified woman's rights. Kelley's defiance of woman's sphere proscriptions had given rise to accusations of her being a vile woman, a Fanny Wrighter, an infidel, a man-woman. Perhaps a more accurate assessment is that recorded by a woman who, although she disagreed with Kelley's public work, found her to be "lady-like in manners. Simple and unaffected. Nothing masculine about her, except that she walks onto the ground which men have occupied alone." Kelley had taught at the Friends' School in Lynn, Massachusetts, before resigning in 1839 to become an antislavery agent. She was an early member of the Lynn Female Anti-Slavery Society and one of several women who spoke at the 1838 national convention of antislavery women, which opened its meetings to men. Her words there so impressed Theodore Weld, general agent of the American society, that he urged her to become a lecturer. Kelley wrestled with the idea for a year before finally surrendering to what she perceived as God's call.[21]

The entire Stone family loaded into two wagons and drove into West Brookfield to hear Kelley. Before the meeting, Stone and her mother went to the front of the hall to greet her, and Stone eagerly told of her interest in woman's rights and plan to attend Oberlin College. Kelley invited Stone to join her in the pulpit but Stone declined, explaining that although she did not believe it, still she had an ingrained feeling that the pulpit was not a place for woman. Perhaps embarrassed by such an excuse, she added that she had ridden three miles and her hair was all blown about. Kelley laughed, "Oh, Lucy Stone, you are not *half* emancipated!"[22]

That winter Bowman became the pastor of the Evangelical Congregational Church in Gardner and married Phebe Robinson, a classmate of Lucy's at Mount Holyoke. About the same time, Frank returned home after seven years in Maine. He had spent four of those years in, but had not graduated from, Bangor's theological course, and he was now thirty-five years old.[23] Lucy renewed her close friendship with her eldest brother. Her chronic headaches, which had begun some years before, were particularly severe that winter. These headaches, which plagued Stone at least into her late forties, seem to have been migraine headaches associated with her menstrual cycle. They usually lasted several days and frequently were so severe as to incapacitate her.[24] When they struck, Hannah administered homemade butternut pills and Frank took his sister's head in his lap and gently massaged it, trying to ease the pain.

The following summer Lucy and Sarah went to Quaboag Seminary in neighboring Warren, founded the previous year by George Trask, the minister under whom Bowman completed his theological studies. Sarah enrolled in the ladies' course while Lucy joined the classical course and studied Greek in preparation for Oberlin College. The eleven-week term ended on November 16, 1842, and then Stone taught another winter term in Paxton.[25]

Between teaching and studying, Stone circulated antislavery petitions, including one for repeal of Massachusetts' ban on interracial marriages. Abolitionists had been petitioning for repeal of that provision, a remnant of Massachusetts' slave code, since 1832. In 1839 the House Committee of the Judiciary issued a report heavy with ridicule and attacking the integrity and virtue of the more than fourteen hundred women who signed the petitions. This contempt toward the petitioners triggered another round of debate on women's political rights and strengthened many women's resolve to exercise their rights. When Stone circulated the petition, a neighbor ordered her off his property and threatened to ride her off on a rail if she ever came back. But she went back every year, and his wife always signed. The ten-year campaign, organized and conducted primarily by women abolitionists, came to a close in February 1843 when the Massachusetts legislature repealed the offending sections of the state statutes.[26] To Stone and other women involved in the effort, the victory must have seemed validation for exercising their right to a voice in public affairs even though some did not want to hear it. The following month she demonstrated her commitment to that ideal.

The abolition controversy had worked its way into West Brookfield's Congregational Church, which Stone had joined four years earlier. Resolutions condemning slavery and dissociating slaveholders had been brought before the congregation in 1841, and although they were soundly defeated, the minister determined to rid his church of abolition activism. After Abby Kelley's visit, he charged Deacon Josiah Henshaw, president of the Worcester County North Division Anti-Slavery Society, with "aiding and abetting the publishing and circulation of resolutions and newspapers and public lectures inconsistent with, and subversive of, the articles and covenant of the Church." Among the cited instances of his "aiding and abetting" were hosting Kelley in his home and transporting her to lectures. After a lengthy period of ecclesiastical maneuvering and repeated church meetings, Henshaw was bought before the congregation for trial, and on March 14, 1843, the congregation voted. Stone raised her hand in the deacon's favor. Seeing her upraised hand, the minister pointed at her and directed the teller not to count her vote. "Is she not a member?" the teller asked. "Yes," the minister replied, "but not a voting member." Deacon Henshaw was ultimately expelled, but it took six votes to accomplish the act, and each time Stone raised her hand in his defense.[27]

Oberlin and Universal Reform

Ten days after her twenty-fifth birthday, Lucy Stone stepped off the train in Albany, New York, the first leg of her journey to Oberlin College complete. Second-class rail passage from Albany to Buffalo cost $1.50 more than taking packets on the Erie Canal, and Stone could ill afford to squander her meager funds; the $70 borrowed from Luther, Sarah, and a neighbor was not enough even for one year's expenses. She planned to work her way through college, confident she could teach district schools during the three-month winter breaks and hopeful the institute would employ her in its preparatory department during the regular term. Bowman had given her a letter vouching for her years of successful teaching, addressed to Oberlin's president, Asa Mahan, who had once preached in Bowman's church at Gardner. She found that although the train cost more, it saved three days' travel and several transfers, thus reducing opportunity for misfortune. Tales of calamity befalling women who traveled alone, eagerly offered by friends and neighbors as she prepared for the journey, had made her apprehensive. But weighing time and convenience against cost, she continued on the train.[1]

As the countryside zipped past her window, Stone studied for the entrance examinations facing her upon arrival in Oberlin. A middle-aged man seated nearby asked why she bothered with Greek. Her answer, that she wanted to learn for herself what Scripture said about woman's rights and duties, amused him, and he suggested physiology might be a more practical subject. Stone said she had already studied physiology. He posed a test question, and her prompt reply convinced him it was all right for her to pursue Greek. Stone's fellow traveler was Francis Elias Spinner, a banker from Herkimer, New York. Conversing as they rode together, the two began a lifelong friendship, and Spinner, who would later serve as a congressman and then as treasurer of the United States, would send Stone copies of documents from Washington that were relevant to her woman's rights agitation.[2]

Through the mistake of the porter, Stone rode from Rochester to Buffalo in the crowded car carrying immigrants inland. At Buffalo, she purchased deck passage on a steamship crossing Lake Erie and bedded down under the stars with several other young women as an older woman kept watch. A stagecoach ride from Cleveland completed her five-day journey. "Mother, there is not a bit of trouble about traveling," she wrote. "I would as soon travel alone from Maine to Georgia, and from there to the Rocky Mountains alone as not."[3] But the trip had cost $16.65, more than a year's tuition or two months' room and board. Despite the ease and safety of traveling alone, she would not return home until she received her degree four years later.

Stone arrived in Oberlin on August 26, 1843, a week after the institute graduated a fourth woman from its collegiate course, and within a few days she was enrolled with seven other women in that same course. "So I am a regular 'freshman woman,'" she announced. Upon acceptance, Stone consulted President Mahan about teaching in the preparatory department. She had learned that teachers received twelve and one-half cents an hour, and at that rate, two classes a day would more than pay her board in the dining hall. But Mahan said the institute did not employ first-year students as teachers because the faculty needed time to be assured of their morals and fitness for the task.[4]

This was a blow to Stone's plans. She still counted on getting a district school during winter break, but the only opportunity to earn money during the regular term was in the manual labor program, and this was not heartening. The manual labor system had been advocated by many progressive educators in the 1830s who held that physical exercise was as important to an individual's development as book-learning. In its early years, Oberlin had required all students to perform four hours of physical labor daily. As at Mount Holyoke, the program provided a way for children of the working class to earn part of their education costs, and its early success attracted many students who expected to do just that. But the depressed economy of the early 1840s made it difficult for the institute to offer enough jobs to meet student demand or for students to do enough work to pay a considerable portion of their expenses. Stone was assigned to straighten the Ladies' Hall sitting room in the morning and dry dishes at night, a total of one hour's work daily for which she received three cents.[5]

Stone shared her room in the Ladies' Hall with the daughter of a slaveholder from South Carolina, who was forbidden to discuss slavery for fear she might become an abolitionist. In addition to educating Negroes, Oberlin was a stop on the underground railroad and 10 percent of the town's fourteen hundred residents were black, including freed and fugitive slaves. Although Ohio had some of the harshest Black Laws in the nation, Oberlin was integrated. "There are a good many colored people here at school," Stone reported to her family, "and they sit some at each table in the dining hall and nobody cares or whines about it either. . . . In church they are on terms of equality; there is no negro pew." Even the town's common school educated black and white children together.[6]

Abolition and reform in general were as much traits of Oberlin Collegiate Institute as was its perfectionist theology. But its reform, Stone soon learned, was decidedly of the anti-Garrison stamp. The day after her arrival she heard a scathing attack against Garrisonian principles from the famous Reverend Charles G. Finney. Of all people, said Finney, the come-outers—always impugning the clergy, violating the Sabbath, and disrupting public assemblies— were most in need of reforming. Stone found that students and faculty in general shared Finney's views. "At the table where I sit," she wrote to her family, "they hate Garrison, but they all acknowledge him a talented man, and they don't know but he may be a Christian." And she found that she was the only person in all of Oberlin who took the *Liberator*.[7]

Oberlin's alignment with "new organization" was only natural, because its early supporters and financial backers came from that circle of New York evangelicals who seceded from the American Anti-Slavery Society in 1840 to form the American and Foreign Anti-Slavery Society. Moreover, Oberlin had a theological seminary, and its leaders had not given up hope of making the church a mighty antislavery force. To them, Garrison's come-outer doctrine not only lacked the requisite posture of Christian benevolence, it was also self-defeatist.

Oberlin had assumed a prominent position in the abolition struggle just two years after its founding when it gave refuge to the Lane converts who, after having been ordered to cease their antislavery agitation, had withdrawn from the Cincinnati seminary as a body. Their demonstration of conviction and courage inspired the admiration and sympathies of eastern abolitionists, who joined the search for a college to train them. Their eyes lighted on Oberlin, whose founders were then in the East seeking financial help. Arthur and Lewis Tappan offered money for buildings if the institute would take the "Lane Rebels" and also agree to admit blacks. It was the Tappans, too, who arranged for Finney to go to Oberlin to mold these men into antislavery leaders.

Oberlin's abolitionists disagreed not only with Garrison's religious come-outerism but also with his political come-outerism. Many faculty members belonged to the Liberty Party and embraced William Goodell's argument that the United States Constitution was an antislavery document. This view, which contrasted with Garrison's denunciation of the Constitution as a "covenant with death and an agreement with Hell," was formally adopted by the Liberty Party at its national convention in August 1843, just as Stone was arriving at Oberlin. Goodell argued that because its preamble proclaimed the Constitution ordained and established in order to "secure the blessings of life, liberty, and the pursuit of happiness" to the people of the United States, any part of the Constitution or act of Congress that conflicted with those principles was null and void. Stone considered this wishful thinking not "in accordance with fact." To Frank, who had advanced from colonization to political abolitionism and who thought Oberlin might undermine her Garrisonian leanings, she wrote that she was still an "old organizationist." She admired the "moral grandeur" of the American Anti-Slavery Society's positions and trusted its leaders. She recognized that the Liberty Party also had worthy men, especially in the West, but its policies were inconsistent. Furthermore, she considered its eastern leaders—who, she thought, had been "pushing their enterprise 'out of spite'" since their separation from Garrison—to be "destitute of moral principle." Nevertheless, she said, "I wish God speed to all they do which is calculated to hasten the day of release to the wretched bondman. . . . I am glad to have anything done for the poor downtrodden slave, and do not care whether it is by Old Organization or New Organization, or no organization, only let it bring freedom to the oppressed."[8]

During her first two years at Oberlin, Stone stood virtually alone as a Garrisonian, although for a few months she enjoyed the company of kindred spirit James Monroe. A young antislavery agent who had lectured at Brookfield, Monroe came to Oberlin in 1844 and joined the class ahead of hers. But by the summer of 1845 he had succumbed to Oberlin's influence and "turned entirely third party." His sudden and complete change amazed Stone, and although she respected him because he acted conscientiously, still she regretted that the "peculiar affinity" was gone.[9]

On the question of peace, too, Stone stood apart. As a nonresistant, she disagreed with the view expressed in Fourth of July orations by Oberlin's leading peace advocates, that war is sometimes necessary. Her view coincided with that of Oberlin's first peace society, formed by students in 1840, that all wars and governments sustained by force were anti-Christian. But Oberlin's faculty had withheld official sanction from that group and bestowed its blessing on a second society, formed in 1843 after Amasa Walker, long identified with the old Massachusetts Peace Society, came to Oberlin as visiting professor of political economy and history.[10]

The Oregon Boundary Dispute and the war fever it generated in 1844 and 1845 enlivened the peace movement at Oberlin. Then followed the war with Mexico in 1846, which reformers opposed on both peace and antislavery grounds. When President Polk asked Congress for two million dollars to acquire territory from Mexico and the Senate twice rejected an amendment that would bar slavery from that territory, many northerners were convinced the war's purpose was to extend slavery and increase southern power. Oberlin students held antiwar meetings and petitioned against the annexation of Texas. Stone was one of thousands across the north who signed a pledge drafted by peace pioneer Elihu Burritt, promising never to "yield any voluntary support or sanction to the preparation or prosecution of any war, by whomsoever, for whatever purpose," and associating herself in a League of Universal Brotherhood, whose object was to use all legitimate and moral means to abolish war and all institutions and customs that did not recognize the equality of all men.[11]

Woman's rights was another reform on which Stone and Oberlin's leaders did not agree. Despite the institute's admission of women to the collegiate course and its defense of educating men and women together, most of its leaders rejected the Garrisonian philosophy of equal rights. Reflecting their connection with the New York reform circle headed by the Tappans, they sought the elevation of woman through issues associated with the New York Female Moral Reform Society, of which the Tappans were the primary financial backers and Finney's wife had been the first president. Prostitution was the great evil targeted by moral reformers, but they blamed female licentiousness on societal factors that made women dependent on men: the limited employments open to women, the meager compensation for women's labor, the frivolous and superficial educations urged upon them. Moral reformers argued that women should have better education, access to more employments, and better pay, not because they had an equal right with men to develop their intellects, exercise their talents and interests, or support themselves, but because without education, jobs, and decent pay, many were forced into prostitution to survive. And women should be allowed to engage in reform movements and petitioning, not because they had a right to participate in public affairs, but because society would benefit from their superior morality. Although some leaders of the moral reform movement were also abolitionists and had participated in the national conventions of antislavery women, few had supported Massachusetts women's calls for equal rights and integration. After the 1840 schism, the *Advocate of Moral Reform* continued to publish articles propounding women's economic independence and right to determine their own sphere, but it did so while disclaiming any connection with the Massachusetts movement. One such article, under the heading "Wrongs of Women," disavowed any interest in the "abstract question of woman's rights" and said that time and energy spent arguing that question could be better spent redeeming women from prostitution and helping them earn an honest living.[12] And because the public associated the very term *woman's rights* with Garrison and his followers, moral reformers carefully avoided using it and substituted the terms *woman's cause* or *the elevation of woman.*

The issues denounced by Garrison's clerical opponents and from which moral reform women retreated became the distinguishing characteristics of Garrisonian woman's rights: women's public speaking, women's interaction with men in public organizations, and the philosophy of men's and women's equal rights. Although Garrison's opponents also denounced women's petitioning, moral reformers had too far committed themselves to that strategy to turn back. Their 1845 petition campaign for the suppression of vice obtained five thousand signatures in New York alone.

Although closely aligned with the New York movement, moral reform at Oberlin had a special mission: to prove to a doubting world that higher education would not "unsex" women, making them unfit for their roles as wives and mothers, and that educating men and women together would corrupt the morals of neither sex. Whereas reclaiming so-called fallen women was the primary object elsewhere, at Oberlin that was secondary to promoting and sustaining moral purity among the virtuous—in other words, ensuring that students did not fulfill the expectations of Lyman Beecher, who opposed the joint education of men and women. "This amalgamation of the sexes won't do," he insisted. "If you live in a powder house you blow up once in a while."[13]

To the prevention of such blowups the Oberlin Female Moral Reform Society committed its all. Women students were expected to join the society, and as members they pledged to refrain from "licentious conversation" and to cultivate and promote purity of feeling and action in themselves and those within the sphere of their influence. They were encouraged to eschew fashions designed to arouse the interest of male students, and they were lectured on such topics as "the connection between the caress, the pressure of the hand, the lounging on each other's shoulders and laps, and the increase of the human species." Because it was women's intrusion into a male system that created the explosive situation, the burden of curtailing the danger fell on them. In addition to Oberlin's prohibition of traveling or walking for recreation on the Sabbath, which applied to all students, Oberlin's female students had to observe several other restrictions on their movements: no walking in the streets with a gentleman except by special permission, confinement to their rooms during evening hours unless attending approved meetings, and set times for retirement. A ladies' board comprised of faculty wives and the principal of the ladies' department supervised the conduct of the women students and dealt with infraction of rules or improper behavior.[14]

Oberlin's seeming preoccupation with the moral conduct of its female students might appear prudish and oppressive by later standards, but its posture as an institution educating adult men and women together placed it far in advance of the rest of the society of its time. To Americans of the 1840s, Oberlin was not at all conservative where women were concerned, but dangerously radical. The eyes of the nation looked suspiciously at the institute, waiting for some scandal to prove their worst fears correct, and Oberlin's regulation of female behavior was its attempt to prove workable and safe a very controversial innovation. Stone and the other women students were aware of their role in this unprecedented experiment, and they were just as eager as college officials to make it succeed. If restriction of their movements was part of the price of obtaining a college education, something they could get nowhere else in the world, it was a cheap enough price to pay. Besides, the advocates of a single, equal-for-both-sexes standard of morality had no desire to set women free to sink to the lower level permitted men; rather, their goal was to raise men to the level of morality expected of women.

Although Stone embraced what were considered the more extreme Garrisonian views of woman's equal rights, at first there was little conflict between her and the institute's protectors of female virtue. Her plan to become an educator of women coincided with Oberlin's elevated view of woman's potential and mission. There was an occasion when she was summoned before the ladies' board for removing her bonnet in church, but when she explained that she must either do that or develop a headache and then waste the rest of the Lord's day, she was permitted to leave it off if she sat in the back where she would not be observed.[15] More serious summons before the ladies' board would come later.

Happily, there was one area of reform on which Stone and Oberlin's leaders were in total agreement—physiological reform. The temperance cause, which was closely aligned with the physiology movement, was a moot issue at Oberlin because the community was dry. But physiology was an active cause. Almost all of Oberlin's founders and early faculty were disciples of Graham. The manual labor program had been instituted as much for health reasons as for economic ones. In 1840, Oberlin secured as its dining hall manager the former editor of Graham's *Journal of Health and Longevity*, who had run a Graham boarding house in Boston. By the time Stone arrived in 1843, though, the dining hall's strict Graham diet had been revised because of student complaint. Evidently Hannah Stone had worried about Oberlin's dietary experiment, for Lucy quickly reassured her, "We have meat once a day, bread and milk for supper, pudding and milk, thin cakes, etc. for breakfast. We shall live well enough."[16] As Stone demonstrated during her journey to Oberlin, she had already studied physiology and knew much about the human body. But it was a required subject, and she attended two classes on the subject weekly.

During Stone's first year at Oberlin, another health system arrived in the United States from Europe and quickly became part of the popular health movement. Hydropathy, a system that stressed the ability of the body to heal itself and treated disease and injury with cold water and exercise, developed in Austria during the 1820s and rapidly gained credence as hundreds of people, including royalty and elite from all over Europe, found healing at the founder's water-cure resort. The first American water-cure opened in New York in 1844, and by 1847 there were twenty-eight establishments in nine states. In the United States, hydropathy was superimposed upon the already well-established Graham system, whose principles of diet, outdoor exercise, fresh air, sexual restraint, and dress reform were as essential to the water-cures' therapeutic programs as baths, showers, wet-packs, and other water treatments.

Oberlin subscribed to *The Water-Cure Journal and Herald of Reforms*, although some people considered the paper risqué because of its drawings of the human body and its discussion of pregnancy and feminine ailments such as obstructed menstruation and uterine disease. Stone readily absorbed the new health principles. During the summer of 1845, her eyes became so inflamed she was forced to stop reading for three weeks and feared she might have to skip the fall term. She thought she could cure her eyes herself if she had good water, but Oberlin's water was so bad she considered going to a water-cure in Vermont. Her letters home also prescribed bathing for Frank's lame back ("Get Harriet to bathe your back often and faithfully in moderately cold water. . . . It will strengthen it") and for her father's illness ("He must bathe a great deal. It is the best thing to prevent and cure fever that I know of"). During her last summer at Oberlin, when an epidemic of typhoid fever claimed the lives of several students and townspeople, Stone reported that she watched what she ate, bathed in cold water every day, and felt perfectly well. She also accompanied other women to Lake Erie to swim, an activity promoted by the physiological movement for both sexes because of its combination of physical exercise and healthful bathing.[17]

Oberlin was in the forefront of every progressive reform associated with evangelical Christianity, and Stone fit in comfortably. While Finney was Oberlin's religious leader, its prophet of reform was President Asa Mahan, former pastor of Cincinnati's Sixth Presbyterian Church and a trustee of Lane Seminary who had come to Oberlin with the Lane Rebels. To Mahan, reform was both the spirit and goal of Christianity, for he saw all desirable reforms as aspects of the greater reform of restoring humanity to the condition designed by God. In Stone, Mahan's teaching concerning the character and manner of a true reformer blended with her Garrisonian principles concerning the equality of human rights. Mahan taught that to be effective, reformers must be motivated by Christian benevolence, loving the oppressor as well as the oppressed and eschewing personal denunciation. They should be open-minded and tolerant, willing to hear and consider opposing views, just as they asked their opponents to be. Reformers must not speak as if having all the answers, but be honest, earnest inquirers after truth, fully aware of the possibility of their own error. They must, of course, be enthusiastic in presenting their views, but must never become dogmatic. Mahan especially warned against "ultraism," which he defined as narrow and fanatic devotion to one special reform, emphasis on form over principle, and impractical ideas pushed in a spirit of denunciation and hate. True Christian reformers, he said, were neither reactionaries nor radicals, but practical moderates seeking "the correction of existing abuses and the conforming of all institutions, domestic, civil, and ecclesiastical, to the fundamental ideals of reason."[18]

Oberlin expected its graduates to become reformers, no matter what they did for their livelihood. By living according to the principles of universal reform and Christian perfectionism, they would become part of the great force working toward the reformation and redemption of the world. To that end, Oberlin taught its students to steel themselves against corrupting influences, not to yield to the pressures of custom and public opinion, to do what they knew to be right and refuse to participate in what they knew to be wrong. But Stone found that sometimes the force she had to defy to remain true to her principles and conscience was Oberlin itself. The first major confrontation came during her second year there, in the winter of 1845.

The eighteen cents Stone earned each week in the manual labor program did not approach her one-dollar charge at the dining hall, so she had resumed her old practice of preparing meals in her room and saved each week more than she could earn in two and a half weeks of manual labor. The low pay for women's work rankled Stone. Men's labor received twice the pay of women's, up to ten cents an hour. Certainly chopping wood and hoeing gardens were more strenuous chores than drying dishes, as she did, but they were no more strenuous than washing and ironing clothes or scrubbing floors, as some of the women did. To earn one's board, a male student had to work only two hours a day; a female student, five. This was the very kind of injustice decried by the moral reform movement. An article in the January 1, 1844, issue of the *Advocate of Moral Reform,* calling the long hours and low pay forced on women workers "an outrage on humanity," could have fueled Stone's simmering rage. At a time when reformers denounced the "mere pittance" of two and one-half cents an hour paid to New York's sewing women, Oberlin paid its female workers just a half-penny more![19]

Sometime in 1844, Stone received the longed-for teaching position in the institute and was one of six women students appointed to teach in the ladies' department. But she did not get the expected twelve and one-half cents an hour pay, for here, as in the manual labor program, women received half pay. The difference in rates was universal wherever women were employed; indeed, in 1844 just the fact of hiring women as teachers was, in itself, a mark of liberality. At Oberlin, the pay a collegiate student received for teaching in the lower departments depended not only on the student's sex but also on the subject taught and previous teaching experience. So Stone, being a highly experienced and successful teacher, received eight cents an hour for teaching arithmetic— *more than half* the twelve and one-half cents paid two less-experienced male students for teaching the same subject.[20]

While teaching a district school during the next winter break, Stone contemplated her situation at Oberlin. Attending lectures, prayer meetings, and various other required sessions consumed the bigger part of each day. She taught two classes daily, worked in the manual labor program, purchased food and prepared her meals, and did her own laundry, ironing, and sewing. This left little time for reading, preparing for recitations, or writing essays. Even rising at two in the morning did not provide enough time for study. Determining that the pay due from the district school, together with what remained of her borrowed funds, would meet expenses through August, she made several decisions. First, wanting both more time and better nutrition, she would resume eating at the dining hall. Second, believing her time to be worth more than three cents an hour, she would quit the manual labor program. Third, believing she deserved the same compensation for teaching as her male colleagues, she would ask for equal pay, and if the board refused, she would resign her classes. And last, she would buy a rocking chair with a writing leaf. It cost four dollars, but in using it to soothe her migraine headaches, she expected to get more than her money's worth.[21]

With the support of Mary Ann Adams, principal of the ladies' department, Stone presented her request for equal pay in February 1845. No record of her words before the faculty board survives, but a few years later when asked for details of her effort, she said she tried to show "that there was no reason, based on justice or common sense, why the same service, equally well performed, should not have the same compensation." The board denied Stone's request, she resigned her classes, and a contest began that lasted three months. Stone was a popular teacher, and her students wanted her back. Evidently impressed more by Stone's description of hardship than by her arguments for fairness, the faculty asked her to teach just one class if she felt she could not manage two. But Stone insisted she would teach only if given the same pay as her male coworkers. The faculty board referred the issue to a committee, and while it pondered what to do, Stone's former students informed the board that if it would not pay Miss Stone what was right, they themselves would! The faculty at length yielded, and in the middle of May, Stone resumed teaching at twelve and one-half cents an hour.[22]

The other women teachers received the higher rate, too, and for at least the next few years, the institute made no distinction in pay between its male and female student teachers. Stone's success was considered a great triumph of principle by much of Oberlin's reform-minded populace, who were still boasting of it a few years later when an English tourist visited the campus. Impressed by the story, the visitor wrote to Stone for the details and published an account in her 1853 travel book, *An Englishwoman's Experience in America.*[23]

This victory was a milepost in Stone's development as a reformer. She had refused to acquiesce to what she perceived as wrong; she had been true to principle and true to herself. Not only did her own self-respect and sense of purpose mature but she also gained the esteem of faculty and students and won the respect and support of her father. Before presenting her appeal to the faculty board, Stone had written home about her difficulties. Francis Stone was moved by his daughter's struggle and shamed by the realization that he contributed to it. "When you wrote that you had to get up at 2 oclock to study your lesson it made me think of the old Tanyard when I had to get up at one and two oclock. I little thought then that I should have children or a child that would have to do the same not the same work but perhaps as hard. . . . Let this suffice. There will be no trouble about money you can have what you will need without studying nights or working for eight cents an hour."[24]

After the standoff was over, though, the higher pay enabled Stone to manage on her own, so it was not necessary to accept her father's offer, at least not for the time being. Francis Stone's promise to supply needed money was the offer of a loan, not an offer to pay her expenses. He had helped his sons through college by supplementing their teaching incomes with loans, which they repaid with interest. This was what Francis Stone promised Lucy—equal treatment with her brothers. Lucy was grateful to have this support to fall back on, for, she said, had it not been for this assurance from "the bank at home" during the weeks her ultimatum was being considered, she could not have withstood the pressure.[25]

During the months Stone did not teach, she caught up on the reading she had not had time for. She spent hours in the reading room of the Ladies' Literary Society, which received thirty-two different newspapers, and bought a year's membership in the college library. But it was that summer, in 1845, that inflamed eyes halted her reading and made her fear she might have to forgo the fall term to seek a water-cure. When her eyes healed, she resumed her independent reading and upon completing the *Narrative of the Life of Frederick Douglass, An American Slave,* exclaimed, "I never read a more deeply thrilling tale. I hate slavery and all its consequences worse than war."[26]

Except for bad eyes and migraine headaches, Stone remained healthy during an outbreak of typhoid fever that struck at least seven women in the Ladies' Hall. Despite the epidemic, life at Oberlin progressed as normally as possible, with classes and meetings held as usual. To one of the Ladies' Literary Society meetings was invited a visiting Englishman, Adolphus Sturge, nephew of Joseph Sturge, one of the school's wealthy benefactors and a leading force against women's admission to the World's Anti-Slavery Convention in 1840. It so happened that Stone had prepared a long composition on the oppression of English mill and factory operatives, miners, and other peasantry. When she finished reading the essay, Sturge sprang to his feet and asked for opportunity to reply. At the next meeting, the president read Sturge's ten-page rebuttal, in which he defended England's honor and capitalistic system and questioned Stone's sources, the accuracy of her information, and her logic and inserted a couple of ridiculing rhymes. Having read the rebuttal beforehand, Stone presented a brief rejoinder. Her reply—forceful, witty, and kind—fully sustained her earlier position, and the audience voted her the winner of the debate. Sturge sent a note of congratulations, praising Stone's personal talents but managing to remind her that she was a member of the "inferior" sex. "I had no idea," he said, "that the intellectual faculties of the 'Ladies' took so high a range, and were so capable of inculcating such excellent precepts."[27]

Both male and female students regarded Stone as a trusted friend and respected advisor. A young man who had been so infatuated with her that he composed a farewell poem to her when he left Oberlin wrote a few months later seeking advice on a career decision. A young woman who felt Stone understood her better than any other "earthly friend" confided a secret romance and showed love letters. Another sought Stone's advice before leaving to teach in Michigan and later reported that she had followed Stone's advice and developed good rapport with her students. Stone was elected secretary-treasurer of Oberlin's Moral Reform Society during her third year and president of the Ladies' Literary Society her senior year.[28]

Stone taught her two arithmetic classes in the ladies' department until the end of fall term in October 1845 and then, turning down job offers at three other schools, taught during the winter break in Oberlin's school for black adults. Liberty Seminary, as it was sometimes called, had operated informally on and off for two years until a committee was appointed in 1844 to manage its operation and find permanent funding. Most of its students had been slaves, some just recently freed or escaped. Many had been sailors; some were old and gray-haired; all were, in Stone's words, "shrouded in ignorance and degradation." At first they did not like having a woman for a teacher, but she persuaded them that knowledge was too important to bother about who imparted it and she quickly gained their confidence. Stone's tenure in Liberty Seminary taught her the power of patience and kindness in, as she put it, "overcoming wickedness." She had one scholar in particular—a large man about thirty years old, a sailor named Robert—who had built a wall around himself she had difficulty penetrating. He sat apart by himself, quiet, uncommunicative, and unresponsive. He seemed to Stone to have steeled himself against kindness as well as cruelty. But Stone took special pains to greet him when he entered and persisted in giving him caring attention despite his coldness. Gradually he opened up, began walking with her after school, confided his life story and plans for the future, and became thoroughly devoted to her. She, in turn, was devoted to her students. She spent hours outside of class writing letters for them, reading the letters they received, calculating their accounts, and listening to them talk about their experiences as slaves. "I believe that my heart sympathizes more fully and deeply with the oppressed from teaching in the colored school," she wrote home, "for I have seen and felt the dehumanizing influences of slavery."[29]

She left Liberty Seminary at the end of January, thoroughly exhausted. During the twelve-week winter term she had spent seven to eight hours a day in the classroom, not including the sessions of letter writing and personal talks, had herself taken French lessons, had made a dress, and had done errands for a feeble old woman whose son was absent teaching. Never in her life, she told her family, had she felt so tired or been so thin. "I grew so poor that my clothes lapped wonderfully and people said 'how poor you grow.'" Having weighed 119 pounds the previous summer, she would weigh in at 106 pounds the next.[30] Stone had expected to resume teaching in the ladies' department, but weary and wanting to concentrate on her own studies, she decided not to teach and to request money from home when her funds ran out.

After a few days' rest, however, she visited the Liberty Seminary and learned that her former students were unhappy with the two men who replaced her. Robert had not read since her departure, and the new teachers, he said, refused to help him with arithmetic. So a few days later when the school committee asked her to return and teach as much or as little as she liked while the other teachers were there, Stone agreed. "I think I can be more useful there than anywhere at present," she explained to her family. "I have acquired (I hardly know how) an almost boundless influence over [the students] and while I retain it, I can do them a great deal of good." So instead of claiming her free time for herself, she taught two hours a day in Liberty Seminary and spent another hour giving private reading instruction to an elderly Negro woman. Commending her decision, Bowman reminded her, "The greatest luxury we can have in this world is in doing good to our fellow men."[31]

The Highest Good

An increasing awareness of her personal power to persuade and inspire, along with a growing disillusionment with progressive thinkers' assessment of women's rights and abilities, nudged Lucy Stone toward becoming a public speaker. She had long intended to devote her life to the elevation of her sex, but until 1846 she planned to do that through teaching. The change in plan grew out of her belief in the ethic of "disinterested benevolence," which taught that the holy person sought the greatest good for the whole of humanity over personal well-being and gain. "The fact that the world is being made better through our influence," she told her new brother-in-law, "is sufficient to make one persevere in well-doing" despite receiving low pay. Urging her father to vote for a new schoolhouse even though he no longer had children to use it, she reminded him that, as lovers of humanity, "we ought to try to promote the highest good."[1] It was this desire to make the world better and accomplish the highest good that had made Stone choose the Liberty Seminary over positions where she could earn more money and why she resumed teaching there despite her need for rest.

Stone had long been aware of the "peculiar power" she had over her students, but the events of 1845—her success with the faculty board over the matter of women's pay, in the debate with Adolphus Sturge, and with Robert in the Liberty Seminary—demonstrated that she could put that power to greater use. In her study of Cicero and rhetoric that spring she probably read *De oratore*, in which the Roman philosopher extolled the orator's power to lift humanity. There was no higher, nobler calling, he argued, than oratory.[2] In February 1846 when Abby Kelley visited Oberlin, Stone hinted that she might take up public speaking, but not until that summer did controversy over Abby's speaking at Oberlin clinch Stone's decision. For it then seemed to Stone that if the country's foremost center of Christian reform could scorn a woman for working according to the dictates of her conscience, then the highest good she could do, both for woman and for humanity, was to help overthrow the ideology that robbed woman of that freedom and humanity of the benefit of her labor.

Abby Kelley and Stephen Foster had been married for two months when they came to Oberlin but had been working together in Ohio for almost a year to convert what had become a new organization stronghold to Garrisonian principles and strategies. These included withdrawing from proslavery churches and refusing to vote or participate in governments that supported and defended the institution of slavery. The shunning of politics and government, embraced as a strategy by only a few abolitionists in 1839, was now widely advocated among members of the Garrisonian wing. Furthermore, many Garrisonians now also advocated *disunion,* or the secession of free states from the Union with slave states. This position had arisen partly in self-defense against the charge that antislavery agitation would provoke slave states to secede. Wendell Phillips had countered that if such effort would dissolve the Union, then let it go! "Perish the Union when its cement must be the blood of the slave!—when the rights of one must be secured at the expense of the other!"[3] Much to the dismay of Liberty Party leaders, Kelley and Foster had great success in Ohio. Assisted by J. Elizabeth Hichcock and Benjamin Jones, another pair of agents who married during their Ohio labors, they established a state society auxiliary to the "old organization" American Society and a newspaper, the *Anti-Slavery Bugle,* as its organ. After a year's work, they had raised such a following in northern Ohio that Liberty Party leaders complained that "the whole Liberty force has gone over to Disunion."[4]

Stephen Foster was a leader of the radical wing of the already radical Garrisonians. In 1843 he published a stinging denunciation of America's churches for their role in slavery, titled *The Brotherhood of Thieves: Or a True Picture of the American Church and Clergy.* While fellow abolitionists saw Foster as one of the most impressive advocates the slave ever had, they also considered him needlessly offensive, so much so that even Garrison wished he would tone down his rebukes. Abby had lectured with Stephen for several months before their marriage, and critics charged that she had adopted his provocative manner.

Oberlin officials were not eager to receive the Fosters. Besides fearing the unsettling influence of Garrisonian principles, they regretted the timing, for the community was engrossed in a fervid religious revival. Resumption of classes after winter break had been postponed so students and faculty could attend the preaching, prayer, and testimonial meetings and concentrate on the salvation of their souls. According to Stone, Oberlin was a "place to harden sinners," because students were forced to hear so much preaching they grew immune to it. But this revival was having dramatic effect. She told her parents the daily meetings were "crowded to excess" and "The Spirit of God seems to be moving on almost every heart."[5] With religious momentum breaking through hardened shells, Charles Finney did not want the distraction of a visit from the Fosters.

But when the Fosters arrived, most of the community extended the Christian forbearance taught by Mahan. They held three meetings, which, to minimize distraction, were arranged as lectures rather than forums for exchange of ideas. No public response occurred until after they had departed and the revival subsided. Initial reaction was mixed. President Mahan said Abby handled her subject ably and that if her premises were granted, her conclusions must be also. But, of course, he disagreed with the premises and defended the antislavery interpretation of the Constitution. The *Oberlin Evangelist* also disagreed with the Fosters' sentiments but conceded that they expounded "great principles of philanthropy and benevolence clearly and cogently." Not all were so kind, however. Despite the general concession that Abby exhibited talent as an orator, some critics insisted that although oratorical gestures and showing emotion were expected of male speakers, from a woman they were not only inappropriate but vulgar and shameless. Stone found a particular criticism of Abby published by the *Evangelist* narrow-minded, cruel, and unjust.[6]

Despite the delayed public reaction, the Fosters awakened much interest in their issues. Stone told them that at first Professor Morgan considered the title of Stephen's *Brotherhood of Thieves* "utterly abominable," but after reading it he thought the title not strong enough. Stone said that although most of the women at Oberlin were not interested in the questions the Fosters raised, Abby had roused their interest in woman's rights. Suddenly there was "a great deal of talking and writing on the subject, and a few are taking the true ground." Stone was encouraged by the working of the "little leaven" the Fosters had brought to Oberlin. Although they had not been able to present their views fully, they had "set a ball in motion that is still rolling," Stone reported a month after their visit. "And it *will* roll, for there are a few who are *pushing* it." Stone, who became a subscription agent for the *Anti-Slavery Bugle*, was one of those pushing it.[7]

In April, Abby wrote to Stone about plans of the new state society to hire more lecturers and, having inferred that Stone was thinking of "trampling on prejudice and taking the field," asked her to leave Oberlin and lecture for the society. But Stone was not about to cut short her college education, and she was not prepared for public speaking. Although theory and practice of public speaking were a standard part of a college education, she found that female members of Oberlin's collegiate rhetoric class did not participate in oral exercises. This was due more to custom than to explicit proscription. When women first entered the collegiate course in 1839, they had been mortified by the suggestion that they read essays to their male classmates and petitioned to remain in the ladies' rhetoric class. Later, when they did move into the collegiate class, they were excused from oral exercises.[8] Although no official policy barred them from participation, the lack of requirement and expectation coincided with the prevailing idea that it was improper for women to participate in oral exercises with men. Aside from the questions of joint activity and female authority over men, women had no need to develop oratorical skill because they would not enter professions that required it. Furthermore, in an age with no amplification systems, speakers had to virtually shout to make themselves heard by large audiences and this certainly did not fit standards of feminine modesty and quiescence. Outside Oberlin's collegiate course, men and women did not study rhetoric together. As at coeducational academies, the men belonged to debating clubs, where they developed speaking skills needed for masculine careers, while the women belonged to literary societies and developed appreciation for literature and religion by reading to each other. Even women's formal so-called discussions and debates consisted of prepared statements rather than extemporaneous argumentation.

If the "great deal of talking and writing" on woman's rights that Stone reported to the Fosters included any suggestion that public speaking be added to the repertoire of the women's literary society, the adoption of a new constitution checked such agitation. The constitution defined the society's purpose as promoting the intellectual and moral improvement of its members, and it lacked phrases contained in the constitutions of the men's societies that committed them to the development of oratorical skills. Nevertheless, two weeks after the women's society adopted the new constitution and formally accepted the restriction, Stone deliberately transgressed it. On May 20 the Ladies' Literary Society held a joint meeting with the men's Dialectic Society, in which the men delivered speeches and held formal discussions while the women listened. To the delight of some and horror of others, Stone participated in the discussion and, like Kelley, punctuated her points with the oratorical gestures taught male students.[9]

Unfortunately, the mood in Oberlin was not receptive to this kind of demonstration, for President Mahan's exposure of several "misstatements and misquotations" in a pamphlet distributed by the Fosters shattered the fragile esteem in which they had been held. The revelation opened a floodgate of bitter personal attacks, especially against Abby, whose public speaking was now denounced as a shocking display of "what woman becomes when out of her place." A rumor circulated that she was pregnant, so her appearance on the platform was indecent. When Stone tried to arrange a second visit for the Fosters, Finney and most of the faculty declared them "unsafe advocates of the slave" and voted not to receive them.[10]

All summer long, controversy raged over whether the Fosters should be permitted another hearing. Soon after Stone's demonstration at the joint literary meeting, a faculty member quoted St. Paul's "Let your women keep silence in the church; for it is not permitted unto them to speak. And if they will learn anything, let them ask their husbands at home. For it is a shame for a woman to speak in the church." This, the students were told, was "a command positive, explicit, and universal." At the next meeting of the women's literary society, in an essay titled "The Province of Woman," Stone challenged that statement. Drawing from Sarah Grimké's *Letters on the Equality of the Sexes*, she offered alternative interpretations for Old and New Testament passages used to rationalize women's subjugation. Male domination over woman was a result of human sin, foretold but not commanded by God, she argued. Although Old Testament law condoned male domination, the New Testament taught that in Christ, there was neither male nor female. The passage about women keeping silent in church, Stone pointed out, was part of Paul's instructions to early church congregations. The Christian Gospel gave women the liberty to read Scripture, a privilege formerly denied them, and they had many questions. The instructions for them to keep silent at church and ask their husbands for explanations at home were probably intended to prevent meetings from being absorbed by the women's questions. Surely, said Stone, Paul could not have intended this instruction to be a comprehensive command against women speaking in church or preaching, for he also said that when the church came together, "ye may all prophesy, one by one, that all may learn and all may be comforted."[11]

Stone's insistence on the right of women to speak in public had the full support of many of her fellow students, male and female. The black community, too, who objected to Oberlin's treatment of the Fosters, sympathized with Stone's stand. In July, a black classmate invited her to participate in the August First commemoration of West Indies Emancipation, an event celebrated by many abolitionist communities and at Oberlin, organized by the black community. It was customary for women who wrote essays for public events to have them read by men. But in accepting the invitation, Stone said she would read her essay herself. The organizers agreed.[12]

Stone's address, titled "Why Do We Rejoice Today?" was her first public speech, not connected in any way with academic activities at Oberlin. The program was held in Oberlin's church and Stone spoke from the pulpit, flanked by President Asa Mahan and Professor James Thome, both of whom supported her course of action. In answering the question she posed, Stone revealed her faith in the Garrisonian principle of moral suasion, or as she termed it, "rectifying public sentiment." They rejoiced, she said, not simply because freedom now presided where slavery once ruled, but "in the greater fact that . . . a public sentiment exists which frees the slave and lets the oppressed go free; which practically recognizes the equal brotherhood and inalienable rights of men." And, she continued, they rejoiced because its influence was not confined to the West Indies. "The doom of slavery everywhere is sealed in the public sentiment which caused England to reach out her hand over the broad Atlantic and lift up . . . the bondman pining there." Expressing her confidence in the power of public opinion, she declared: "A rectified public sentiment always has been, and must ever be, the sovereign remedy for existing evil. It matters not though the strong arm of the law may be around systems of wrong, nor though they may be hoary with age . . . Let but the indignant frown of a virtuous public be concentrated upon them, and they must inevitably perish." Stone would later tell a friend, "To make the public sentiment on the side of all that is just and true and noble is the highest use of life."[13]

A Cleveland newspaper reported Stone's part in this celebration: "The third and last essay, 'Why do we rejoice today?' was read by one of New England's white girls. She is a member of the junior class in this college, and the way she answered the question . . . gave evidence that a mind naturally brilliant had not been dimmed, but polished rather, by classical studies and the higher mathematics. . . . She is one of those who believes that neither color nor sex should deprive of equal rights, and true to her principles, she ascended the stand and in a clear full tone, read her own article."[14]

Telling her family of the event, Stone said two other women wrote for the occasion but did not read, "for it is not considered proper here for women to do anything of the kind, but I thought it *was right*, and so read. I expected to be reproved for it, but I have not been scolded at all, and presume I shall not be." Although Stone was not formally reprimanded by the ladies' board, some of its members tried to impress upon her that what she had done was unbecoming. Asked if she did not feel ashamed or embarrassed to occupy the pulpit with men, she replied, "Why, no. It was only President Mahan and Professor Thome, whom we all know and like so well. I did not feel any more uncomfortable with them than if I had been with them in class." Stone told her parents, "On the whole, I think they respect me more for carrying out my principles. They think I am honest, but say they are sorry I believe as I do. Father told me once, 'So long as you have a good reason, stick to it,' and it has helped me to stick to, since I came here, where I differ entirely on many questions from the people. They hate Garrison and woman's rights. I love both, and often find myself at sword's point with them, but I have a good reason and so I stick to."[15]

Shortly after the Emancipation Day celebration, President Mahan overrode the faculty vote against the Fosters, and Stone arranged meetings for them in September. Afterward, Finney continued his attack against them, denouncing their Unitarian beliefs and saying, according to Stone, that they were headed straight for hell. The controversy nudged Stone from Congregational trinitarianism to Unitarianism. As late as February during the revival, she had still clung to orthodox beliefs despite her acceptance of Finney's Christian perfectionism and Garrison's views on a popular ministry. She had repeatedly reminded family members to cultivate their religious life, confided her own feelings of unworthiness, and asked them to pray for her. But now, in the summer of 1846, hearing the Fosters denounced as unchristian and the Bible quoted to defend woman's subjugation, Stone commenced an earnest reexamination of long-held beliefs. Ironically, she credited Finney himself with converting her to Unitarianism. She said his lectures and subsequent class discussions on the Trinity left her a Unitarian and entirely clear about it in her mind.[16]

In the summer of 1846, Stone befriended a newcomer to Oberlin, Antoinette L. Brown, who had arrived in the spring, right after the Fosters' first lectures, and enrolled in the ladies' course. Brown was from Henrietta, New York, in an area Finney had stirred with religious revivals during the 1820s, and she admired him with a fervor that rivaled Stone's for Garrison. Her brother William had graduated from Oberlin's theological department in 1841, and although she did not let it be known at first, she intended to study theology, too. On her way to Oberlin, Antoinette had been warned about a student named Lucy Stone, who "believed so strongly in the rights of women that she was making herself the center of irrepressible agitation on the subject" and was therefore "a rather dangerous person, not exactly one to be avoided, but best treated with a distant and wise discretion." Brown's curiosity piqued, she had Stone pointed out to her in the dining hall and, watching her talk with several men, quickly decided she talked "altogether too much and with an unfitting absoluteness of conviction and authority" for a young girl. Brown judged Stone to be about sixteen, and when she later learned that Stone was actually a mature twenty-seven, she changed her opinion.[17]

The two young women became acquainted during a summer outing to Lake Erie and became good friends during the following weeks. Taking long walks together and sitting for hours watching clouds and sunsets, they engaged in intense discussions about religion, abolitionism, and woman's rights. Brown, eight years Stone's junior, was an unshakable orthodox trinitarian, while Stone was shaking off orthodoxy. Although they read Ralph Waldo Emerson's essays together and laughed over passages they found incomprehensible, Stone was moving toward transcendentalism and the belief that God's truth could be discerned through spiritual intuition and nature. By the end of the year, she would proclaim herself a "natural worshiper," and she later recorded that she often "worshiped" outdoors where she found God's "unwritten revelations." Stone believed the church itself was experiencing a reformation, similar to but greater than that instigated by Martin Luther, through which "pure Christianity" would overthrow the institutionalized church and reform every aspect of society.[18]

Although both women were staunchly antislavery, Brown was a "voting abolitionist" and did not share Stone's admiration for Garrison. There were other issues on which they did not agree, but when it came to woman's rights they were of one mind. One evening as they discussed what the future might hold for women, Antoinette confided that she wanted to become a minister. Stone thought the clergy would never ordain her and advised her to become a woman's rights lecturer along with her.[19]

Their discussions reveal that by the summer of 1846 Stone had definitely decided to become a woman's rights reformer. The question of woman's rights had been simmering for ten years and interest was so widespread that Stone said she could scarcely pick up a paper that did not contain an article on it. Reacting to losses in the recent depression, legislators were seeking ways to protect the property of married women from their husbands' creditors. Massachusetts passed a law in 1845 giving women ownership rights to property they brought to their marriage if secured by a prenuptial agreement, and another in 1846 securing their earnings. Mississippi, Michigan, and Ohio passed similar laws. Commenting on these legal changes in the *Liberator*, Wendell Phillips hailed the "progress of public opinion" regarding the legal position of women. The restoration of woman's "full and unfettered control of all her property and earnings," whether married or unmarried, was the first of woman's rights to be secured, he said. Next came the ballot. "So it has always been with all disfranchised classes; first property—then political influence and right; the first prepares for, gives weight to, challenges, and finally secures the second."[20]

As Phillips's editorial reveals, the issue of woman suffrage was gaining interest, too. Reformers such as John Neal, editor of the journal *Brother Johnathan*, were increasingly blaming laws that treated women unfairly on women's exclusion from the law-making process. As early as 1840 when the Liberty Party formed, some within its ranks wanted to make universal suffrage, including woman suffrage, part of its platform. It remained an issue within the party throughout the decade, and in 1846 an offshoot, the Liberty League, petitioned Congress to extend the vote to women so they could be represented in "State and National Councils." Responding to the growing interest, New York jurist Elisha P. Hurlbut set out to present all the reasons women should not vote, but when he found he could easily counter each point, he made his 1845 book, *Essays on Human Rights,* an argument in favor of woman suffrage instead. Also in 1845, reacting to the fact that New York had just ratified a new state constitution without giving its female citizens any voice in the process, Samuel J. May appealed for woman suffrage from his Syracuse pulpit. His sermon, "On the Rights and Condition of Women," excerpted in many newspapers and widely circulated in pamphlet form, was one of the works that caught Stone's attention in the summer of 1846.[21]

Stone found newspapers filled, too, with a new reform that touched on the issue of woman's equality—Associationism. The American version of the French Fourierist movement, Associationism was a cooperative social and economic system introduced by Albert Brisbane, who had studied under social philosopher Charles Fourier and wanted to make the United States the proving ground for his ideas. According to Fourier, society's progress through various stages of development could be measured by the degree to which it allowed individuals to exercise their natural human impulses and instincts, which he termed "passions." Indulgence of these instinctual forces allowed individuals to reach the highest level of development of which they were capable, while restraint caused not only individual pain and unhappiness but also all of society's ills. Higher social orders, therefore, harmonized the interests of the individual with the interests of society. Fourier said the present social order, although more advanced than earlier stages, still doomed its members to misery by isolating them in separate households and businesses, which fragmented industry, duplicated effort, wasted time and resources, and condemned individuals to the drudgery of work with no opportunity to develop their interests and talents. His remedy was a system of "associative living." In his proposed cooperative communities, which he called "phalanxes," members lived independently but "in association" with each other under one roof in a "unitary building," sharing the work essential to providing the necessities of life. This "associative system" reduced the workload for everyone, allowed members to choose their work according to their interests, and provided time and opportunity for individuals to exercise their intellectual, artistic, and creative passions.[22]

Introduced to Americans in 1840 through Brisbane's book, *The Social Destiny of Man, or Association and Reorganization of Industry,* Fourier's ideas immediately attracted the attention of farmers, laborers, and businessmen displaced or disillusioned by the depression, as well as of reformers, who saw in Association a system that might "accomplish all other reforms—abolition, peace, temperance, woman's rights, health." Horace Greeley, editor of the newly established *New York Tribune,* helped spread Association ideas by carrying a weekly Brisbane column on his paper's front page, printing Brisbane's weekly journal, and publishing his second book in 1844. Parke Godwin, editor of the *Path-Finder,* carried weekly translations from Fourier's work and published his own *Popular View of the Doctrines of Charles Fourier.* Spread by newspapers and lecturing agents, enthusiasm spawned numerous Fourier societies and culminated in the formation of a national society in 1846. By then, two dozen Fourierist communities existed in ten states. Even Massachusetts' famed transcendental Brook Farm had reorganized as a phalanx.[23]

Associationism intrigued those interested in woman's rights because Fourier not only recognized the absolute equality of the sexes, but also measured the historical progress of society by the degree to which women could exercise their freedom as individuals. Like moral reformers, Associationists blamed prostitution on society's failure to provide women the means of earning a living, but it also said this degradation would not be eliminated until society recognized "the independent right of woman to existence and happiness." Some Associationists said the present social order doomed the institution of marriage itself to what Harriet Martineau called "legalized prostitution," for as long as wives remained dependents, marriage could not rise to the "mystic and divine union of soul and body of which St. Paul speaks." Associationists generally agreed that by keeping married women isolated in separate households and absorbed by housekeeping and child rearing, society prevented them from developing their intellect and talent. Fourier's plan of industrial organization was the only social system that could change that, they said.[24]

Articles such as these helped shape Stone's ideas. On September 16, during the week of the Fosters' second visit, Stone delivered another essay before her literary society. Although it does not survive, its title, "Wasted Intellect," suggests inspiration from a passage in May's sermon, and it was probably an elaboration on an idea expressed in her earlier essay. May had stated that the exclusion of women from public affairs kept them from developing their minds and that this "waste of intellect and moral sense" cost humanity dearly in lost benefit.[25] Stone had touched on that theme in her essay "The Province of Woman," saying that as long as women were taught they had a duty *not* to use their intellect or to follow their conscience, few would do it. And so long as they did not, "so long will the great end of woman's existence be unattained, and society will suffer just in proportion as she does not occupy the station which God designed she should occupy as an intellectual and accountable being." The idea that humanity suffered from the wasted intellect, talents, and energies of half its members could only have reinforced Stone's resolve to help set those resources free and her perception that it was in such a crusade where her personal talents could best serve humanity—where she could do "the highest good."

Once certain of her calling, Stone wrote to her family of her decision. Her brothers were immediately supportive. Frank said he had no objection to women lecturing, and "If you think you have got brass enough, and can do more good by giving public lectures than any other way, I say go to it." "I think you should do that which you think to be your duty," said Bowman. "No one can be truly happy who neglects to do what he feels he ought." Although her father did not like the idea of her lecturing, he encouraged her to do what she thought was her duty. But Hannah Stone was aghast at her daughter's plan. "Now Miss Lucy," wrote her father, "you will hear what Mother thinks about your Public Speaking. Mother says she had rather you would [have] married Walker and had a pair of twin babes every year. She did not say how many years."[26]

Despite her father's levity, Stone knew that the preferred fate of marriage and constant maternity ranked, in her mother's estimation, only a little higher than death. The wish effectively communicated Hannah's anguish over her daughter's announcement. Lucy tried to assuage her distress:

But Mother, do you really wish that I had married Walker, with such results as you said, than have me open my mouth for the dumb? You have often told me you hoped I never would be married and I have as often told you that I would not. I mean to obey you too in this particular. But shall I not also obey God? He tells us to open our mouths for the dumb and plead the cause of the poor and needy. He makes no exception, but leaves each one to choose his own way to do it in. Now Mother, the way I have chosen is the one in which I think I can do it best, and would you have me act contrary to the dictates of my conscience?[27]

Lucy probably anticipated her mother's reaction, but not her sister's. Sarah said she had suspected Lucy was preparing to become a public speaker but had hoped she was mistaken. Although she certainly believed women had a right to speak in public, she considered lecturing "a great many grades below" what Lucy was qualified to do. As far as working "for the restoration and salvation" of the female sex, Sarah hardly knew what Lucy meant but concluded she meant a salvation from "some thralldom imposed by man." "Now my sister," Sarah protested, "I don't believe woman is groaning under half so heavy a yoke of bondage as you imagine. I am sure I do not feel burdened by anything man has laid upon me." Of course women could not vote, but Sarah cared nothing about that; she would not vote if permitted. She knew women received lower wages than men for the same work, and that was unjust. But that was the only way she knew of in which women were oppressed, and women had only themselves to blame for that, she said. "If as a general thing they had qualified themselves, as men have, they would command the same price; but they have not, and the few who have are obliged to suffer on that account."[28]

Lucy was astonished by Sarah's perception of woman's position in society. "Why, Sarah my dear sister," she replied, "the time was when you did not think as you now do. When you knew, and felt too, the crushing power of the unjust restraints of the unnatural position we are compelled to occupy." Lucy wondered what "sorcery" had blinded Sarah's vision. Was it her own domestic bliss in a new marriage that made her forget "the untold wrongs . . . under which the mass of women are suffering?" How could Sarah say women had not qualified themselves for teaching as men had, when she knew there was "but *one* institution in the world where equal advantages for obtaining such an education are afforded, with the additional fact that while the board, tuition, books etc. of a woman cost as much as those of a man, *she* must labor the live-long week and perhaps longer for a compensation which *he* receives for a single day."

There was "not a single position—social, civil, or ecclesiastical—in which equal rights and privileges are enjoyed by the different sexes," said Stone, but this would not always be the case. Women and men would one day enjoy equal rights by virtue of their common humanity. But it would take a long time to effect the change because women's subjugation was so universal and deeply rooted. Everywhere, said Stone, women "hug their chains" while men divert them from exalted and worthy lives, pulpit and press combine to crush their intellect, and "the whole machinery of society" drives them into a "system of legalized adultery to which we rush rather than starve." When Stone saw all of this, she said, her blood leapt like wild fire through her veins and she pledged her whole being to lifelong effort.[29]

Stone sent her family a copy of May's sermon as a means of explaining the work she intended to do, hoping, too, that it would calm her mother's fears. But Hannah could not reconcile herself to Lucy's plan. She wanted Lucy to consider whether she might be able to do more good by teaching, or if she might be able to do more good by going from house to house, as some other reformers did, than by addressing public audiences.[30]

Stone replied:

I know, Mother, you feel badly about the plan I have proposed to myself, and that you would prefer to have me take some other course if I could in conscience. Yet, Mother, I know you too well to suppose that you would wish me to turn away from what I think is my duty and go all my days in opposition to my conscience. I surely would not be a public speaker if I sought a life of ease, for it will be a most laborious one; nor would I do it for the sake of honor, for I know that I shall be disesteemed, nay, even hated, by some who are now my friends, or who profess to be. Neither would I do it if I sought wealth, because I could secure it with far more ease and worldly honor by being a teacher. But, Mother, the gold that perishes in the using, the honor that comes from men, the ease or indolence which eats out the energy of the soul, are not the objects at which I aim. If I would be true to myself, true to my Heavenly Father, I must be actuated by high and holy principles, and pursue that course of conduct which, to me, appears best calculated to promote the highest good of the world.[31]

"All Lucy Stone's Doing"

In the fall of 1846, Lucy Stone wrote to several known advocates of woman's rights seeking advice on how to begin her crusade. One of those to whom she wrote was Samuel J. May, the Syracuse minister whose sermon advocating woman suffrage suggested some of the work to be done. Another was Hannah Tracy of nearby Rochester, Ohio. A thirty-one-year-old widow with three children, Tracy supported her family by writing for area newspapers, through which she had gained a respectable status as a minor literary figure in the West as well as a reputation for her views on woman's rights. This common interest had already drawn the two women together, and they had become good friends. To Stone's query about how to begin her work, Tracy replied that she must rouse women to desire their freedom and suggested a "quiet but thorough agitation" starting with the women at hand. Excited by Stone's plans, she came to Oberlin after the winter break, opened a boarding house, enrolled in the ladies' course, and helped Stone begin deliberate agitation at Oberlin.[1]

Few of the replies Stone received addressed what she believed to be the root cause of woman's oppression. Tracy emphasized education as a remedy, but Stone thought education alone could do little to lift beings whose souls and intellects had been deadened by society's expectations. What was needed, she believed, was a concerted attack on the idea that marriage and home were woman's sole domain and that a married woman's identity, interests, and rights were the same as her husband's. This idea, taught by the church and embraced by American society, was seemingly also embedded in law, as indicated by Sarah Grimké's quotation from Blackstone, that a married woman's legal existence was "incorporated or consolidated" into that of her husband. Legal commentator Edward Deering Mansfield agreed: "The first principle of Scripture, the unity of husband and wife, is repeated in the law. They are *in law,* one person."[2]

This religious and legal merging effectively denied women basic civil and human rights. With no legal right to property or earnings, a married woman must rely upon her husband to provide for her needs and protect her interests. But men were taught to consider their wives as possessions, whose purpose in life was to please them. Although frequent pregnancies and childbirth endangered women's health and lives, pregnancy was almost an annual occurrence for married women, and men frequently married three or more times as, in succession, they lost wives to childbirth or its complications. Even so, men believed they had a right to their wives' bodies, and women were taught they had a duty to submit, regardless of their feelings or concerns. Wives had not only the duty to submit but no practical alternative, because law authorized husbands to wrest submission through physical force. If a wife ran away, law enabled her husband to force her return and allowed him to lock her in his house. Divorce was not a viable option for an unhappy wife. In the few states that permitted women to divorce their husbands, the wife must appeal to the state legislature and make her most private matters public. If granted a divorce, she must forfeit possessions, the product of her labors before and during marriage, even her children, for these belonged to her husband. And society withheld from her the means of living independently, denying her virtually all avenues of employment except factory work and sewing, at which, even if she toiled from sunup to sundown, she could earn barely enough to pay room and board. Yet attempts to grant women rights independent of their husbands, such as married women's property bills, drew opposition because of their perceived threat to "marital unity."[3]

Stone saw this subjugation of wives as a corruption of what God intended marriage to be. Remembering the injustice of her mother's pecuniary subjugation and the stealth it bred, Stone advised her sister on the eve of her marriage in 1845 to establish a "perfect open-heartedness" with her husband that recognized her equal right to the family purse. During her final year at Oberlin, she contemplated women's marital subjugation and its remedy. Carrying on a lively correspondence with Mercy Lloyd, a young Quaker Garrisonian from Salem, Ohio, Stone developed ideas on what she termed "moral reform in marriage," which focused on the wife's right to control her own body. The two women were undoubtedly influenced by the writing of such reformers as Orson S. Fowler, who divided the indicators of love between men and women into a lower portion for mere animal passion and an upper portion for pure platonic affection. Lloyd postulated that although sexual attraction originated in the "animal feelings" and that there was nothing degrading or unnatural in their indulgence, true married love could exist only when these initial impulses were matured by "perfect sympathy" and "subject to the direction and control of the higher feelings." Agreeing that husbands and wives must let their "higher feeling" of reason rule over their "animal feeling" of passion, Stone arrived at several conclusions: Couples should control their sexual appetites and restrict the frequency of their sexual relations to space children about three years apart; it was wrong to have sexual intercourse if conception would injure the wife's health; wives had not only the right but also the moral duty to refuse sexual intercourse that conflicted with their judgment or emotions; sexual relations that were forced, or were engaged in when the couple did not want to conceive, were "adultery"; and, to avoid temptation, husbands and wives should sleep in separate beds.[4]

These ideas were not out of line with what other reformers of Stone's day advocated. Sylvester Graham taught abstinence before marriage and moderation afterward for health reasons. Many progressive thinkers valued spiritual, platonic love above physical love. Harriet Martineau held that "true marriage" was based on spiritual mutuality more than physical or sexual attraction. Associationists, too, believed that the marriage relationship was a "mystic and divine union of soul and body" that could not be achieved until "regulation of the Affections" was committed to woman. In 1854, Henry C. Wright would publish a book on marriage and parentage that combined many of the ideas Stone advocated. Wright said that because marriage and parental relations were the most powerful and enduring of all human relations, men and women should place sexual instinct and reproduction under the control of reason, conscience, and forethought. He taught that conception was the result of a human act, not of God's will, and that couples must accept responsibility for the result of their sexual relations. Insisting that every child should be a welcomed child, he said it was a crime for men and women to give existence to children they could not or would not provide for. Moreover, in a society in which abstinence was virtually the only method of birth control, Wright taught men that love of a woman found expression more in control of sexual impulse than in indulgence and taught women that it was their duty to themselves and their children not to submit to their husband's desire if they could not happily respond. Wright also taught that because woman bore the consequences of the sexual act, it must be she who governed the couple's sexual relations.[5] In the 1840s and 1850s, ideas of sexual restraint and feminine control represented neither Victorian prudery nor women's desire to dominate men. Based on health concerns and progressive views of marriage rather than ideas about sexuality or sexual politics, they were radical new ideas advanced more by male doctors and reformers than by women.

Stone tested her ideas on her family. Although Sarah saw some truth in Lucy's views, she did not think sexual intercourse within marriage could ever be called adultery. She discussed it with their mother, who quoted the passage, "To avoid fornication let every man have his own wife." As Hannah Stone pointed out, "nobody ever committed fornication for the sake of offspring." Sarah's husband, Henry Lawrence, thought there was more virtue in resisting than in avoiding temptation, and said that if to avoid temptation husbands must not sleep with their wives, they must also stop looking at them. Luther suggested it was as sinful not to use one's sexual organs at all as to use them too much.[6]

Frank found little in Lucy's ideas with which he could agree: "This waiting three years, Sis, as you intimate is all nonsense. Have [children] as fast as you can if you can take care of them, and if you can't, trust Providence and obey the command given to our first parents to multiply and replenish the Earth and subdue it." To the suggestion that couples should engage in sex only for the sake of offspring, he asked if that pertained as well to couples who could not conceive. Did people eat three meals a day only to stay alive, he asked, or to satisfy hunger? So, too, he supposed, couples engaged in sexual intercourse not for the sake of children alone, but to satisfy a natural hunger. And as to Lucy's claim that it was wrong to impair a woman's health through childbirth, he pointed out that risking injury once in three years would not be less wrong than risking it more often. So was childbirth itself to be considered wrong? he asked.[7]

Bowman answered with a bit more levity. Although he agreed that whatever injured health was wrong and that many people did injure themselves through excess, still, he believed husbands and wives should sleep together and nothing was wrong that resulted from their doing so. "God has joined them together and nothing should separate them from the same bed, especially on cold winter nights."[8]

But Lucy thought the measures she advocated would enable a wife to control her own body, and this right of autonomy, she believed, underlay all other questions of woman's rights. No woman could control her life if she could not control her own body. This was the primary issue she intended to agitate when she began lecturing, although Bowman warned that she might quickly become discouraged because she would have no way of ascertaining her effect. Not waiting until she could lecture, however, Stone began promulgating her ideas among Oberlin's women students. As a result, she was again summoned before the ladies' board, and this time reprimanded for advancing ideas contrary to accepted views of marital duty and for counseling about matters of which she, as an unmarried woman, could have no knowledge. Stone defended her views and objected to the idea that only married people were competent to speak about marriage. That was as absurd, said she, as requiring a physician to have had smallpox before attempting to cure it in others.[9]

In addition to developing ideas on marriage, Stone spent a large part of her senior year trying to gain practical experience in public speaking. The previous spring she had drawn Hugh Blair's *Lectures on Rhetoric and Belles-Lettres* from the library and begun a private study of oratory.[10] But to develop the skills required of a reformer, she needed opportunity to apply the principles and techniques about which she read. The idea of forming a women's debating club came during winter break, through correspondence with Antoinette Brown.

Brown taught during the break at an academy in Rochester, Michigan, run by a "woman's rights man" who encouraged her to lecture to the women students and the whole school as often as she pleased upon any subject she chose. In the women's literary society, Brown reported to Stone, students enthusiastically participated in declamations and discussions. "I have never before improved so rapidly in my life in the use of the tongue." Brown said the society frequently discussed woman's rights and many students were becoming advocates. And, she said, alluding to the movement Stone had in mind, she expected some of them to "go out in the world pioneers in the great reform which is about to revolutionize society." Brown wished Oberlin had a society where women could freely discuss such ideas and develop speaking skills.[11]

When Brown returned at the end of January 1847, she and Stone began plotting how they could circumvent Oberlin's restrictions on women's speaking. At the first meeting of the Ladies' Literary Society, Stone again defied the injunction against female oratory by memorizing her composition and presenting it as a speech. Shortly thereafter, the two called a meeting of the women students and proposed the formation of a club, independent of the institute, where women would be free to discuss any ideas they wanted, as well as to practice declamation, oratory, and debate. Stone reminded them that although they would leave Oberlin with the reputation of having a thorough college education, not one of them would have any elocutionary training. If, as Professor Morgan maintained, half of a person's education was obtained through discussion and debate, then they were being denied half their education. She, for one, refused to be defrauded of it. Pointing out that not one of them could state a question or argue it in successful debate, Stone proposed they create their own debating club. She had discussed the idea with James Thome, professor of rhetoric, and he had agreed to provide the club instruction.[12]

Few of the women, however, were interested in learning to speak, and those who agreed to join the club preferred to forgo the assistance of Professor Thome, in whose presence they would feel uncomfortable speaking. The club met privately, in the home of the elderly black woman who was Stone's reading student or, when weather permitted, in the woods near campus. Hannah Tracy and Helen Cook regularly joined Stone and Brown in weekly exercises, but others attended sporadically, sometimes participating in oral exercises but mostly just lending their moral support by listening. After acquiring some measure of skill and confidence, Stone and Brown asked Professor Thome for permission to debate each other in the collegiate rhetoric class, and he scheduled them for the following week. News of the impending debate spread, and many students who were not members of the class came to observe. The assault on custom backfired, though. When the ladies' and faculty boards heard what had happened, they formally banned oral exercises by women in coeducational classes.[13]

But the two women continued to think up ways to gain the experience they needed. Night after night Brown left the dormitory and joined Stone in her room at the home of Professor Henry Whipple, where, wanting her final year to be free of the distractions of dormitory life, Stone had begun lodging after winter break. Lying awake into the wee hours of the morning, they planned various assaults on Oberlin's vision of woman's sphere and discussed their plans for the future and how they might get money to carry them out.[14]

Brown's recollection of spending nights in bed with Stone, together with expressions of love for each other in their correspondence, led at least one twentieth-century scholar to surmise that the two women were lovers, "bound together by sexual intimacy as well as by emotional ties."[15] But there could not have been two less likely candidates for a lesbian relationship than Lucy Stone and Antoinette Brown. Believing that individuals must govern their "animal feeling" of passion with their "higher feeling" of reason, and that it was wrong even for married men and women to have sexual relations for mere sensual gratification, Stone was not likely to have engaged in sexual activity with anyone outside of marriage, male or female. Brown was so firmly orthodox in her religious views that she could not support the demand for easier divorce because of scriptural proscription against it; she could have felt no less aversion toward sexual activity considered sinful. In the nineteenth century, men commonly slept in the same bed with other men, and women with women. Dormitory rooms were furnished with one bed for two occupants, and nearly all students—at Oberlin, Mount Holyoke, and other boarding schools—slept with their roommates. Stone and Brown were part of a culture that distinguished between feminine love and masculine love. Feminine love—which was seen as emotional, intellectual, and spiritual—was considered pure and on a much higher plane than masculine love, which was considered tainted by sexual desire. As historian Carol Smith-Rosenberg has demonstrated, "deeply felt same-sex friendship," in which girls routinely expressed intense love for each other, held hands, hugged and kissed each other, and "curled up together in bed at night to whisper fantasies and secrets," was considered natural in the nineteenth century and carried no implication of homosexuality. Stone and Brown's intimacy was intellectual and emotional rather than sexual, grounded (in Stone's words) in the "knowledge that in the wide world *one* heart understands me, can *feel* what I feel, and sympathize with me."[16]

In March, Stone launched another attack against restrictions on women's public speaking. At Oberlin's graduations, a number of the graduating class, selected by their classmates, presented essays as part of the public exercises. The men delivered theirs as orations, but, according to custom, faculty members read the women's. As the time for electing that year's essayists approached, Stone drew up a petition asking that the women be permitted to read their own papers, obtained the signatures of most of her classmates, and presented it to the faculty and ladies' boards. The petition was denied, so when Stone was elected she declined the honor. Although classmates, Professor Whipple, and President Mahan urged her to let Professor Thome read her essay, Stone explained that to do so would be to accept "the principle which takes away from women their equal rights and denies to them the privilege of being co-laborers with men in any sphere to which their ability makes them adequate." "No word or deed" of hers, she said, would ever approve such a principle. Supporting Stone's position, three of the other four women and two of the eight men elected to write essays declined their appointments, as did those named as replacements.[17]

Stone was soon offered another opportunity to debate—this time in public, and with a man for an opponent. The topic of woman suffrage was gaining interest in the West, especially among Liberty Party men, many of whom wanted woman's right to vote and hold office to be made part of the Liberty Party platform. A newcomer to Oberlin, formerly the editor of a county newspaper in the central part of the state, believed he could easily knock down any arguments in favor of woman suffrage and challenged Stone to a debate. He boasted beforehand that he was "double-loaded to the muzzle" with arguments to prove that voting would "wholly unsex women." But after he presented his objections, Stone took the platform and thoroughly riddled his arguments with wit, logic, and eloquence that brought cheers from the audience. The next day, some who had missed the debate asked the editor how he had done with his "unsexing" arguments. He replied humbly that Lucy Stone had not only "unsexed" *his* arguments, but had "swept them away like chaff before the wind."[18]

In June, Stone and Brown spearheaded a project of another nature—the establishment of a women's newspaper at Oberlin. Prominent players in this enterprise were Brown, Hannah Tracy, and Josephine Penfield, with Stone staying in the background. The women met with a printer to discuss terms for a contract and then presented the plan to the women's literary society, which voted themselves into an Association of the Oberlin Ladies Banner and appointed Tracy editor. But the faculty and ladies' boards denied permission. For a while, the women still hoped to bring their plan to fruition, Brown writing to Stone that she could get several subscribers in her hometown in Henrietta, New York, but without the boards' approval, they could not proceed.[19]

During Stone's last summer at Oberlin, typhoid fever struck again and claimed the lives of several students and townspeople. Guarding her health by bathing daily in cold water and watching her diet, Stone taught in the Liberty Seminary, studied for final examinations, and made a black bombazine dress for graduation. But as graduation neared, she could not decide what to do after leaving Oberlin. All year, she had been pondering whether to begin lecturing right away or teach first to repay her college debt and whether to return to Massachusetts or stay in Ohio. She had managed to finance her education by herself until the previous summer, when she accepted her father's offer and allowed Luther to bring funds as he passed through Ohio on his way west. Her father also paid off her previous notes, so her debt to him was well over $150. She could repay him by teaching a year or two, and figured that if she gave an occasional lecture while teaching she could refine her skills before attempting a regular speaking career. Sarah urged her to come home and not worry about repaying the debt, since it was only their father she owed. But Lucy considered the obligation to repay him as sacred as it would be to anyone else.[20]

In April while Stone was contemplating her options, she received an appeal from Abby Foster asking her to work for the Massachusetts Anti-Slavery Society. The great tide of opposition against the abolition movement made it difficult to find lecturers equal to the emergency, said Foster, but Stone's course at Oberlin had demonstrated she possessed the requisite energy and determination. Another reason she wanted Stone was to keep a woman's voice in the field, for "that which was reported falsely last summer is true now." Abby Kelley Foster was pregnant.[21]

Before Stone could reply, Samuel Brooke, general agent of the Western Anti-Slavery Society, asked her to lecture for them. His recruitment spoke directly to Stone's plans. The Western Society was planning a special campaign to begin that summer when Garrison came to Ohio, aimed at organizing antislavery societies in every county and town in the state. Stone's participation would give her ample opportunity for speech-making among people not as accustomed to accomplished speakers as easterners were. By working for them, she could get the lecturing practice she wanted, gain confidence, and earn income toward her debt while rendering a greater service to humanity than she could by teaching. The society would also employ Mercy Lloyd as her traveling companion.[22]

Elizabeth Jones, who had followed close upon Abby Kelley's heels into the lecturing field and was an agent for the Western Society, urged Stone to stay in Ohio and take up abolition instead of woman's rights. Was it not better, she asked, for women to seize their rights, demonstrate their independence, and show men that they were not intellectually inferior, than to discuss the question with those who would keep women down? "When men shall see that we despise their flattery and gallantry," Jones said, and "that we prefer our rights and ask nothing more . . . then shall we begin to have legislation on the subject and the rights that we now claim shall be acknowledged by all." Insisting that "[w]omen must place themselves in the position they ought to occupy," she argued that women lecturers such as the Grimkés and Foster had done more to advance woman's rights than they could have by agitating the question directly.[23]

Even Stone's brothers, who fully supported her decision to lecture, thought she should speak on abolition instead of woman's rights. Frank considered the question of woman's rights a "rather lean one," and Bowman thought that slaves "sighing for deliverance" had a stronger claim on her efforts than women who "hug their chains." Stone considered working for the Western Society but finally decided to stay focused on woman's rights, for it was just such attitudes as Frank's, and the truth of Bowman's observation that many women did hug their chains, that made a woman's rights crusade all the more imperative.[24] It was not a matter of which cause was more worthy or important, but of where she personally could have the greater effect, where she could do the highest good. Abby Foster mourned the small force laboring to break the slave's bonds, but there was no force of any size laboring to break woman's bonds. After much soul-searching, Stone decided to leave the antislavery field to the hundreds of workers already laboring there, return to Massachusetts, pay off her debt, and begin her woman's rights work there.

On the morning of Wednesday, August 25, 1847, twenty-nine-year-old Lucy Stone received her bachelor of arts degree from Oberlin Collegiate Institute, along with seven other women and seventeen men. Joining a small circle of women college graduates, she was the first from Massachusetts to achieve that distinction. Another Massachusetts woman would have graduated with her but had died a few weeks earlier during the typhoid epidemic. Despite the initial rush of essay resignations by sympathetic classmates, Stone's protest had no visible effect on the ceremonies. Seven men and four women wrote essays; the men delivered theirs and faculty members read the women's. On the preceding day, Antoinette Brown and eight other women read essays at graduation exercises of the ladies' department, and even though there were men in the audience, their doing so was deemed entirely proper. Oberlin officials issued a formal statement a few years later to explain the seeming inconsistency: Tuesday was a ladies' meeting; Wednesday, a gentlemen's meeting. On Tuesday the Female Principal presided, the ladies' board occupied the stand, young ladies sang and filled the orchestra, and none but ladies appeared before the audience. If gentlemen mingled in the audience, they came to attend a ladies' meeting, "in which the most fastidious cannot object to having ladies read their essays." But on Wednesday, a gentleman presided, gentlemen filled the stand, the speakers were gentlemen who did not read essays but delivered them "with whatever rhetoric they may be able to command." These circumstances, said the officials, made a wide difference between the two occasions that ought to be obvious and appreciated by all.[25]

A college graduation was an important event in 1847. Clergymen, businessmen, farmers, and friends traveled great distances to attend Oberlin's daylong festivities. Among the four thousand people on hand for the afternoon exercises of the theological department were Stone's friends Stephen Foster and Samuel Brooke, accompanying William Lloyd Garrison and Frederick Douglass, who were scheduled to hold meetings in Oberlin three days later. Stone was thrilled to meet Douglass, whose life story had so moved her. When she read his book in 1845, Douglass was in England, where he had been forced to flee to avoid recapture. While there, British abolitionists raised funds to purchase his freedom, and now, having just returned to the United States, he joined Garrison on his western tour. Stone was thrilled, too, to finally meet her long-revered idol, William Lloyd Garrison, a balding, bespectacled forty-three-year-old man whose gentle, benevolent manner seemed incompatible with his fiery reputation. On August 26, the day after Stone's graduation and the day before her departure, she had a long talk with the band of antislavery crusaders. Recalling their meeting many years later, Douglass said that although he met Stone as one entering the field of equal rights for women, he was pleased to find that she was also an abolitionist. Garrison wrote to his wife: "Among others with whom I have become acquainted is Miss Lucy Stone. . . .

She is a very superior young woman, and has a soul as free as the air, and is preparing to go forth as a lecturer, particularly in vindication of the rights of woman."[26]

Stone returned to Massachusetts leaving an indelible woman's rights mark in Ohio. In addition to the equal pay victory and women's debating club, both of which continued after her departure, other agitation she initiated was taken up by others. Antoinette Brown and Helen Cook continued discussions on woman's rights with Oberlin students and reported to Stone a year later that the cause was progressing "finely" there. When appointed to write compositions for meetings of the Ladies' Literary Society, several women insisted on delivering them as orations. Brown enrolled in the theological course and was admitted to the Theological Literary Society, which allowed her to participate equally in oral exercises. And the college decided to let professors decide individually the question of women's oral participation in their classes. The question of women reading their own graduation essays continued to be agitated until 1859, when the institute finally allowed the practice.[27]

Stone arrived at her New England home to a family much changed from the one she had left four years earlier. Her parents, now sixty-eight years old, had turned the farm over to Frank, who had married Harriet Blake and now had a four-month-old daughter named Rhoda. Two previous children had died in infancy.[28] Bowman and his wife, Phebe Robinson, had two sons, three-year-old Frank and one-year-old Eddy. Their first child had died at birth. Luther and his wife, Phebe Cutler, who had married before Stone left for Oberlin, were there to greet her, too, having just returned from Louisiana. Their twin daughters, born in 1844, had died in infancy. Sarah and her husband, Henry Lawrence, who as yet had no children, were living in Gardner near Bowman. One of Eliza's daughters had died, and Aunt Sally, too, was gone.

After getting reacquainted with her family, Stone began teaching school in North Brookfield while boarding in the home of Amasa Walker. Walker had served as a visiting professor at Oberlin, usually teaching only in the summer, and his trips between Oberlin and Brookfield had enabled him to serve as courier between Stone and her family. He arranged a select school for Stone and placed his own children under her tutelage.[29]

A few weeks after her return, Bowman gave his sister her first opportunity to speak publicly on woman's rights, from the pulpit of his Evangelical Congregational Church in Gardner. Her speech does not survive, but it was probably the same one she gave a little later in Warren, which a witness recalled years later as having been titled "Woman's Place" and was probably an adaptation of her essay "On the Province of Woman."[30] Because so much opposition to woman's equal rights was based on Scripture, Stone felt it necessary to tackle those objections head on and later made the "Bible Position on Woman" one of her standard lectures.

When Stone lectured in Warren, the hall was filled with earnest listeners as well as a few rowdies intent on disrupting the meeting. Ignoring the hissing and stomping from the back benches, Stone calmly delivered her address on woman's equal duties and rights. Among those impressed by her arguments was the superintendent of Warren's Sunday School, who asked a young woman of the congregation, Anna Watkins, to read a Bible passage at a service the following week. But even such minor female participation in a public meeting was so uncommon that it startled the community. The minister called on Anna's mother to remonstrate against the daughter's conduct, but Mrs. Watkins replied that if women were equally bound with men to obey the Bible, they ought to be able to read it as freely. The controversy raged for weeks, and all over Warren people shook their heads and lamented: "This is all Lucy Stone's doing."

Anna Watkins had been an academy classmate of Stone's, and when she came to West Brookfield to visit the superintendent's widowed sister, she invited Stone to join them. When the older woman suggested to Stone that the uproar in Warren might deter her public speaking, Stone answered, "Not at all. It only shows me how much work there is for me to do."[31]

Part Two

The Power of an Orator

Antislavery Agent

During the winter of 1847–48, while living in North Brookfield and teaching the select school Amasa Walker arranged for her, Lucy Stone participated in Massachusetts' antislavery movement, attending meetings, circulating petitions, and raising money for special projects.[1] In debt and needing more speaking experience before starting a lecturing career, she planned to teach another year and hone her skills on her students. But those plans changed when she attended the New England Anti-Slavery Convention in Boston in May.

The Massachusetts Anti-Slavery Society had not given up hope of recruiting Stone despite her rejection of their offer a year earlier, and from the moment she arrived in Boston its leaders showered her with hospitality. Garrison invited her to dine with his family and insisted she stay at his home. James N. Buffum, another of the state's leading abolitionists, invited her to spend the weekend at his ocean-side home in nearby Lynn. Maria Chapman spent an evening getting to know her over dinner. At the convention, activists whose names she had been reading in the *Liberator* for years greeted her warmly and placed her on the business committee. Stephen Foster made her promise to stop in Worcester on her way home to see Abby and their infant daughter.[2]

At that visit, Abby asked Lucy to lecture during the summer as part of the society's "One Hundred Conventions" campaign. Lucy protested that she was not ready, but Abby assured her she would learn all she needed to know in the field. Besides, lecturing required more than giving lectures. Auditoriums needed to be booked; advertising, travel, and accommodations needed to be arranged. Unless Stone had the backing of an organization, she would need a network of local contacts to help with arrangements, and an antislavery agency would help her develop one. Stone hesitantly agreed and soon received a letter confirming her appointment from the society's general agent Samuel May Jr., a cousin of Syracuse's Reverend Samuel J. May.[3]

May assigned Stone to the eastern series of conventions, along with Stephen and Abby Foster, James Buffum, Charles Lenox Remond, William Wells

Brown, and Parker Pillsbury. This group would cover eastern Massachusetts, Connecticut, Rhode Island, Maine, and parts of New Hampshire, while another band worked central and western Massachusetts, Vermont, and the remainder of New Hampshire. The agents would travel and lecture separately or in pairs most of the time and join each other for two-day county conventions. The eastern series opened on June 17 at Stoneham in Essex County, but the first record of Stone's participation was a week later at the annual meeting of the Essex County Anti-Slavery Society in Lawrence.[4] She offered brief remarks a few times but concentrated on observing and learning how to conduct a convention. The object of these meetings was to convert, to rouse public sentiment and produce active abolitionists, so they were designed to make individuals think about slavery, grapple with the issues, and determine their own position in regard to them. The first session usually opened with the singing of abolitionist hymns before the agents stated the purpose of the convention and laid the issues before the people. At subsequent sessions, they presented resolutions, spoke in their favor, invited opponents to express contrary views, and then tried to reveal the error in opponents' thinking. At the last session, the audience was asked to vote on each of the resolutions. This forced individuals to weigh the arguments they had heard and to take a stand. After the votes, the agents took a collection and solicited subscriptions to the *Liberator*. The meeting closed with a stirring appeal designed to move the audience to active commitment.

Although Stone agreed to work for the society, she refused a salary until she had learned enough to be an asset. In giving notice of the first conventions, therefore, the *Liberator* did not identify her as an agent, but said the meetings would be attended by "Parker Pillsbury and William W. Brown, agents of the Massachusetts Anti-Slavery Society, and Miss Lucy Stone." But she soon proved her worth. At Georgetown, three days after the Lawrence meetings, neither Pillsbury nor Brown had arrived by the appointed hour, so Stone took charge of the meeting and delivered an address on the duties of individuals in regard to the slavery issue. An observer said that although she uttered the most radical sentiments, her words were persuasive and well received. With Brown's arrival the next evening, the convention formally organized. After he presented the resolutions and spoke in their support, the audience called enthusiastically for Stone. She stepped forward to "rapturous applause," said the report to the *Liberator*, and "held the vast assembly in breathless silence for nearly half an hour. No speaker has been better received in Georgetown than Miss Stone." The next issue of the *Liberator* identified Stone as an agent of the Massachusetts Anti-Slavery Society.[5]

In her first two weeks with the society, Stone proved to be an effective speaker, popular with the limited audiences she reached. But it was her appearance at a grand Fourth of July rally at Abington that introduced her to the wider antislavery movement. Independence Day was a big occasion in New England, where Puritan descendants took great pains *not* to observe religious holidays, which they considered "papist festivals." Being a secular holiday, Independence Day set loose pent-up festive impulses. Pealing bells and firing cannons ushered in a day of great patriotic fervor. Everyone turned out of doors for the communal festivities: parades, games, picnics, drinking. Each town secured the best speaker it could afford and turned out en masse to listen to two-hour-long orations extolling the virtues of the young nation, its founders, and its leaders. Abolitionists held their own observances and made them grand antislavery rallies. Organizers secured special half-fares on the railroads from the cities to the groves where they were held. Choirs roused the crowds with stirring antislavery hymns, and a loud, bold voice read from the Declaration of Independence that all men are created equal and have an inalienable right to liberty.[6]

At Abington, Stone appeared on the speakers' platform with Garrison, Wendell Phillips, and other antislavery notables before an audience of three thousand people. The *Liberator*, the *Anti-Slavery Bugle*, the *Pennsylvania Freeman*, the *National Anti-Slavery Standard*, and other reform papers introduced her to thousands of other abolitionists scattered across the northern states:

The speaker last named is a graduate of the Oberlin Collegiate Institute, where, having pursued a thorough course of study, she received the degree of A.B. . . . Her appearance is striking. Tried by the standard of the novelist, she could not be called handsome; but her countenance is marked with a serene thoughtfulness and an earnest sympathy which tender it far more attractive than anything that the world generally calls beauty. . . . Her manner was not only free from offensive boldness, but gentle, calm, dignified, earnest. She spoke extemporaneously, but with a quiet self-possession that was perfectly charming; her voice was clear and sonorous, her enunciation distinct, though quite rapid, and her gestures natural and graceful. Her speech was remarkably coherent—having beginning, middle, and end—while the language in which she clothed her thoughts was exceedingly chaste and beautiful. In listening to her, we felt that in thus coming before the world as the advocate of the enslaved, she had not in any degree compromised the modesty belonging to her sex.[7]

In a day when public speaking was a primary form of entertainment, voice, appearance, style, delivery, form, and audience reaction were evaluated as much as content—much like theater and motion picture reviews of the twentieth century. And in a day when critics were especially harsh toward the few women lecturers there were, the reform press were protective of their honor and capabilities. The curiosities of a "female speaker" and a college-educated woman were part of what attracted crowds to Stone during the next weeks. Taking note of this fact, the *Blackstone Chronicle* commented: "We hope the day may soon come when a thoroughly educated woman shall not be a rare phenomenon, a being to be stared at like a lion or an elephant."[8]

Parker Pillsbury and William Wells Brown, Stone's most frequent coworkers, attracted crowds for other reasons. Brown had escaped from slavery fourteen years earlier and had been an abolitionist lecturer for nine years, during which he had enjoyed relative safety and security. But early in 1848 he published a narrative about his life as a slave and his escape, and suddenly he became the object of much attention. His former master contacted him and offered to sell him his freedom, but Brown denied the man's right to own, and therefore to sell, him and refused to pay. During the months Stone lectured with him, slave catchers kept him under surveillance.[9] Pillsbury, like the Fosters, was vociferous in denouncing the church and political parties for their collusion with slavery. He saw no need for conciliatory language, so his meetings were always explosive and attracted those who wanted to add to the fireworks.

Stone quickly learned how dangerous it could be to appear with Pillsbury and the Fosters. At a convention in East Bridgewater, where Pillsbury had roused emotions with his characteristic denunciations, a band of hecklers came to the final session. "Our friend Lucy Stone opened the meeting with an address characterized by her usual mildness and gentleness," said Pillsbury's report to the *Liberator*, "and yet those characters insulted her in a manner too shameful to name." Throughout the meeting, the rowdies threw dried fruit, smoked fish, and tobacco quids at the speakers but failed to halt the proceedings. Then a prayer book came sailing from the back and hit Stone in the face. Had her shoulder not broken the force of the blow, said Pillsbury, it would have prostrated her on the floor.[10]

Traveling by coach or wagon over rough roads to get from one appointment to the next, Stone maintained an exhaustive schedule throughout the summer, rarely having a full day in which to rest. As a lecturer for the Massachusetts Society, she promoted the principles of Garrisonian abolitionism: that the Negro race was entitled to all human rights claimed by the white race; that physical force was an unacceptable means for ending slavery; that individuals should refuse to support institutions that participated in or defended slavery; that the United States Constitution and the federal government legitimized and protected slavery and thus made the entire nation morally and politically responsible for it; and that free states should therefore sever their union with the slave states.

The call for disunion and opposition to politics as a viable means of combating slavery were shaped by what Garrisonians saw as the slave states' ever tightening grasp on national politics and the increasing willingness of antislavery politicians to compromise away the very point of the antislavery movement—the abolition of slavery. Over the past decade a group of antislavery congressmen had developed a moderate antislavery position that rejected positions at both ends of the abolition spectrum. Disagreeing on one hand with those who denied the validity of constitutional clauses that legitimized slavery and insisted the Constitution was an antislavery document, and on the other hand with Garrisonians, who recognized the Constitution's proslavery provisions and urged dissolution of the Union, the congressional antislavery bloc accepted the proslavery clauses of the Constitution but tried to use them against slave interests. Under the leadership of Ohio Congressman Joshua R. Giddings, they insisted that the Constitution required federal neutrality concerning slavery and that every action of the federal government that supported slavery outside the original slave states was unconstitutional.[11]

Sympathy with this approach had grown. Between 1842 and 1848, several northern legislatures passed personal liberty laws denying state aid to the federal government in enforcing the Fugitive Slave Law of 1793, but Washington continued to force compliance. Congressional rejection of the Wilmot Proviso, which would have barred slavery in the territories acquired from Mexico, fueled resentment against what was increasingly being viewed as southern political aggrandizement. Then the Whig and Democratic parties shaped their 1848 platforms and slate of candidates to suit the South, the Democrats nominating slaveholder Zachary Taylor for President. Northern hostility to southern political clout led antislavery politicians from all parties—"Conscience" Whigs, "Barnburner" Democrats, and even abolitionists from the Liberty Party—to form a new coalition, the Free Soil Party, committed to defending northern political interests against the encroachment of slave interests. While the new party demanded a halt to the spread of slavery, it pledged noninterference with the institution in the slave states.[12]

To those who sought an end to slavery, the Free Soil Party was no more antislavery than the American Colonization Society had been, and every bit as much an obstacle to the goal of total emancipation. So Parker Pillsbury and Stephen and Abby Foster did not hesitate to heap as much vitriolic denunciation on the antislavery politicians as they did on slaveholders and their defenders. Stone shared Garrisonian distrust in political antislavery but could not acquiesce in personal attacks on antislavery politicians and frequently tried to mellow Pillsbury's or the Fosters' extreme denunciations.

Toward the end of August, at a convention on Cape Cod, Stone experienced one of the most violent episodes of her career, triggered by one of Stephen Foster's attacks on the church. When an angry auditor rushed from the back of the assembly shouting that he would defend the church against Foster's accusations, the roused audience became a mob. Cries came from all sides: "Down with them," "Tar and feather him," "Haul them out!" Dozens of men rushed toward the stage, and Stone urged Foster to leave. "But who will take care of you?" he replied. At that moment a club-wielding rioter bounded onto the platform and headed toward them. Stone grabbed the man's arm, looked calmly into his face, and said, "This gentleman will protect me." And he did! The diverted rioter escorted Stone to the edge of the grove while pandemonium broke loose around them. A group of sympathizers sprang to Foster's defense, formed a circle around him, and fought off attackers who succeeded only in ripping off his coat. Other friends coming to Foster's aid were mistaken for assailants and also beaten off. Brown was pitched over the back of the platform, some six or seven feet to the ground. Pillsbury was dragged from the platform and beaten, he all the while yelling, "Strike, but hear me!" Before long, someone cried falsely that Foster was being run out of town on a rail, and the rioters ran from the grove to witness the sight, leaving the abolitionists to make their escape.

All this time Stone talked calmly to her protector, sympathizing with those whose loyalties had been offended but deploring their refusal to hear differing views and their violent recourse. The rioter-turned-protector agreed that abolitionists deserved a respectful hearing, and because Stone was the only one remaining in the grove, he rounded up an audience to hear her. Lifted onto a tree stump, Stone spoke to the remnants of the once-large gathering. When she finished and asked for a collection, she received twenty dollars, more than enough to buy Foster a new coat.[13]

Although Pillsbury and the Fosters were notorious for their virulent attacks, Garrisonian lecturers as a class were denounced for their use of "harsh language." Even so popular an orator as Wendell Phillips recommended "rough instruments for rough work." Antislavery sentiment, he pointed out, was no more acceptable to the slaveholder "wrapped up in honied phrase" than expressed in "rough old Saxon." Stone, too, defended the use of antagonistic language by reformers whose goal it was to change ideas and feelings. To effect this change, she said, "a thorough discontent with the existing wrong must be created, and this is done by depicting it in all its naked deformity—calling every crime and every criminal by the right name, and if anger most intense swell the bosom of the wrong-doer, it is proof the Truth's barbed arrow is fast in the right place."[14] But while defending such language, Stone, like Phillips, exhibited a speaking style very different from that of Pillsbury and the Fosters. She became known for expressing the most radical Garrisonian principles in a calm and respectful manner. Her teaching experience had demonstrated that learning did not occur in a climate of antagonism, that one kind word accomplished more than a stream of angry chastisements. She knew that thundering attacks upon individuals and their revered institutions roused not only anger but also defenses that deafened auditors to any truth there might be in them. So her style was to exhibit empathy with her audience's feelings and positions, to gain their respect and trust, and then to lead them gently to her point of view.

In addition to this exhibited goodwill toward her audiences, many other qualities merged to give Stone an unusual power over her audiences. Her manner was simple, unpretentious, sincere, yet forceful. She was a "little meek-looking Quakerish body, with the sweetest, modest manners and yet as unshrinking and self-possessed as a loaded cannon," wrote one new admirer. From her father she had learned the art of storytelling, and her vivid descriptions moved her audiences to tears or laughter as she willed. The tenor of her voice, described by her contemporaries as "like a silver bell," was one of her assets. "No more perfect instrument had ever been bestowed on a speaker," said one.[15] Her calm air of assurance and authority, her broad knowledge, and her skillful use of facts and statistics all served to make Stone a supremely effective speaker.

When the summer campaign ended, Stone no longer felt the need to teach another year and agreed to continue working for the society during the November–April lecture season. On December 1, she spoke in her hometown of West Brookfield. Her father was in the audience, slumped rather embarrassedly with elbow on knee and cheek on fist. During the course of her speaking, Lucy looked every now and then to see how he received her words. As it became evident to him that she was master of both her subject and oratory, he straightened up and Lucy could tell he was well pleased. Later he apologized for opposing her public speaking and admitted she was doing valuable work. The support of her father and brothers was a great satisfaction to Stone, one to which she frequently referred during her lectures in the years ahead as she urged men to assist women in the fight for their rights. Stone's lecture in West Brookfield also changed Hannah Stone's mind about her daughter's speaking. When neighbors called on her to commiserate about Lucy's unseemly conduct, Hannah defended her and in so doing converted herself.[16]

Working with the Fosters in the neighborhood of West Brookfield, Stone again experienced the hostility they seemed to accept as normal. At Warren, rowdies tried to silence Abby with the usual pranks of sprinkling pepper on the floor, showering the audience with corn and beans, and overturning benches. Then someone fired a gun and the bullet barely missed Abby. When she appealed to the audience for protection, no one moved. Refusing to capitulate to the rowdies, Stephen conducted the rest of the stormy session.[17] With such experiences, it is no wonder Stone developed a strong preference for lecturing alone.

She also traveled alone. The society offered to pay the expenses of a companion, for it was not considered proper for a woman to travel by herself. Mercy Lloyd had agreed to accompany her in Ohio but could not come to Massachusetts, and Sarah Lawrence declined her sister's invitation to travel with her. So Stone, who had experienced no unpleasantness journeying to and from Ohio, decided to go it alone.[18] Boldly traveling by herself throughout Massachusetts, Rhode Island, and New Hampshire, she maintained a hectic lecture schedule that found her speaking six days a week, usually in a different town each night.

Lecturing for the Massachusetts Anti-Slavery Society gave Stone a strong foundation upon which to build her woman's rights work. Besides teaching her the mechanics of spreading ideas and organizing agitation and enabling her to develop into a powerful orator, it put her name before the public as a champion of human rights and introduced her to progressive thinkers throughout New England. One new contact was Anna Parsons of Boston, former member of the failed Brook Farm Phalanx. Like many enthusiasts of the nearly defunct Association movement, Parsons had looked to that movement to achieve "the elevation of woman to independence and an acknowledged equality with man."[19] That bright flame of hope was about to be extinguished—killed by controversy over the sexual theories and practices of the movement's founders. Although American Associationism centered on "cooperative industrial arrangements," from its beginning it had had to repel charges of being a free-love movement. In the summer of 1845 reports of Fourier's ideas on sexual freedom, stories of Albert Brisbane's affair with a married woman, and rumors of sexual promiscuity at the phalanxes had scandalized the country. Despite the fact that the American movement had always disclaimed Fourier's sexual theories and distanced itself from Fourier at the founding meeting of the American Union of Associationists in 1846, political enemies of Horace Greeley, who was second only to Brisbane in promoting Associationism in the United States, nursed the controversy to discredit him. In the winter of 1846–47 and again in the summer of 1848, Greeley's opponents charged him and the Association movement with being antichurch, antimarriage, and antifamily. Although Greeley championed marital fidelity and opposed divorce, those who disliked his growing influence in the Whig Party accused him of being a Fanny Wrighter and insisted on linking Associationism not only to Fourier's but also Robert Owen's and John Humphrey Noyes's theories of "non-exclusive" love. A translation of the French *Love in the Phalanstery* fueled the controversy, and the stigma of free love became the final deathblow to a movement already suffering economic failure. But even as the movement disintegrated, women clung tightly, unwilling to let go of what seemed to offer the only workable alternative to woman's domestic bondage and pecuniary dependence. Women dominated the diminishing ranks of Boston's Associationists and appealed to other women to help make that movement the vehicle for achieving their emancipation.[20] But during the months of Stone's antislavery agency, both the American Union of Associationists and its organ, the *Harbinger*, were dying, and only William Henry Channing's Religious Union of Associationists and *Spirit of the Age*, both based in Boston, continued to carry the Association banner. Through her antislavery work, Stone met Parsons, Channing, and other Associationists who would eagerly support her effort to organize a woman's rights movement.

But foremost among Stone's supporters, after Garrison himself, was Wendell Phillips, the young Boston patrician and lawyer who had given up a life of prestige and security to labor for the slave. Phillips had led the effort to get the women delegates, including his wife, admitted to the 1840 London convention, and he was an early advocate of woman suffrage who would soon be drafting petitions for Stone. Two other men who would become devoted supporters were Thomas Wentworth Higginson and Francis Jackson. Higginson, in his first year as pastor of a church in Newburyport where Stone lectured in September, had been mildly interested in woman's rights since his adolescence, but Stone won him to the cause completely. Jackson, a wealthy Boston merchant and president of the Massachusetts Anti-Slavery Society, had long supported the struggle of abolition women to claim and exercise their rights. He would become one of Stone's most reliable financial backers as well as a source of ideas and information for her lectures.

As Stone built a network of supporters among New England reformers, several influences combined to create a favorable climate for her new crusade. The highly publicized failure of Elizabeth Blackwell to gain admittance to several medical schools in 1847 had spurred what one writer to the *Liberator* called "some desperate and effective struggles for freedom and equality of intellectual privileges." During the winter of 1847–48 a number of women began lecturing on physiology to female audiences in Boston and Providence, in an effort to give women knowledge about their own bodies that society seemed intent on denying them. Providence women formed a Physiological Society to advance this work, and Boston women tried to get up a petition to the legislature to establish a school to educate women physicians. In 1845, Massachusetts had passed an act significantly improving the rights of married women, and in the spring of 1848, both New York and Pennsylvania followed that example. Also in the spring of 1848, women in western New York formally appealed to their legislature to recognize women "as the equals of men" in all areas of law. Interest in woman suffrage continued to grow, particularly in western New York where the Liberty Party had held its national convention the previous fall and a number of delegates had pressed for adding woman suffrage to the party's platform. From her home near Rochester, Antoinette Brown informed Stone that the issue had been the topic of student essays and literary society debates all winter long. And on May 31, 1848, a convention of Liberty Party loyals led by Gerrit Smith who refused to join the Free Soil Party met in Rochester and passed a resolution calling for "universal suffrage in its broadest sense, including women as well as men." Several weeks later, antislavery women of western New York held two woman's rights conventions, one in Seneca Falls and the other in Rochester, and began circulating woman suffrage petitions.[21]

Shortly after Stone renewed her agency with the Massachusetts Anti-Slavery Society, she received a letter from Phoebe Hathaway of Farmington, New York, one of the women connected with these conventions, asking her to lecture for them. Stone quickly accepted, for to begin her work with the backing of a society would make it much easier. But, she told Hathaway, she could not come to New York until her agency with the antislavery society ended in April.[22]

Although Stone committed herself to work for antislavery for the next six months, she also began organizing woman's rights agitation. That winter the Massachusetts legislature received its first petition for woman suffrage, headed by the signature of William Lloyd Garrison. Although no documentary evidence links Stone to the petition, there can be little doubt that she initiated it. Over the past decade, several leading Garrisonians had publicly stated their belief that women should have the right to vote, but abolitionists had not agitated for woman suffrage because they pressed only for rights that would enable women to serve their cause, and voting was not one of their strategies. It was not until Stone appeared on the scene that petitions for woman suffrage began arriving at Massachusetts' State House. Legislators set Garrison's petition aside, refusing even to consider it, but the effort roused public consciousness. An anonymous writer to the *Liberator* protested: "Why should women be taxed for the support of institutions for whose advantages they are not candidates? Indeed, why, unrepresented, should they be taxed at all?"[23]

In April 1849, Stone made a three-week visit to Philadelphia to lecture under the auspices of that city's Female Anti-Slavery Society. There she found ready sympathizers with her cause, women who had been involved in the movement for woman's rights since the eruption of the woman question. But compared with Massachusetts, Pennsylvania was a conservative state, in its reform as well as politics and social arrangements. So reticent were the city's women reformers that after the Seneca Falls woman's rights convention a city paper boasted that its women would not get involved. "The Boston ladies contend for the rights of women. The New York girls aspire to mount the rostrum [and] to do all the voting." But Philadelphia women, it said, were "celebrated for discretion, modesty, and unfeigned diffidence."[24]

Stone's visit stirred things up. The host society advertised her first lecture on April 18, as it did all its meetings, as "for women." But this segregation ran counter to Stone's principles, and notice of her second lecture stated that it was "expressly but not exclusively for women." The rest of her lectures in Philadelphia and surrounding towns were open to everyone.[25]

Lucretia Mott took advantage of Stone's presence to call the state's first woman's rights meeting. Since returning from the New York conventions, she had tried in vain to rouse interest for a similar meeting in Philadelphia. Stone provided the needed impetus. A meeting "to consider the duty and position of woman" was held on Friday, May 4, at Philadelphia's Franklin Hall. Mott spoke first, showing from Scripture the right and duty of woman to "share the labors of the pulpit with her brother." Stone followed with an address on woman's social and civil status, showing that society considered woman merely man's appendage, even calling her, after her husband's death, his "relict," or remnant. In what were to become her forte as a woman's rights lecturer, Stone's vivid stories and illustrations revealed the effect of discrimination on women's lives, and Mott said it was from Stone that she learned the depth of woman's degradation.[26]

Stone did not reenlist as an antislavery agent. After stopping in New York and Boston for the conventions of the American and New England antislavery societies, she went home to prepare for woman's rights work in New York.

Organizing a Movement

Among works Lucy Stone consulted in the summer of 1849 as she prepared for her New York agency was Edward D. Mansfield's 1845 *Legal Rights, Liabilities and Duties of Women*. Despite steady improvement during the 1840s in property laws affecting married women, the idea of a woman's actual *right* to control her property was not one whose time had come, and Mansfield's views reflected predominant legal thought. Commenting on legal provisions that vested a woman's personal property "immediately and absolutely" in her husband when she married, Mansfield asserted that they had "all the authority of human and divine law." These provisions reflected "the first great principle of Scripture, the unity of husband and wife"—that husband and wife are *one person*. Laws that seemed severe and harsh toward women, he said, were "but necessary and inevitable results of this principle."[1]

Reading this, Stone wrote to Antoinette Brown, "It seems to me that *no* man who *deserved* the *name* of MAN, when he knows what a *mere thing* the law makes a married woman, would ever insult a woman by asking her to marry." Since leaving Oberlin, Stone's resolve not to marry had remained firm, telling Brown she thought more than ever she would never marry, and Brown responding that the two of them should stand alone and prove the worth of an independent woman. Stone regretted the December 1848 marriage of Mercy Lloyd and hoped Helen Cook would not follow her, for, said Lucy, "'Tis next to a chattel slave to be a *legal* wife."[2]

And yet Stone longed for the love and intimacy she saw in marriages around her. "I have not yet reached the place where I need no companionship as you have," she told Brown. "It is horrid to live without the intimate companionship and gentle loving influences which are the constant attendants of a true love marriage." Stone had developed a close relationship with fellow antislavery agent Charles C. Burleigh and often stayed in his home, where she had become a close friend of his wife and observed their effort at an egalitarian marriage. Burleigh believed that men should adopt simple habits to ease their wives' housework, that men should share the care of their children, and that women's parental responsibilities should not interfere with cultural and intellectual pursuits. The marriage of Charles and Gertrude Burleigh was probably one of the two among Stone's acquaintances she considered "true marriages." Stone craved such a relationship. "My heart aches to love somebody that shall be all its own," she confided to Brown. She found single life a "wretchedly unnatural way of living." But there were so many legal obstacles to "a married woman having any being of her own" and nothing could be worse than being "a *thing*, as every married woman now is in the eye of Law." The only solution to the dilemma, as she saw it, was for Brown and her to "get down these laws, and then marry if we can."[3]

Stone did not lack opportunity to marry. Samuel Brooke, who had resigned his position as general agent of the Western Anti-Slavery Society and come to Massachusetts, was just one of her suitors. He worked with her at several antislavery meetings, visited at her parents' farm, and friends noticed the developing one-sided "love affair."[4] But if Stone's resolve to remain single had softened at all, her study of laws affecting women bolstered it, and she became more strongly convinced that she could not marry until laws changed.

To "get down these laws" was the work for which Stone now prepared, and she urged Brown to make it her work, too. Brown was studying theology at Oberlin, but under special status granted her as "resident graduate," official admission to the theological seminary having been denied. Adamantly opposed to Brown's religious studies, the ladies' board eliminated her anticipated source of income by passing a rule prohibiting resident graduates from teaching at the institute. Nevertheless, Brown had persevered and was beginning her final year in the program. Stone regretted that Brown was wasting three years studying an "old, musty theology" when she could be making a valuable contribution as a reform lecturer. Brown had already demonstrated her speaking ability. During a visit home in March, she had lectured on woman's rights for a group of Henrietta reformers and then, needing to return to Oberlin, declined an invitation from women in nearby Rochester. But, she told Stone, perhaps both of them would be lecturing on woman's rights within a few months.[5]

For some unknown reason, Stone's woman's rights agency did not materialize. The lost opportunity had to have been a great disappointment, for she was not prepared to lecture without such backing. As summer turned into fall with no word from New York, she accepted invitations for antislavery work and by October was back to a full-time schedule. Meanwhile, she proceeded with woman's rights agitation in Massachusetts, drafting a second suffrage petition and sending printed copies to friends across the state. Wendell Phillips wrote an accompanying appeal for circulation, explaining why those who refused to vote themselves should nonetheless demand that right for women, and Garrison published the petition in the *Liberator* for volunteers to cut out or copy. Stone circulated it during her antislavery labors, and when she sent the petitions to the legislature in February 1850, over half of them were from towns where she had lectured. This year, they were referred to the Judiciary Committee before being tabled.[6]

As she traveled throughout Massachusetts, Connecticut, Maine, and Pennsylvania, a few community lyceums invited her to speak, and if they did not specify a topic, she spoke on woman's rights. Even when lecturing on antislavery, she often included ideas aimed at raising her audiences' consciousness. When the nominations committee at a county convention listed women nominees under their husbands' given names, Stone suggested it might be more appropriate to identify them by their own names. Agreeing, the committee revised its report.[7]

Two events renewed interest in woman's rights outside New England that winter. The first was publication of Elizabeth Wilson's *Scriptural View of Woman's Rights and Duties, in all the Important Relations of Life,* the product of a ten-year study inspired by the controversy of the late thirties. The *National Anti-Slavery Standard* and the *Liberator* published excerpts and resurrected the biblical debate, which continued for several months and elicited widespread notice of the book. Stone's copy probably came from Lucretia Mott, who helped arrange publication and sent copies to friends for them to sell. Although Stone hoped the day was not far off when the question of human rights would be allowed to "rest on its own merits," she thought the book would be influential among those who relied on scriptural authority. The second event that sparked interest in woman's rights was debate in the Tennessee legislature on a married women's property bill. Among arguments opponents used was one to the effect that women should not be allowed to control property because they had no souls. After lengthy debate on whether women possessed souls, the honorable body concluded they did not and rejected the bill. Reports of the debate served as a wake-up call to many women who had held their distance from the woman's rights cause, including Amelia Bloomer, editor of a temperance newspaper in New York, who responded with a spunky editorial calling on women to open their eyes, see where they stood, and begin demanding their rights.[8]

Perhaps it was the Tennessee legislature's vote that spurred Ohio women to action. With a constitutional convention scheduled to meet that summer, women associated with the Western Anti-Slavery Society called a state convention to organize petitioning for securing to women the same legal and political rights guaranteed to men, as well as for woman and Negro suffrage. Although New Yorkers had held two woman's rights conventions, they had been local meetings with little advance notice. This was a state convention, and Stone hailed it as an important beginning. "Massachusetts ought to have taken the lead in the work you are now doing," she told organizers, "but if she chooses to linger, let her young sisters of the West set her a worthy example; and if the 'Pilgrim spirit is not dead,' we'll pledge Massachusetts to follow her."[9]

Many of the organizers of the Ohio Woman's Rights Convention, which

met on April 19 and 20, 1850, were friends of Stone's. The president, Betsy
Mix Cowles, was a protégée of Abby Kelley's, a graduate of Oberlin's ladies'
course who had returned to Oberlin during Stone's last year, enrolled in the
collegiate course with her, and watched her battle for woman's rights. The
keynote speaker, Elizabeth Jones, was the friend who had tried to persuade
Stone to lecture on antislavery instead of woman's rights. She had since surrendered her own antislavery agency and begun lecturing on women's physiology. Mary Ann Johnson, who drafted the suffrage memorial, had just moved
to Ohio from New England with her husband Oliver Johnson, with whom
Stone had worked at antislavery meetings. As new editor of the *Anti-Slavery
Bugle*, he helped promote the convention. These leaders wanted Stone and
Lucretia Mott to plead their cause before the constitutional convention in Columbus, but Stone believed appeals to lawmakers should come from their own
constituents. Urging Ohio women to proceed on their own, she said, "Now is
the time, while the old Constitution is being removed and the new making, to
strike for equal rights. It is an important moment. No more favorable can ever
occur. I need not tell you that I am with you heart and soul. If I were one of
you, I would serve you to the best of my ability. As it is, while grateful for the
confidence you have given me, I must decline going to Ohio."[10]

Immediately, Stone began making plans to carry out her "pledge to follow."
What she wanted, however, was a convention to formally organize the woman's
rights movement. Usually such meetings were called by existing societies from
several states, but in 1850 there were no woman's rights associations. She
sought advice from Garrison, and it was probably he who suggested she hold
a meeting during Boston's anniversary week that, attended by reformers from
several states in town for other meetings, could issue a call for a national
convention. Stone found a ready helper in Paulina Wright Davis, another of
Abby Kelley's early converts. Paulina had become a physiology lecturer after
her first husband died in 1845 and had tried to rouse interest in holding a
woman's rights convention then. Now married to a leading political abolitionist, she had served with Stone on a committee at the American Anti-Slavery
Convention in May.[11]

The two women appeared before a large audience that occupied both levels
of Boston's Melodeon Hall on the evening of May 30, 1850. Davis presided
while Stone spoke on the need for a formal woman's rights movement and
proposed calling a convention to establish it. Henry C. Wright, Samuel Brooke,
and Garrison gave seconding speeches, Garrison suggesting that the first thing
women should do was to demand political enfranchisement. Explaining to nonvoting abolitionists in the audience why they should support that demand, he
compared the question to abolitionist efforts to repeal laws that barred blacks
from state militias. Although he himself was a pacifist and did not want anyone
enrolled in the militia, still, he said, he hated the law that barred blacks from
serving. Black men should be able to decide for themselves whether to serve,
with no opprobrium thrown upon them on account of their complexion. So it

was with women. "I want the women to have the right to vote, and I call upon them to demand it perseveringly until they possess it. When they have obtained it, it will be for them to say whether they will exercise it or not."[12]

The assembly voted to call a convention and appointed five women—Abby Kelley Foster, Harriot K. Hunt, Eliza J. Kenney, Dora Taft, and Eliza H. Taft—to assist Stone and Davis with arrangements. Hunt was a Boston physician and medical lecturer. Thwarted in attempts to acquire formal medical training, she had studied on her own and established a successful career. Kenney and the Tafts were active abolitionists, and Kenney had also taken leading roles at Association conventions. Consulting together in an anteroom after the meeting, the women decided to hold the convention at Worcester in October and assigned Stone and Davis to prepare the call and serve as a Committee of Correspondence.[13]

Stone and Davis asked William Elder, a retired Philadelphia physician who had assisted both Elizabeth Blackwell and Davis with their careers, to help with the call. The women outlined points to be included but left actual composition to him. Then they returned to their homes and began writing to friends of the cause across the country, soliciting signatures to the call and recruiting attendance and speakers. "We need all the women who are accustomed to speak in public, every stick of timber that is sound," Stone said in asking Antoinette Brown to speak. Although it might not have been good in olden days to "number the army," it was necessary now, said Stone. "We want to know upon whom we can rely."[14]

After finishing her part of the correspondence, Stone left for Ohio and Illinois, expecting to return by mid-August. She had planned to spend the summer writing woman's rights speeches and had arranged to study at a private library in Providence, but an "iron necessity" compelled her to go to Cincinnati instead. What exactly that necessity was is uncertain, but it seems to have been an engagement with the Western Anti-Slavery Society. Samuel Brooke had accompanied her home from Boston and stayed for a brief visit during which the idea of her going west seems to have emerged, and Brown recalled that after stopping for a brief visit in Oberlin, Stone continued on to a speaking engagement somewhere in Ohio.[15]

From Cincinnati Stone went on to Hutsonville, Illinois, a settlement just across the Indiana border where her brother Luther operated a store. Within days of her arrival, however, Luther died of cholera. Left to sell his business and accompany his frail and pregnant widow back east, Stone feared she might not be able to return home for three months and wrote to Paulina Davis asking her to complete convention arrangements without her. Finding among the locals an intense hatred of slaves but not of slavery, Stone lectured on antislavery as she settled her brother's estate. Reporting her work to Samuel May, she added that it was very "sickly" in Hutsonville: "There have been three fatal cases of cholera. The small pox, measles, mumps, whooping cough and other diseases abound. The weather is excessively hot, and the water miserable. It will require all our knowledge of physiology to keep well, and perhaps we cannot even then do it."[16]

Weighing the risk of staying in such a place against the rigors of travel, Lucy and Phebe set off by stage coach across Indiana on August 20. They had traveled only three days when Phebe went into labor and delivered a premature stillborn son. Lucy buried the baby and nursed her bed-ridden sister-in-law until she herself contracted typhoid fever. For the next three weeks she drifted in and out of consciousness as innkeepers nursed her and neighbors came to stare and ask, "Do you think you shall live?"[17] Near the end of September, however, both Lucy and Phebe were well enough to resume their journey.

They arrived at Coy's Hill, both very frail, just two weeks before the convention. Stone's name had headed the list of signatories on the convention call, and she would be expected to play a major role in the meetings. But neither her legs nor her voice would hold long enough for a major address. Although she had felt it important to know in advance on whom she could rely, she now had little idea of whom or how many to expect. So on the morning of October 23, she went to Worcester with a heavy heart, nearly despairing that the meeting would be a failure.[18]

She need not have feared. Entering Worcester's Brinley Hall, she found a sea of sympathetic faces. There, of course, were such stalwarts as Garrison, Phillips, Mott, Abby and Stephen Foster, and Anna Q. T. Parsons, who, although not a member of the planning committee, had helped Davis with final arrangements. There were longtime friends like Josiah Henshaw and his wife, Elizabeth, and newer friends like Thomas Earle, editor of the *Worcester Spy,* and his wife, Sarah. From her antislavery network were Samuel May Jr. and his wife, Sarah; Charles and Gertrude Burleigh; Parker and Sarah Pillsbury; Oliver and Mary Ann Johnson; William Henry Channing; James Buffum; Frederick Douglass; and Ernestine Rose, another lecturer with whom Stone had worked at antislavery conventions in New York. Also from New York was Joseph C. Hathaway, whose wife had contacted Stone about lecturing there two years earlier, and Antoinette Brown. Among the many people she had never seen before were two sisters from Cincinnati—Emily and Marian Blackwell— who would become her sisters-in-law. Response to the call had exceeded Stone's highest hopes. Over one thousand people crowded into Brinley Hall, designed to hold eight hundred, while hundreds more had to be turned away from the opening session. Managers tried to move the afternoon and evening sessions to the much larger City Hall, but renovations made it unavailable and the convention had to proceed where it was, with every inch of space occupied and many disappointed people denied admittance.

Paulina Davis presided. Her opening address intended to set the woman's rights movement on the firm basis of the common humanity of the sexes, their equal rights and partnership in all things, and counter the impression that it was a *women's* movement and antagonistic toward men. The declaration of sentiments adopted by the New York conventions two years earlier had denounced men as tyrants. The Ohio convention, although called to promote the equal rights of women with men, had, according to custom, excluded men from its deliberations. Stone's advisors cautioned against letting this meeting take a similar stance. The sexes "must labor together for the benefit of the race," Sarah Grimké said. "They are a unit and can only make true progress by working harmoniously." Stone and Davis wanted to define this movement not as a battle between the sexes but as a joint battle of men and women to uplift humanity.[19]

Davis also wanted to set the movement's tone as one of charitable understanding and forbearance. Alluding to the document issued by the first New York convention, which had elicited strong criticism and ridicule, Davis said it was one thing to issue a declaration of rights or wrongs but quite another to present the subject in such a way as to command public acceptance and consideration. "Harsh judgments and harsh words will neither weaken the opposition nor strengthen our hands," she cautioned. The public mind would be more receptive to their ideas if they treated opponents with understanding and respect, for prejudices were sincerely held and customs had foundations that at one time may have been necessary. Davis also objected to the adage repeated by Garrison at the preliminary meeting that those "[w]ho would be free, themselves must strike the blow." She considered this a barbarous principle, one that justified the rule of might over right and condemned the contented slave to slavery and the ignorant man to darkness. This attitude must be done away with, said Davis; men must learn to give justice rather than insist that rights be wrested from the powerful.[20]

Davis's appeal came across to some as criticism of Garrisonians and their techniques, and it probably was. Her friendship with Abby Kelley Foster had cooled since their early days together. As a pioneer woman lecturer herself, she had seen how difficult it was to gain access to the public ear and how easy it was to lose it once obtained. In towns where Foster's invective had preceded her, she had found it difficult to obtain either hall or audience. She did not want champions of this new movement to needlessly close doors. But both Abby Foster and Lucretia Mott took exception to what they saw as an appeal for meekness. At the afternoon session, in a speech that does not survive, Foster objected to Davis's request for a conciliatory attitude, in language that must have offended some of the audience. Following shortly thereafter, Mott defended Foster's language, saying she feared some might have misunderstood her as advocating "the use of violence and bloodshed" to obtain these rights. But Mott explained that their weapons were spiritual, not carnal, and that they "must fight with the sword of the spirit." Like Foster, she was opposed to any "twaddle" on the subject. "We want to speak earnestly and truly the words of honest and sober conviction. We want to speak in tones of reproof to those on whom the guilt of these wrongs rests. We want to say as Jesus did: 'Ye fools and blind,' 'Ye hypocrites,' and to our Sisters who are still indifferent and contented with their position: 'O, thou slothful and slow of heart, rise up in the strength of thy womanhood, and Christ shall give thee light.'"[21]

At the evening session, Wendell Phillips supported Davis's appeal for forbearance when he said that the work of this new movement was to reform the customs and institutions that kept women down. Denying that the male sex alone was to blame for those customs and institutions, he said both sexes were, in part, "creatures of circumstances; we are what the past has made us." Injustices had developed and continued to exist not because of intentional wrongdoing, but out of ignorance. "We have inherited these customs," he said; "very few men ever get beyond the smoke of their father's cabins." The remedy, he said, was to "run the ploughshare of reform deep through the soil which has given growth to our present institutions and customs." That soil, he said, was public opinion. "It is public opinion that deprives Woman of most of her rights. When this public opinion is reformed the barriers and restrictions thrown around Woman will fall almost imperceptibly."

Again Mott disagreed. She did not believe in abstract wrong. Where wrong was done, there was a wrongdoer. She thought the wrong in this case clearly rested on man, and he should be held responsible for it. She also objected to the idea, implied in Davis's opening address, that women should *ask* that their rights be *given* to them. Mott insisted that women *demand* their rights be *yielded* to them on the ground of common humanity.[22]

Here at the outset of the organized woman's rights movement was disagreement on its desired character and tone: Some refused to hide their anger over woman's oppression and did not hesitate to blame and denounce men for it, while others considered such attitudes unworthy, inexpedient, and even counterproductive. This difference over style and tactic would continue throughout the decade, and the century, sometimes dividing the ranks. But there was no disagreement on the movement's ultimate goal. The first resolution presented from the business committee concisely defined the movement's objective: "to secure for [woman] political, legal and social equality with man, until her proper sphere is determined by what alone should determine it, her powers and capacities, strengthened and refined by an education in accordance with her nature."[23]

From her position on the business committee, Stone helped draft this and other resolutions that articulated the movement's principles and goals. One set of resolutions put forth woman's claim for equal civil and political rights and demanded that the word *male* be stricken from every state constitution. Other resolutions addressed specific issues of property rights, access to education, and employment opportunities. And others defined the movement as an effort to secure the "natural and civil rights" of *all* women, one declaring the goal to be equality before the law without distinction of sex *or* color, and another specifically including the rights of the one-and-a-half million women held in slavery.[24]

All these resolutions passed without dissent, although not everyone in the audience agreed with them. Of the more than one thousand people who attended, fewer than two hundred enrolled as members and were therefore entitled to vote. But everyone was urged to participate in discussion and invited to send written questions to the speakers' platform. When someone asked how the demand for women's equality could be reconciled with certain biblical passages, Antoinette Brown was called to the platform. She had completed her theological studies in August, but since the institute had not officially enrolled her in its seminary, it also refused to award her a diploma or to permit ordination. Nevertheless, Lucretia Mott introduced her as one who had prepared for the ministry. Brown gave several examples of distorted translation and misinterpretation, trying to show that rightly interpreted, the Bible described equality between the sexes. Burleigh seconded Brown's premise, giving additional examples. But on the last evening Stephen Foster, that great critic of orthodox religion, said he believed the Bible did decree woman's subjugation, and he started to digress into a discussion on the question of inspiration and equal authority of all parts of the Bible. A spirited debate ensued until he was forced to yield the floor. Mott had the final word on the subject, in the convention's closing speech, attempting to remove what would remain a thorn in the side of the woman's rights movement.[25]

In addition to discussing the principles and goals of the new movement, the assembly considered how best to organize to promote them. Among supporters of woman's rights were many individuals who objected to having their beliefs defined and actions prescribed by others, and thus considered organizations oppressive. Mindful of their concerns, Phillips said there was no need for a formal association or founding document. No organization was needed other than annual conventions and a standing committee to arrange them, and the resolutions and speeches could serve as a declaration of principles. Agreeing, the business committee proposed a central committee to serve as the movement's executive body and, reflecting its egalitarian principles, appointed nine women and nine men. Other committees, on Education, Industrial Avocations, Civil and Political Functions, and Social Relation, were appointed to gather information useful for guiding public opinion "upward and onward in this great Social Reform of establishing Woman's Co-equal Sovereignty with Man." Stone was named to the Central Committee and the committee on Civil and Political Functions.[26]

Until the last session, Stone had addressed the convention only briefly as a participant in discussions. But before Lucretia Mott delivered the convention's closing address, she took the podium and, contemplating what had just been accomplished, confessed the doubt and apprehension she had felt the previous morning and the joy she now felt at the convention's great success. Addressing what had been a point of contention—whether women should ask men to give them their rights or just seize and exercise them—she said women should take what rights they could and demand those they could not. To this end, she proposed that members of the convention petition their respective state legislatures for the right of suffrage, the right of married women to hold property, and as many other specific rights as they felt practical to seek in their respective states. She then gave a short address, ending with the assertion that women should be more that appendages of men. "We want that Woman should be the co-equal and helpmeet of Man, in all the interests, and perils and enjoyments of human life. We want that she should attain to the highest development of her nature; we want that when she dies, it may not be written on her gravestone that she was someone else's 'relict.'"[27]

Word of this convention spread across the United States and, carried by a full report in the *New York Tribune* for Europe, across the Atlantic. It inspired women in Sheffield, England, to call a meeting, draw up a petition for woman suffrage, and present it to the House of Lords the following February. It also elicited a lengthy analysis of its principles and demands, published nine months later in England's *Westminster Review*, which heartily concurred with both. Thus it was, as Elizabeth Cady Stanton would write twenty years later, that the 1850 National Woman's Rights Convention in Worcester, Massachusetts, gave birth to the woman's rights movement both in America and England.[28]

Speaking for Women

In October 1850, Lucy Stone was too weak to resume the work of a lecturing agent. Traveling by train, coach, and open wagon through all kinds of weather, speaking night after night in cold and drafty lecture halls projecting a voice loud enough to be heard over the commotion of detractors, and walking great distances to post placards, make arrangements for a meeting hall, or find accommodations was exhausting work. On one occasion the previous year, when the town hotel was closed against them, Stone and Parker Pillsbury had walked a mile and a half through muddy fields in pitch dark to reach overnight lodging. Another time, when advertising placards sent ahead had not been posted and the requested announcement not given in the churches, Stone spent the entire day before her lecture putting up her own bills and going door to door to recruit an audience. Then she trudged up a long hill to the hotel to get something to eat and tended the proprietor's children while a meal was prepared. Presented a plate of hash with pieces of a dish cloth chopped in with the meat, she went to her lecture hungry. Lecturing in New Hampshire during a bitter cold spell, she stayed at a home where she had to wash at an outdoor spout a great distance from the house. Such incidents were routine for an antislavery agent, so, still weak from her nearly fatal struggle with typhoid fever, Stone apologized to May for being unable to work. "My teeth almost chatter when I remember the *cold beds* and the *cold rides* . . . of last winter. I must be hardier than at present before I shall be able to endure it again."[1] It would be six months before she regained sufficient strength to resume her work.

From the National Woman's Rights Convention, Stone went home to convalesce. The winter was not one of inactivity, however. Besides spending two months nursing her sister through the final stages of pregnancy and then caring for a new niece, she conducted another petition drive. The newly appointed Woman's Rights Central Committee recruited people to circulate petitions in eight states, and Stone took charge of the work in Massachusetts. She drew up a petition similar to her previous ones and, unable to circulate it at speaking engagements as before, sent printed copies to friends and had it published in the *Liberator*. Presented to the legislature in February and March, the petitions were referred to the Judiciary Committee, which reported it "inexpedient to legislate thereon."[2]

While Stone recuperated, Antoinette Brown made her lecturing debut. She had accepted a position with the American Female Guardian Society, formerly the New York Female Moral Reform Society, hoping to make Sunday preaching part of her mission work in New York City's slums. Her employers disapproved of female preaching, however, so, with financial backing from a woman prominent in that society, Brown left and began lecturing independently.[3]

Stone was eager to return to the lecturing field, too. "It does seem a pity for even the weakest of us to be on our oars now when so many are ready to hear," she told May.[4] Passage of a new Fugitive Slave Law in September 1850 had angered many northerners and made them more receptive to antislavery lectures. The law, part of the omnibus bill known as the Compromise of 1850, empowered federal marshals to enter free states in pursuit of runaways and required citizens, under penalty of fines and imprisonment, to assist in their capture. Since captives were not entitled to a jury trial or to testify in their own behalf, not only were fugitives doomed to reenslavement, but free blacks claimed as runaways were also imperiled. Newspapers reported many "kidnapings" that winter, as well as defiant rescues by sympathizers. Despite anger over the Fugitive Slave Law, people were sharply divided over the Compromise of 1850 as a whole. Desperate for a peaceful resolution, many blamed abolitionists for keeping the conflict alive. In New York City, where economic and social ties to the South were strong, opposition to abolitionists was so keen that officials closed public halls against them, forcing the American Anti-Slavery Society to move its May anniversary to western New York.

Amid this mixed anger, Stone resumed her antislavery agency in April 1851. Resolutions passed at meetings she attended denounced the Fugitive Slave Law as unconstitutional and the Fillmore administration as an "absolute despotism." But the strongest condemnation was still directed toward churches and religious leaders who refused to condemn slavery. Stone served on the business committee of the Worcester County Anti-Slavery Convention that drafted a resolution branding as "a hireling, or a wolf in sheep's clothing, every pulpit occupant who remains dumb in view of our great national sin." Two months later, she received notice from the West Brookfield Congregational Church that because she had "withdrawn from the communion" of that church and "engaged in a course of life evidently inconsistent with her covenant engagement" to it, she was no longer a member. Stone asked for an opportunity to show that her actions were not only consistent with, but demanded by, her covenant with the church, but she did not receive a hearing.[5]

In May 1851, Stone ended her three-year agency with the Massachusetts Anti-Slavery Society so she could lecture full time on woman's rights. The national convention had formally launched a woman's rights movement, but it had no treasury to hire agents. Stone had acquired the speaking ability and organizational experience needed to work on her own, but independent work would be difficult. She would have to engage halls and pay rent out of her own pocket, arrange her own transportation and lodging, and generate whatever notice and publicity she could as a lone lecturer. And unlike Antoinette Brown, she would have no financial backing. But an incident at the New England Anti-Slavery Convention propelled her ahead.

Hiram Powers's statue of the *Greek Slave,* being shown in Boston after a nationwide tour, had evoked rapturous praise for its beauty and pathos, but also controversy over its nudity. Some cities required men and women to view it in separate groups. Going to the exhibit early in the morning, Stone and Brown were able to view the sculpture by themselves in complete silence. It was the first life-size statue Stone had ever seen, and it moved her profoundly. In depicting a female prisoner of war placed by her captors on the Turkish slave market, her hands fettered and face half averted, Powers combined in the figure's stance and expression a bitter despair for her plight and a scorn for all around that made her oblivious to her nakedness. It represented, Powers said, "the embodiment of enslaved Greek womanhood."[6]

To Stone it embodied *all* enslaved womanhood. When she spoke that night at the convention, she poured out her heart about the *Greek Slave* "so emblematic of woman," with a stirring eloquence that excited even herself. Afterwards, Samuel May praised the speech but said that however true, it was out of place at an antislavery meeting. Stone recognized that May was right. But, saying, "I was a woman before I was an abolitionist," she insisted "I must speak for women," and resigned her antislavery agency.[7]

Stone began making arrangements for woman's rights lectures in several towns in the eastern part of the state. She kept antislavery appointments made for her during the summer but told May she would not be available after the first week of September. Unwilling to accept her resignation, May continued to press assignments upon her and she finally agreed to help with Sunday meetings. Although Garrisonians routinely held reform meetings on Sundays, it was still a controversial practice that Stone did not plan to use in her independent work. Telling May she would accept antislavery appointments on Sundays, she insisted that the week days were reserved for woman's rights and there was no reason the two should interfere with each other.[8]

The sudden illness and death of two of Frank and Harriet's children postponed the inauguration of Stone's woman's rights lectures. Before beginning her work in the eastern part of the state, she gave her new lecture at Ware on October 1, then on successive nights in Warren and North Brookfield. The next week she was at Lynn, Salem, Beverly, Dedham, and Millville.[9] At these lectures Stone appeared in a new style of dress that had become a fashion rage during the summer. Consisting of a pair of baggy trousers under a skirt that reached just below the knees, the new costume was variously called the "short skirt and trowsers"; the "Turkish dress," because of its Turkish-style pantaloons; the "American dress," as contrasted with French fashion; the "Bloomer dress," after Amelia Bloomer, who helped popularize it; or simply the "reform dress" or "new style." Although it had captured the attention of the popular press only that spring, Stone had donned it as a health measure during her convalescence and had been wearing it for almost a year.

The dress was a product of the health movement, and Stone had probably read descriptions of it in the *Water-Cure Journal*. Graham disciples had worn it in the mid-forties at Brook Farm, and articles advocating it for outdoor exercise appeared in various newspapers at least as early as the summer of 1848. But not until October 1849 did the *Water-Cure Journal*, decrying the debilitating effects of the current popular fashion, call for a deliberate dress reform movement. The fashionable dress health reformers condemned consisted of a skirt that fell six inches beyond floor length, worn over several layers of starched petticoats with straw or horsehair sewn into the hems, which the wearer was obliged to lift with both hands. In addition to these heavy, trailing skirts, it also had a long, whalebone-fitted bodice that accomplished the desired "long-waist" effect by pushing the wearer's internal organs out of their normal place. The result was a feminine population that, as one medical professor warned his students, was of no use as cadavers with which to study human anatomy.[10]

Urged to invent a style of dress that would allow women the free use of their legs, readers of the *Water-Cure Journal* offered many ideas, all including some form of pants. Within months, women as far west as Michigan and Wisconsin were wearing some form of pants and short skirt, and staff and patients at the water-cures adopted different versions of it. Although most donned it as a walking and exercise dress or as a house and gardening dress, a letter writer to the National Woman's Rights Convention urged women to adopt it as their common attire. It was after this convention, when Stone retreated to her parents' farm to convalesce, that she made herself a dress of short skirt and baggy pants.[11]

Stone was just one among many who donned the reform dress in the winter of 1850–51. With the coming of spring, astonished newspaper editors in several states reported sightings of women in the strange attire. In March, Amelia Bloomer, the editor whom the Tennessee legislature had shocked into a strong stand on woman's rights, announced that she and other Seneca Falls women had adopted the costume. She had been championing the new style for several months in her temperance newspaper, the *Lily*, and now her lively promotion of it attracted the attention of hundreds of women not connected with the health movement. She printed a description of her dress and instructions on how to make it, and soon newspapers dubbed it the "Bloomer dress."[12]

The reform dress became a fad during the summer of 1851. Mary Gove Nichols, now a hydropathic physician and proprietor of a New York water-cure, gathered signatures to a "Declaration of Independence from the Despotism of Parisian Fashion." Managers of Lowell's textile mills gave a banquet for employees who adopted the safer dress before July Fourth. Dozens of women turned out in Turkish costume at one of Toledo's grandest social events. The Springfield Water-Cure in western Massachusetts held a large dress reform celebration, with speakers, resolutions, and toasts, and supporters planned an even grander festival at New York City's Broadway Tabernacle. The dress received warm support from many quarters. A month before the *Water-Cure Journal* published its first illustrations of the dress, *Harper's Monthly* presented a sketch of one version for "fair reformers" to copy. Criticizing the long-flowing skirt as "among the silliest foibles of Fashion," it praised those who adopted the "far more convenient, equally chaste, and more elegant" reform dress. Garrisonians were among the costume's prominent promoters. Dr. William Elder spoke at a dress reform meeting in New York, and the Reverend Samuel J. May and William H. Burleigh, brother of Charles Burleigh, helped organize a dress reform society in Syracuse. Ebenezer D. Draper, an antislavery activist and supporter of woman's rights, offered silk to any of his friends who would make it into short skirt and trousers for a public dress, and Stone accepted the offer.[13]

By the time she began wearing the dress in public, however, backlash had begun. Championing the new style as a freedom dress did nothing to recommend it to critics of the woman's rights movement, who saw it as a usurpation of the symbol of male authority. They called meetings to put down the fad, and some of the very same editors who had previously praised the dress began to waffle on the "somewhat delicate and rather vexed question" of "Bloomerism." *Harper's Monthly*, which had encouraged women to adopt the dress, now ran cartoons ridiculing it.[14]

Surprising objection came, too, from Jane Swisshelm, editor of the *Pittsburgh Saturday Visiter*. Although an advocate of woman's rights, she had become a severe critic of the organized movement. After the National Woman's Rights Convention, she rebuked its leaders for introducing the question of slavery and converting it into an "abolition meeting." Then, after attending a woman's rights convention in Akron, Ohio, she pronounced it mismanaged and said she would have nothing more to do with the movement. And now, after trying out the "freedom dress," Swisshelm declared it impractical. There were a variety of reasons why women should not wear it, she said. If the trousers were worn straight and loose at the ankle, they went "flip flap," and if they were worn gathered at the ankle, they went "slip, slap." If a short-skirt wearer stooped to pick up a thimble from the carpet, the back of the skirt rose above the knees to expose the front part of her underskirts. Then, too, Swisshelm found, it was much easier to maneuver through a briar patch in a long skirt than in a short. And—now, here's the rub—Swisshelm thought the announcement of her wearing such a dress would injure her influence.[15]

Although the *New York Daily Tribune* had declared Bloomer-wearing "too general to excite surprise or ridicule," when Stone lectured in the short skirt and trousers in the fall of 1851 (with the straight, loose trouser legs that purportedly went "flip, flap"), it was the first time most of her audiences had seen the new style. Whispering and snickering greeted her entrance, but once she began to speak her attire was forgotten. The *Lynn Democrat* said Stone was "very tastefully and appropriately dressed," without specifying that she wore short skirt and trousers, while the *Salem Observer* noted the Bloomer costume without further comment. The dress was becoming on her small frame, for at this time Stone was "a tiny creature" who "could not have weighed more than a hundred pounds."[16]

Completing her first series of woman's rights lectures on October 10, Stone turned her attention to the second National Woman's Rights Convention, scheduled to meet the next week. Jointly with William Henry Channing, she had assumed the post of secretary of the Central Committee, replacing Sarah Earle, who had held it during her convalescence, and Stone had spent much of the summer lining up speakers and soliciting letters. Among those who responded was Ralph Waldo Emerson, whom she had visited in March and had hoped to enlist in the cause. Although he declined to speak, he sent a brief letter of support and confided to his journal at the time of the convention that he did not believe women were on "right footing" as long as they were denied equal property rights and the right to vote.[17]

The National Woman's Rights Convention that met at Worcester on October 15 and 16, 1851, was one of the most successful of the decade—in its attendance, its array of talented and eloquent speakers, its articulation of the principles and goals of the movement, and the extensive and favorable press coverage it received. Three thousand people crowded into Worcester's City Hall. In addition to Stone, Davis, Channing, Rose, Phillips, Foster, and Brown, convention speakers included Abby Price and Emma Robinson Coe, both of whom had begun lecturing on woman's rights since the last convention. New to the platform were Clarina I. H. Nichols, editor of the Vermont *Windham County Democrat,* who was already known for her woman's rights writing but now made her debut as a public speaker, and Elizabeth Oakes Smith, a contributor to magazines such as *Godey's Lady's Book,* who was making inroads for women on the lyceum circuit, where women's reading of essays on literary topics was becoming quite respectable.

Several women wore the new style, and some expected the dress question to be a prominent issue at the convention. During the summer, Davis had discouraged the calling of a dress reform convention, saying the matter was sure to be discussed at the woman's rights meeting. But the issue received very little and only incidental attention. Alluding to the dress question in one of her speeches, Stone cited women's willingness to risk their health to attract husbands as one of the ills that grew out of the idea that women were to live solely as companions for men. As long as women were taught that their chief end in life was to get married, said Stone, they would continue to try to please men who sought wives "in the shape of wasps and hour glasses."[18]

The business committee set the agenda for discussion with a series of resolutions authored by Wendell Phillips. Although in 1846 Phillips had considered suffrage second in importance to securing property rights, now, like Garrison, he proclaimed it the cornerstone of the woman's rights movement. The ballot would not only empower woman to sweep away all unequal laws relating to marriage and property, said Phillips, but also stimulate her to seek more education. Phillips's resolutions laid out the principles upon which the movement based its claims for woman's political, legal, and social equality, and charged with "gross dishonesty or ignorance" any who might contend that the word *men* in the Declaration of Independence did not mean *the human race,* or that "life, liberty, and the pursuit of happiness" were not the inalienable rights of the entire race. In a speech that became one of the movement's primary tracts, he explained how the woman's rights movement furthered the ideals upon which Western civilization had been built.[19]

In the report from the Committee on Education, Paulina Davis noted the recent establishment of a medical college for women in Philadelphia, which had been championed by opponents of coeducation such as Sarah Josepha Hale, and reminded the audience that separate schools for women were not what the woman's rights movement sought, for although they provided training denied women elsewhere, they were based on false precepts concerning women's interests, capacities, and duties. The demand for coeducation rather than special schools for women was one that woman's rights leaders found themselves having to explain repeatedly. When the Reverend Samuel J. May appealed for women's colleges at the next convention, Stone objected. "We don't want woman's schools or colleges," she said. "There are very good schools and colleges already built and endowed, with excellent apparatus and professors, and they have room for more students. . . . What we want is to gain admittance to these."[20] A lifelong opponent of sex-segregated schools, she refused to send her daughter to the any of the newly established women's colleges and sent her instead to Boston University, coeducational from its founding in 1869.

Presenting the report from the Committee on Industrial Avocations, Abby Price appealed not only for opening occupations and professions to women but also for equal pay and woman's "pecuniary independence." But, she declared, meeting in conventions, complaining of wrongs, and arguing equality of rights would not secure the desired result. Rather, women must assume responsibility for their own lives, break out of the present confines of feminine employment, and boldly enter new occupations. Taking up the appeal for individual responsibility, Stone agreed women must be their own saviors. Men could not feel the misery of woman's lot, she said, because when a young man goes forth to make his way in the world, he "sees no height to which he may not aspire, no place of honor which he may not fill. No matter how poor or lowly born, his opportunities are as large as his aspirations." But, said Stone, when his sister goes out into the world, she finds her options limited to the "petty details of domestic life" or the "wasting toil" of working for pay insufficient to sustain life. Stone told of a young sculptor from Beverly who had created a beautiful

bust that showed talent perhaps as great as that of Hiram Powers. But she could
not develop her skill or earn a living by it, for she received neither encouragement nor patronage. "We want this woman to come here and speak to us of
what the heart feels when the knell of dead hopes is rung," Stone said. She
wanted every woman in the audience to feel that this work rested on her
shoulders. "If you have a thought that seeks expression, utter it boldly. If you
remember the millions of slaves . . . and your heart prompts you to plead for
these millions, speak out fearlessly. If your taste is to sculpture, work out your
bust and let it stand there to speak for itself until it shall speak for you. No
matter what it be that you wish to do, if it be high and noble, go and do it.
When we can do this, our acts will be living epistles, known and read of all
men."[21]

Stone's words were chosen to rouse and inspire women. Her style was indeed
different from that of Abby Foster, who also spoke on individual responsibility
but framed her thoughts in words calculated to inflict discomfort. Foster introduced a resolution blaming women's lack of rights on their own lack of a sense
of responsibility. She said women must feel themselves equally bound with
men to provide for the necessities and luxuries of life. They must feel as deeply
as men the responsibility for intellectual, moral, and religious elevation of the
race. Then they would seek out and enter paths of labor that would elevate
them and secure their independence. Earlier, Price had alluded to Foster as the
woman whose self-sacrifice had won for all women the right to speak in public.
But Foster said women would not need to mount the speakers' rostrum if they
spoke through their everyday actions. "For fourteen years I have advocated
this cause in my daily life. Bloody feet, sisters, have worn smooth the path by
which you have come hither." Foster's words were an eloquent reminder of
her contribution to winning woman's rights, but that was not her point. Rather,
like Stone, she wanted women to take personal responsibility—in their own
lives, through their own action—for securing their rights. "Let us then, when
we go home, go not to complain, but to work." Foster said many women who
worked for a pittance felt they were suited for something better, but when she
urged them to open shops and do business for themselves they said they did
not want the responsibility, it was too much. To such women Foster said, "Well,
then starve in your laziness."[22]

Foster was impatient with women talking and whining while doing nothing
for themselves. She was outspoken and blunt, but her message was a valid
counterpoint to any who thought woman's rights could be won through beautiful essays in popular women's magazines. Her speech offended many, but
Stone recalled it as *the speech* of the convention."[23]

The resolutions, committee reports, and speeches of this convention presented the principles and goals of the woman's rights movement with a thor-
oughness, clarity, and cogency that changed minds. One convert was the editor
of the *New York Christian Inquirer,* who had severely criticized the movement
the previous year. Now, after reading the proceedings, he declared this conven-

tion perhaps "the most important meeting since that held in the cabin of the Mayflower." There could be "no more practical or tremendous revolution" than the one this convention sought. "To emancipate half the human race from its present position of dependence on the other half; to abolish every distinction between the sexes that can be abolished or which is maintained by statute or conventional usage; to throw open all the employments of society with equal freedom to men and women; to allow no difference whatsoever, in the eye of the law, in their duties or in their rights—this," he said, was a "reform surpassing in pregnancy of purpose and potential results any other."[24]

After the convention, Lucy Stone and Antoinette Brown set off on separate woman's rights tours, Stone in Massachusetts and Rhode Island, Brown in New York. At first, Stone's attendance was so slight that proceeds failed to cover even hall rental, let alone traveling expenses, and her attempt to increase attendance by not charging an entrance fee produced no larger audiences. Her arrangement with Samuel May turned out to be a great boon. Whereas she had been paid six dollars a week as a full-time antislavery agent, she now received four dollars for Sunday work alone, and by arranging woman's rights lectures in the vicinity of antislavery assignments, she reached more places than she could have without them. Satisfied with her first attempt at independent work, she said if Brown was having similar results, they both could "be proud and take courage."[25]

13

Divergent Paths

By the summer of 1852, the woman's rights movement had taken on more of a national character. Ohio activists had organized a state woman's rights association in May, Pennsylvanians had held a state convention in June, and preparations were under way to organize a state society in Indiana that fall. To increase the movement's visibility, the Central Committee decided to move the national convention out of New England and chose Syracuse, New York, for that year's meeting. As they corresponded about the program, committee members considered whether it was time to establish a national society. Disagreement on this and other questions created a division between Paulina Wright Davis and other leaders and led to her withdrawal from the annual meetings.

In the weeks preceding the 1851 convention, someone on the Central Committee, arguing that Abby Kelley Foster's prominence in the movement kept many influential women from joining, had asked other members to help persuade Foster not to attend. But Foster had gone and, at the committee's preliminary meeting on the day before the convention, this person asked that she not be seated on the speakers' platform. The proposed ostracism of the very woman who had forced the most radical reform movement of the day to acknowledge woman's equal rights, and who had borne all manner of abuse and scorn to exercise those rights, was a cruel irony and a move to which neither Lucy Stone nor others would accede.[1]

Although there is no definitive identification of Foster's opponent, evidence points fairly conclusively to Davis, whose second marriage had given her social position and a penchant for respectability. Davis agreed with Swisshelm that the woman's rights movement was too closely associated with Garrisonianism and, as long as it was so, doomed to failure. Seeing no need to burden the movement with all the "unpopularities of the abolitionists," she had determined—unlike Swisshelm who washed her hands of it—to work from within to diminish their influence.[2]

Intent on refurbishing the movement's image, Davis wanted to install Elizabeth Oakes Smith as one of its prominent figures. Smith had made a name
for herself as a writer for women's magazines and a literary lecturer on the
lyceum circuit, and her widely excerpted *Woman and Her Needs,* published in
1850, established her as a woman's rights advocate. How it was that she came
to the movement, whether on her own or through Davis's recruitment, is not
clear, but in the weeks preceding the 1851 convention Davis circulated a prospectus for a woman's rights journal to be edited by Smith and then brought
the prospectus, along with the proposed editor, to Worcester and arranged for
her to lecture on the evening before the convention as well as at its closing
session.[3]

Although many women had come to that convention in short skirt and
trousers, Davis and Smith were not among them. Both had advocated the dress
early in the summer before vocal opposition erupted, and Davis had worn it at
home but not as a public dress. "I have felt that if I put on this dress," she
confided to a friend, "it would cripple my movements in relation to our work
. . . and crucify me ere my hour had come." Furthermore, Davis said, Mary
Gove Nichols, a leader in the dress reform movement, neither had "good taste
in dress" nor was "a person of any style," and she would not be followed by
the "better class of women." It was this better class of women—refined upper-
middle-class women with whom Davis now associated—that she wanted to
bring into the woman's rights movement, but the reform dress was one of
several associations with the movement that repelled them. Determined to do
her "utmost to remove the idea that all the woman's rights women are horrid
old frights with beards and mustaches," Davis wanted a formal association and
an official journal, both managed by the better class of women.[4]

Stone had a different vision. Underlying her hesitancy to form a national
society was her desire to make the movement a venue through which all advocates for woman's rights could work together, regardless of differences, and
her fear that an attempt to define and limit the movement through a constitution might generate more factionalism than unity. As in the antislavery
movement, there was not total agreement among activists on the nature or
character of the movement, the best methods to achieve its goals, or even what
its goals were. There were pragmatists, such as Davis, who were anxious to
make the movement palatable to the public, and idealists, such as Mott, who
considered rectitude more important than public favor. There were some, such
as Phillips and Garrison, who considered suffrage the cornerstone of the movement, and others, such as Davis and Clarina Nichols, who cared little for voting
and viewed woman's social and pecuniary independence the primary goals.
Some, such as Antoinette Brown, were sensitive to society's reliance on biblical
authority, while others, such as Rose and Mott, saw no need of reconciling the
movement with Scripture. Stone feared that, as in the antislavery movement,
factionists might use a written constitution to try to impose their views and
strategies on others and thus alienate needed workers.

Other members of the Central Committee agreed. Mott thought holding conventions in different parts of the country would be as effective as establishing a formal association and less likely to sow "seeds of dissolution." Phillips said their "loose committee way" was all that was needed at present. "Organize, and you will develop divisions among ourselves; a thing not to be evaded when it results from steps that are necessary, but organization is not yet so needed as to counterbalance that end." Brown wanted the freedom to act independently and yet feared that failure to organize might also invite discord. If they did not form an association "upon true grounds," she asked, might not somebody "get up a narrow minded partial affair of some stamp that will shame the cause" and force them to organize a rival society in self defense? Despite the majority decision not to organize, Davis issued a convention call announcing it time to consider establishing "a thorough and efficient organization."[5]

Because of their different visions for the woman's rights movement, Stone and Davis found themselves at cross purposes at Syracuse. The first manifestation of this tension came in the selection of a convention president. Invited by Davis to preside, Elizabeth Oakes Smith came to the convention fully expecting to do so. But instead of proposing a slate of officers as it had previously done, the Central Committee deferred nominations to a convention committee. One reason might have been to avoid the mistake made the previous year of putting forth persons not in attendance, but another reason seems to have been a strong undercurrent against having Smith preside. When the nominations committee selected Mott, she hinted at behind-the-scenes rivalry by acknowledging possible objection to her nomination and asking the convention to vote for president separately from the rest of the slate. Only one person—her husband—voiced dissent. Although Davis did not publicly object, she considered Mott every bit as offensive as Foster.[6]

Exactly why Smith was rejected is unclear, but many activists evidently considered her unsuitable as either a spokesperson or a figurehead. Divorced after many years of marriage, she read essays on the popular lecture circuit to support herself and her children. Despite experience at the rostrum, however, there was genuine concern over her ability to communicate effectively and make herself heard, although her unpopularity seems to have had less to do with ability than with personality. One activist criticized her "aping of court ceremonies" and described her as "thoroughly self-intoxicated." Stone thought she possessed noble qualities despite her defects.[7]

Although Davis refrained from voicing dissent during the convention, in an open letter sent to the *Liberator* afterward she revealed that the rebuff of Smith was just one of many actions that upset her. Another was the introduction of politics. With the convention held in the Liberty Party stronghold of western New York in the midst of congressional election campaigns, and with a prominent party figure one of the movement's own, it was surely too much to expect the Liberty Party not to use the opportunity to drum up support. Its chairman sent a donation and a letter affirming the party's official support of woman's rights, and a member offered resolutions recommending support of its candidates. Gerrit Smith, a member of the Central Committee who served as a convention vice president and member of its business committee, was the party's candidate for Congress from western New York. With the Liberty Party thus promoted at the convention and Davis's husband running for Congress as a Democrat, it is not surprising that she disapproved of the meeting's "political tone."[8]

Davis also disliked the introduction of a new tactic of agitation—tax resistance. Although resolutions and speeches at the first two conventions had asserted that because women were taxed, they were, under American principles of government, entitled to vote, no one had suggested that women refuse to pay taxes until permitted to vote. But now Stone did exactly that. Francis Jackson had suggested the strategy to her the previous December when he supplied statistics about tax-paying women in Boston. "During the ten years' agitation which preceded the American Revolution of 1776," he told Stone, "the continual 'rub-a-dub' cry of 'no taxation without representation' . . . did more to ripen public sentiment for that successful struggle than any other four words. The same words will do as much for the greater revolution which you have in hand." So among the resolutions Stone sent from the business committee was one asserting the right of every property holding woman "to resist taxation till such time as she is duly represented at the ballot box." Stone appealed to women property owners to nobly and heroically refuse to pay taxes, even though it might cost them friends and reputation as well as property, and then to take their cases to court and plead their case on the self-evident truth that taxation and representation are inseparable. Just one such resistance, along with its reverberations, said Stone, would do more toward winning suffrage than all their conventions and resolutions. Much to the dismay of Paulina Davis, who considered the strategy antagonistic, the convention adopted the resolution.[9]

The convention's suspension of customary business procedure—suggested and defended by Stone as encouraging free discussion—also upset Davis. Neither did she like the fact that resolutions were presented without going through the business committee, for she did not want the movement held responsible for ideas not endorsed by that body. A major complaint, however, was something that happened not in the convention, but in press coverage of it. Expecting the reform dress to be the target of press ridicule, Davis and Smith had worn elegant, fashionable dresses to counterbalance the unfavorable image sure to be created by the short skirt and trousers. But instead of ridiculing Bloomer-wearers, the *Syracuse Standard* criticized the women who obstructed aisles and stairways with skirts that covered "at least three steps of the stairway." These skirts were a "great annoyance to those who are not fond of going through the world at the slow and stately pace of a fashionable lady," said the reporter, and he advised the wearers of such dress to "don the Bloomer costume without delay." Stung by the criticism, Davis said public judgment of women's attire was "so revolting to a woman of true delicacy" that she shrank from public duties with "more dread than she would from the rough abuse of a mob."[10]

The final sessions of the convention did nothing to soothe her wounded pride. Discussion on whether to organize a national association opened with a letter from Angelina Weld advising against such action. "The tendency of organization is to kill out the spirit which gave it birth," she warned. "Organizations do not protect the sacredness of the individual; their tendency is to sink the individual in the mass, to sacrifice his rights." Nevertheless, a motion to establish a national society came from the floor, and both Smith and Davis spoke in its favor. In the debate that followed, some speakers flatly opposed organization; others thought that although a society would be useful, the movement was not yet strong enough to sustain one. Davis amended her motion to appeal for the formation of state societies. Samuel J. May seconded the motion, saying that because circumstances and needs varied from state to state, state associations could best determine appropriate agitation. Stone summarized the discussion, sympathizing with those who had experienced the pain of permanent organizations, agreeing that organization would be both useful and necessary at some point, but also agreeing that that time was not at hand. The appeal for state societies was adopted, and Mott declared that the national structure of annual conventions and Central Committee would continue as before. In the afternoon, Stone invited members of the Central Committee to retain their membership and sought additions that would give it at least one member from each state represented at the convention. When Mott's list of new appointees did not include Smith, Davis resigned as committee chair and moved that Smith be appointed in her place. The convention acquiesced.[11]

There may have been tension among movement leaders, but the convention itself proceeded calmly, with none of the open argument characteristic of many men's meetings. On the last day, however, a minister denounced the convention and its leaders in language so offensive that the audience shouted him down. The incident created fodder for local editors, who seemed to delight in the disruption of an otherwise seemingly uneventful convention, and it pushed the last major agenda item—whether to establish an official organ for the movement—to the convention's final session.[12]

Davis read the prospectus she had presented the previous year for a weekly paper to be called the *Elgeria* and asked the convention to adopt it as its official organ. With few sources of revenue and more debt than cash on hand, Stone was undoubtedly concerned about the convention committing nonexistent resources to the support of a newspaper.[13] But again she let others debate the pros and cons of such a move. Davis said that with Smith as editor, the paper would begin with a good literary reputation, but Smith, obviously aware of the feeling against her, offered to withdraw and let the convention determine editorship. There was almost universal agreement on the good a paper could do, but speaker after speaker felt the convention could not sustain the enterprise. Finally, Davis said the paper could be established if two thousand dollars were raised by a stock company, five hundred of which had already been pledged. Stone urged the friends of woman's rights to support that enterprise and the convention passed a motion urging the formation of a stock company.

It was 9:30 before business was completed and Mott could introduce the evening's featured speaker, Elizabeth Oakes Smith. But because Smith's address required well over an hour to read, she declined taking the podium and left the convention hanging without a closing speaker. After a brief pause, Stone stepped forward and, no stranger to improvisation, delivered a rousing half-hour speech. If the convention had not gone as Davis wished, this final turn of events was more than she could bear. A convention's closing address was a major event, assigned to one of the most noteworthy speakers in attendance and attracting the largest audience of its several sessions. Davis had looked forward to Smith filling this honored position and going forth through the press as a spokesperson of the woman's rights movement. But instead of the press acclaiming Smith's highly polished literary essay, it effusively praised Stone's extemporaneous substitute remarks.[14]

Upset with the way the convention was managed and the actions it took, Davis aired her grievances in an open letter published in the *Liberator*. Responding to a convention critic, she lamented the convention's political tone and spirit of antagonism, its refusal to assume financial responsibility for a woman's rights journal, its decision to convene in Cleveland the next year, and the lack of thoughtful preparation by speakers. She regretted the emphasis placed on suffrage at the expense of "bitter social wrongs" where "woman is most defrauded of her rights, where her bondage is most keenly felt." Influenced greatly by Association ideas, Davis believed women's liberation lay more in rectifying the distorted marriage arrangement than in political enfranchisement. But, although she saw economic dependence upon man as one of the wrongs imposed upon women by the current marital system, she found offensive the talk about women entering marriage for financial security rather than for love, a minor debate that had stemmed from a remark of Stone's. She also regretted the antagonism exhibited in the talk of women refusing to pay their taxes. "I would excite no new strife, nor look to any force," said Davis. "I would not resist taxation, but I would remonstrate with clear, cogent arguments that would ultimately prevail." And Davis did not like extemporaneous speaking. "It will scarcely do for undisciplined minds to trust to the inspiration of the moment," she complained. Those who wanted to be heard should "learn system with the pen in hand . . . take up points on which they are most interested, and digest their subject thoroughly, and not attempt to go over the whole ground, giving us identically the same thought year after year."[15]

Davis's letter shocked Stone. "I don't know when I have been so pained," she wrote to Antoinette Brown. "I could not help saying, 'Save us from our friends.' . . . Her vexation at not having Mrs. Smith president made everything seem wrong side out to her, and her influence since the convention has been wholly against it." The tension among convention leaders had been disillusioning, and Stone confided to Brown that she found "so much selfishness instead of real interest in the cause" that she hardly dared "speak freely to anyone."[16]

Davis's public complaints were mild compared with those she expressed privately. "The conventions have become unwieldy," she told Caroline Dall, critic to whom her open letter was a reply. "There is a class of women filled with personal ambition and they can show off in them." She wanted neither Rose nor Mott to preside at the meetings. Rose had no position or influence and Mott was "in her dotage" and gave "no high character" to the chair. Telling Dall she "wear[ied] of the strife," she said she would have nothing more to do with the meetings. And indeed, although she soon reclaimed her position as head of the Central Committee, she never attended another national woman's rights convention.[17]

Although the call for contributions to a joint stock company failed to produce the needed funds, Davis forged ahead with her journal. A small inheritance allowed her to pay printers but not an editor, so she undertook the work herself. Relating her new plans to Stone, who had written trying to smooth over their differences, Davis said she expected assistance from Stone as both a writer and a subscription agent.[18]

The first issue of Davis's *Una* appeared on February 1, 1853, and listed Stone as a correspondent. Addressed to the women Davis hoped to attract, it was a careful balance of woman's rights articles with literary subjects. But the attempt to attract both the mainstream readers of popular ladies' magazines and the more reform-minded readers of the *Lily* made the *Una* acceptable to neither. Although Stone promoted the paper during her lecture tours over the next few years, selling subscriptions as far west as St. Louis and even in Canada, the *Una* attracted no great following. It could not compete with the *Lily*, whose circulation had jumped to four thousand and was still growing, and which began appearing twice a month. Achieving neither a wide readership nor a sound financial footing, the *Una* spent its short existence struggling to stay alive.

14

The Converting Voice

Moving the 1852 National Woman's Rights Convention to New York took Lucy Stone and her growing reputation as an effective speaker to a wider audience. Until then, she had worked primarily in New England, venturing outside the region for only brief lecture tours in Pennsylvania and the May anniversaries of the American Anti-Slavery Society in New York City. The Syracuse convention gave New York reformers a taste of Stone's speaking power, and they began asking her to lend that power to their causes.

By the fall of 1852, Stone's ability as a persuasive speaker was fully developed. Describing his reaction to hearing her, the editor of the *Syracuse Chronicle* said he had gone to the woman's rights convention strongly opposed to the movement and "prejudiced in particular against this wholesale sortie of women upon the public rostrum." But Stone, he said, melted away "every particle of our hostility." Pleading for the right of women to use the talents God gave them, she related her oft-used story about the woman "whom God made a sculptor." When she closed, said the editor, "after having held an immense audience for more than an hour in breathless attention, we turned away in a state of subdued perplexity, saying softly to ourselves: 'Well, whether we like it or not, little woman, God made you an orator.'"[1]

An antislavery lecture given after the convention's close moved another Syracuse editor to declare that he had never seen an audience "so absolutely in the possession of the orator." Stone "threw her voice over the assembly," he said, "and swayed it with pity, and grief, and scorn, and indignation, as if it was the helpless plaything of her inspiration," and he appealed to "the whole country, far and near" to make every effort to hear her. Two weeks later, Stone shared the podium with Frederick Douglass at a grand antislavery rally and captivated the audience of fifteen hundred. One auditor said that although Douglass's speech was "the thunder of the gods," Stone surpassed him in reaching the hearts of their listeners.[2]

Even though Stone distrusted politicians and had little faith in the usefulness of politics to end slavery, she joined Antoinette Brown lecturing in western New York for Gerrit Smith, who was running for Congress on a platform that included woman suffrage and opposition to the Fugitive Slave Law. She stumped for the issues rather than the candidate, but when he was elected, the two women were credited with "arousing and molding the public feeling" for the victory. A correspondent to the *New York Tribune* said Stone attracted large numbers of people who would never attend antislavery lectures given by men and won more converts than any three male lecturers could have done.[3]

While canvassing western New York, Stone attended meetings in Seneca Falls to assist New York women with two causes they were agitating—protecting the provision for coeducation in the prospectus of a state-supported industrial college, and gaining acceptance of women's participation in the state temperance movement.

The People's College movement had begun in 1850 with the proposal of a public college where practical industrial courses would be taught along with regular college fare. Horace Greeley, who looked to rural and agricultural expansion as a remedy for urban congestion and poverty, suggested that it also offer agricultural instruction. He became one of the college's prominent promoters and drafted its prospectus, which called for admitting both women and blacks. Sympathizers formed an association to promote the college, and agents held meetings in different parts of the state to raise public interest and recruit subscriptions for an endowment. Because it proposed coeducation, Amelia Bloomer championed the college in her *Lily* and urged women to attend the regional meetings to show support for the admission of women. At a meeting in Elmira she had helped fend off opposition to admitting women and, expecting similar opposition at the Seneca Falls meeting, she and her associates requested help from the National Woman's Rights Convention. Stone was among the large number of women at the October 13 meeting of the People's College Association, and when discussion on the practicality of teaching women the same courses as men arose, she was called on to defend equal education. So effectively did she make her case that the meeting voted not only to retain the provision admitting women but to strengthen it by changing the wording from "suitable" facilities for women to "equal" ones.[4]

The next day, Stone attended the convention of the New York Women's State Temperance Society to try to persuade members not to retreat on the issue of equal rights. Organized in April, the society had sent Greeley, Bloomer, and Susan B. Anthony as delegates to the annual meeting of the State Temperance Society in June. But the all-male association rejected the women delegates and denounced them for disrupting the meeting. In the flood of criticism that followed, many temperance women began to waver, and some, quite satisfied working apart from men, criticized their leaders for attempting integration. Although not involved in the temperance movement herself, Stone tried to help head off retreat. Appointed to the convention's business committee, she offered a resolution "that every reform movement is best forwarded by cultivating . . . that independence of character which, without stopping to count the consequences, demands that 'justice be done though the heavens fall.'" Then in a speech that was probably a version of one she gave to abolitionists the following spring, she entreated the women to persevere in what they knew to be right. "It costs something to be free," she said. "Dare to differ from the fashion and custom and opinion of those about you, and just so surely are you made to smart. . . . The world may sneer at the nobleness of soul it cannot imitate; friends may rebuke that which they cannot comprehend; and even affection may be blind to the deep mysteries and high and noble purposes of life; but the consciousness of rectitude is its own exceeding great reward." No amount of ridicule or malice, she said, could stop a soul "animated with a holy purpose." Stone's impassioned appeal moved the temperance women not only to reaffirm the executive committee's action in sending delegates to the state convention, but also to adopt a resolution declaring that the men's actions demonstrated their need of "enlightenment," which women could provide through unwavering labor.[5]

Stone remained in New York after the congressional elections and continued to attract large audiences and more invitations than she could accept. But when word came of the critical illness of Bowman's wife, she canceled three weeks of engagements and headed home. By the time she arrived, however, Phebe Robinson Stone was in her grave. Taking time to mourn her friend's death and to rest from weeks of hard labor, Stone sorted through appeals for her assistance and pondered where to resume work. Brown urged her to come back to New York. Clarina Nichols wanted her in Vermont to support a petition asking that women be allowed to vote in school elections. Benjamin Jones wanted her in Ohio to prepare the way for a state woman's rights convention in the spring and the national convention in the fall. From far-off Wisconsin, a woman who had read about her in the *New York Tribune* asked Stone to bring her woman's rights lectures west. But finally she decided to stay in Massachusetts and direct her winter labor toward a constitutional convention slated to convene the next spring. Just as she had encouraged Ohioans to use the redrafting of their state constitution to try to secure woman suffrage, so she embraced the opportunity in her own state. And not wanting delegates to have the same excuse given by some in Ohio—that although they favored woman suffrage in principle they felt compelled to vote against it because of insufficient public demand—Stone decided to create demand by lecturing throughout the state. "A proposal is made to amend our State Constitution," she wrote to Antoinette Brown, "and if it is within the bounds of possibility, I mean to have the franchise secured to women. Massachusetts *ought* to do it first." [6]

One of the first events of her campaign was a December lyceum engagement in Beverly, where she sparred with a "respectable and gentlemanly antagonist on the question of Woman's Rights." Afterward, a local editor declared Stone's "higher powers of debate" nearly matchless and pronounced her "one of the most accomplished speakers now living." For the next four months, Stone lectured almost every evening, generally giving two lectures on successive nights at one place, the first titled "The Position, Rights, and Duties of Woman" and the second, "The Legal Disabilities of Married Women."[7] Wanting to reach as many people as possible, she did not charge admission, but collected free-will offerings that barely covered expenses. Midway through the campaign, however, collaboration with the Hutchinson Family Singers, a popular quartet who mixed music and reform, convinced her that people would pay to hear her speak. At New Bedford, her first lecture fell on the same night as a concert by the Hutchinsons. The competition resulted in small audiences for both, but Stone had a respectable audience of four hundred at her second lecture. To recoup lost income, the Hutchinsons asked her to appear with them the following night, she speaking on antislavery and they singing their best abolition songs. More than eight hundred people gladly paid twelve and one-half cents for the combined attraction, and thereafter Stone charged admission to her lectures.[8]

As Stone labored in Massachusetts, appeals for help continued to arrive from other states. Among those wanting her aid was temperance activist Susan B. Anthony, who had heard Stone speak at the Syracuse convention and again at the Seneca Falls meetings. Although Anthony had read reports of earlier woman's rights conventions and sympathized with most of their goals, not until she heard Stone at Syracuse did she believe women needed the right to vote. Coming from a family of nonvoting Quakers, she had seen little value in the ballot, but Stone convinced her that suffrage would enable women to secure other rights and was therefore the right needed above all others. Stone also converted her to the controversial Bloomer costume. Although Anthony had been working with several women who wore the reform dress, including Bloomer herself, it took the experience at Syracuse—newspaper criticism of Davis's and Smith's high fashion versus accolades for Stone's practical dress—to persuade her to don it herself. Having fallen under Stone's converting power, she would soon be urging her to help win over two married sisters as well.[9] But for now, as one of the organizers of a women's temperance convention at Albany, Anthony wanted Stone to lend that converting power to the temperance cause.

In January 1853, temperance societies from all over New York would converge on the state capital to try to persuade legislators to pass a "Maine Law," prohibiting the manufacture and sale of alcohol. The women's society had gathered one hundred thousand signatures to their petitions and wanted to present the petitions to the legislature themselves, because the previous year, after allowing their petitions to be combined with those gathered by other workers, the State Temperance Society took credit for the entire effort and denounced women's activism.[10] Now, as president of the women's society, Elizabeth Cady Stanton had prepared an appeal to be read at an anticipated hearing, and she wanted it followed by an eloquent speech by Stone. Other leaders of the women's society wanted one of their own members, H. Attilia Albro of Rochester, to address the legislature, but because it would be the first time a woman addressed the New York legislature, Stanton and Anthony wanted a "speaking" woman instead of one who would read a written address. Stone agreed the occasion called for a public speaker but believed, as she had earlier told Ohio reformers, that legislatures should be addressed by their own constituents. She suggested Antoinette Brown, who was not only an orator but also a resident of New York and an ardent temperance advocate. If Brown could not go to Albany, said Stone, then she would speak at the convention but not at the hearing.[11]

The day after mailing her reply, Stone received yet another appeal from Anthony urging her to attend a January 12 meeting of the People's College Association. The association had drafted a new constitution that was, said Anthony, a "miserable non-committal sort of thing" as far as women's admission was concerned. With this added incentive, Stone agreed to go to Albany and scheduled several lectures in the vicinity. But when the time came, a hard headache sent her home instead. Brown accepted Anthony's invitation and traveled to Albany expecting to address the legislature. But the society insisted on having its own members—Albro, Bloomer, Mary Vaughan, and Emily Clark—present the petitions and plead their case before the legislature.[12] In addition to missing the Albany convention, Stone missed the People's College meeting. Anthony's fear that the association was scuttling coeducation was well-founded, and Stone probably could have done nothing to save it. In April, the college was incorporated with no provision for admitting women, and women reformers halted their efforts in its behalf.[13]

After a brief recuperation, Stone headed for Brattleboro to assist Clarina Nichols's school suffrage drive. On her way, she stopped in Worcester to recruit support for her own campaign from Thomas Wentworth Higginson, newly installed pastor of that city's Free Church. To assist her Vermont mission, Higginson dispatched a letter to his Brattleboro sisters urging them to attend Stone's lectures there on February 1 and 2. Although strongly prejudiced against the woman's rights movement, the sisters went and were thoroughly converted. Using their first-hand testimony, Higginson sent a letter to the *Liberator* extolling Stone's power to "reverse the public sentiment of a whole town," and urging friends of the cause to arrange for her to speak in all of Massachusetts' towns before the Constitutional Convention assembled in May.[14]

Around the first of February, Stone began circulating a petition addressed to the Constitutional Convention. Like those she had earlier sent to the legislature, the petition sought to secure women's right to vote and serve in public office. But by asking the convention to strike the word *male* from wherever it occurred in the state constitution, it also aimed at securing women's full political and legal equality. Wendell Phillips had drafted the petition for her, along with an eloquent appeal urging Massachusetts citizens to sign it, to which Stone obtained the signatures of reformers willing to lend the influence of their names to her effort. Besides circulating the appeal at her lectures, she sent printed copies to friends and reform papers across the state.[15] A series of woman's rights tracts just off the press also aided her work. The previous fall she and Samuel J. May had collected an assortment of convention speeches and letters, arranged them into ten tracts, and with funds from the Syracuse convention, published them together in one volume. By February they had twenty thousand copies in circulation.[16] Soliciting editorial support, Stone found a number of newspapers willing to publish suffrage articles if provided. She asked two activists known for their effective writing—Caroline Severance and Elizabeth Cady Stanton—to supply material for her but received no response. She also asked Antoinette Brown to lecture with her, but Brown had begun working with Amelia Bloomer and Susan Anthony and would not leave New York.[17] So Stone worked on, aided only by a small circle of friends who circulated petitions.

In mid-March, exhaustion and another migraine headache forced Stone to retire to the Boston home of Francis Jackson. "I am tired of the hard labor of stirring this state to do something before the Constitutional Convention," she wrote to Anthony. "If Nettie only could see how important it is that much should be done right now, she would come. But I can't get her." Unable to get the assistance she needed, she felt the full weight of her solitary campaign. "I am tired and nervous, and half sick, too, and just this minute can't help wishing that my body was safely at rest," she wrote. A few days later, however, welcome support came from Theodore Parker, the eloquent but controversial Unitarian minister who, barred from orthodox pulpits, preached radical sermons at Boston's Music Hall. Having already signed her appeal, he delivered a sermon titled "The Public Function of Woman," giving religious and moral reasons for extending suffrage and equal legal rights to women, which Garrison immediately published in pamphlet form. After a couple of weeks' rest, Stone resumed her "suicidal process," as Brown called it, and interrupted the campaign again only for a brief trip to New York City.[18]

Immensely pleased with the effect Stone had had in the western part of the state in the fall, Samuel J. May had persuaded her to let him arrange lectures for her in New York City, where they would be heard by some of the nation's largest audiences and broadcast by far-reaching newspapers. So on April 25 and 26, Stone gave New York City its first lectures on woman's rights since Fanny Wright shocked it with her version of the issue twenty-five years earlier. The first night Stone argued for opening all fields of employment to women, using stories to illustrate the wrongs and hardships suffered by women denied the right to earn a living. Woman's labor, like man's, she said, "should be bounded only by her capacity, for where God has conferred a power, there also is His certificate of the right to its use . . . Whatever woman can do and do well, either by head or hand, she has a right to do." In her second lecture, Stone grounded the demand for women's political and legal equality on the nation's cherished political ideals—that governments derive their just powers from the consent of the governed and that taxation and representation are inseparable. Although their leaders would not proclaim that these principles applied to all except women, such was the message of their acts, Stone said. She asked only that the self-evident truths of the Declaration of Independence be made actual fact.[19]

In a glowing report carried to more than one hundred thousand *Tribune* subscribers, Horace Greeley said that to all Stone's questions concerning women's labor and property rights, there was no just answer that did not condemn existing laws. Agreeing also with her points on women's legal disabilities, he said her speech was one of the best he had ever heard, "surcharged with the eloquence of heartfelt conviction and an indignant sense of wrong." After reading Greeley's report, Anthony exulted that, as expected, Stone's lectures were "not only spoken to the thousands in the metropolis" but also carried to remotest parts of the nation and even across the Atlantic. "Verily, those lectures have been given to the whole civilized world."[20]

Not all press reports were as glowing as Greeley's, however. The *New York Daily Times,* no friend to the woman's rights movement, acknowledged Stone's power as an orator but said she erred when she turned away from the sanctities of domestic life to become a "public haranguer." It could not help but regret that such "a delightful woman was spoiled when Miss Lucy Stone abandoned good sense, society, and duty, and addicted herself to Woman's Rights." Another critic said that if some in her audience were not fully convinced, at least they were pleased, for "Miss Lucy is a very captivating little woman in spite of her trowsers. She is brim full of good sense and womanly feeling. Her manner is subdued, but graceful and self-possessed; and her voice is musical as a bird's. In short, if she would only eschew that abominable innovation of Mrs. Bloomer, and return to the petticoats of her mothers, she would be irresistible."[21]

Sight of Stone's lamentable "trowsers" was destined to reach a much larger audience than that of New York's Metropolitan Hall, however. Also among her auditors was Phineas T. Barnum, editor of the nation's first pictorial weekly, the *Illustrated News.* Although now remembered almost exclusively as a showman—owner of New York's museum of curios, promoter of strange and exotic acts, and later founder of the first multiple-ring circus—Barnum was as much a sympathizer with the vast pallet of social reforms as he was a caterer to popular appeal. In May his *Illustrated News* carried Stone's speeches to its 150,000 subscribers, along with a drawing based on a Matthew Brady photograph of Stone clad in the controversial reform dress.[22]

As soon as Massachusetts' Constitutional Convention assembled on May 4, Stone began sending it petitions while friends tried to arrange a hearing for her. The first installment of the petition, headed by Francis Jackson's signature and signed by over fourteen hundred men and women, was presented on May 12 and referred to the Committee on the Qualification of Voters. Although another fourteen hundred signatures were on the way, the committee promptly issued a negative report before all were received. To keep the issue alive, another petition was quickly drawn up, asking that when the revised constitution went to the people for ratification, women be permitted to vote on it. The first installment of this petition, signed only by women, was presented on May 23 and also assigned to the Committee on the Qualification of Voters. Although Stone had attended antislavery and temperance meetings in New York City during the second week of May, she now turned down all appeals for aid and refused to leave Boston while waiting to learn if a hearing would be granted.[23]

The meetings in New York City had brought Stone additional newspaper attention. Her speech before the American Anti-Slavery Society had both shocked her audience and provoked "floods of tears." Describing the tragic flight of a fugitive slave whose child was shot by slave-catchers as she ran with it on her shoulders, Stone used such graphic detail that the *New York Independent* denounced her "terrible distinctness." But newspapers carried the "fugitive mother speech" across the land and, alluding to it many years later, Frederick Douglass said that like Harriet Beecher Stowe's *Uncle Tom's Cabin*, it fit well "the extreme needs of the time."[24] The speech was just one of many that contributed to Stone's growing reputation. Elizabeth Stanton later said that because no reporter could do justice to Stone's speaking, her eloquence could not be judged by printed record. But newspapers carried countless testimonies of her eloquence and power to convert even hostile auditors. A Canadian editor said that although he had heard much about Stone's speaking ability, he had not realized "the full power of her logical deductions and dispassionate reasoning" until hearing her himself. "She enchained the attention of her hearers, now touching a tender chord in their bosoms and anon convulsing them with laughter," he said. "She is evidently something of an adept in her art, and thoroughly understands how to manage an audience." While some cited her "solid Seward-like logic," others said it was the "grandeur of her character," a "nobility and honesty of purpose," or the magnetism of her "rare and remarkable voice" that disarmed opposition and inspired confidence.[25]

A practical test of that power came on May 27, 1853, when the Massachusetts Constitutional Convention granted Stone a hearing, and several hundred men and women crowded into the Senate Chamber of Boston's State House to hear her address the Committee on Qualifications of Voters. Although no text of her speech survives, one newspaper described it as "simple and clear as daylight, strong in its array of pertinent facts and plain, forcible exposition and application of principles," with passages of touching pathos that at times moved her audience to tears. Many newspapers reported the event, for as the *Liberator* noted, "Never before, since the world was made, in any country, has woman publicly made her demand in the hall of legislation to be represented in her own person, and to have an equal part in framing the laws and determining the action of government." Writing for the *Pennsylvania Freeman*, Charles Burleigh said the scene ranked with other forward steps of humanity commemorated in grand historical paintings. The time would come, he predicted, "when the world will be glad to have . . . a faithful picture of the first appearance of a woman before the framers of the fundamental law of the State, to demand for her sex that equality with men in political rights which is the inevitable logical inference from the political theories of our nation." Wendell Phillips followed Stone with "one of his noblest efforts," and a week later Higginson, who had sent the convention an elaborate essay in support of women's suffrage, joined Theodore Parker at a second hearing.[26]

In their decision issued on July 1, the committee restated the propositions Stone and her colleagues had put forth at the hearings:

1. That women are human beings, and therefore have human rights, one of which is that of having a voice in the government under which they live and in the enactment of laws they are bound to obey;
2. That women have interests and rights which are not, in fact, and never will be, sufficiently guarded by governments in which they are not allowed any political influence;
3. That they are taxed, and therefore, since taxation and the rights of representation are admitted to be inseparable, they have a right to be represented;
4. That so far as education and general intelligence is concerned, they are as well qualified to exercise the elective franchise as many who now enjoy that right;
5. That in mental capacity and moral endowments, they are not inferior to many who now participate in the affairs of government;
6. That there is nothing in their peculiar position, or appropriate duties, which prevents them from taking a part in political affairs.[27]

But the committee said they were not obliged to base their decision upon the validity or fallacy of these arguments. Rather, stating that "[a]ll questions involving the rights and interests of any part of the human family should ever be determined by some well-established and generally recognized principle or fundamental maxim of government," the principle on which they chose to base their decision was the very one that Stone had been preaching demanded equal rights for women—that "governments derive their just powers from the consent of the governed." The committee pointed out that Massachusetts women had always enjoyed and often exercised the right of petition, through which they made their wants known to the government. There were almost two hundred thousand women over the age of twenty-one in Massachusetts. Only two thousand had signed Stone's suffrage petitions, whereas fifty thousand had recently petitioned for the enactment of a law prohibiting the sale of alcohol. From these facts, the committee inferred "that a great majority of the women of Massachusetts do willingly consent that the government of the State should be, as it hitherto has been, in the hands of their fathers, husbands, brothers, and sons . . . and therefore, that the powers exercised by the government of this Commonwealth over that class of its population are 'just powers,' and it is inexpedient for this Convention to take any action in relation thereto." Despite an attempt to rescue the measure when it went to the floor on July 12, the convention upheld the committee's finding.[28]

Thus, when a Massachusetts body was first called upon to vote on the issue, it rejected woman suffrage not because it disagreed with any of the principles underlying the demand, but because only two thousand women asked for the right by signing a petition. Reporting the result to a friend, Stone wrote, "The women who asked our Constitutional Convention for the right to vote were coolly 'allowed to withdraw.' We shall do it, and renew our forces to such an extent that they will not again dare to insult us."[29] But when the convention's report came in the middle of July, Stone was already at the center of another battle, this one taking place in New York—for woman's right to participate on equal terms with men in the temperance movement.

15

Temperance and Woman's Rights

The temperance work for which New York women sought Lucy Stone's assistance was part of a prohibitionist wave that swept the country during the 1850s. For several decades reformers had tackled America's drinking problem with moral suasion, trying to create public scorn for alcohol and promoting voluntary abstinence. But during the 1840s, temperance activists shifted their focus to legislative remedies. Maine's 1851 passage of a law prohibiting the manufacture and sale of alcohol touched off a frenzy of agitation for similar laws in other states. In January 1852, temperance activists held a grand rally in Boston and marched to the State House with petitions for a Maine Liquor Law bearing 130,000 signatures. Six months later Massachusetts became the third of thirteen states and territories to enact prohibition laws in the early 1850s.[1]

Because the nation's rampant alcoholism greatly affected the lives of women—increasing the incidence of domestic abuse and abandonment—they took special interest in the temperance cause. Fifty thousand of the signatures presented to the Massachusetts legislature were of women, those referred to by the Constitutional Convention in rejecting woman suffrage. Although Stone was not involved in temperance agitation herself, many woman's rights activists were. Clarina Nichols was a prominent temperance advocate in Vermont. Hannah Darlington, Ann Preston, and other women identified with the woman's rights movement in Pennsylvania were leaders of women's temperance work there. Among those who organized an Ohio Women's State Temperance Society in January 1853 were Caroline Severance, Elizabeth Hitchcock Jones, and Frances Dana Gage. And in New York, woman's rights advocates Amelia Bloomer, Mary C. Vaughan, and Elizabeth Cady Stanton were among the organizers of the Women's State Temperance Society.[2]

But in New York, the efforts of the women's organization to be accepted under the umbrella of the State Temperance Society had created a public controversy from which many women recoiled. Susan B. Anthony sought reinforcement from the National Woman's Rights Convention at Syracuse, experienced Stone's converting power, and urged her to assist the New York women. Stone supported their work by speaking at the October meeting in Seneca Falls and by referring them to Antoinette Brown for their Albany convention. Then, in early May 1853, just as Stone was sending her suffrage petitions to the Massachusetts Constitutional Convention, Anthony asked her to attend two temperance meetings where she expected confrontations: a May 12 meeting of temperance delegates in New York City to plan a World Temperance Convention, and the first annual meeting of the Women's State Temperance Society in Rochester on June 1 and 2.

The women's temperance society had appointed six delegates to the planning meeting, but because their delegates to the state convention the year before had been rejected, they feared similar treatment in New York City. Anthony asked Stone to become a delegate from a Massachusetts temperance society so she could attend the meeting. Because she and other women activists would be in New York anyway, to attend the American Anti-Slavery anniversary on May 11, Anthony hoped they would aid the temperance women. "I look to the Antislavery friends to sustain us in our claim that woman shall be represented at the World's Convention," she told Stone. "Were it not for the hope of their presence I should shrink from going into that meeting."[3]

Anthony expected two battles at the Women's State Temperance Society's annual meeting in June. First, wanting to place the society on the "higher ground" of equal rights, she was going to ask the society to amend its constitution to allow men to hold office. And second, although most of the society's leaders did not want to attach the controversial topic of divorce to their movement, Stanton wanted the society to press for making habitual drunkenness grounds for divorce.[4] Both controversies had been brewing since the society's formation a year earlier.

At the organizing convention, some women objected to segregating the sexes and proposed that they press for admission into the State Temperance Society instead of establishing their own organization. Others argued that although that society might welcome women's membership dues, it would not receive them as equal members, and as long as men refused to cooperate with them, women should work by themselves. The convention established a new society, named it a women's society, but encouraged men to join. Although admitting men and affirming their right to speak and vote at meetings, the constitution provided that only women should serve as officers. Responding to critics of this feature, Bloomer said the decision to exclude men from office was made with "much and serious deliberation, and adopted with few dissenting votes." Antoinette Brown, who was elected a vice president, was among those who objected to the restriction. The turn-about exclusion seemed to her "a shrewd good joke in a convention (perhaps)" but inappropriate in a state organization, and she told Stone she would "protest against it zealously." Whatever protest she made was ineffective, and she declined membership in the society.[5]

When Anthony attended the National Woman's Rights Convention in Syracuse five months later, she was surprised to learn that it disapproved of the temperance women's policy. Introducing herself as an agent of the New York Women's Temperance Society, she presented a series of resolutions sent by Stanton, one of which sought endorsement of the society. But Catherine Stebbins, who had been an officer at the 1848 Rochester Woman's Rights Convention and signer of its Declaration of Sentiments, pointed out that in denying men equal rights, the women's temperance society violated the principles of the woman's rights movement. The convention adopted all of Stanton's resolutions except the one endorsing the women's society.[6]

The convention's insistence on equal rights was also the basis for rejecting a suggestion Anthony made during debate on whether the convention should establish a paper. Saying woman's rights principles were sure to progress whenever women edited newspapers, she proposed that activists support existing papers edited by women instead of establishing another. Clarina Nichols, herself a newspaper editor, objected to the idea that support of a paper should be determined by the sex of its editor. She pointed out that many papers edited by men supported woman's rights and reached audiences women's papers could not. Benjamin Jones, former editor of the *Anti-Slavery Bugle*, reminded them that the paper edited by Jane Swisshelm, mentioned by Anthony as worthy of support, opposed the woman's rights movement and did more harm than good. Anthony left the convention with a new understanding of the principle of equal rights. Her association with Brown after the Albany convention helped her recognize the inconsistency of the women's society asking men to grant women equal rights while restricting men's rights. So in asking Stone to attend their annual meeting, she said she intended to place the society "on higher ground [and] admit *all* on terms of perfect equality."[7]

The other issue for which Anthony sought Stone's support was the demand that habitual drunkenness be made grounds for divorce. A bill to this effect had been introduced in the New York legislature and Stanton had argued in its favor in addresses and appeals as president of the society. But most temperance women opposed the bill. Clarina Nichols, Amelia Bloomer, Mary Vaughan, and Antoinette Brown thought the best way to rescue the wife of an alcoholic was to secure her legal control over her own person, earnings, property, and children. Although the October meeting in Seneca Falls passed a resolution on divorce drafted by Stanton, some resented the way it had been forced through late in the last session after many delegates had left. In March 1853, when Anthony wrote to Stone about the divorce controversy developing within the women's temperance movement, Stone said she agreed with Stanton's position. She thought injured spouses should have a second chance at finding "true love," and marital separation denied that opportunity. Urging Stone's presence at the meeting, Anthony said some members wanted to "stave off the divorce question" but Stanton was determined to raise it and "anxious to have those present who can discuss it fully and ably."[8]

During the second week of May, thousands of people from across the country were in New York City to attend the various meetings of "anniversary week." Although four thousand people would attend the American Temperance Union's convention on Wednesday evening, only seventy-three representatives met that morning at New York's Brick Church to plan the world convention. Stone, Abby Kelley Foster, and six delegates from the New York women's society were the only women there. Stone enlisted the support of Thomas Wentworth Higginson, a temperance leader in Massachusetts, and Dr. Russell T. Trall, an early temperance leader in New York and founder of a medical school based on water-cure principles. After Trall engineered the women's admission, Higginson tried to get them recognized as equal members by asking the chair to appoint Anthony to the business committee. His proposal roused immediate controversy, which the chair tried to end by saying he had appointed one representative from each state and the committee was full. Higginson resigned his appointment and moved that Stone be appointed to represent Massachusetts in his place. Heated debate followed, and the convention tried to settle the matter by rejecting Higginson's resignation. But Higginson insisted he would not serve where woman's voice was denied. After a rancorous exchange between the women's opponents and supporters, the women themselves having been ordered to remain silent, the convention revoked their membership. Realizing further effort was futile, Higginson made one last motion— that the excluded delegates and all who objected to their exclusion withdraw and meet at Dr. Trall's Water-Cure Establishment for a meeting of their own.[9]

When the seceding delegates met that afternoon, they were reinforced by many sympathizers, including some of the most prominent temperance leaders in the country. About fifty men and women representing eleven states enrolled as members. The business committee concluded that because the assembly included those persons delegated to plan a world convention who had remained true to the letter and spirit of the call, it had the authority to organize a World Temperance Convention. Voting to proceed, the assembly appointed organizing committees. Higginson and Anthony served on the correspondence committee, while Stone headed the committee on the call.[10]

The schism between temperance leaders and the astonishing fact that now *two* World Temperance Conventions were being planned attracted three thousand people to an indignation meeting at Broadway Tabernacle on Saturday night. Stone explained that the seceders from the Brick Church meeting simply asked that when the world came together to consider the urgent problem of drunkenness, women be recognized as part of the world. The convention they were planning, she said, would be a world convention true to its name—a "whole world" convention, rather than the "half world" convention insisted upon by others. Newspapers carried reports of these events across the nation. Some criticized the women for disrupting the planning meeting and blamed Stone for instigating the whole sequence of events. One described the confrontation as a "Battle of the Sexes" in which Stone and her sisters had "thrown down the gauntlet" to the temperance cause. It praised the Brick Church stalwarts for declining "Miss Lucy's company and that of other talking ladies who would have been dragged in clinging to Miss Lucy's skirts."[11]

Back in Massachusetts the next week, as Stone began soliciting signatures to a call for the Whole World Temperance Convention, which, like its rival, would be held in New York City during the World's Fair that fall, she proposed to members of the Woman's Rights Central Committee that they move their convention from Cleveland to New York. Although she herself had earlier argued for Cleveland over the East, she now believed the World's Fair and temperance convention offered important opportunities they should not pass up. While sending off her correspondence concerning the two conventions, Stone anxiously awaited word from the Constitutional Convention on her request for a hearing. Unwilling to leave Boston while it was pending, she told Anthony she could not attend the June 1 meeting of the Women's State Temperance Society. But Anthony insisted she come. Friends could telegraph her if a hearing were granted and she could be back in Boston in less than twenty-four hours. "Oh, Lucy, I do so hope you will be here next week. It seems to me we shall have no meeting at all without you." Stone had urged the delegates to make a "grand exposé" of their treatment at Brick Church, and Anthony pleaded, "Who but Lucy Stone can do the subject justice?"[12]

With the hearing granted on May 27, Stone went to Rochester five days later. There she met Elizabeth Cady Stanton for the first time. Although Stanton had been the main force behind the Seneca Falls Woman's Rights Convention in 1848, when Stone met her in the spring of 1853 she was neither a major figure in the movement nor widely known outside New York. Her father, Daniel Cady, was a New York Supreme Court justice, and her husband, Henry B. Stanton, who had worked so diligently to undermine Garrison's influence and then become a "new organization" leader, was now a Democratic state legislator. Both opposed Stanton's involvement in woman's rights agitation, so after her brief flicker of activism in 1848 she had retreated to domesticity. Comparing herself to the sunflower, passing through life "unnoticed and unknown . . . though possessed of so many noble virtues and valuable properties," she submitted anonymous articles to the *Lily* under the pen name "Sun Flower" and later under her initials. Not until 1851, in the midst of the Bloomer craze, were readers informed of the identity of Sun Flower and E. C. S.[13] It was these articles in the *Lily* and her promotion of the reform dress that put Stanton's name before the public as a woman's rights advocate. She had not been mentioned in press accounts of the Seneca Falls convention, which identified Lucretia Mott as the convention's moving spirit. Stone knew her primarily as a correspondent to the National Woman's Rights Conventions, for although Stanton did not attended them, she sent letters of support to each. Since meeting Anthony, Stone had learned of Stanton's family situation. A year earlier, when Stanton was pregnant with her fifth child, she had complained to Anthony that although she longed "to be free from housekeeping and children," perhaps it was best for her to suffer "the trials of woman's lot" so she could eloquently proclaim them when her time came. Meeting Stanton at Rochester, Stone found her to be a talented but frustrated woman. In rejecting a suitor later that summer, Stone said that marriage prohibited women from pursuing a public life and cited Stanton's situation as example.[14]

At the opening session of the Women's State Temperance Convention, William Henry Channing, newly installed minister of Rochester's Unitarian Church, presented a series of resolutions dealing with the incident at Brick Church and the right and duty of women to help determine public policy on drunkenness. Stone spoke in support of these but, because she was not a member of the society, did not participate in discussion on Anthony's proposal to amend its constitution. Slated to address the convention at its public session that evening, she used that forum to speak on what Anthony and Stanton expected to be the firebrand of the convention—the divorce question.

Although most temperance leaders called for prohibition legislation like the Maine Law, Stone did not advocate legislating temperance. Trusting moral suasion over legal force, she attempted to go "behind the law, to the people's hearts." Relating one of her pathos-filled stories of a young bride whose seemingly happy future became a life of misery through her husband's addiction to drink, Stone concluded that it was cruel to compel a person to live as the spouse of a "confirmed drunkard." Common justice and a true understanding of marriage demanded not only a legal separation, but the right of divorce. But she said reformers' concern must be not only with the spouse of the drunkard, but with the drunkard himself. She enumerated efforts made over the past decades to stem the tide of drunkenness: pledges of temperance, pledges of total abstinence, cold-water armies with banners and songs, the Sons of Temperance and Daughters of Temperance, petitions by the hundreds of thousands, the Massachusetts law prohibiting the sale of individual drinks, then the Maine law prohibiting the manufacture and sale of liquor. None of these had been effective. But, said Stone, give a man the prospect of losing his wife and children and he would have great reason to foreswear drink. "Make this temperance question a matter of divorce, and the battle is half or wholly won."[15]

Despite a spirited, unscheduled rejoinder from Clarina Nichols, Stone carried the audience. Her idea that the risk of losing family could be an effective deterrent put a new slant on divorce as a temperance issue. She roused such interest that discussion carried over to the following two nights and she was asked to speak on the issue at Syracuse. Her speeches won both converts and admiration for herself. A visitor from Michigan wrote home that she had met several prominent women at the convention, but the "*great* woman" was Lucy Stone of Massachusetts. And Stanton, who felt vindicated by Stone's success with the divorce question, wrote, "How proud I felt of her that night! We have no woman who compares with her."[16]

Anthony's attempt to remove the constitutional barrier against male officers, however, did not meet with similar success. Stanton introduced the issue in her opening address, explaining that the restriction against men had been intended to force women to take charge of the society. Because its leaders were now well skilled in the practical business of getting up meetings and executing campaigns, she suggested they consider removing the exclusionary feature and appointed a committee to recommend appropriate action. The committee produced opposing reports. Presenting the majority opinion, Anthony recommended changing the society's name to the *People's* New York State Temperance Society and striking the clause requiring the society's officers to be women. The minority report recommended keeping the name and constitution unchanged.[17]

The issue immediately polarized the assembly. Some opposed letting Brown speak to the issue, but Stanton ruled that although only members could vote, anyone could speak. Brown pointed out the inconsistency of the society's demand that women be accepted on equal terms with men in the broader temperance movement while denying equal rights to its own male members. Most of the society's leadership, however, opposed a change. Debate carried over to the second day and turned rancorous, with someone suggesting that those who did not like the society's structure leave and form their own society. Fearing a vote might cause division or dissolution, Frederick Douglass moved that decision be postponed until the next annual meeting. His motion carried.[18]

But that afternoon when Anthony was reelected recording secretary, she announced that because the society had taken a position in violation of equal rights, she must decline the office. An astonished Douglass urged her to reconsider, but Anthony said her soul was no longer with the society and she resigned her membership. When Stanton was elected first vice president, she also resigned.[19]

Stanton's election as vice president followed her defeat for a second term as president in an election that revealed a concerted effort to replace her. Her ouster was probably due less to her opinions on woman's rights, divorce, and the church—as she later contended—than to her habit of presenting her opinions as the views of the society. The demotion upset Anthony, who asked Stanton a few weeks later if she wasn't "plunged in grief" at her defeat. "Not at all," she replied. "I am only too happy in the relief I feel from this additional care. I accomplished at Rochester all I desired by having the divorce question brought up and so eloquently supported by dear little Lucy Stone."[20]

The suggestion that those dissatisfied with the constitution withdraw and form their own society took hold in Anthony's mind, no doubt encouraged by the recent secession of temperance men from the planning meeting and the success in calling a rival world convention. Within a few weeks she was wanting to form a new temperance society in which men and women could work together as equals. When Stanton, burdened with domestic responsibilities and glad to be rid of public ones, refused to have anything to do with it, Anthony sought Stone's advice on how to proceed. But Stone advised that if there was insufficient interest, it was best to wait. Meanwhile, she suggested, Anthony might create interest by holding meetings and speaking on equal rights.[21]

When Stone returned home from New York, she learned that her idea of moving the National Woman's Rights Convention had met resistance. Elizabeth Oakes Smith disliked the conspicuous role Stone had played in the temperance schism and did not want the woman's rights movement further identified with it. She had already issued the call for Cleveland and refused to change it. But others favored Stone's idea, and Phillips suggested she organize a convention in New York "wholly independent of the society."[22]

Just as Stone began planning an independent woman's rights convention, a crisis concerning the temperance convention confronted her. The "half world" organizers had issued a call inviting "all temperance organizations" and promising their delegates "a cordial welcome." Some of the "whole world" organizers wanted to accept the call at face value and cancel arrangements for a competing convention, although they waited to hear from Stone before acting. Higginson was sure the women would be rejected again. But if they were, he said, they and their supporters could withdraw to a prearranged place and effect an even better schism than the first! Outraged, Stone reminded Higginson and the others that the decision to call the "whole world" convention had been made by vote of a large meeting, and that no committee had the right to cancel it and deliver the women again "into the camp of the enemy." Furthermore, after their public protest, it was due "both to the principle involved and to our own self-respect not to back out." She for one did not want to offer herself again to be insulted. In her indignation, she wrote to Garrison and Phillips, asking them to confront certain organizers, "take [them] over the coals" for their willing capitulation, and convince them that they must adhere to their set course. She described the situation to Anthony, who discussed it with Frederick Douglass and wrote back that Douglass thought she should issue the call on her "individual responsibility."[23]

Whether Stone issued the call on her own or waited to hear from the other members of her committee, by the time she received Anthony's encouragement she had already sent the call to the *New York Tribune*. In an accompanying editorial, Horace Greeley acknowledged plans for the other world convention but reminded his readers that it was being organized by those who had denied women any recognition as public laborers, insulted them, and driven them from a meeting to which "all friends of temperance" had been invited. On the other hand, said Greeley, "We who meet on the 1st and 2nd days of September know no test of Temperance Orthodoxy but devotion to the cause of Total Abstinence; no test of fitness to participate in Temperance councils but inclination and ability to labor. . . . Distinctions of Sex, or Creed, or Caste have all their proper place; but we perceive no relevancy in any of them to the deliberations and acts of the World's Temperance Convention." When Anthony saw the *Tribune*, she wrote to Stone with gratitude: "My eyes have feasted on the Call for the Whole World's Tem[perance] Con[vention]. Who but you, Lucy, could have braved and conquered the objection of such an array of men?"[24]

All these difficulties and the attention they required of Stone came at the very time the Massachusetts Constitutional Convention was acting on her suffrage petitions. When the committee issued its report and supporters in the larger convention failed to pass woman suffrage over the adverse recommendation, Stone was too absorbed in pushing through the call for the Whole World Temperance Convention to be distracted by the disappointing, but not unexpected, culmination of her winter labors.

After issuing the call for the temperance convention, Stone left further arrangements to the organizing committees and turned her attention to her independent woman's rights convention. Using a draft sent by Phillips, she quickly composed a call, gathered signatures, and sent it to a number of papers. The announcement of a woman's rights convention in New York City after Elizabeth Oakes Smith had announced one at Cleveland created confusion. Knowing that Stone was trying to move the convention, Bloomer withheld Smith's call and told *Lily* readers it seemed certain the site of the National Woman's Rights Convention had been changed. So Stone sent out press notices clarifying that there would be two conventions, the one in New York serving as a "John the Baptist" to the one in Cleveland, and she urged attendance at both.[25]

Stone resumed lecturing in August, working in Vermont and Rhode Island, where she urged a temperance audience of two thousand to send delegates to the whole world convention. Even while traveling, she continued making arrangements for the woman's rights convention, lining up speakers, seeking someone to preside, and asking Brown to help manage the proceedings. When her note to Stanton requesting a speech at one or both of the conventions brought no reply, Anthony explained, "Mrs. Stanton I dare say cannot *find time* to answer your note. She says she will not attend a con[vention] nor write a line to one until this baby is on its feet and she freed from household chores." Anthony tried to persuade Stanton to finish an address on divorce she had already started, but Stanton would not be moved. Bidding "adieu to the public for a while," Stanton told Anthony, "My ceaseless cares begin to wear upon my spirit. . . . I do swear . . . that while I am nursing this baby I will not be troubled with suffering humanity." Disappointed but sympathetic, Stone wrote to her, "We shall sadly miss the brave, true words you have been wont to send us. When your children are a little more grown you will surely be heard, for it cannot be possible to repress what is in you."[26]

Stone arrived in New York at the end of August for a full week of meetings. There was the Whole World Temperance Convention on Thursday and Friday, a banquet of the American Vegetarian Society on Saturday, to which she and other reform leaders were invited; a Sunday morning sermon at Metropolitan Hall by Antoinette Brown; a meeting to benefit the New York Women's Temperance Society on Monday, and finally the woman's rights convention on

Tuesday and Wednesday. She also fit in a night at the National Theater for the stage adaptation of *Uncle Tom's Cabin* and a visit to one of the city's homes for abandoned women.

Delegates from seventeen states and at least three foreign countries, some of whom would also attend the "half world" convention the following week, attended the Whole World Temperance Convention at Broadway Tabernacle on September 1 and 2, 1853. Stone, Higginson, and Mary Vaughan, new president of the women's society, had worked all summer to get more women delegated from existing societies, and as a result, a large number were present. Clarina Nichols of Vermont, Lucretia Mott of Pennsylvania, Caroline Severance of Ohio, and Frances Dana Gage, now of Missouri, were elected vice presidents along with fourteen men. Secretaries included Anthony of New York and Mary Jackson of Wakefield, England, a temperance speaker for over twenty years who had been delegated by five English temperance societies to represent them at the World Temperance Convention, but whose voice would be denied at the "half world" meeting.

Because arranging the woman's rights convention required so much of her time, Stone had hoped she would not have to address the temperance convention. But when she learned Stanton would not attend, she knew the subject of drunkenness as grounds for divorce would not be raised unless she did it herself. So while others appealed for Maine Laws, Stone repeated the appeal she had made at Rochester for "creating a public sentiment" that would demand for women, and men, the right to divorce a drunken spouse. Horace Greeley, as firm a defender of marriage as he was of woman's rights, disagreed with Stone's proposal. As chair of the business committee, he had authored resolutions calling for government action to abolish the liquor traffic and had already spoken in their favor. Now, arguing for the sanctity of marriage, he seconded Stone's plea for strong public sentiment but asked that it be directed toward the ballot-box instead of divorce law.[27]

Such disagreement was common at reform conventions and in no way marred the calm proceedings of the convention, which was spared the orchestrated disturbances that afflicted subsequent meetings. The presence in New York City of William Lloyd Garrison, who arrived Thursday to attend the Whole World Temperance Convention and stayed over for the woman's rights convention, attracted the attention of friends and foes alike. Taking advantage of his presence, the New York Anti-Slavery Society arranged meetings on Sunday afternoon and evening at which he would speak. This was all that was needed to activate the city's "public defenders"—hired troops of illiterate day workers who broke up meetings city leaders considered harmful to the community. Directed by Isaiah Rynders, a leader in Tammany Hall politics who had worked his way up from boatman through the ranks of boxer and professional gambler, their strategy was to create such commotion that speakers would have to leave the platform unheard. Among those from whom Rynders took his cue was James Gordon Bennett, editor of the *New York Herald* and

one of America's pioneers in sensational journalism. While denouncing abolitionists for their "traitorous" attacks on religion, government, and the South,
Bennett praised the mob action of Rynders's followers as "patriotic
expression."[28]

Rynders's men were among the four thousand people who filled Metropolitan Hall on Sunday morning for Antoinette Brown's service. Although she
espoused orthodox Christianity, the mere fact that she presumed the right to
preach was considered blasphemous by city leaders, whose agents drowned her
out with catcalls, hisses, shouts, laugher, and stamping feet. Next, the rowdies
took their protestations to the antislavery meetings and created a commotion
that one paper said was "as boisterous as was possible to be without a riot."
After assaulting the preliminary speakers with noise-making of all sorts, one
of them mounted the platform while Mott was speaking, sat close to the edge
and, acting drunk, elicited such peals of laughter that Mott gave up and took
her seat. Stone was the next speaker. After initial volleys of hisses and catcalls,
the hecklers quieted down and allowed Stone to give what friends considered
her most eloquent speech to date, voicing only sporadic protest to points they
found particularly objectionable. When Stone finished, however, they resumed
their noise-making and created such bedlam that the managers adjourned the
meeting with addresses from Brown and Garrison unattempted.[29]

The *New York Evangelist* denounced the "disgraceful violation of the Lord's
day" and the "violent interruption of the right of speech," but it blamed the
disturbances on Brown's "shameless" public appearance and the abolitionists'
blasphemous ravings. The *Herald* cited Stone's call for disunion as an example
of traitorous talk that justified people taking action into their own hands. If
Garrison, Greeley, and Stone were punished as they deserved, said Bennett,
they would be imprisoned and whipped. But because martyrdom would only
rouse misguided sympathies, he commended the rowdies' "sensible restraint."
"No violence, no blows," he urged, only "pungent remarks, well seasoned with
the wit of Atticus, and an occasional volley of hisses." He encouraged Rynders's
troops to extend their "sensible restraint" to Tuesday's woman's rights convention, noting that among the announced speakers was Ernestine Rose, an
unabashed atheist whose last public appearance had been at an "Anti-Bible
Convention" two months earlier. Adding that this meeting would be an extension of the Worcester conventions, "with all the latest improvements," Bennett
also invited visitors from the South, as yet unexposed to the new movement,
to "walk in and see the fun."[30]

Despite these invitations, the opening session of the woman's rights convention was not disturbed. Hecklers did try to disrupt the afternoon session
several times, but with little effect. That evening, though, Rynders's men were
out in great force, aimed, it seems, at Bennett's suggested target—Ernestine
Rose. While shouts and hisses and foot-stamping interrupted all the speakers,
when Rose took the rostrum the disturbance became so great she could not be
heard. The assault continued on the second day and drowned out several speak-

ers. A tense moment came when a journalist known as a vocal opponent of woman's rights asked to speak. Stone had issued her customary invitation at the opening session, asking the audience to participate in discussions and saying the platform was not reserved for those who agreed with the convention's positions. With everyone expecting a witty attack, loud cheers erupted as the journalist took the floor. He responded, however, to the second part of Stone's invitation. She had said that although critics were welcome to explain their opposition, if convention speakers succeeded in taking "their reason from under their feet, we want them to admit it fairly, and thenceforth to support us like true men and women." The journalist acknowledged that for the past two years he had been ridiculing the woman's rights movement for the very journal that gave "the cue to the hisses in the gallery." But he had seriously studied its claims, changed his views entirely, and now raised his voice in its behalf. He knew not only that his former opinions were wrong, but that this movement was one that could not be stopped. Nevertheless, the rowdies continued trying.[31]

Despite rumor that Rynders's troops had been offered a bonus if they broke up the convention before its scheduled end, their commotion so far had not forced the suspension of any session. Expecting an all-out effort on the last evening, Stone called on the mayor and chief of police to get their help in maintaining order. Mott opened the meeting with an announcement that although police were on hand, she hoped they would not be needed. The response made it clear that police presence would make no difference. Screeches and howls accompanied the vocalist who opened the proceedings with a reform anthem, and then boisterous laughter and mocking cries of "Encore!" followed.[32] Mathilde Francesca Anneke, editor of a women's paper that had been repressed by German authorities, attempted to speak in her native tongue with Rose translating, but a frenzy of stomping feet, rapping canes, laughter, shrieks, and shouts forced them to withdraw. The police were called on to restore order, and a few arrests brought a brief break in the commotion. But a resurgence of noisy protestations cut Phillips short, too. Then Stone came forward, and her first words were also lost in a din of cat calls and jeers. But as on Sunday, the longer she spoke the quieter the hall became, until at last she held it in rapt attention. As soon as she finished, however, the noise resumed. Unable to restore order, Mott adjourned the meeting.[33]

While Rynders's ruffians had been trying to silence the women at Broadway Tabernacle, a different sort had been trying to silence women at Metropolitan Hall. Instead of attending the woman's rights convention on Tuesday, Antoinette Brown went to the (Half) World Temperance Convention, acting on its invitation to delegates from "all temperance societies." Convention officials accepted her credentials—from a society in South Butler where she would soon be ordained as minister of its Congregational Church and from a society at Channing's church in Rochester—and Neal Dow, author of the Maine Law, invited her to sit on the speakers' platform. However, a resolution inviting participation from all delegates "without respect to age, sex, color, or condition" provoked loud and prolonged debate until at last, amid cries for order, it was tabled.

Although the assembly refused to invite women to participate, it had not actually barred them, so when Dow was elected president he ruled that Brown, as a duly authorized delegate, was entitled to speak. Most of the delegates refused to hear her, however, and created such an uproar she had to take her seat. They then passed a resolution restricting the platform to officers and invited guests, forcing Brown from it, and then another, drafted by General S. F. Carey, a leading temperance figure from Ohio, that although they appreciated the cooperation of their wives, mothers, and sisters, they believed the public platform was not "the appropriate sphere of woman."[34]

Brown reported these proceedings to the evening session of the woman's rights convention, after which several people decided to help her challenge the Carey resolution. Organizing themselves into a temperance society, they delegated Wendell Phillips and a few women to represent them. The next morning, these new delegates sat with Brown who, shortly into the proceedings, asked permission to speak. Dow again invited her to the platform and, over another onslaught of protests, ruled that despite the Carey resolution, the convention call had invited all temperance societies and therefore the convention must allow the delegates of all societies to be heard. This time, a slim majority sustained Dow's ruling, but when Brown attempted to speak, a roar of hisses, shouts, and foot-stomping silenced her. Phillips took up the battle to win equal rights for the women, but his attempts so exasperated the majority of delegates that they voted to exclude the representatives of new society—including Phillips—from the remaining sessions.[35]

Along with his report of Brown's treatment at the (Half) World Temperance Convention, Horace Greeley published a statement from Brown explaining why she had pressed for the right to speak there. She tried "to assert a principle," she said, "that the sons and daughters of the race, without distinction of sex, sect, class or color, should be recognized as belonging to the world." She asked no favor or privilege as a woman, but only the rights of a citizen of the world at a world convention. To those who thought it inappropriate to press the claim at that particular time and place, she answered that she pleaded for equality whenever and wherever she had the opportunity. Earlier that year, "when woman claimed the supremacy—the right to hold all the offices in the Woman's State Temperance Society," she had contended for the equal rights of men. Everywhere, she said, she claimed "the equality of humanity in Church and State."[36]

Assessing the events of the week and their treatment by the press, Greeley concluded that both would advance the cause of woman's equal rights. "Nothing is so good for a weak and unpopular movement as this sort of opposition," he said. Knowing that newspapers across the nation would reprint the reports, along with the calls for disruption and the ridicule, Greeley said, "The mass of people throughout the country who might otherwise not know of [the move-ment's] existence will have their attention called and their sympathies enlisted on its behalf." Predicting that opponents would never again resort to such extreme tactics to silence women, the *Anti-Slavery Bugle* declared woman's right to the platform "henceforth vindicated in America."[37]

Both papers were right. As Stone lectured across the country during the next few years and other women ascended the public rostrum, the question of woman's right to speak in public seemed settled.

16

"A Hearing Ear" in the West

Soon after the tumultuous week in New York City in September 1853, Lucy Stone embarked on a tour that gave the woman's rights cause its widest hearing. The tour developed from an invitation from Henry B. Blackwell, a young man she had first met in 1850 as she passed through Cincinnati on her return from Illinois. She met him again in the spring of 1853, with his sister Ellen at the New York antislavery offices during anniversary week, and then at the New England Anti-Slavery Convention in Boston. Two weeks later, on the very day she returned home from the Rochester temperance meeting, he appeared on her doorstep with a letter of introduction from Garrison and a proposal of more than just lecturing.[1]

At age twenty-eight, Henry Blackwell was eager for marriage and, having grown up in a reform family with one sister who had participated in the early woman's rights agitation, another who had overcome great obstacles to become the first woman to be granted a medical degree, another who was following in those footsteps, and two others who through necessity and principle were supporting themselves, he was attracted to women of independent character. Blackwell had followed Stone's public career through various reform papers, but when he actually heard her speak in New York he was smitten. He followed her to Massachusetts, watched her at the New England Anti-Slavery Convention, and attended her hearing before the Constitutional Convention. Then he went to Garrison to learn if she was involved in a relationship and decided to press his suit despite being told that she was intent on remaining single and had already turned away several suitors.[2]

As they walked together over the countryside surrounding Stone's home, Blackwell revealed his romantic interest and asked Stone to be allowed to court her, saying at the same time he was not yet in an independent position from which he could ask her to marry him. Stone said she was not interested in marriage, and although she welcomed him as a friend, she would not accept him as a suitor. Blackwell left the encounter undaunted. In an exchange of letters over the summer, the two discussed the character of the antislavery and woman's rights movements and the nature of the marriage institution—actual and ideal.[3]

Blackwell's proposal that Stone lecture in the West where he could use his business connections to make arrangements for her was motivated partly by his desire to demonstrate how useful he could be to her work. Part of Stone's rejection of marriage was her belief that it so restricted women that they could not carry on a career such as she had chosen. She gave as examples Angelina Weld, who had withdrawn from public labor after her marriage, and Elizabeth Cady Stanton, whose domestic bondage kept her from taking the active role in reform she desired. To answer this objection, Blackwell visited the Welds, talked with them about why they no longer participated in reform, and told Stone that their retreat was due to factors that had nothing to do with marriage. As for Stanton, Blackwell believed she and her husband were simply mismatched. Although a woman "unsuitably married like Mrs. Stanton" might find herself fettered, a woman married to "a fellow worker with sufficient means and position to prevent the necessity of her drudging" and permit her to come and go as she pleased—this woman would be no less influential than a single woman, he argued.[4] Fully aware of the design behind Blackwell's invitation to Cincinnati, Stone was hesitant to accept. As she worked her way toward Ohio for the National Woman's Rights Convention, she had not decided whether to continue to the southern part of that state.

Stone had begun her 1853–54 lecture season in August, speaking in Rhode Island, Vermont, and Massachusetts. After leaving New York City, she lectured at Newark, New Jersey, and at several cities in New York. Speaking in Albany on September 15, she missed the historic ordination of Antoinette Brown at South Butler. No American woman had been formally admitted to the Christian ministry before, and when Stone announced the pending ceremony at Broadway Tabernacle, the orthodox press immediately denounced as infidel any woman who would seek ordination and any church that would ordain her. Knowing how the press would react to any affiliation she had with the ceremony and not wanting to precipitate controversy at the beginning of her friend's pastoral career, Stone stayed away. After engagements at Rochester and Syracuse, she finished her westward trek through New York at Niagara on October 3 and then boarded a train for Cleveland.[5]

Although the preceding national conventions had all been in the East, it was Ohio that had taken the lead in organizing woman's rights agitation. After holding the first state convention in May 1850 and petitioning their constitutional convention, Ohio activists continued to hold state conventions annually. In 1851 they appointed a standing committee to direct their work and in 1852 organized the first state woman's rights society, hired lecturers, published tracts, and held county conventions. At its first annual meeting in May 1853, the Ohio Woman's Rights Association launched a second petition drive, this one directed to the state legislature. Its activities combined with publicity of the New York events to create great interest in Ohio. More than three thousand people attended the evening sessions of the fourth National Woman's Rights Convention on October 5, 6, and 7, making it the largest woman's rights convention to date.[6]

Stone was reunited with several western friends who had not made it to the eastern conventions. Oberlin colleague Hannah Tracy Cutler, first president of the Ohio Woman's Rights Association, had recently remarried and moved to Illinois but returned for this national gathering. Another Oberlin ally, former president Asa Mahan, took this opportunity to publicly voice his support for the movement. Stone stayed at the home of Caroline Severance, whom she had met at the Syracuse convention. Chair of the executive committee and author of the first tract published by the state association, Severance was one of the women Stone had asked to supply articles for her suffrage campaign the previous winter. Among western leaders Stone knew only through correspondence was Frances Dana Gage, a columnist better known to readers of the Ohio *Cultivator* as "Aunt Fanny." Although she had moved to St. Louis in March, Gage remained one of the most prominent of western leaders and was chosen to preside.[7]

A major objective of this convention was to mobilize petitioning in as many states as possible. After the spurt of activity stimulated by the first National Woman's Rights Convention, only Stone had continued annual drives. She was planning to expand her effort to all the New England states, Ohio was putting together another campaign, and the Central Committee wanted to widen the effort. A letter from William Henry Channing urged the convention to draw up model petitions and made suggestions concerning form. Stone and Indiana activist John O. Wattles presented a model based on Phillips's petition asking legislatures to remove the word *male* from state constitutions. Emma Robinson Coe, who with Caroline Severance was preparing an address to the Ohio legislature in anticipation of a hearing, read the petition they would be circulating that winter. Unable to reach consensus on form, the convention rejected uniform petitions and encouraged state activists to draw up their own.[8]

The convention also decided to publish reports on the status of women. Stone read a letter from Thomas Wentworth Higginson urging the convention to move beyond abstract arguments for equal rights and publicize the facts and statistics of woman's wrongs. He proposed that it commission three reports using data gathered from the various states: one on laws pertaining to women, one on women's education, and one on women's employment and compensation. Describing these reports as an "arsenal of arms" for woman's rights advocates, he asked the convention to authorize the expenditure of $100 on each. Stone reported that Wendell Phillips had already hired a Boston lawyer to do the legal study and asked the convention to assume responsibility for the other two. Arguing for more "light," she related the story of a woman she had met at a home for abandoned women in New York who had become a prostitute because she could not feed her children through honorable labor. While women were forced to struggle for survival and neglect the "deathless part of their natures," should they not "let the world know?" Stone asked. Approving the project, the convention immediately took a collection to finance it. As baskets passed among the audience, a call came from the gallery that some young men would contribute only if Lucy Stone came up and asked them. Without hesitating, she ran up the stairs to receive the money. Eighty dollars was collected on the spot, and Stone, Mott, Rose, Higginson, and Phillips were assigned the job of gathering statistics and publishing the reports.[9]

The convention also considered adoption of a formal Declaration of Woman's Rights. Because the national conventions had decided not to organize as an association, they had drafted neither a constitution nor a statement of principles and purposes. Declarations of sentiment had been adopted by the conventions in New York in 1848 and by Pennsylvania's state convention in 1852, but the national movement had not offered the public any statement of definition. So Channing's letter, in addition to urging petition drives, asked the convention to adopt and print for wide circulation a distinct declaration of woman's equal rights in all areas of human activity. Lucretia Mott presented the Declaration of Sentiments written by Elizabeth Cady Stanton for the New York conventions, but there was strong objection to it. Some delegates pointed out that in addition to containing factual errors, it was more a list of grievances than a statement of principles or goals. Some feared that, as a parody of the Declaration of Independence that declared all laws made by men "of no force or authority," it would elicit more ridicule than serious consideration. Others objected to its implication that man had "purposely played the tyrant" and was solely to blame for society's restrictions on woman.[10]

Debate on its merits called forth once again the question of men's culpability in woman's oppression and the tone the movement should adopt concerning the male sex. Rose said it was bad laws that made men tyrannical. Certainly men made the laws, but they had made them "in ignorance." Garrison insisted on holding classes responsible for their actions. Just as he did not excuse the ignorant slaveholder, he would not excuse the ignorant male. "Unless the men of this nation are made by woman to see that they have been guilty of usurpation, and cruel usurpation, I believe very little progress will be made," he said. Stone saw validity and utility in both arguments. "We talk of the wrongs we suffer in one direction, and in another of the rights we ought to have. . . . And the people listen." But quoting Tennyson, she reminded the assembly that woman's rights was not a question of women versus men: "The woman's cause is man's: they rise or sink together, dwarf'd or godlike, bond or free." After much deliberation, the convention rejected the New York declaration and appointed a committee—Stone, Mott, Garrison, Brown, and Rose—to draft an original statement.[11]

Prolonged debate on another thorny issue—the Bible's position on woman's rights—absorbed both the morning and afternoon sessions of the convention's final day, and the committee's draft was not presented until the closing session.

A motion was made to adopt it, but Stone suggested that an official statement such as they intended required more deliberation than they could give at that time. The convention deferred further action to a subsequent convention. Although the 1855 convention adopted a series of resolutions as a partial "Woman's Rights Platform," intending subsequent conventions to add to it, the National Woman's Rights Convention never adopted a formal declaration of sentiments or principles.[12]

Stone closed the convention with one of her famous motivational speeches, urging young women to speak out and make their wrongs known to the world. "Make your claims to a college education known, and present them in a determined manner," she exhorted young women in the audience. Among her auditors was sixteen-year-old Sarah Burger, a student at Cleveland High School whose family would soon return to Ann Arbor, Michigan, where, three years later, she would lead an effort to open the state university to women. It was this speech of Stone's, Burger said, that persuaded her to do it.[13]

Henry Blackwell, still strongly in pursuit of Stone, had attended the first day of the convention and been elected one of its secretaries. In a speech addressed as much to Stone as to the audience, he argued that giving women the vote would help not only to combat unjust laws, to open college doors, and to secure equal pay for equal work, but also to dignify the marriage relation by making woman an equal partner. The *Cleveland Plain Dealer* described his speech as "excessively radical" and much too long, but it evidently hit its intended mark. Instead of attending that evening's session, Stone accompanied Blackwell to the bluff overlooking Lake Erie to watch the sunset. The next day, he headed for Cincinnati to make arrangements for her visit there. At Stone's continued uncertainty about going to Cincinnati, Blackwell had suggested she ask other women to come along and hold a woman's rights meeting. Lucretia Mott and Lydia Jenkins agreed to go if Sarah Otis Ernst, Cincinnati's matriarch of reform, thought it a good idea. Blackwell went directly to see Ernst and wrote back that the way was prepared.[14]

Located on the Ohio River, Cincinnati had long served as a gateway for settlers moving west. The arrival of the railroad in 1843 boosted it as a center of commerce and manufacturing, and now with a population of 160,000, it was both the economic and cultural center of the West. Having strong ties with its Kentucky neighbor as well as with the proslavery population of southern Illinois, Indiana, and Ohio, the city was guarded in its antislavery interest. Garrisonian abolition found such little sympathy that when the Ladies' Anti-Slavery Society proposed inviting Garrison to speak at their annual convention the previous spring, nay-sayers predicted his presence would so divide the community that they would never be able to hold an antislavery meeting again.[15] But Garrison had come and the community had survived.

Cautious though Cincinnati was on antislavery, it seemed quite eager to hear about woman's rights. The press gave friendly notice that the city's first woman's rights meeting would be held on Friday evening, October 14, and would be addressed by "the young and popular female lecturer, Lucy Stone, and the venerable Lucretia Mott," long known for her advocacy of various reforms. To counteract their influence, a local preacher began a series of sermons on "the moral, social, and religious duties of domestic life" and urged those who wanted to know the "natural and most important sphere of woman" to attend his meetings instead of the women's. Nevertheless, an hour before the appointed time, the hall was filled to overflowing, with hundreds standing in the aisles and hundreds more—perhaps a thousand, said Mott—unable to get in. Stone's fame had spread through reports of the stormy New York meetings, and many people were surprised to find her "not a masculine-looking virago," as they had supposed, but rather "a small and fragile woman . . . quite feminine" despite her short hair and "unmistakable pants."[16]

The women preached woman's rights for two nights, and then on Sunday while Mott traveled up river to visit relatives in Maysville, Kentucky, Stone and Jenkins lectured on temperance. In Maysville, Mott she gave two lectures: one in the afternoon on reform in general and another in the evening on woman's rights. The afternoon lecture included antislavery, and yet she received a calm, attentive hearing, a surprising feat for someone known far and wide as an abolitionist, and one that perhaps could have been accomplished only by a sixty-year-old Quaker matron. The reception of woman's rights was no less remarkable, for in the South as in much of the North, the two causes were inextricably linked. Newspaper report of a married women's property bill in Georgia noted that the bill was awakening earnest discussion on woman's rights in the South, where that topic had been "rendered contraband" by its connection with abolitionism. But Maysville showed such enthusiastic interest that Mott volunteered that Lucy Stone, too, would lecture for them.[17]

Despite Blackwell's prodding for a western tour, Stone had written to her mother when she left Cleveland that she would be in Cincinnati only a few days before returning to the northern part of the state. But after Mott's success in Maysville, Stone let Blackwell make arrangements for her in Louisville and other nearby communities. So as the Mott party left town, Stone moved her trunk from Mrs. Ernst's into the Blackwell home on Walnut Hills, two miles out of town. Three years earlier when she and Phebe had stayed in the neighborhood, Stone had passed the modest brick house in awe, knowing it to be the home of Elizabeth Blackwell. Now that she was a guest in the house, she quickly got to know the family.

The Blackwells had emigrated from England in 1832, when Henry was seven. His father, Samuel, had been a sugar refiner and abolitionist, interested in developing a substitute for slave-grown sugar, and had transplanted those interests to the United States. Settling just outside New York City in New Jersey, the family had witnessed some of the violence of the early antislavery years, and Garrison, Theodore Parker, Theodore Weld, and Samuel J. May had been visitors in their home. The family had also taken a keen interest in the first stirring of the woman's rights movement. The eldest daughter, Anna, attended the Anti-Slavery Convention of American Women in 1837, drafted its letter thanking John Quincy Adams for his support of women's petitioning, and served on the central committee set up for New York.[18] But the panic of 1837 and resultant depression destroyed the family's resources, and Samuel took his wife, Hannah, his sister, and nine children to Cincinnati in 1838. He died shortly thereafter, and the family had been struggling ever since. The daughters taught and the sons pursued business. Continuing interest in woman's rights influenced Elizabeth to attempt the feat she did in achieving a medical degree in 1849, and when the first National Woman's Rights convention was held in 1850, daughters Marian and Emily attended.

Anna and Howard now lived in England, Marian was away from home teaching, Elizabeth ran a medical clinic for poor women and children in New York City, and Emily, who was pursuing a medical education in Cleveland, was at the moment in New York with Elizabeth. Stone renewed her acquaintance with Sam, whom she had met during her brief stay in Cincinnati in 1850, and with Ellen. She also met twenty-one-year-old George, the only family member born in the United States. The Blackwells were quickly captivated by Henry's intended. "She is a most admirable woman," Sam wrote in his diary. "By her quiet decision, steady purpose, and lofty principle she reminds me strongly of Elizabeth . . . We have quite adopted her."[19]

On Tuesday, October 18, Stone lectured on antislavery, and two days later she was the featured attraction at Cincinnati's Anti-Slavery Fair.[20] On Friday she left for nearby New Richmond, Ohio. As the boat pulled away from the wharf, word quickly spread that she was aboard, and a minister left the men's cabin to seek her out. The women invited him into their quarters, and in a suffocating crowd they listened as he attacked Stone's wearing of the Bloomer, her views on slavery and religion, and the "troublesome" practice of women standing with uncovered heads in the presence of men. Stone's witty responses brought cheers from the women, and the preacher shot back, "How can you possibly get over the scriptural text which says a woman shall not speak in public? I advise you to look into these matters more, to study the Scriptures more thoroughly."

"I have looked into them," Stone replied. "I have studied them in their original. I have read them in Greek, and can translate them for you."

"Had a thunderbolt fallen at the Reverend's feet," said a reporter for a Columbus paper, "he could not have been more astounded." Stone explained how she thought that particular text should be translated, and before the boat docked, "Miss Lucy had added an extra leaf or two to her laurels, for, merciless creature that she is, she was not content to merely show up the important divine as utterly ignorant of the Scriptures in their original, but [also showed that he] actually knew but little of them as rendered in our own tongue."[21]

At New Richmond, she spoke twice on woman's rights and once on antislavery, with Blackwell joining her at the podium on the last night. Upon their return to Cincinnati, she lectured in one of the black community's churches.

The woman's rights meetings had been held in a hall that did not admit blacks. Upon learning of that policy, Stone changed to a different hall for her subsequent lectures, but a number of blacks wanted to hear what they had missed. So on Thursday, October 27, she gave a benefit lecture on woman's rights, with all proceeds going to Cincinnati's orphanage for black children.[22]

Blackwell scheduled four nights for Stone in Louisville, for she had two new lectures to add to those of the previous season. News of her impending visit electrified the city. "Miss Lucy Stone, the beautiful Miss Lucy Stone, the strong-minded Miss Lucy Stone, the eloquent Miss Lucy Stone, the long and anxiously expected Miss Lucy Stone is at last among us and will deliver a lecture tonight at Mozart Hall upon Woman's Rights," a city paper announced on November 2. Warning that there might be "no getting along with the Louisville ladies" after they heard Stone, the paper nevertheless urged women to "go and hear her" if their husbands would let them, "and if they won't, go anyhow." The standing-room-only audience that turned out despite a "rainy, muddy, sloppy" evening astonished the editor of the *Louisville Courier*, as did the speaker who, he said, demonstrated "powers of extempore address rarely the birth-rite or acquired property of even celebrated male orators." This assessment was shared by the editor of *Prentice's Daily Journal*, who called Stone's speech "one of the ablest, clearest, most forcible and beautiful productions we ever heard." A more critical editor attributed the size of the audience to "novelty of the subject, the singularity of the Bloomer, [and] the boldness of the lecturer in stepping from the sphere usually assigned to women." Nevertheless, he acknowledged that whatever one thought of Stone's "ultra" doctrines, her talent as a speaker could not be denied.[23]

Stone's subsequent lectures, the "Legal and Political Disabilities of Women," the "Bible Position on Woman," and "Marriage and the Injurious Consequences of Too Early Marriages," attracted even larger audiences. A note delivered to her room and signed by "many Ladies" asked her to give an afternoon lecture. Other women, who missed the first lecture because of the rain, asked her to repeat it, and Stone complied, urging them to have short dresses made for the occasion in case it rained again. Told she was doing more good in Louisville than she could anywhere else, she was begged to repeat the entire course. Amazed by the enthusiastic reception of her ideas, Stone mused that Kentucky might give "political and legal equality to its white women sooner even than Massachusetts."[24]

The rights of its black population were altogether a different matter. Visiting Stone before her first lecture, newspaper editor George D. Prentice warned her not to attempt an antislavery lecture, for the people would not listen to a word about abolition. But if she did not raise that subject, his reports would open the door for her everywhere throughout the South. Such a tour did not interest Stone, but the "hearing ear" she found in the West excited her, and she agreed to let Blackwell make arrangements for her in Indiana, where she would be free to speak on either of her subjects.[25]

Stone opened her Indiana tour at New Albany, home of the Albany Female College, where interest was so great that she sold all her remaining woman's rights tracts. A correspondent to the *New York Tribune* said she dissipated the prejudices created against her by abusive articles in the Eastern papers and reported that her lectures were received with almost universal commendation. But editors in other towns remained wary. One denounced her "brazen and unblushing effrontery" and another warned, "You she-hyena, don't you come here!" A third printed a rumor that Stone had been seen in a tavern smoking a cigar and "swearing like a trooper." But the people of Madison welcomed her and asked her to add an afternoon lecture for children. When Stone learned that several black women had been denied admittance to her lecture, she went immediately to see the doorkeeper and convinced him that whoever rented a hall had the right to determine who should be admitted. He agreed not to turn anyone away but warned that attendance would be adversely affected and asked her to state publicly that it was not his fault that colored people were admitted. Stone sent tickets for the next lecture to the women who had been excluded, and to her subsequent audiences, which were indeed smaller than the first, she announced that she spoke only in halls that were open to all.[26]

At Indianapolis, according to the *Weekly Journal*, Stone "set about two thirds of the women in town crazy after women's rights and placed half the men in a similar predicament." She stimulated a lively newspaper debate on woman's rights that raged for weeks after she left. After lecturing for Terre Haute's historical society, she completed her Indiana tour in Evansville, and then headed for St. Louis, where after prolonged effort, Blackwell had succeeded in arranging lectures.[27]

Stone's first lecture on December 18 attracted the largest crowds ever assembled in St. Louis, according to local papers, filling the city's largest auditorium beyond its capacity of two thousand. Classes at the McDowell Medical College were suspended so students and faculty could attend her subsequent lectures, and one minister, with the consent of his congregation, canceled the annual Christmas eve service so they could hear her. Responding to unexpected interest and excitement, she remained nine nights and gave eight lectures, including one on temperance by request. [28]

Stone stayed at the St. Louis home of Frances Dana Gage, who reported to the *New York Tribune* that Stone was stirring the West on the subject of woman's rights "as it is seldom stirred on any subject whatsoever." Her home was "thronged with visitors from all classes—lawyers, doctors, and some clergymen; ladies in high life and in its midway walks, school teachers and maidens—all giving the hand of sympathy and urging [Stone] to talk on." Gage said that although most St. Louis papers had not written favorably on woman's rights before Stone's arrival, now every daily gave "fair and approving" reports of her lectures.[29]

Indeed, almost everywhere she spoke in the West, Stone was treated with respect. One paper boasted that westerners "disdained to follow the rowdy footpaths" recommended from New York, where it seemed women could not speak without being mobbed. Another said, "So persevering, indeed, if not malicious, have been the jibes and derision with which the Woman's Rights movement has been everywhere met, it is fair to assume that a majority of Miss Lucy Stone's audiences had prejudged her cause and went . . . from curiosity alone, and to obtain fresh occasion for renewed and mayhap original wit at the expense of Woman's Rights." But, it said, "if any went to deride, they derided not. Their premeditated mockery yielded gradually to a deep and heartfelt admiration." The papers continued to express surprise at Stone's personal appearance. "She is by no means lacking of good looks. She has a medium stature, good figure, rather a round face, small, pretty hands, and a soft, womanly voice." Several remarked on her hair style—"short hair, parted in the middle and combed close down behind the ears, reaching only to the neck and lying close thereon." One writer said the style disappointed imaginations used to dwelling on flowing hair and "dancing curls." On the other hand, he said, Stone's plain looks served to "sober" her hearers' minds so they could concentrate on her message.[30]

Just as ridicule of the speaker and her views was absent from most western press coverage, so, too, was ridicule of her dress. Stone wore only the short dress and trousers during her western tour, finding them practical and convenient for travel and for getting around in rain, mud, and snow. Although Professor McDowell, who helped arrange the St. Louis lectures, pleaded in vain for her to wear a long skirt, nowhere did she receive the taunts and jeers that the dress sometimes attracted in the East.[31] Stone found that audiences received her respectfully, and when papers did take note of her dress, they usually did so in matter-of-fact comment, often adding that it was quite becoming on her.

With the Ohio River frozen and steamboat travel back to Cincinnati impossible, Stone headed for Chicago and its rail connection with the East. Noting the arrival of the "celebrated and efficient advocate of Woman's Rights," a Chicago editor asked Stone to favor the town with a lecture. "We can promise her as much as the St. Louis papers did—that she shall be treated with all the courtesy due her sex; we can promise our readers a little more, and that is, that Miss Lucy can talk. . . . [V]ery few of her male enemies would like to meet her in argument."[32] Although she had not intended to speak in Chicago, Henry Blackwell, who brought her trunk from Cincinnati, helped her arrange lectures before proceeding to Wisconsin on business.

Again praised as the best of the season, Stone's Chicago lectures inspired discussion and debate in the city's homes and meeting places. She found volunteers to gather statistics from Illinois for the reports on the status of women, recruited others to distribute tracts and circulate petitions, and won the support of a local lawyer who invited her to draw upon him for money for the cause whenever she deemed it necessary. Reports of her lectures generated interest in other places, too, such as Muscatine, Iowa, where the Young Men's Debating Club took up the question of woman's rights on January 7.[33]

When Stone ended her western tour and headed east, she left behind incalculable influence. As Elizabeth Stanton would write fifteen years later in *Eminent Women of the Age*, "Lucy Stone was the first speaker who really stirred the nation's heart on the subject of woman's wrongs." Her ideas were not original, but she took ideas garnered from many thinkers and writers on woman's rights to audiences across the country. Her logic, wit, pathos, humor, and mastery of facts and arguments; her confident, sincere, and simple style; her open and tolerant manner; her ability to demonstrate empathy with her audience and win their good will; her petite stature and girlish appearance; her wonderfully melodious voice—all combined to give her a charisma that disarmed prejudice and converted thousands. The effect she had was so general that forty years later friends of equal rights across the country ascribed their conversion to some meeting of Stone's that they attended during this or subsequent lecture tours. Dr. Caroline B. Winslow, for example, said that although she had struggled to acquire a medical education, not until she heard Stone in Cincinnati did she understand that all women wanted and needed what she was fighting for individually.[34] There is no way of knowing how many young women in her audiences, like Sarah Burger, Stone persuaded to "knock at the door" and finally push it open.

Encouraged by the great interest in woman's rights in the West, Stone wished the cause had more lecturers. "My heart runs over with gratitude that this cause, so full of blessings to the race, is being so candidly heard. But I do not forget that there are long days, aye, years, of hard toil before us, and the last worker in the cause is not yet born."[35]

17

"Heart and Soul"

Leaving Chicago and her triumphal western tour on January 6, 1854, Lucy Stone headed east toward engagements in Pennsylvania, Washington, D.C., New York, Rhode Island, and Maine. Her widely reported activities of the previous year had not only prepared a hearing ear in the West, but also opened new doors in the East. Bundles of mail forwarded to her in Indiana and Illinois brought invitations from popular lyceums, all asking specifically that she speak on woman's rights. On January 10 she opened a course of lectures sponsored by Pittsburgh's Young Men's Mercantile Library Association and then stayed over to lecture independently. A week later she was in Washington, D.C., where Congressman Gerrit Smith arranged that city's first lecture on woman's rights. Then she went to Philadelphia for a lecture arranged by James and Lucretia Mott.[1]

Arriving at the Motts' on the afternoon before the lecture, Stone busied herself with last-minute preparation. Wanting the city's black population to understand the claims of the woman's rights movement, she set about sending complimentary tickets to Sarah Douglass for distribution in the black community. But the Motts' daughter said the auditorium reserved for her did not admit Negroes. Stone was stunned. When the Musical Fund Hall had been suggested, she was told it could be booked for woman's rights but not for antislavery. This stipulation had not bothered her. If woman's rights had been excluded and temperance allowed, she later explained, she would have lectured there on temperance, if that had been the topic on which she wanted to speak, "for each good cause helps every other." But speaking where blacks were excluded was a different matter. Recalling how easily she had persuaded the Indiana doorkeeper to admit them, she believed she could accomplish the same here. Lucretia encouraged her, for, she said, just as New York's Broadway Tabernacle had changed its policy against antislavery meetings, so the Musical Fund Hall might be open to change. So Stone sent the tickets, and Lucretia penned an accompanying note saying she hoped the recipients would not suffer the indignity of a refusal.[2]

Accompanied by James Mott, Stone visited the curator of the hall who, despite all their arguments, refused to set aside its "established rule." By the time they left, it was too late to change location, so Stone decided to proceed with the lecture and incorporate a public protest against the hall's segregationist policy. That night, as feared, several black people bearing complimentary tickets were turned away. At the close of her lecture, Stone protested their exclusion and promised never again to lecture where people of all races were not admitted. "The woman does not deserve her rights who is willing to secure them by trampling upon or ignoring those of any other," she declared. The following morning, she sent a written protest to the *Daily Register*. Later, a delegation of blacks called on her. The doorkeeper had told them their exclusion was with Stone's consent and, not having heard her protest, they objected to her complicity in racial discrimination. Stone's explanation did nothing to placate their leader, Charles L. Reason, who blamed the Motts for booking the hall and Stone for going ahead with the lecture. Stone apologized for the injustice they had suffered but said she believed her protest called more attention to it than canceling the meeting could have done. And she repeated her promise to never again lecture where they were not welcome.[3]

She repeated the protest and promise again two days later from the podium of New York City's Broadway Tabernacle, where she spoke in a prestigious antislavery course. The next day, suffering physical pain from head and back, and no doubt emotional pain from the incident, she canceled engagements at Auburn and Ogdensburg and went home.[4] There, she received additional reaction against her Musical Fund Hall appearance. Dissatisfied with her explanation, Charles Reason sent his own protest to the *Daily Register*, charging both Stone and the Motts with forsaking their black friends for the benefit of woman's rights. Frederick Douglass published the protest in his paper, added his own condemnation of Stone's "dereliction from duty and principle," and attributed her "corruption" to the enthusiastic praise bestowed upon her in slave states.[5]

Unfortunately, Stone's Philadelphia lecture came on the heels of an acrimonious four-month exchange between Douglass and Garrisonians, and the attack on her, it seems, was another volley in the crossfire. The feud had begun two years earlier, when Douglass converted to political abolition and merged his *North Star* with the *Liberty Party Paper* to become *Frederick Douglass' Paper*. At first he remained friendly to the American Anti-Slavery Society, attending its meetings and respectfully challenging its positions, but gradually he began attacking persons as well as policies. Criticizing Garrisonians for foisting the woman question upon the antislavery movement, he blamed Abby Kelley for causing the 1840 division and declared that he would have allowed his right arm to be cut off before he would divide "the ranks of freedom's army." Then, in the summer of 1853 he denounced Henry C. Wright, Stephen

Foster, and Parker Pillsbury as infidels whose antireligion preachments brought irreparable harm to the cause, and attacked black Garrisonians Charles L. Remond, William C. Nell, and Robert Purvis as "contemptible tools" and enemies of their race. In the fall while Stone was in the West, the *Anti-Slavery Standard* accused Douglass of succumbing to "worldly ambition" and attributed his changed temperament to the influence of Julia Griffiths, an Englishwoman who had come to the United States to assist with his paper. Garrison also blamed Griffiths and, giving credence to rumors that had circulated among abolitionists for two years, accused her of causing discord in the Douglass home as well. Although Garrison subsequently apologized for bringing up personal matters, Douglass was still smarting when Stone lectured in a hall that excluded blacks.[6]

James Mott counseled Stone to ignore the criticism, saying Douglass seemed intent on alienating all his friends. But she received a remonstrance she could not ignore. Lydia Mott, a friend and coworker from Albany, called Stone's appearance in Musical Fund Hall a "very great error" that would injure her influence if she did not acknowledge it forthrightly. Hurt by the lack of confidence from one so close, Stone sent a detailed account of how the incident had developed and the actions she had taken, and said that regardless of what others thought, she felt "fully justified" in all she had done.[7]

Douglass, however, continued to question Stone's integrity. A few years later, after she returned from a brief residence in Chicago, several papers published a letter purportedly from Senator Stephan A. Douglas declining her invitation to address a woman's rights convention there. Friends immediately recognized the letter as a "ridiculous forgery" and "transparent hoax." Aside from the certainty that Stone would not seek support from the politician responsible for the Kansas-Nebraska Act, the senator's signature was misspelled (two S's instead of one) and there was no such event to which he was allegedly invited. Frederick Douglass, however, never questioned the letter's authenticity and again accused Stone of sacrificing antislavery principles in a "feverish desire for prominence and popularity."[8]

Besides forcing her to cancel lyceum engagements at Auburn and Ogdensburg, Stone's illness prevented her attendance at a series of important events in Albany, the climax of a two-month petition campaign organized by Susan B. Anthony and William Henry Channing. Upon returning from the Cleveland convention, Anthony had consulted Channing about executing his petition proposal in New York. They called a state convention, which authorized a campaign, and Channing drew up petitions for suffrage and equal legal rights. An organizing committee hired lecturing agents to circulate the petitions, lined up legislators in both houses to introduce them, and asked Elizabeth Stanton to compose an appeal to accompany them to the legislature. As a grand finale, they scheduled a convention at the state capital, which would present the petitions to the legislature, and asked Stone and Wendell Phillips to speak at it.[9]

Hired to manage the campaign, Anthony also asked Stone to lecture in the state's larger cities and help roll up a long petition, for they did not want their legislators to use the same excuse Massachusetts had given—that all women would be denied their rights because only a small minority asked for them. Stone already had a full schedule when she received Anthony's request but agreed to circulate petitions at her New York engagements. Illness forced her to cancel those lectures, however, and once at home she realized she could not go to Albany, either.[10]

Stone followed proceedings of the Albany convention through newspaper reports and letters from Anthony. It opened on Tuesday, February 14, without its target audience, for in a move some suspected a deliberate "dodge" of the woman's rights forces, the legislature recessed to permit lawmakers to be in their home districts for meetings and elections on a canal question. A snowstorm prevented the return of enough legislators to make a quorum, so the petitions were not presented until the following Monday, after the convention was over and most attendees had gone home. The senate assigned the suffrage petitions to a select committee, which Channing and Ernestine Rose addressed the following week. Rose and Anthony appeared before a select committee of the assembly, to which the equal rights petitions were sent. But this committee dismissed the petitions saying that because men and women were not equal, inequalities in the law were inevitable.[11]

Anthony's letters also relayed some astonishing sentiments concerning the reform dress. When Anthony told Stone that Elizabeth Stanton was going to attend the Albany convention, she reported that Stanton had resumed the long dress. Suffering bitter criticism from her family, she had tried to please them by lengthening her skirts a few inches and leaving off the pants. But the compromise had not worked and, having decided that the convenience was not worth the persecution, she had given up the reform dress altogether. And just as she had urged Anthony to "come out" with her in the compromise dress, she now pleaded with her to resume the long skirt "for the sake of the Cause." Anthony found the pressure so straining that for the last ten days, she told Stone, "my heart has almost failed me, and but for my reliance on my own convictions of right and duty, [I] must have sat down disheartened and discouraged."[12]

Stone dismissed the idea that the reform dress hurt the woman's rights movement. "It is all fudge for anybody to pretend that any cause that deserves to live is impeded by the length of your skirt," she assured Anthony. "I know, from having tried through half the Union, that audiences listen, and assent, just as well to one who speaks truth in a short as in a long dress. Did you see any want of willingness on the part of the people to hear us at Syracuse, New York, or Cleveland? No, no, Susan, it is all a pretense that the cause will suffer." On the other hand, Stone acknowledged that the dress did produce a string of petty annoyances. She was often bothered during her travels by people who recognized her from her clothes and then monopolized her time and attention. She could avoid much of this if she dressed like others. Then, too, when she wanted to explore a new city, hordes of jeering boys followed her around, calling attention to her presence. And when she was a guest in others' homes, she felt the uneasiness the dress caused her hosts. Stone told Anthony about her stay with the Motts in Philadelphia, where her short skirt and trousers had caused the Mott daughters much embarrassment with callers. And disliking the attention the dress attracted in public, they refused to accompany her on the street. Stone told Anthony she was thinking of adding a long skirt to her wardrobe for occasional use, simply to save her friends embarrassment and herself a great deal of annoyance.[13]

Anthony received Stone's letter after bearing an entire day of stares and taunts, and it triggered a release of pent-up emotions. "If Lucy Stone, with all her reputation, her powers of eloquence, her loveliness of character, that wins all who once hear the sound of her voice, cannot bear the martyrdom of the dress, who, I ask, can?" She took Stone's letter to Stanton and Brown, who sent responses full of sympathy. Stanton empathized with what she thought Stone must suffer "among fashionable people," said she felt "a mental freedom" among her friends that she had not known during the previous two years, and urged Stone to "lay aside the shorts," too. "Not for the sake of the cause, nor for any sake but your own, take it off. We put the dress on for greater freedom, but what is physical freedom compared with mental bondage?" Stanton asked. Brown, who had never worn the dress, added her exhortation not to "suffer martyrdom over a short dress or anything else that can be prevented."[14]

Expressions such as *martyrdom* and *mental bondage* astonished Stone. "I am sure you are tired and all worn out," she wrote Anthony, "or you would not feel so intensely about the dress. I never shed a tear about it in my life, nor came within a thousand ages of martyrdom on account of it." Stone hastened to clarify that the Mott daughters had not wanted to accompany her in public only because of the "staring and impertinence of rude people . . . They felt kindly to me personally." As for "laying aside the shorts," she had no intention of doing so. To have to travel in rain and mud and snow in a long dress, she said, would be far greater inconvenience than a few unpleasant remarks, of which she usually took no notice. Far from the short dress being any kind of bondage, she believed it was the *long dress* that restricted women, for it hindered their engaging in business and industry that would make them financially independent. So surely those who realized this could put up with a little annoyance in order to set an example through which women could more easily work out their own emancipation. "With this feeling, added to my own greater comfort in the short dress," said Stone, "I have a strong aversion to change." She intended to make a long skirt simply to have the choice of wearing it on particular occasions. Before Anthony received this reply, however, she had let out her hems and was "dragging around" in the long dress and suffering the "humiliation" of defeat.[15]

Meanwhile Stone had recuperated and, still clad in short skirt and trousers, gone to Maine, stopping briefly in Providence to deliver a lyceum lecture and, to Paulina Davis, nearly two hundred *Una* subscriptions sold in the West. Stone spent three weeks in Maine. Her lectures at Bangor, held as a charity benefit, attracted the city's largest crowds of the season. Her lectures at Rockland, she was later told, inspired a young woman to take employment in her father's counting room and two others to seek jobs at the local printing office, where they were hired. A year earlier, said Stone's correspondent, most townspeople would have disapproved of women engaging in such work. Now they not only supported them, but also rallied a strong counter force to prevent the removal of a woman hired as Registrar of Deeds, whose critics charged it was unconstitutional for a woman to hold office.[16]

Stone was elated with the growing support for woman's rights. While she was in Maine, its senate passed a bill giving married women the right to their own earnings. Friends in Vermont, where she had previously lectured on slavery, asked her to come back and lecture on woman's rights, saying that although it would have been folly to attempt it earlier, now it would do much good. And in Connecticut, P. T. Barnum wanted her to lecture on woman's rights as a benefit for the new Methodist church at Bridgeport. The time was ripe for her plan to expand petitioning throughout the region. Stopping in Boston on her way home, she reserved a hall for Boston's anniversary week and, with the aid of Phillips, Higginson, and Paulina Gerry, sent out a call for a New England Woman's Rights Convention.[17]

Taking a few weeks off before embarking on another lecturing tour, Stone made herself a new dress that, according to papers in Cincinnati where she first wore it, sported a "long skirt" and disappointed all who expected to see her "*a la Bloomer.*" The dress was not at all in the fashionable "draggley" style, however. Like Stanton's compromise dress, Stone's skirt skimmed her high-topped shoes, still several inches above the ground, retaining the Bloomer's ease of movement while attracting less notice. Newspaper reports of Stone's new dress fueled a rumor, spreading among reform circles since her correspondence with Anthony, that she had abandoned the reform dress. "Oh dear, I wanted to cry!" Elizabeth Buffum Chace wrote to her after being persuaded it was true. Although Chace wore the short skirt around the house, she lacked courage to adopt it for general wear and had looked to Stone to establish the right of women to dress according to their own taste. Now she regretted that she and other women had left Stone to bear the burden of innovation alone.[18]

Although Stone had not abandoned the short dress and trousers, she wore the new above-the-ankle dress throughout much of her work in April. After speaking in Cincinnati at the Ladies' Anti-Slavery Society's convention, she spent three weeks lecturing on woman's rights in Ohio. While at Columbus, she received an urgent appeal for help with a crisis at nearby Mt. Vernon, where Amelia and Dexter Bloomer had relocated their newspaper operations. Amelia had hired a woman as compositor of the *Lily*, whom Dexter's printer had agreed to train, but his typesetters refused to work with her and extracted pledges from other local printers to unite against the female intrusion. Despite the Bloomers' promise that the woman would work only on the *Lily* and not infringe upon the men's jobs, the strikers remained resolute. So the Bloomers fired them, hired women as replacements, and brought a journeyman from Columbus to train them. Local papers published the strikers' grievances but none of the Bloomers' explanations, criticized the women typesetters for taking men's jobs, and denounced the "Woman's Rights humbug" for causing the conflict.[19]

The conflict in Mt. Vernon was not merely a question of male versus female employment, however. Although the decade of the 1850s was a time of prosperity for landowners and manufacturers, for northern tradesmen and craftsmen it was a period of widespread unemployment, job insecurity, and drastically reduced wages caused by a glut of immigrant labor. Tradesmen tried to protect their livelihoods by forming unions, but most strikes failed because the men were quickly replaced by workers willing to accept low pay. Immigrants were not the only competition. Women had eagerly replaced Pittsburgh printers who struck for higher wages just a few months before the Mt. Vernon strike, and in Boston, where female printers received two-thirds the pay of their male counterparts, two hundred worked in printing offices previously staffed by men. The right of workers to a living wage and their displacement by those willing to accept lower pay were as much issues in the Mt. Vernon conflict as was the question of women's employment rights, for although Amelia had promised her compositor pay equal to that of her coworkers after one year, Dexter's fellow publishers accused him of paying scab wages to undertrained women. Most townspeople sympathized with the men who had lost their jobs and blamed the Bloomers for the hardship forced on their families. Learning of Stone's presence in Columbus, Amelia Bloomer asked her to come and "vindicate the principle involved."[20]

On April 22, Stone lectured at the Mt. Vernon Congregational Church on "Woman and Her Employments." Presenting the Bloomers' side of the controversy and pleading for woman's right to labor in any field for which she was suited, she subdued the excitement and anger, alleviated ill feeling, and won support for the women workers. Her words, Amelia Bloomer told *Lily* readers, "were like soothing oil on the troubled waters." The controversy dissipated, and the *Lily*, printed by an all-female staff, grew in circulation from four to five thousand subscribers by the end of the year.[21]

A month after completing her Ohio tour, on June 2, Stone opened the first New England Woman's Rights Convention in Boston, which she had called to organize petitioning in the six New England states. After dispatching with preliminary matters at the morning session, however, she postponed further business until the evening, for that afternoon, after nine days of near-riotous excitement that included a failed rescue attempt, Boston was forced to surrender a fugitive slave to a ship that would carry him back to slavery in Virginia. Many convention-goers joined the angry throngs lining the streets as twelve hundred armed troops marched Anthony Burns from the courthouse to the wharf. That evening they listened in somber resolution as Stone read a letter from Higginson who, indicted for his role in the rescue attempt, could not show his face in Boston. Higginson said that although Negro slavery commanded immediate and urgent attention, the convention's work was essential because women's slavery was more firmly fixed in the social system and yet not readily acknowledged. Directed by Stone as chair of the business committee, the convention appointed standing committees to organize woman's rights work throughout New England.[22]

Wanting some degree of uniformity in the work in New York and New England, Susan Anthony asked Stone whether they should have separate petitions for suffrage and legal rights or "ask all in one." Stone and Phillips had used just one petition, but Channing thought the demand for equal property rights should not be burdened with the more controversial claim for woman suffrage. The difference of opinion remained, for New York proceeded with two petitions while Stone continued with one.[23]

Congratulating Stone on the success of the New England convention, Antoinette Brown observed that the "little Woman's Rights ball" continued to grow instead of "unraveling in long and tangled yarns" as critics predicted. "But don't you get tired of pushing it on?" she asked. Stone showed no signs of letting up, however. As she turned her attention to the fall National Woman's Rights Convention, she received a letter from Elizabeth Blackwell, who, emboldened by her brother's association with Stone, urged her to suspend the annual meetings. Blackwell said many women sympathized with the cause but considered the conventions a "theatre of vanity and petty ambitions," "mere discussions of abstract principles," and a "waste of time [that] injured the cause rather than benefitting it." She thought Stone's lectures did more to influence public opinion than all the woman's rights conventions ever held. Stone replied that the conventions could not be considered a "waste of time" if one noted their results, with which she was well satisfied. She pointed out the positive reception of the movement's ideas, the wide discussion in public newspapers, the encouraging action of several legislatures, the formation of societies in some states and standing committees in others, the rapidly widening sphere of women. All these, Stone said, gave the movement "as much 'body' as could have grown in so short a time." And although individual effort such as her own was essential to the movement, conventions made it easier and more effective by preparing the way and securing a hearing.[24]

Having reaffirmed her confidence in the effectiveness of conventions, Stone forged ahead with that year's preparations. At the request of James Mott, who was in charge of local arrangements, she had already decided basic details of time and place and cleared up confusion over who should issue the call. Now, as she recruited people to preside and write resolutions, she also tried to solve the problem of how to publish needed literature despite an empty treasury. The cost of printing the Cleveland *Proceedings* had exceeded the committee's meager funds, and she had paid the difference from her own purse. But with newspapers giving their meetings extensive and favorable coverage, these reports were in little demand. Believing their limited funds could be put to more effective use, Stone proposed that the committee pay for a fuller report in the *New York Tribune* and not publish one themselves. At the same time, she wanted a new supply of woman's rights tracts, which she had nearly depleted during her western travels. Raising the needed funds herself, she selected three articles from the first series and added Parker's sermon "The Public Function of Woman" and Higginson's "Woman and Her Wishes," the essay sent to the Massachusetts' Constitutional Convention in support of her suffrage campaign, and printed them together in a book titled *Woman's Rights Tracts,* which she had ready for distribution at the convention in October.[25]

The fifth National Woman's Rights Convention met in Philadelphia during the third week of October 1854. Presenting her new tracts to the assembly, Stone urged their circulation along with petitions as the most practical means of advancing the cause. And she proposed another type of literature as an effective addition to their arsenal—fictional stories depicting in personal terms the effect of injustices women suffered. Undoubtedly impressed by the success of Harriet Beecher Stowe's *Uncle Tom's Cabin,* she thought stories about woman's wrongs could have similar effect on public opinion and, urging the convention to solicit stories and award prizes for those it selected for publication, she pledged five hundred dollars toward a prize fund. The convention adopted the project and appointed a committee to judge submissions.[26]

Most of the convention's leading women stayed at the home of James and Lucretia Mott, which boasted all the latest conveniences, including gas lighting, the strangeness of which nearly dealt a costly blow to the movement's leadership. One night after several of the women had stayed up late talking over various issues and then retired to their rooms, Frances Gage frantically summoned Stone to come see "what ailed the gas." Unfamiliar with the new technology, Gage had blown out the flames without turning off the gas, and the air was rapidly becoming noxious. Stone quickly roused Martha Wright to help turn off lamps and open windows and doors, and then the three retired amid profuse apologies from the flustered Gage.[27]

Although several leading figures were not at the convention, Stone rejoiced that there were so many new faces no individual was missed. Thomas Wentworth Higginson filled Wendell Phillips's place writing resolutions and giving great speeches and counsel, while Susan B. Anthony rendered important service as a member of the finance committee. Nevertheless, Stone was still the movement's central figure. Calling her the "observed of all observers," a reporter for the *New York Tribune* said it was remarkable "to notice how the public mind instinctively fastens upon this little person as being, what she really is, the heart and soul of this crusade."[28]

"Heart and soul" was an apt description of what Stone was to the woman's rights movement. In the seven years since she gave her first lecture in her brother's pulpit, she had emerged as its most visible leader and primary spokesperson. But she was also its behind-the-scenes manager. It was she who carried out the work of the poorly functioning Central Committee, organized and managed the national conventions, and directed the allocation of funds, sometimes paying movement expenses out of her own pocket. It was she who set the movement's agenda, soliciting proposals from others and then through eloquent appeals urging their adoption. And it was she from whom workers in the various states sought advice and assistance.

By the fall of 1854, Stone's name was a "household word" across the land. Northern papers praised her courage and devotion to righteous causes, while those south of the Mason-Dixon line denounced her as "the most prominent advocate at the North of all those wild and depraved schemes which offend every sentiment of virtue and invite the just indignation of every Southerner." Even Canada knew her as the "chief-ess" of America's "valiant band of unsexed women." Admirers wrote poems celebrating her "majesty of mind" and "impulse true and pure," while detractors sang a parody of a popular song that expressed opposite sentiments:[29]

> I just come out before you
> To make a little moan;
> I'll put it in the Boston Post,
> And call it Lucy Stone.
>
>> So hold your tongue, Miss Lucy;
>> Don't talk so much, Miss Stone;
>> Your tongue is ever wagging;
>> Do let us men alone! . . .
>
> Oh would that she were married,
> And had a house to care.
> Will no one sacrifice himself
> To save us from despair?
>
>> A name like Curtius' shall be his
>> On fame's loud trumpet blown,
>> Who with a wedding kiss shuts up
>> The mouth of Lucy Stone!

In the fall of 1854, neither the public nor most of her friends realized how near to fulfillment was the wish to have Lucy Stone married.

Lucy Stone, early 1850s (Copyright National Portrait Gallery, Smithsonian Institution/ Art Resource, NY)

LUCY STONE

Is a native of West Brookfield, Mass.; graduated from Oberlin College, Ohio, in 1847, since which time she has devoted herself mainly to the cause of those considered by her the oppressed.

She recently gave two lectures in Metropolitan Hall, in this city, on the claims of women. In the first, she argued that, since man and woman have the same physical, mental and moral parts, and since whatever supplies these parts, is as expensive for woman as for man, there ought, of right, to be for her, equal facilities for obtaining their supply—she should be denied no industrial pursuits for which she has taste and capacity; instead of being confined to the needle, and the schoolroom, and receiving the meagre compensation which must always result, when any kinds of labor are over-stocked with workers, she should be admitted with printers, jewellers, daguerrean artists, designers, post-masters, ticket-masters at the railway stations, phrenologists, merchants, physicians, lawyers, ministers, sculptors and painters. In a word, the sphere of her activity should be bounded only by her capacity, for where God has conferred a power, there also is His certificate of the right to its use in harmony with the laws of benevolence. Whatever woman can do and do well, either by head or hand, she has a right to do.

Miss Stone also demanded equal educational facilities for woman;—that when she has been taxed to build and endow a college, and then asks to tread its halls with her brothers, she shall not have its door shut in her face, and to the injury the insult added, that she is man's inferior; nor, having obtained a scholastic education, should she be prevented from applying it in any direction she chooses.

Miss Stone's second lecture covered the political and legal disabilities of woman. She based her claim to the right to vote, and to be voted for, on the admitted self evident truth, that, "governments derive their just powers from the consent of the governed," and urged that, while drunkards, negroes and foreigners give their consent to the laws under which they live, the right to give that consent should not be denied to woman. She showed that the interests of woman have not been protected by men's legislation; that in every state, the "custody" of the wife is given to her husband, so that he is literally her *keeper*. In the greater part of the States, a wife loses all right to her personal property—her husband may use it, in the payment of his debts, *will it* away from her and her heirs forever, and she can't help herself; he may spend her hard earnings upon his mistresses, and give her children, without her consent or knowledge, to the worst enemy of their mother.

In view of these legal wrongs, said Miss Stone, wrongs which would never have existed had women been allowed to protect her own rights, and which plainly show us that one class cannot be trusted to legislate for another class, we demand, continued Miss Stone, and will continue to demand, that the grandest words our fathers ever uttered, the admitted self evident truths of the Declaration of Independence, shall become a practical fact. To *them* was given the announcement of the great idea, that the people are sovereigns. To us is entrusted the nobler mission of making their spoken word an *actual fact*, and *we will do it.*

Men of this day, continued the lecturer, surely would not be willing to hang up in Independence Hall a new declaration, which should say "Governments derive their just powers from the consent of all the governed, except women." "Taxation and representation are inseparable, except in the case of women." Yet such *is* the language of their acts—acts which wrong the mother, degrade the sister, and leave the daughter without the right to protect herself. It cannot be in the heart of manhood, when all the facts are before him, to persist in the wrong. We expect that the true and the noble of men will rally to our sides, as helpers, and that at a day not far distant, there will be neither political or legal distinctions based on sex.

Miss Lucy Stone is apparently youthful as well as good-looking, and was habited in a Bloomer costume of black silk and velvet. She is graceful in her manner, easy and appropriate in her gestures, fluent in her speech, chaste in her language, and altogether prepossessing as a public speaker. She interspersed a variety of singular facts, illustrative of her peculiar views, throughout her discourse, that added materially to its general interest, and for two hours enchained her audience in the deepest attention to her cogent arguments and felicitous conclusions.

cient usage practised of wa by the side of the grave. ments of mourning, but loss of their kindred by length.

The Mahommedan's hea

LUCY STONE.—FROM A DAGUERREOTYPE BY BRADY.

From *The Illustrated News*, No. 22, Vol. 1, p. 245, May 28, 1853 (Minnesota Historical Society)

The Constitutional Convention and Equal Political Rights.

FELLOW CITIZENS :—In May next, a Convention will assemble to revise the Constitution of the Commonwealth. At such a time, it is the right and duty of every one to point out whatever he deems erroneous and imperfect in that Instrument, and press its amendment on public attention. We deem the extension to woman of all civil rights, a measure of vital importance to the welfare and progress of the State. On every principle of natural justice, as well as by the nature of our Institutions, she is as fully entitled as man to vote, and to be eligible to office. In governments based on force, it might be pretended, with some plausibility, that woman, being supposed physically weaker than man, should be excluded from the State. But ours is a government professedly resting on the consent of the governed. Woman surely is as competent to give them consent as man.

Our Revolution claimed that *taxation* and *representation* should be coextensive. While, then, the property and labor of woman are subject to taxation, she is entitled to a voice in fixing the amount of taxes, and the use of them when collected.—While she is liable to be punished for crime, she is entitled to a voice in making the laws that regulate punishments.

It would be a disgrace to our Schools and civil Institutions, for any one to argue that a Massachusetts woman, who has enjoyed the full advantage of all their culture, is not as competent to form an opinion on civil matters, as the illiterate foreigner, landed but a few years before upon our shores, —unable to read or write,—by no means free from early prejudices, and little acquainted with our Institutions. Yet such men are allowed to vote.

Woman, as wife, mother, daughter, and owner of property, has important rights to be protected. The whole history of legislation, so unequal between the sexes, shews that she cannot safely trust these to the other sex. Neither her rights as mother, wife, daughter, or laborer, have ever received full legislative protection. Besides, our Institutions are not based on the idea of one class or sect receiving protection from another ; but on the well recognized rule, that each class or sect is entitled to such civil rights as will enable it to protect itself.

The exercise of civil rights is one of the best means of education. Interest in great questions, and the discussion of them under momentous responsibility, call forth all the faculties, and nerve them to their fullest strength.

The grant of these rights, on the part of society, would quickly lead to the enjoyment by woman of a share in the higher grades of professional employment. Indeed, without these, mere book study is often but a waste of time. The learning for which no use is found or anticipated, is too frequently forgotten almost as soon as acquired.

The influence of such a share on the moral condition of society is still more important. Crowded now into few employments, women starve each other by close competition; and too often vice borrows overwhelming power of temptation from poverty. Open to woman a great variety of employments, and her wages in each will rise ; the energy and enterprise of the more highly endowed will find full scope in honest effort, and the frightful vice of our cities will be stopped at its fountain head.

We hint, very briefly, at these matters. A circular like this will not allow room for more.

Some may think it too soon to expect any action from the Convention. Many facts lead us to think that public opinion is more advanced on this question than is generally supposed. Beside, there can be no time so proper to call public attention to a radical change in our civil polity as now, when the whole framework of our Government is to be subjected to examination and discussion. It is never too early to begin the discussion of any desired change. To urge our claim on the Convention, is to bring the question before the proper tribunal, and secure, at the same time, the immediate attention of the general public.

Massachusetts, though she has led the way in most other reforms, has in this fallen behind her rivals, consenting to learn, as to the protection of the property of married women, of many younger States. Let us redeem for her the old preeminence, and urge her to set a noble example in this, the most important of all civil reforms. To this end, we ask you to join with us in the accompanying petition to the Constitutional Convention.

ABBY KELLEY FOSTER,	ABBY H. PRICE,	HARRIET K. HUNT,
LUCY STONE,	JOHN PIERPONT,	ELIZABETH SMITH,
THOMAS W. HIGGINSON,	A. BRONSON ALCOTT,	ELIZA BARNEY,
ANN GREEN PHILLIPS,	ABBY MAY ALCOTT,	JOHN W. BROWNE,
WENDELL PHILLIPS,	JOSIAH F. FLAGG,	WILLIAM C. NELL,
THEODORE PARKER,	MARY FLAGG,	ROBERT MORRIS,
WILLIAM I. BOWDITCH,	THOMAS T. STONE,	SAMUEL MAY, Jr.,
SAMUEL E. SEWALL,	FRANCIS JACKSON,	ROBERT F WALLCUT,
ELLIS GRAY LORING,	WM. LLOYD GARRISON,	CHARLES K. WHIPPLE,
	ANNA Q. T. PARSONS.	

TO THE CONVENTION ASSEMBLED TO REVISE THE CONSTITUTION OF THE COMMONWEALTH :

The undersigned, citizens of Massachusetts, respectfully ask that you will report an amendment to the Constitution, striking out the word ' MALE' wherever it occurs in that instrument.

Appeal and petition sent to the Massachusetts Constitutional Convention of 1853 (Library of Congress, Manuscript Division, Blackwell Family Papers)

"Representative Women." Lucretia Mott, center, and clockwise from top, Harriet Beecher Stowe, Abby Kelley Foster, Lucy Stone, Lydia Maria Child, Antoinette Brown Blackwell, and Maria Weston Chapman. Lithography by L. Grozelier, 1857 (Massachusetts Historical Society)

"Heralds of Freedom, Truth, Love, Justice." William Lloyd Garrison, center, and clock-wise from top, Ralph Waldo Emerson, Wendell Phillips, Joshua R. Giddings, Theodore Parker, Gerrit Smith, and Samuel Joseph May. Lithograph by L. Grozelier, 1857 (Massachusetts Historical Society)

Henry B. Blackwell as a young man (Library of Congress, Manuscript Division, Blackwell Family Papers)

Lucy Stone and daughter, December 1857 (Library of Congress, Manuscript Division, Blackwell Family Papers)

Susan B. Anthony, ca. 1850 (Special Collections, Vassar College Libraries)

Thomas Wentworth Higginson, 1857 (Mary Thacher Higginson, *Thomas Wentworth Higginson: The Story of His Life*. Boston: Houghton Mifflin, 1914, facing p. 180)

Lucy Stone, ca. 1866 (Library of Congress, Manuscript Division, Blackwell Family Papers)

Henry Blackwell, ca. 1866 (The Schlesinger Library, Radcliffe Institute, Harvard University)

Part Three
Testing a Wife's Autonomy

Romance and Politics

Henry Blackwell was a reluctant businessman. Although raised in the liberal tradition of aspiring to a life of personal development and dedication to human progress, necessity had placed him in what he considered "the paltry avocations of business."[1] He was only thirteen when his father died, and although his mother and older sisters decided he should become a lawyer and sent him off to college, financial difficulties forced him to return home and take a job at a flour mill at age sixteen. Five years later, hoping to set the family on surer financial footing, he went to New York City to learn sugar refining and then tried to establish a refinery in Cincinnati. The enterprise failed, he returned to New York seeking some other route to financial independence, and when gold fever gripped the country in 1849, he announced his intention of going to California. His alarmed mother dispatched a visiting English cousin to dissuade him, and when Henry insisted he must do something to secure the family's financial security, Kenyon Blackwell persuaded him to accept a $5,000 loan and join his brother Sam in buying into a wholesale hardware business.

At age twenty-four, Henry became the traveling partner of Coombs, Ryland, and Blackwells, twice a year making two-month-long horseback journeys through Ohio, Indiana, and Illinois, selling hardware to country merchants and collecting payments due the firm. Although he now possessed the means of getting ahead, he still had nothing but disdain for business. "Surely the day will come when the mere acquisition of the means of living will be only incidental to life itself," he wrote during one of his journeys. He longed for the day when he would have enough wealth to devote his life to nobler aims.[2]

Although precariously close to poverty during their early years in Ohio, the Blackwell family possessed the cultural values of the English middle class. All of the siblings subscribed to a philosophy of personal improvement and altruism, and all had passionate interests and varying abilities in art, music, literature, and languages. The sisters taught music and art, and Anna, in addition to being an exceptional pianist and vocalist, translated the George Sand novel

Jacques into English. Although necessity channeled the brothers into business, they helped organize the Cincinnati Young Men's Literary Society where they read, wrote, and discussed literature. Possessing a special passion for literature, Henry spent his spare time writing poetry and always carried several books with him to make every spare moment "useful" and "self-improving."

By the time he was twenty-eight, Henry felt stifled by his occupation. "I am approaching the meridian of physical life with the bitter consciousness of neglected opportunities and undeveloped powers, blighted possibilities," he wrote to a family friend in April 1853. "I am full sufficiently conscious of my faults to feel self-contempt, of my capabilities to feel restless." Resolved to grapple with his "false position," he went east to seek a publisher for his poetry, which he considered his only worthy accomplishment, and to widen his circle of acquaintances and form, if he could, "a few elevating friendships."[3]

It was during this trip that Blackwell was mesmerized by Stone and her "fugitive mother" speech; followed her to Massachusetts, where he tried to attract her attention by speaking at the New England Anti-Slavery Convention and jealously watched Charles Burleigh hover over her at the Constitutional Convention hearing; consulted Garrison about rival suitors; and then boldly showed up at her door.[4] But it would take eighteen months of persistent wooing to overcome Stone's deep-seated revulsion against placing herself in the legal position of a wife.

Blackwell conducted the first months of his suit by correspondence. Because Stone had not rejected him personally, but rejected marriage because she believed no one should form a connection that required the sacrifice of one's "highest aims," he determined to convince her that marriage need involve "no sacrifice of individuality, but its perfection; no limitation of the career of one or both, but its extension." Like Stone, he believed in the philosophy of a "true love" marriage—that mystic and divine union of two souls that ennobles the character and secures the greatest happiness and usefulness of each. Like Stone, he believed that most marriages were corruptions of the ideal, and that laws and customs treated women unjustly. But he believed the parties to a marriage determined its nature. "Marriage is as imperfect as the people themselves—no more," he said. He agreed it would be wrong to form a union that kept either partner from attaining his or her highest aims and said he had no intention of luring Stone into such a union. He would not want her to become a "drudge" like Mrs. Weld or homebound like Mrs. Stanton. What he wanted was a relationship that would enable both parties to "study more, think more, talk more, and work more than they could alone."[5]

Blackwell argued that the love between man and woman was "a want of our nature," necessary to the highest development of the soul, and that marriage, therefore, was "a duty of our very organization," necessary for a "symmetrical" life that was "true to all our faculties." And, because human beings were capable of ordering the circumstances of their lives to balance noble pursuits with the responsibilities of domestic life, he saw no reason why Stone should deny herself those essential relations. Stone agreed with Blackwell's philosophy of love and marriage but was resigned to living a single life regardless of the loss she might suffer to her personal development. "The objects I seek to accomplish will not be attained until long after my body has gone to ashes. While so few can or are willing to give themselves wholly to the work the world so imperatively needs, all the more necessary it is that those who can do so should not falter," she said.[6]

Blackwell appreciated Stone's willingness to sacrifice the lower for the higher but thought she ranked "the sacred law of affections" too low. Besides, her circumstances might change: her voice might fail, or she might determine that she could influence more people by writing than by speaking. She could not always "lecture five times a week, ten months in the year. . . . Such excessive and continuous labor of one kind will give place to a more varied and different sphere of duty." Her present occupation, he said, was but one chapter in her "book of life," and like all chapters must come to an end and give way to another. But no matter what argument he used, he could not dent Stone's certainty that she should not marry. Her chosen life had privations and isolation, she said, but these she had learned to endure and did not regret, while the certainty that she was living a useful life brought "a deep and abiding happiness."[7]

Besides trying to convince Stone that she should marry—if not him, "then a better person"—Blackwell tried to establish whether they were suited for each other. He openly revealed his aspirations and dreams as well as his self-perceived faults and deficiencies, saying he hoped to be ennobled by Stone's friendship. He confessed that he envied her position as a lecturer engaged in advocacy of great although unpopular ideas. He found the very isolation that resulted from her unpopular opinions, occupation, and dress "strangely attractive," for he himself was such a "social being, loving too well the high regard of others," that he loved all the more Stone's devotion to truth regardless of cost. Although he did not consider it a "selfish love of money" to "choose not to be poor and dependent," still he felt guilty for pursuing material gain instead of working for the good of humanity, and he questioned the validity of his excuse—that he must wait until he acquired the requisite wisdom and independence. Seeing the complexity of the slavery issue and being uncertain of the answer, he did not feel ready to try to influence others. When he was ready, he must be free to speak according to his conscience, and this freedom required command of one's own time and action—"pecuniary independence." He hoped to fill his obligations to family and business partners and earn such an independence within three years. Was he not right, he asked, to continue three years as he was despite his preferences?[8]

"Questions of duty should always be settled by one's own convictions," Stone replied. Although she agreed that financial independence was desirable, she considered moral independence more important. As for waiting for wisdom, she suggested he consider the advice Wendell Phillips gave at the first woman's rights convention: Because it is impossible to foresee the ultimate consequences of any great social change, individuals faced with a decision concerning it should ask themselves "if there be any element of right and wrong in the question, any principle of clear natural justice that turns the scale. If so, take your part with the perfect and abstract right, and trust God to see that it shall prove expedient."[9]

Blackwell was charming; he was serious, open and frank, and witty and playful, and he had a delightful sense of humor that leapt from his letters. But he seemed to lack the moral independence Stone valued, the willingness to act according to one's conscience regardless of what others thought. Blackwell's uncertainty concerning his role in antislavery agitation reflected a different orientation from Stone's. He believed in resolving the slavery question through political action, using elections and legislation to achieve desired ends. Stone believed in using moral suasion, creating personal conviction and public sentiment that would not tolerate slavery. "The politician, as the creature of the public sentiment, never goes ahead of it, because he depends on it," she said. "He who creates and controls that public sentiment is much greater than a politician, as the creator is greater than the thing created. To make the public sentiment on the side of all that is just and true and noble is the highest use of life."[10]

As a politician, Blackwell was wary of causing offense. He agreed with Garrisonian principles but saw among his southern contacts that Garrisonian methods did as much harm as good, for stern denunciations embittered rather than softened the prejudices of people born and raised amid slavery. It was the same with the woman's rights movement, Blackwell said; to produce conviction, reformers should avoid unnecessarily rousing prejudices. Stone disagreed. It was the reformer's task, she said, to create a "thorough discontent" with existing wrong, and one way to do this was by calling "every crime and every criminal by the right name." It was inevitable, she said, that those who create this discontent should be hated and scorned. They would be considered "too severe and denunciatory while the contest is waging, but posterity will marvel that the censures fell so far behind the dreadful reality."[11]

In the fall of 1853 when Stone began her next season's labor after three months of correspondence with Blackwell, she was no more receptive to his suit than she had been in June. In her speech at the New York Woman's Rights Convention she declared: "I have said to the men, instead of asking woman to marry, go first and strike off the statute books those barbarous enactments, then come back and ask women to be your wives; and if all women were of my mind, they would make you wait until you had done so." And two weeks later, when she received a request from Blackwell to be allowed to meet her at Niagara for a "good talk," she replied that although she would not let a friend's sex debar her of his companionship, she thought he knew her well enough "to put the right construction" on her consent to meet him. "But believe me, Mr. Blackwell, . . . I have not the remotest desire of assuming any other relations than those I now sustain. I would incur my own heavy censure if by fault of mine you did not understand this."[12]

With his summer business journey over, Blackwell shifted his suit from discussing the abstract nature of marriage to demonstrating how helpful he could be to Stone's work. After meeting her at Niagara, he accompanied her to Cleveland, where he served as a secretary of the woman's rights convention and gave his first woman's rights speech. Then in Cincinnati, before Stone moved to the Blackwell home, he met her every evening after her lectures, and as they rode together in a buggy he outlined his ideas for her western lecture tour. He wrote to his sister Elizabeth about the resolve of his new acquaintance to remain single and showed Lucy her response. Although they had never met, Elizabeth said she had a real respect for Stone and at an earlier stage in her life would have agreed about the nobility of sacrificing love for higher aims. But she had learned it was futile to deny any "essential part of human nature." The love between a man and woman, she said, was a "central truth of life," and the mystic union that existed in a true marriage was a "constant inspiration" and "exhaustless source of blissful strength" to "efforts for humanity or self-progress." So Elizabeth thought it a "painful mistake" for Stone to deliberately shut her soul against "this God-given source of growth." Stone found Elizabeth's description of the benefits of marriage so beautiful she copied it before returning the letter to Henry. But it did not pierce her resolve. At the bottom of her copy, which she sent to her sister for safekeeping, Stone wrote that she was still convinced her road in life would be a solitary one.[13]

During the next two months, Blackwell made the arrangements for Stone's lectures, writing business acquaintances in Ohio and Indiana to engage halls and place newspaper notice, and printing and mailing broadsides to be posted. He supplied her with law books needed to adapt her lectures to Ohio and Indiana audiences, and other books to read while traveling, for her personal "improvement." In every way he tried to demonstrate his usefulness and to make himself worthy of her friendship and affection. They corresponded almost daily, with Lucy now addressing him as "Harry" rather than "Mr. Blackwell."[14]

When they met at Chicago in December, Stone was exhilarated by the tremendous success of her tour and filled with gratitude and genuine affection toward Blackwell for having made it possible. Their rendezvous was an intense and intimate one, during which she gave him her picture and some "manifestation" of affection—perhaps a kiss? After he left and her lectures were over, she spent an entire day alone in her hotel room thinking seriously of their relationship, of the "possible and impossible."

But a note from Blackwell broke the spell, and she replied, "I am glad that your visit here gave you so much happiness. It was good for me too. I have only this regret in regard to it: that the manifestation of the affection which I really feel for you lures you to hopes which can never be realized." Although she did love him, more than her dearest friends, still, she explained, that love did not approach what she believed was required for a marriage relation. "You are very dear to me Harry. For weeks you have been surrounding me with kindnesses. With more than brotherly solicitude you have planned for my usefulness, happiness and success. How can I help [but] love the hand that blesses me? You have shown me noble and generous traits of character, and I both admire and love them." Nevertheless, she said, she valued his happiness too much to attach to him a life she was convinced did not belong to him. "Harry, human love is a treasure which ever enriches him who gives and him who receives it; hence, I have been glad that I could love you and be loved by you, and have reverently accepted it knowing that we should both be happier and better for it. Wedded love is a pearl of still greater price. I hope we may both be able to find it, but do not let us mock ourselves by even a *good* counterfeit. If there were real affinity between us—the elements by which a true marriage could be made—I do not think that I should so instinctively recoil from the thought of it. But Harry, we are capable of being friends, and in this relation it will always be a joy to me to be able to add sunshine to your lot."[15]

What a blow this letter must have been to Blackwell, coming after the breakthrough intimacy of the visit. After seven months of passionate wooing, Lucy was still insistent that their relationship be nothing more than friendship. And yet her letter indicated two significant changes. She acknowledged that she loved him, and she not only said she had considered the possibility of marriage with him but she also hoped *each of them* would find wedded love.

Blackwell wrote a long reply, restating her objections as he understood them, and said she could continue living her life only for others, but sooner or later she would learn that individuals have a duty to themselves as well. He believed human beings were created "as positive *ends* as well as means. We have a right to be happy in and for ourselves. If not, what a stupid thing to try to make *other people* happy." If she did not love him enough to marry him, then, he said, "Wait till you do. . . . You cannot love by your simple will any more than you can see. But you can let yourself love or prevent yourself from loving, just as you can open or shut your eyes. Dear Lucy, love me if you can. I will endeavor to give you no cause to regret having done so."[16]

Lucy said that even if her affection for him deepened, still she would not marry, for her very being recoiled at the idea of placing herself in the position of a "legal wife." Would *he* marry, she asked, if law placed husbands in the same position it placed wives? Yes! he answered. "If the marriage were harmonious, the laws would not exist as far as we were concerned, because the provisions only apply where appeal is made to them." But because the law did indeed meet out injustice when an unhappy marriage appealed to it, he would take certain precautions to protect his interests. He would require from her a prenuptial promise not to avail herself of laws giving her control of more than half his earnings. And he would put all his present property in a trusteeship beyond her control. If the marriage proved discordant and she should lock him up, he would let himself out by habeas corpus and sue her for assault and battery. He would take at least half of their children and put her to the trouble and expense of a law suit to get them back. "In short," he said, "I should be my own master." Observing that her perception of marriage was "warped by the unfortunate impressions" of her childhood, he suggested that she exaggerated "the scope and force of external laws at the expense of internal power." For although most marriages were far from ideal, still he believed marriage could provide the most beautiful and desirable relationship possible, and denying oneself that relationship because laws regarding it were unjust was to "subject oneself to a more abject slavery than ever actually existed."[17]

Stone wanted to believe that women could marry without sacrificing independence. Her aversion to marriage sprang from her great repugnance to the idea of surrendering her autonomy, of being forced to accept the debilitating dependence and loss of individual rights that she had witnessed in her mother, Aunt Sally, Lucy Lamberton, and the countless other women whose plights she had heard of during her travels. But deep within her still burned the longings she had confided to Antoinette Brown five years earlier for the "intimate companionship and gentle loving influences" of a "true love marriage." Although she had accustomed herself to the idea of living alone rather than become the "mere thing" that law made all married women, still her heart ached "to love somebody that shall be all its own." Henry Blackwell's love rekindled those longings. Lucy's sister advised that if she loved Henry she ought not to refuse him. But whenever Lucy entertained the hope that marriage might be possible for her, the old objections reasserted themselves and snuffed it out.[18]

Blackwell understood the conflicting sentiments tearing at Stone's mind and was willing to wait until she was certain, confident that at last she would be. "A woman runs a terrible risk in marrying unless she knows intimately and esteems fully the character of her love," he wrote to Sarah Lawrence after spending time with Lucy in Cincinnati in April 1854. "We are in many respects different, and I never try to conceal those differences from her. I want her to understand me as I understand her. . . . However, I am most happy in knowing that Lucy does love me, and would love me much more if her judgment and will were not so much on the other side. She warns me not to hope, but she might as well warn me not to breathe."[19]

For Lucy, her weeks in Ohio after that rendezvous were a time of great indecision and wavering. In one letter, she asked Henry to come east in May so they could talk more fully, then in the next said she thought it would be best if he did not. Still, if he did come, he would have a glad greeting and get the lock of hair he requested. Another letter discouraged him from wasting money on a trip when he would not like the result. For however much she loved him, she wrote, "the horror of being a legal wife, and the suffocating sense of the want of that absolute freedom which I now possess, together with the revulsions of feeling which continually recur, and the want of certainty that we are adapted," would never let her be a wife.

Now Harry, I have been all my life alone. I have planned and executed, without counsel and without control. I have shared thought and feeling and life with myself alone. I have made a path for my feet which I know is very useful; it brings me more intense and abundant happiness by far than comes to the life of the majority of men. . . . I have lived alone, happily and well, and can still do it. . . . My life has never seemed to me a baffled one, only in hours that now and then come when my love-life is consciously unshared. But such hours are only as the drop to the ocean. The great whole of my life is richly blessed. Let it remain so.[20]

She did want to see him again for one more frank talk and wished there was a way they could get together without scandal before she left Ohio, but there was not. So she left it up to him whether to come east or not.

"One or two things I want you in the outset to understand," Blackwell wrote to Stone before joining her at her sister's home in Gardner. "I do not want you to fetter yourself one particle for my sake. I do not want you to forego one sentiment of independence, nor one attribute of personality. I want only to help you, as best I can, in achieving a really noble and symmetrical life. I want you also to help me to do the same. We can help each other, I am sure, not merely as friends, nor as lovers, but as husband and wife. . . . I do not want that we should endorse the present unjust laws, but by making our public and outside contract, enter a practical and efficient protest against them."[21]

For two days they talked over the possibility of their marriage. When they parted, Blackwell was more confident than ever they would marry, but Stone was not. The summer of 1854 was an agonizing one for her. A battle raged between her emotions, which drew her toward Henry and marriage, and her rationality, which required a feeling of absolute certainty before she could make a decision of such consequence. The "old paining hesitation" would not go away, and it seemed to her that "some inherent want of affinity" must be the basis for it. At one point she wrote: "Believe me dear Harry, we do not belong together as husband and wife. If we did, I should not so often feel my spirit protesting against it." But on the other hand, she had come to realize that marriage to the right person would not necessarily preclude her public work, and she did want to be married. "Do you suppose, dear Harry, that now when I believe I have a *right* to the marriage relation, after having spent half my days in the barren desert of an unshared life, that I would voluntarily shut myself up to its utter loneliness still longer if I knew any true door to escape? O no!"[22]

Finally accepting that she "had a right to be a wife," with Henry so persistently and lovingly seeking her to be his, and conscious of her own very real and growing affection for him, Lucy was determined to discover what their "natural and true relations" were. And so she asked for another meeting at which one more "candid, honest conversation" might lead to a "permanent understanding." When Henry said he could not come east again until January, she replied, "I *must* see you. . . . If there *can* be a *true* marriage between us, it is as much for *my* happiness and interest to assume it as for yours. And if there cannot be, it will be *your* gain not less than mine to avoid it." If full assurance of their affinity came to her, she would accept it as the "best blessing" of her life.[23] And so as Stone began scheduling her work for the fall, she sought a time and place where they could meet.

Meanwhile, the nation experienced a turbulent summer, too. On May 30, three days before Anthony Burns was returned to slavery, President Franklin Pierce signed into law an act opening for settlement the Indian territory west of Missouri, removing the ban against slavery north of the 36°31' line that had been part of the Missouri Compromise of 1820, and leaving the question of slavery in the new territories of Kansas and Nebraska to be decided by their inhabitants. Proposal of the bill—which would repeal the settlement of a divisive question that had been painfully worked out by legislators and just as painfully accepted by the nation's populace—had triggered massive protest meetings and a flood of opposition petitions. So across the North, on the day of Burns's rendition, stores closed, doors and windows were draped in black, and church bells tolled while indignation meetings hanged effigies of President Pierce and Senator Stephen A. Douglas, author of the Kansas-Nebraska Act. In June, Massachusetts citizens petitioned Congress for repeal of the Fugitive Slave Law and the state legislature incorporated an Emigrant Aid Society to recruit and assist settlers to the new territories who would vote to keep them free.[24] During the next several months, scores of cities, states, and private efforts organized emigrant aid societies, and hundreds of northerners began moving to Kansas and Nebraska.

Passage of the Kansas-Nebraska Act created unprecedented sympathy for the Free Soil movement, which attracted northern Whigs, antislavery Democrats, and members of the American Party, dubbed the Know Nothings, into a new anti-Southern political alliance that would become the Republican Party. Garrisonians stood firm against the swelling tide of sympathy with a movement that pledged not to interfere with slavery in the South and put economic factors above moral issues. They continued to denounce the Free Soil position and to call for "No Union with Slaveholders." At a Fourth of July celebration at Framingham, Stone joined other abolitionists renewing their assertion that the only way the free states could keep from being forced to serve slave interests was to secede. The issues of disunion and political antislavery action were ones on which Stone and Blackwell disagreed. Blackwell was a member of the Free Soil Party and had defended its position at abolition conventions in New York and Boston. Although Stone respected his conviction and praised him for defending his views, she hoped he would come to see that defending a "Union cemented by wrong," as he agreed it was, created a "moral cancer" that ate away at the nation's vitality.[25]

In response to Blackwell's expectation of being ennobled by her influence, Stone had urged him to cultivate a "love of and trust in the Truth, *without regard to consequences*," and following her advice not to await financial independence before taking unpopular action, he had helped organize an anti-

Nebraska meeting in Cincinnati in the spring and was preparing to lecture on antislavery that fall.[26] Then at the end of summer, his participation in a slave rescue seemed to indicate he was at last willing to "[l]et justice be done though the heavens fall."

On August 28, 1854, the Western Anti-Slavery Convention in Salem, Ohio, received a telegram that a young slave girl, traveling with a couple to whom she had been given as a nursemaid, was aboard a train that would pass through Salem en route to Memphis that afternoon. This presented opportunity for implementing Ohio's recently enacted Personal Liberty Law, which held that, because slavery was a matter of state authority, Ohio considered free any slave voluntarily brought into the state. The convention appointed a delegation of four men to board the train, locate the girl, and ask her if she wanted her freedom. Henry Blackwell was one of the four.

It so happened that Blackwell was the first to come upon the party. He asked the eight-year-old girl if she wanted her freedom, lifted her from her seat, and passed her to others who hustled her off the train to an awaiting carriage. News of the event was immediately telegraphed across the country. In the South, initial reports described the rescuer as a huge black man who tore the girl away from her mistress, struck the woman and knocked her baby to the floor, and carried the crying slave girl off the train under his arm while flourishing a revolver in the other hand. But several Cincinnatians aboard the train recognized Blackwell and fingered him as the culprit. A protest meeting in Memphis offered a $10,000 reward for his capture, and for months Kentuckians came into the hardware store to stare at him so they could recognize him if he ever appeared on their side of the river. Southern sympathizers threatened to destroy his business by circulating accounts of the "kidnapping" in Illinois and Indiana. The girl's master threatened to sue him for assault but dropped the charges when witnesses corroborated Blackwell's version of the incident. As to the little girl, she was named Abby Kelley Salem, placed in a foster home and enrolled in school, and within weeks was reported to be happily adjusted to her new home.[27]

"What a change in her destiny!" Stone wrote after reading of the girl's rescue but before learning of Blackwell's role in it. "I would rather have been a helper in her rescue . . . than to be president of any slaveholding confederacy." When Blackwell wrote about the threats he was receiving, Stone reassured him that even if his enemies succeeded in injuring his business, he would be richer in self-respect. "The only safe wealth, after all, is that which 'does not perish in the using.'"[28]

Satisfied with his action, Blackwell was not at first disturbed by the persecution. But he soon had second thoughts and regretted his "indiscretion." The change of heart disappointed Stone. When he first wrote to her of his role in the rescue, she thought he had "deliberately made up his mind to abide by his highest convictions" and she had felt closer to him than ever before. Had he been her husband, she said, "I would have gathered you to my heart of hearts, with more lovefull trust and tenderness than ever, sure that such high heroism and great fidelity to yourself might be trusted to the utmost." But now she found in him that which she had feared—the inability "to sacrifice all that must be sacrificed, and to accept the consequences of the carrying out of his real ideas at whatever cost." This one "really most serious defect" in Blackwell's character was difficult for her to accept, and she advised him to pay more attention to it than to the "lack of self-control" he now thought he had exhibited. She had wanted to see this trait in him so much she had gladly accepted his role in the rescue as exhibiting it, and now that she learned otherwise she felt it as a loss. Nevertheless, she said, "the deep, intense, constant yearning which I feel that you should be sound in this vital part shows me how very dear you are to me."[29]

Blackwell's involvement in the rescue did nothing to alter Stone's ambivalence toward him. On one hand, both her feelings toward him and her desire to marry were growing stronger. "You do not desire true relations for yourself and me, Harry, more earnestly than I do," she wrote him. "You can scarcely tell me anything I do not know about the unfitness of a single life. I have tried it longer than you. I know how every joy in life may be intensified by being shared, and every pain made less." On the other hand, she was not convinced that she and Henry had the requisite "affinity" for a true marriage. Perhaps he would find greater happiness with a woman who shared his personal ambition. But, she said, "I should be gladder than I can express if *we could* be everything to each other . . . I love you, love your interests, love your *possibilities* and should dearly love in any way to aid you and to be aided by you— whatever our relation may be."[30]

So she still wanted to meet for a long talk. "I want to see you. I want this suspense which haunts me, sleeping and waking, over." Letters flew between Cincinnati and wherever Stone was lecturing, as the couple tried to determine where and when to meet. Although rumors about their romance had been circulating for months, Stone was careful not to lend them credence. She wanted their rendezvous somewhere where they would not be noticed and planned to wear her long dress so as not to be recognized. And if a sudden change in plans was necessary, she would telegraph him over an alias.[31]

They met in Pittsburgh at the end of October and spent three days talking. Again they discussed their "natural defects," because if these could weaken their love for each other, "it should be now rather than hereafter." Lucy admitted as a very real defect her "limited literary culture," although she believed it was due only to the lack of opportunity. She did not think the "essential elements" of her being were wanting, for "with no external helps and everything to contend against" she had yet wrought out for herself "a far better life than thousands who have every facility." Henry thought Lucy overestimated her defects, and in response to her serious recitation of imperfections, he jestingly added that he wished she could sing like Jenny Lind, possessed perfect grace and beauty, and was ten years younger. Lucy replied that in all but the last she expected somewhere in the ages to find herself greatly improved. Their age difference—Stone was seven years older than Blackwell—was perhaps their "greatest actual barrier," Lucy explained. Because excessive work and grief had given her a "premature womanhood," she expected also "premature physical decay." In addition, she reminded Henry, "a man is younger than a woman of the same age." They discussed Henry's deficiencies and whether Lucy could "trust in the nobler purposes and upward tendencies" of his soul. And they talked about how they might shape their life together. Agreeing that they wanted "simple habits and a quiet mode of life," they would have a little farm where they could produce their few wants themselves. Henry and Sam were trying to sell their shares in the hardware firm, after which the Blackwell family wanted to move east and Henry to take time to decide what to do next—whether to reenter business or seek a new direction.[32]

Despite Stone's hope that they might reach a "permanent understanding," when they parted she was still undecided. After lecturing several more weeks in Pennsylvania and New Hampshire, she went to Gardner and stayed with Sarah, who was awaiting the birth of a baby before joining her husband in a little town near Cincinnati where he had taken a teaching position. Sarah had been Lucy's confidant throughout the courtship, and now the two sisters talked over Lucy's conflicting desires and fears. The idea of becoming a "legal wife" still pained her, and she had apprehensions about becoming a mother. Besides her age—she was now thirty-six years old—Lucy worried about some "hereditary tendency" that might produce "defective" babies. Although Lucy nursed Sarah through a stillbirth, their talks calmed her fears. Believing that the love she and Henry shared already united them, she accepted her own oft-given advice to act on what she believed right and trust it to prove expedient. She wrote Henry a short note agreeing to marry him.

As Stone resumed lecturing in December, she began buying silverware, blankets and sheets, and little things for their future home. When she won a footstool at the Christmas antislavery bazaar in Boston, she took it as a happy omen. The preceding week she had told Antoinette Brown and a few others of her engagement, and the news had spread so fast that when her name was announced as raffle winner, the entire hall rang with cheers.[33]

That evening, friends came to her room to offer happy commendations of Henry Blackwell and blessings for their marriage. After everyone had gone, though, a little sadness mingled with her thoughts of the future, for she knew that, despite their intentions to the contrary, marriage could not help but curtail her work. Martha Wright could opine upon hearing the news of Stone's engagement, "Dear little soul, how glad I am for her to have the prospect of being 'no more,' as she expresses it, after having been *so much*, so long. The nursery and the cradle and the 'blank oblivion' of Matrimony must seem delightful after the journeyings, the lecturings and the continued excitements of conventions." But the constraints of "nursery and cradle" held no such attraction for Stone, and she confided to Antoinette Brown that although she wanted a baby right away, she hoped to have twins, for she wanted "about four children and would like to dispatch matters so as to gain time."[34]

Although Stone jested about becoming "no more," she worried about the prospect. Writing to James and Lucretia Mott that they need not keep her secret any longer, she told them she hoped marriage would make both her and her future husband more productive but added, "the future is all unknown." And relating the lingering fear to Blackwell, she said, "My heart turns trustingly to you, dear Harry, to help make my future still more useful."[35]

Forging a True Marriage

During the months of personal deliberation at the end of 1854, Lucy Stone maintained her usual public schedule, lecturing in Vermont, Delaware, Pennsylvania, and New Hampshire. After attending Sarah at Gardner, she worked in Massachusetts and Maine before accompanying her sister and four-year-old niece to Cincinnati in January. Then she spent February lecturing in Michigan and half of March in Ontario. Intense headache cut her work short, however. After an engagement in Syracuse she spent four days in bed at the Albany home of Lydia Mott and then, still ill, she went home to West Brookfield.[1]

While Stone was on the road lecturing, Blackwell was traveling, too. So it was through correspondence that they tried to arrange not only their wedding date and place, but also the terms of a marriage contract, the prenuptial agreement Blackwell had earlier suggested to protect her property and earnings. Blackwell thought a true marriage should be like a business partnership in monetary matters, the husband and wife being "joint proprietors of everything except the results of previous labors." He advised Stone to secure all her money in the hands of a trustee for her benefit. While married and living together they would share earnings, but if they should separate, they would relinquish claim to the other's subsequent earnings. In case of death, either party could will his or her property to whomever he desired, unless there were children.[2]

Early in their discussions Stone had said she would not be supported. She believed wives should retain their financial independence, and if marriage was to be a truly equal partnership, they should also be responsible for their own support. Blackwell objected. "Even among birds it is the office of the male to bring food and assistance to the female while she is rearing the family," he insisted. To expect wives to support themselves while caring for children would be a "monstrous injustice . . . far worse than the present imperfect system." He thought the only equitable provision was appropriating all earnings to family expenses, with the surplus divided and credited to each partner.[3]

Although he had not yet achieved the financial independence he wanted,

Blackwell anticipated no problem in supporting a family. Besides drawing a comfortable income from the hardware firm, he had acquired new assets that promised considerable future income. In December 1853 he had become the agent of a group of Cincinnati businessmen wanting to purchase land in Wisconsin, where the government was selling forty-acre tracts on thirty years' credit. All that was required to buy a section of 640 acres worth $800 was $20 for government land warrants and $56 for the first year's interest. There were, of course, annual costs of interest and taxes to hold the land, but because its value would rise rapidly as settlers filled the state, this was an excellent short-term investment. Blackwell and his siblings had been investing their spare dollars in Illinois land during the past year, so he had little cash to invest in Wisconsin. But the Cincinnati investors offered him—as compensation for going to Wisconsin and selecting land for them—10 percent of the land he registered. In this way, he became the owner of over forty-eight thousand acres of Wisconsin land in January 1854. Sent again the following winter, he increased his holdings with just the expenditure of more time and energy. By the spring of 1855, in addition to land elsewhere, Blackwell owned over $7,000 worth of land in Wisconsin, which he expected to triple or quadruple in value within a few years.[4]

Although Stone valued working for humanity over the "struggle for material wealth," she realized that business and money-making were necessary and conceded to Blackwell that those who created wealth contributed to society too. "Money is power," she had told the Cleveland Woman's Rights Convention, and improving women's access to money-making opportunities was a goal of the woman's rights movement. She had told Cincinnati's black women that their first priority after getting an education should be to get money, invest it in land, and thus secure their pecuniary independence. Despite her low opinion of commerce, she readily accepted investment assistance from Blackwell. Acting on his suggestion, she purchased 160 acres along the Central Railroad about a hundred miles south of Chicago.[5] According to the terms of their marriage contract, neither would have claim to lands belonging to the other, nor any obligation for the other's costs of holding them.

In addition to financial independence, their agreement also set terms for personal independence: "Neither partner shall attempt to fix the residence, employment, or habits of the other, nor shall either partner feel bound to live together any longer than is agreeable to both." Blackwell assured Stone that she would "break no faith and violate no compact" if she should leave him at any time either before or after their wedding. "You are your own mistress and always will remain so." And, he said, she would choose "when, where and how often" she would "become a mother."[6]

This last provision, more about sexual relations than about motherhood, was very important to Stone, who would tell Antoinette Brown later that summer: "It is very little to me to have the right to vote, to own property, etc., if I may not keep my body and its uses in my absolute right. Not one wife in a thousand can do that now, and so long as she suffers this bondage, all other rights will not help her to her true position." When Stone and Blackwell were considering the possibility of marriage in the spring of 1854, she gave him a copy of Henry C. Wright's recently published book, *Marriage and Parentage; Or, The Reproductive Element in Man as a Means to His Elevation and Happiness,* and asked him to consider the correspondence in that book as "indicative of what should be between husband and wife." The correspondence was the second part of the book, presented as letters between a husband and wife who considered the "natural laws by which the sexual element should be governed in the marriage relation," among them, female control of sexual relations. The man told his wife to give to him "whatever thy nature prompts thee to give as a wife" and to "yield nothing merely to gratify him when thy nature cannot happily respond."[7]

In committing their sexual relations to his wife, Blackwell by no means relinquished any expectation of a satisfying sex life. Unlike separate spheres enthusiasts, who thought women were not interested in sex, Blackwell believed in women's "natural" and "normal" sexual desires. As Stone's correspondence with Mercy Lloyd reveals, she also viewed sexuality as a natural, albeit "lower," part of one's humanity and did not consider sexual desire an unfeminine instinct. She was comfortable with "the sexual aspect of marriage" but viewed spiritual love as higher than physical love, and spiritual mutuality as more essential to the relationship of husband and wife than sexual gratification. This is not to say she had no reservations about sex. Now thirty-six years old, she worried that she might be too old to bear healthy children and questioned "the propriety" of their trying to have them. Blackwell understood Stone's misgivings and told her not to feel badly on his account. "I would rather wait *ten years,*" he assured her, "and have no children than give you *any* unhappiness." But he did not think abstinence would be necessary. He had some information, he said, that should ease her fears, that made him believe she could become "a cheerful and happy mother" by him. He asked only that she put aside her fears until after they were married. Then they would consider the matter together and do as they both felt right. Regardless of their decision, she would "be a loved and cherished and happy wife."[8]

In addition to drawing up a marriage contract, Blackwell proposed drafting a document through which they might protest the laws that deprived married women of their equal rights. To Stone's continued revulsion at the thought of assuming the legal position of a married woman, Blackwell said, "There is no degradation in being unjustly treated by others. The true degradation and disgrace rests not with the victim but with the oppressors. . . . The Law, by clothing me with unjust powers, puts me in the position of the wrongdoer." So he wished, "as a husband, to *renounce* all the privileges which the law confers upon me which are not strictly mutual," and as part of his marriage vows, to make "a brief enumeration of the usurpations and distinctly pledge myself to never avail myself of them *under any circumstances.*"[9]

Blackwell worked on his protest while Stone labored in Michigan and Ontario, fighting off physical exhaustion and the onset of headache. When she
told him she was too ill to continue, he became alarmed. Unaccustomed to her
periodic headaches, he diagnosed her ailment as "brain fever" and offered to
come east to nurse her. He thought her illness might be exacerbated by anxiety
over their approaching marriage. Perhaps he was right, but it seems more likely
that it was the result of months, or years, of excessive labor. Severe headaches
had frequently interrupted her work and would continue to plague her over
the next several years. Thomas Wentworth Higginson, who saw Stone the
second week of April, described her appearance and speech as "the inevitable
result of physical and mental fatigue" and implored her to take a long period
of "entire rest and peace" after the wedding.[10]

After considering various forms and places for their marriage, the couple
decided to wed after an antislavery convention in Cincinnati, with Antoinette
Brown officiating. But when another headache struck, Lucy asked Henry to
come east. The wedding took place at the Stone home on Coy's Hill at seven
o'clock in the morning on Tuesday, May 1, with Thomas Wentworth Higginson
officiating. The couple stood before a small gathering of family and friends
while Henry read the protest both had signed:

While acknowledging our mutual affection by publicly assuming the relationship of
husband and wife, yet in justice to ourselves and a great principle, we deem it our duty
to declare that this act on our part implies no sanction of or promise of voluntary
obedience to such of the present laws of marriage as refuse to recognize the wife as an
independent, rational being, while they confer upon the husband an injurious and unnatural superiority, investing him with legal powers which no honorable man should
possess. We protest especially against the laws which give the husband:

1. The custody of the wife's person.

2. The exclusive control and guardianship of their children.

3. The sole ownership of her personal and use of her real estate, unless previously settled upon
   her or placed in the hands of trustees, as in the case of minors, idiots, and lunatics.

4. The absolute right to the product of her industry.

5. Also against laws which give to the widower so much larger and more permanent interest in
   the property of the deceased wife than they give to the widow in that of the deceased husband.

6. Finally, against the whole system by which the legal existence of the wife is suspended during
   marriage, so that, in most States, she neither has a legal part in the choice of her residence, nor
   can she make a will, nor sue or be sued in her own name, nor inherit property.

We believe that personal independence and equal human rights can never be forfeited
except for crime; that marriage should be an equal and permanent partnership and so
recognized by law; that until it is so recognized, married partners should provide against
the radical injustice of present laws by every means in their power.

We believe that where domestic difficulties arise, no appeal should be made to legal
tribunals under existing laws, but that all difficulties should be submitted to the equitable adjustment of arbitrators mutually chosen.

Thus, reverencing law, we enter our protest against rules and customs which are unworthy of the name since they violate justice, the essence of law.[11]

Then followed the vows. Although Lucy had some scruples about the form, she was mindful of her mother's wishes and had the traditional ceremony except for the promise to obey. After the couple promised to "love, honor, and cherish" each other, Higginson joined their hands and pronounced them husband and wife. Charles Burleigh gave a brief speech, laid his hands on their heads, and bestowed a benediction so heartfelt and appropriate that Higginson said he felt it was Burleigh, rather than he, who had united the couple.[12]

News of the Stone-Blackwell marriage flashed across the country. Higginson sent an announcement and a copy of their protest to the *Worcester Spy*, and from there it spread like wildfire. Critics of the woman's rights movement gloated that Stone had shown "a true woman's nature" and yielded "to the promptings of the affections and the heart." The *Weekly Chicago Democrat* took note of their joining "under protest" and predicted they would "separate by mutual dissent in less than a year." Some papers charged that the protest was "as much the offspring of a love of notoriety as of principle." The *Washington Union* noted: "Mr. Blackwell, who last fall assaulted a Southern lady and stole her slave, has . . . married Lucy Stone. Justice, though sometimes tardy, never fails to overtake her victim."[13]

But many papers praised the protest. Jane Swisshelm, who had criticized Stone's wearing of the Bloomer and called her "deficient in true womanly instincts" for mentioning the plight of a prostitute in her lectures, said that however much she was at odds with Stone on some points, she heartily agreed with her on this one and honored Stone and her husband for making the protest. No woman, said Swisshelm, should resign her legal existence without such formal protest against the despotism that forced her to forgo marriage and motherhood or submit to the unnecessary and oppressive degradation in which law placed a married woman. "Long life, longer dresses, honor and prosperity to Mrs. Blackwell and her chosen companion in life's journey."[14]

The protest evoked nationwide attention. "No event of the year," said Frances Gage, had stirred up St. Louis "like this 'protest' against bad laws." Although men sometimes discussed these laws, this was the first many women had ever heard of them, she said, and everyone—women calling on friends, shopkeepers and their customers, school girls and their teachers, women and men at the hotel table, husbands and wives at home—was discussing the protest and arguing its points. The protest also inspired followers. The following summer, Higginson married another New England couple who made a similar protest part of their ceremony. In reporting this marriage, the *Sibyl*, a new woman's rights paper published in Middletown, New York, urged other women to remember the justice due them when "entering the sacred bonds of marriage." It reported several such "woman's rights marriages" over the next years. The protest of an Ohio couple contained phrases lifted verbatim from the

Blackwell-Stone protest. A Pennsylvania couple protested every law and custom that placed "woman in an inferior position to man, civilly and socially" and pledged, as part of their ceremony, all their influence to secure "equal rights and privileges."[15]

In the summer of 1855, while the nation gossiped about their marriage and protest, the newlyweds settled into the Blackwell home in Cincinnati and, after two years of discussing the characteristics of a true love marriage and months of defining the terms of their partnership, set about putting their principles into practice. Many of the articles about their marriage referred to Stone as "Mrs. Blackwell." But she had no intention of assuming her husband's surname and began signing her correspondence "Lucy Stone (only)." She had given the matter of a married woman's name much thought long before she decided to marry, starting perhaps when an Oberlin professor remarked that women were more "sunk" by marriage than were men. She had asked why that was so, and among the reasons he gave was the fact that by becoming part of her husband's family and adopting his name, a woman lost her previous identity. During one of her early lecturing years Stone fastened onto an idea presented in Lydia Maria Child's *History of the Condition of Women,* which she recorded in a notebook: "Moorish women do not take the name of their husband, but retain that which they received in their infancy."[16]

Stone was not alone in considering the custom of a woman taking her husband's name as degrading. After the 1848 Rochester Woman's Rights Convention, a local editor asked why the women had not protested the custom. "This merging of their individuality into that of their husbands, even to the loss of the good name they are heirs to by birth, is certainly as humiliating as any of the grievances under which they labor." The memorial of the 1850 Ohio Woman's Convention had also objected to name loss as "emblematic of the fate of [a married woman's] legal rights" and the divestiture of her "distinct individuality."[17] To Stone, the question of a married woman's name represented the principle that underlay the entire woman's rights movement—woman's right to self-sovereignty.

But it was not long before Stone's right to her name was challenged. Shortly after the wedding she bought land in Appleton, Wisconsin, and when Blackwell attempted to register the deed, officials insisted she add "Blackwell" to her signature. The couple consulted Blackwell's longtime friend, Salmon P. Chase, a prominent Cincinnati lawyer and newly elected governor of Ohio who would later become Chief Justice of the United States Supreme Court. Chase had no ready answer but promised to look into the matter. He must have advised Stone to use the Blackwell name in the meantime, though, because for the next several months she submitted to custom and signed correspondence, the call to the National Woman's Rights Convention, and a petition to the Ohio legislature as "Lucy Stone Blackwell." It would be several months before she received assurance of the legality of her birth name.[18]

Regardless of her name, Stone maintained her personal independence. In

August, still weak from her spring illness and hoping to recuperate in a cooler and healthier climate, she went east to visit family and attend two conventions. Earlier in the summer, she had received a letter from Susan Anthony urging her to get Henry's permission to attend a convention in New York that she and Brown were planning. "Don't do me the injustice, Susan," Stone replied, "of expecting disabilities *now* for me which are not called for by my free will. I yet keep my own custody and all that pertains to it." She told Anthony that when she showed the letter to Henry and asked if she might go to the convention, "Only think of it, he did not give me permission but told me to ask Lucy Stone! I can't get him to govern me at all!"[19]

In addition to retaining authority over her coming and going, Lucy kept control of her body. True to his promise, Henry did not press for sexual relations before she was ready. Although Lucy had told Antoinette Brown she hoped to get pregnant right away, when she left for New England in August, she and Henry had not yet consummated their marriage. Friends' insinuations that maternity would force her to neglect duty made Lucy wonder if her desire for children was selfish, and she suggested to Henry that perhaps they should renounce parenthood and devote the whole of their lives to the good of humanity. Henry replied that "the noblest preaching is incomplete without the noble life to exemplify it. To reform others we must try to reform ourselves, by assuming the natural relations of humanity and acting our part well therein." He thought even the recorded life of Jesus was imperfect as an example, because it did not show him in the relationship of son, husband, or father.[20]

Reassured in her desire for children, Stone returned to Cincinnati intent on becoming a mother. But she was home only a few days before Henry had to set off on a two-week trip. He was home again for just another two weeks before she left for a month-long lecturing tour. Naively, Lucy expected immediate results from their brief time together and a week after her departure notified Henry with great disappointment that "our hopes of parentage are so far [in] vain." Resolved not "to lose any opportunity of securing the blessing of motherhood" after her return to Cincinnati in December, she lectured the next month only in nearby towns where an overnight stay was not necessary. When the desired result had not been achieved by mid-March, she began to fear she might never have children.[21]

Meanwhile, Blackwell assisted his wife's work however he could. Although summer was normally a time of rest for Stone and the summer of 1855 found her still weak from her spring illness, she and Blackwell lectured together in and around Cincinnati during the first two months of their marriage. In the fall, he had to be away while she made final arrangements for the sixth National Woman's Rights Convention, which met in Cincinnati in October, but he returned in time to help her manage it. He arranged a November lecture tour for her in Wisconsin and in January helped arrange lectures in Indiana, writing letters to engage halls and arrange newspaper advertising, sending handbills and tickets in advance of her arrivals, and forwarding incoming invitations. With deep-felt appreciation Stone wrote, "Harry dear, you are the best husband in the world. In the midst of all the extra care, hurry, and perplexity of business, you stop and look after all my little affairs . . . doing everything you can to save me trouble."[22]

January 1856 brought two major events to the Blackwell family. After more than a year of actively trying to get out of the hardware business, Henry and Sam found a buyer for their shares. This meant the family could complete their move east. Elizabeth and Marian were already settled in New York City, where Elizabeth had established a medical practice and Marian a boarding house. Emily planned to join them there after completing medical training in Europe. Henry stayed with the business a few months to introduce its new partner to his routes and help it through some unexpected difficulties. But Sam was free, and he headed east to take a bride—Antoinette Brown! The pending marriage came as a complete surprise to Lucy, who learned of it only as Sam left. Sam had proposed shortly after Henry and Lucy's marriage, and although Antoinette had confided the proposal and her indecision to close friends, she had kept her eventual acceptance and the continuing romance a secret, meeting Sam so discreetly that friends thought the relationship was over. The couple were married on January 24, and Antoinette, who had resigned her pastorate over a theological issue, moved into the Blackwell home for the few months remaining before the family's relocation. When the bridal couple arrived in Cincinnati, Lucy was lecturing in Indiana but had already written welcoming Antoinette into the family and assuring her that the "full sympathy and love of Sam" would enable her to do her work even better. Both Lucy and Antoinette found marriage to a man who supported their work to be a "blessing," and when they heard rumors that Susan Anthony, too, might take a husband, Antoinette urged her to be sure to "get a good husband, that's all dear."[23]

Lucy succeeded in maintaining her financial independence as well as her personal independence. Refusing to be supported, she insisted on paying half their joint expenses, including trips Henry made to attend to their investment properties. Henry objected but acquiesced: "I have pursued the course of *even* and *exact* justice in charging you with one half of my expenses in visiting the land," he reported after returning from Wisconsin, "so never reproach me again with cheating you, little one!" He, in turn, laid claim to half *her* expense in visiting an area in New Jersey where they thought of settling. Henry tried to persuade Lucy that being supported would not threaten her independence and that she should feel no more "subservient" accepting his money than she did accepting his caresses. "*Any* marriage not consecrated by love is monstrous," he said, "and the *presence* of love makes dependence *mutual* and financial details simply *trivial*."[24]

Lucy's insistence upon paying her own way hurt Henry's husbandly pride. When she suggested during her eastern recuperation that she arrange a few lectures to raise funds for their Appleton taxes, he urged her not to let the need for money determine her actions. If she wanted to pay with her own money, the interest she earned on money she had deposited with the hardware firm was more than sufficient to cover her taxes. As for her paying any of *his* costs, that was out of the question. "If you are not willing that your husband should support you, at least do not think it will ever be necessary to support him. Lucy dear, Lucy Stone Blackwell is more independent in her pecuniary position than was Lucy Stone," he assured her. Although their marriage might result in the forfeiture of her name, which at the time seemed a possibility, he did not want that loss to make her "feel less free." He did not want her to be driven by the necessity of earning an income, for monetary gain seemed to him a factor "unworthy to enter into [her] calculations."[25]

If monetary gain was unworthy as a consideration in scheduling her public work, it was, nonetheless, something Stone sought. Not wishing to ever become dependent on her husband, she wanted to build her own financial security, and in the mid-1850s land investment was the surest way to multiply one's assets. In December 1854, land that Elizabeth Blackwell bought in Illinois a year and a half earlier at $2.50 an acre was worth $10 an acre. In the spring of 1855, George and Ellen sold land for more than three times what they had paid, and a little later a tract Ellen bought for $75 brought $400. With land prices in Illinois spiraling, the Blackwell clan began selling off holdings there and re-investing the proceeds in Wisconsin, where similar growth was expected. Henry was convinced that purchasing, improving, and trading western land was the best business he could undertake to establish his coveted financial independence, but he could not do this while tied to the hardware firm. His younger brother, though, had no such restraint, and in the fall of 1855 Henry helped twenty-three-year-old George Blackwell set himself up as a grain broker and land agent in Lyons, Iowa, near the corners of Minnesota, Wisconsin, and Illinois, where he could easily operate in the four-state region and take over Henry's management of family investments.[26]

Once in the Blackwell family, Stone joined in the investment enthusiasm. When Ellen could not decide whether to reinvest proceeds from a sale or hold them for her trip to Europe, Lucy offered a true investor's solution. Advising Ellen to let Henry reinvest the money so as not to miss out on the profit, she offered to supply any funds Ellen might need later on and take a corresponding interest in the new investment. When George sent word of what he considered an exceptional investment opportunity—the purchase of a 120-acre farm near Lyons for just over $15 an acre—Lucy bought it. And when neither she nor Henry had cash for final payments on her Appleton land and Henry suggested selling an interest to Ellen, Lucy sold bank stock rather than relinquish any part of the investment.[27]

Lucy and Henry generously helped each other resolve cash-flow problems with their individual investments and sometimes entered joint investments. In November 1855 he paid $450 toward her Lyons farm, and the following summer she gave him $500 to develop a farm on some of his Wisconsin land.

During the first nine years of their marriage, while they tried to develop their investments and establish a home—first during a national panic and depression and then through war—keeping property and funds separate was difficult. But they kept track of who owed whom what, and after achieving financial independence in 1864 they kept their incomes separate in order to ensure Stone's autonomy.[28]

The allegation that Blackwell squandered Stone's money on land speculation and personal debt is unfounded. Stone had about $6,000 when she married, $4,000 of which was invested in the Coombs, Ryland, and Blackwells hardware company. When that partnership dissolved and a new one formed, the debt to Stone was split. The brothers assumed responsibility for half, and the purchaser of their interest, L. A. Ostrom, gave Stone two $1,000 notes for the other half. In 1857 Lucy traded the Blackwells' note for half interest in her and Henry's house, which Henry purchased with some of his Wisconsin land. She received interest on the Ostrom notes until he defaulted. The Illinois farm he had put up as collateral was then deeded to the Blackwells, and she traded her interest in it for sole ownership of her and Henry's residence. The rest of her premarital assets were invested in bank stocks and various land holdings.[29]

In the spring of 1856, with the hardware firm sold, Henry and Lucy could consider with more certainty two aspects of their marriage that they had been discussing ever since their engagement—what Henry would do in the future, and where they would live. According to their prenuptial agreement, neither partner would "attempt to fix the residence, employment, or habits of the other."[30] But these matters were, after all, central to their life together and in a "true marriage" required mutual consent.

Blackwell had long looked forward to the day when he could quit commerce and "leave the society of country merchants for the choice spirits of literature."[31] He thought business had no appeal to him except as a means of accumulating enough wealth to leave it. But his great success with land investment revealed that he possessed the sound judgment and interpersonal skills that could make him a successful businessman. His siblings were so convinced of his "superior business talents" that Elizabeth urged him to settle in New York City where he could make the best use of them and Ellen suggested that their brother Howard, who was experiencing financial difficulties in England, spend a year under Henry's tutelage. When Henry received a letter at the beginning of 1855 with an enticing business offer from an English cousin, it caused him to pause and reconsider his "true path." He was then engaged to be married, committed to supporting more than himself, and he had to be practical. Although he viewed business as "a very low and mean object of thought," he also realized that he was suited for it, and that his natural and acquired abilities for "a more intellectual career" were such that he would probably fail at that. "Now to excel in the most common and merely temporary human avocation," he told Lucy, "is to my mind better and more honorable than to achieve mere respectable mediocrity in a higher one. . . . I think I can actually succeed in business in accumulating wealth, and with wealth how much good may be done and how much power may be exerted."[32]

Lucy had discouraged this leaning. She knew he had an aptitude for business and might excel in that department but, she said, there were many people who could make money, not so many who could inspire "the world to a higher thought . . . ; fewer still, whose life of sublime devotion to the highest right . . . wins followers and so makes the world better." She had hoped they both would give themselves "to the great moral movements of the Age." Henry had sent Lucy copies of essays he had written for his literary society, and seeing that he was a good writer, she suggested his true calling might be as a newspaper editor, in which capacity he might fulfill his desire to serve humanity.[33]

Uncertain what to do, Blackwell left the decision of his future course until after he was free from business and had time to contemplate in leisure. Having labored hard since his youth, he looked forward to a period of rest, and Lucy was sure such an interlude would help him find his "true sphere." Henry thought that after selling the business he and Lucy would probably live in New York, on a railroad line a little way from the city, but whether he would reenter business or work and study on their small farm was a question yet to be decided. They might even use that time to make a trip to England to lecture together on woman's rights.[34]

But the sale of the hardware firm did not supply the cash Blackwell needed for an interval of contemplation. The brothers received over $12,500 for their shares ($10,000 of which they owed to their cousin), but it was paid in land and notes—land that required payment of taxes and interest to hold, and notes bearing interest insufficient to live on. Anticipating such a settlement, Blackwell had taken steps to obtain investment income he hoped would eventually cover both investment and living expenses. He had established a farm in Wisconsin with one of his investment partners, which produced a modest income. Hoping for a steady stream of land sales, he had put his town lots in Cincinnati and in Viroqua, Wisconsin, on the market, listed his remaining Illinois land with agents in four cities, and made a trip east in search of buyers for his "wild" Wisconsin land. Finding the market glutted, he determined to gain an edge by supplying detailed descriptions of each parcel he offered for sale. So now, in the spring of 1856, he suggested that Lucy accompany him on a six-week tour of their properties, lecturing along the way to pay expenses. While he surveyed their land and wrote up descriptions, they could determine if any of their properties offered an inviting temporary home from which they could develop more of their holdings into income-producing enterprises.[35] In the final month before they were to leave Cincinnati, as Henry went to Wisconsin on another assignment from his investment partners, Lucy prepared to go east for the May anniversaries and look for home sites there before joining Henry in Wisconsin. She advised him to take time to consider some definite plans for his future, for where they settled would depend on that. She was eager to find "that little spot . . . unknown to us yet existing somewhere" where they would "be able to live nearer our ideal, to make more of our time, and to achieve what is more worthy of us." What she wanted was "to have land enough to grow so large a part of our subsistence that we need not depend on the public—with a little income from rents or interests, and be free to study, to think, to grow unitary and symmetrical, and be ready to give occasional help to any great Cause."[36]

By the time Stone left Ohio, Salmon P. Chase had supplied the legal assurance she wanted—that no law required a woman to take her husband's name. Slated to speak at the anniversary of the American Anti-Slavery Society on May 7, she used that occasion to make a public announcement that her name had not changed.[37]

Some of Stone's friends had little appreciation for her decision to keep her birth name. Mott suggested she insert Blackwell between her names "as the French do—Lucy Blackwell Stone." But Elizabeth Cady Stanton recognized the significance of her decision: "Nothing has been done in the woman's rights movement for some time that has so rejoiced my heart as the announcement by you of a woman's right to her name," she wrote. "It does seem to me a proper self-respect demands that every woman may have some name by which she may be known from cradle to grave." Stone did not object to being called *Mrs.*; that title should be used for all mature women, she explained, and *Miss* reserved for young girls. Nor did she challenge the custom of giving children the father's name. To her it did not matter what name a child was given; the point was that once given a name, each person had a right to it, and a bride should no more change her name than a groom should change his. Once again, Stone instructed her correspondents to "[n]ever add Blackwell to my name" and often added a brief explanation of the injustice of that custom.[38]

The marriages of Lucy Stone and Antoinette Brown upset some who had looked to them to establish the fact that marriage was not woman's only option. When Martha Wright's daughter complained that "as soon as women begin *to be* anything, they are married," Wright responded that what women wanted was "to be *something after* they are married, as well as before." During Stone's winter labors she had met an old friend who, seeing marriage as the "annihilation of a wife," lamented that Antoinette Brown, too, had "gone down into the abyss." Relating the encounter to her husband, Stone said they must "prove the contrary." Her insistence that she was still, as before, Lucy Stone, demonstrated that aim.[39]

The Marriage Question and Woman's Rights

The protracted discussion between Lucy Stone and Henry Blackwell on the nature of marriage, the faults of the institution as viewed and sanctioned by their society, and how they might themselves achieve a "true marriage" was not a unique phenomenon. America had been discussing and debating marriage for over two decades, and at the time of the Blackwell-Stone courtship it was still an area of highly charged examination. A spate of newspaper articles and books, among which Henry C. Wright's *Marriage and Parentage* was only one, explored the nature of marriage and the rights of the marriage partners. In the spring of 1853 when Blackwell began his courtship of Stone, the "marriage question" was one of two controversial issues considered by the General Assembly of the Presbyterian Church, the other being slavery.[1] Bills aimed at broadening the grounds for divorce were before several state legislatures, eliciting heated arguments between their sponsors and those who viewed marriage as an insoluble bond and remarriage as adultery. The demand for making habitual drunkenness grounds for divorce that was so controversial among New York temperance women was part of this debate.

Challenges to the traditional view of marriage came in many forms. Reformers such as Harriet Martineau and Henry C. Wright taught that true marriage was a spiritual merging of two souls, a union made by God rather than human institutions, that existed with or without legal or religious sanction. Quaker couples such as Theodore Weld and Angelina Grimké or Stephen Foster and Abby Kelley married themselves, without benefit of clergy or public official, and the legality of their marriages was not questioned. Those who propounded the philosophy of "true marriage" viewed the marriage relationship as one of mutual dependence in which neither partner was superior or subject to the other, and they maintained that if a true, divine love existed between a man and woman, they were married regardless of religious or legal sanction, and if such love was absent, they were not married regardless of religious or legal release.

Both Stone and Blackwell ascribed to these views. During her wrestling with the question of whether to marry, Stone said that if she had been the novel heroine Jane Eyre, whose wedding ceremony was halted by the revelation that the groom was still legally bound to a mad woman, she would have "turned from that half-finished ceremony . . . to the love-altar in my own soul, and there (not only as *our right*, but as a *sacred* duty imposed by our mutual love) . . . I would have consecrated myself to the solemn yet joyful duty." Stone believed "the mere existence of such love is proof of its right to be," and her support for divorce rather than legal separation sprang from that belief. To Blackwell, too, marriage was a matter of private agreement. When he and Stone were trying to settle on a date for the "public recognition" of their marriage, he told her, "Now you are my wife in sight of God, by the divine tie of affection, I can wait as long as you please for its manifestation in this way." He had also been receptive to Lucretia Mott's suggestion that they marry at her home in a ceremony conducted by themselves without clergy.[2]

Those who held this view of "true marriage" saw traditional marriage, in which man and woman assumed a "relation of master and servant," as the corruption of a holy relationship.[3] Agreeing with this assessment but settling on a different remedy was another group of marriage critics, the free-lovers. Whereas true-lovers wanted to reform the marriage institution, free-lovers sought to do away with it altogether. Among the first antimarriage advocates in America was the Scottish reformer Robert Owen, who in 1826 established a communitarian settlement in New Harmony, Indiana, and preached against the "trinity of evils" that afflicted humanity: private property, organized religion, and marriage. When Frances Wright came to the United States shortly thereafter, she embraced Owen's ideology, incorporated it into her experimental community in Tennessee, then wrote and lectured against marriage. But public furor against her demonstrated that few Americans were ready for such ideas.

Another critic of traditional marriage was John Humphrey Noyes, pioneer in perfectionist theology and founder of a utopian community in Vermont. After 1840 he began teaching that no man had exclusive right to one woman, and when his community began practicing his theories, he and his followers were driven out of the state. Resettling near Syracuse, New York, they established the Oneida Community in 1848, where each member was married to all others. The idea at Oneida was not *no* marriage, but "complex," or group marriage.[4]

Another attack on the institution of marriage came in the 1840s, from the Fourier movement. Promoted in America as an economic system based on associative labor—with nothing said about Fourier's philosophy of "Passional Attraction" or sexual license—it spread across the country with the recommendation of prominent leaders such as Horace Greeley. The first presentation to the American public of Fourier's ideas on love, sex, and marriage came in 1844 with publication of Parke Godwin's *Popular View of the Doctrines of Charles Fourier.* Fourier believed that because the "erotic impulse" was a nat-

ural element of humanity, every man and woman had a right to sexual gratification, and civilization was wrong to restrict it to the confines of monogamous
marriage. Subordinated to the narrow utilitarian purpose of Christian marriage, the sex drive was perverted, its natural development arrested, its vast
potential for social good destroyed. Fourier believed sexual gratification could
be made to foster social harmony and economic well-being but that marriage
stood as an obstacle to that high good.

If the theories of the movement's founder were not enough to implicate the
Association movement, the news that Fourier's chief apostle in America, Albert
Brisbane, was teaching and practicing those theories, was. Reports of Brisbane's
open affair with a married woman shocked the nation and gave ammunition
to the political opponents of Horace Greeley, who soon found himself under
attack for promoting free love. Understanding Association only from its economic standpoint and unfamiliar with Fourier's sexual philosophy, Greeley
unwisely agreed to a newspaper debate on Fourierism in 1847. It was through
the debate articles written by Henry J. Raymond in the *New York Courier and
Enquirer* that the wider American public—and Greeley himself—were introduced to Fourier's and Brisbane's sexual philosophy. Raymond compared Fourier's theories to the antimarriage sexual license of Fanny Wright, and Greeley
quickly severed his connection with both Brisbane and the Association
movement.[5]

But Fourierist ideas on woman's rights and associative households had already interested a large number of women, and many of them were drawn also
to its Passional Attraction theories. Among those who continued to be devoted
disciples of Albert Brisbane was Anna Blackwell, Henry's eldest sister, who in
the 1840s was a member of the Brook Farm Phalanx. During the summer of
1845, while Elizabeth Blackwell was studying in Philadelphia and the scandal
of Brisbane's affair was at its peak, Anna brought Brisbane and a few other
friends for a visit. Elizabeth was horrified by Anna's new doctrines. "Simple
constancy she laughed at, advocated a continual change of lovers as fancy dictates, thought it right that a woman should love one man for his beauty, another for his fortune or rank or talent, that it was natural and proper that a
woman should unite with a man because he could make her the mother of
beautiful children," and that "when women are better developed, their passion
will be as great as man's, and that this highest enjoyment and most beautiful
act of life should be cultivated and refined with the utmost care." Anna told
Elizabeth she "worshiped" Brisbane's ideas and considered him her "dearest
friend on earth." Although he was accused of being a notorious libertine, Anna
said he never in his life seduced a woman, but if a woman gave herself to him,
he "reciprocated" her passion and accepted her "offering." Elizabeth had always
cherished the ideal of "eternal constancy, a beautiful union of two souls made
for each other," but as she observed Brisbane's tender relationships with Anna
and other women she began to "understand how rich life might be where these
free beautiful relations prevailed." She not only saw that the isolated household

was a prison, she began to see that marriage was "a hopeless slavery." Within a few years, though, some internal controversy caused both Anna and Elizabeth to disassociate themselves from the movement, Anna fleeing to England and Elizabeth declaring the Associationists "generally a very poor set of people" and resuming her former view of marriage as a "divine institution."[6]

Discussion of love and marriage reached great intensity in the 1840s and was part of the backdrop against which Stone formed her ideas on "moral reform in marriage" and decided to become a woman's rights reformer. "A wife's right to her body"—that is, the right to decline sexual intercourse and decide whether to subject herself to the possibility of pregnancy—had been the intended focus of Stone's work, but she had not yet brought it openly onto the woman's rights platform. During her travels she learned of appalling abuses of the right that Scripture, law, and custom gave the husband. "One noble woman," she confided to a friend, "told me how she fled from her husband to the Shakers because he gave her no peace either during menstruation, pregnancy, or nursing. And on the application of such a brute to our legislature, the laws of divorce were so modified that that man, and others like him, might sooner be enabled . . . to claim 'a husband's rights.'" Saying she knew of "many similar cases," Stone asked: "Shall we keep silence when such curses are inflicted through woman upon the race?" And yet, as of 1853, despite the urging of William Henry Channing and Paulina Wright Davis, Stone had not brought the issue to the woman's rights conventions. Although she agreed with Davis's assessment that marriage was where "woman is most defrauded of her rights, where her bondage is most keenly felt," and believed that this question was the most basic of all their claims, she knew, too, that it was the most radical. On all their other demands—for suffrage, for property rights, for equal guardianship rights, for equal education and employment opportunities, for equal pay—society seemed ready to move. She did not want to endanger progress on those issues with premature introduction of this other.[7]

Elizabeth Cady Stanton also wanted the marriage question raised, but her venue was the temperance movement and her vehicle, the demand for the right of divorce on grounds of habitual drunkenness. Shortly after a meeting at which her resolution on divorce created an uproar among temperance women, Stanton told Anthony that although the world might not be ready to discuss the marriage question, she felt certain the thoughts she sent the convention were true. "It is vain to look for the elevation of woman so long as she is degraded in marriage. I hold that it is a sin, an outrage on our holiest feelings, to pretend that anything but deep, fervent love and sympathy constitute marriage." Like the Quakers, Stanton saw no need for laws concerning marriage. "Remove law and a false public sentiment," she said, "and woman will no more live as wife with a cruel, bestial drunkard than a servant, in this free country, will stay with a pettish, unjust mistress." She believed men had monopolized the question long enough; it was time women rose up and gave it a "thorough, fearless examination." She believed the entire question of woman's rights turned on the marriage relation, and sooner or later it must be discussed.[8] Learning through Brown and Anthony that Stone shared her views, Stanton asked her to attend the June 1853 annual meeting of the temperance society to support her position on divorce.

During the summer of 1853 as Stone made arrangements for the Whole World Temperance Convention, Anthony informed her that Stanton, after her resignation from the Women's State Temperance Society, had bid "adieu to the public" and would not write for or attend any more conventions. Having become acquainted with former Association leader William Henry Channing, Stanton was "all taken up with Association ideas; sees no other way for woman to be developed." Burdened with domestic and maternal responsibilities, she saw no hope for woman except through associative households and was, she told Anthony, "so full of dreams of the true associative life" that all other reforms seemed "superficial and fragmentary." Nevertheless, Stanton urged Stone to speak on the sexual rights of a married woman at the Whole World Temperance Convention, arguing, "Does not the fact that the truth has come to you show that God says the time also has come to utter it?" But Stone said that if she spoke at all at the temperance convention, she would speak on drunkenness as grounds for divorce, because that issue ought to be heard there and no one else would do it. As for a wife's sexual rights, Stone said, "I do not think, let truth come from what source it may, that anyone has a right to keep it. But I do think that a premature announcement of it is possible. . . . One who is in total darkness finds his eyes pained by the sudden admission of bright light, and closes them." Stone wished a mature woman such as Lucretia Mott, "whose name and age would add weight to her words," would take up the question. She told Stanton she would be "glad to receive [her] thoughts, for there is not another woman in our ranks who thinks or who dares speak what she thinks on this topic."[9]

As Stone was being pressed to speak out on a wife's sexual rights, publication of a book by Brisbane-disciple Stephen Pearl Andrews, *Love, Marriage, and Divorce, and the Sovereignty of the Individual,* heated up public debate on the marriage question. Andrews declared that a man and woman who loved each other could live together in purity without the blessings of any religious body or ceremony, and he called for the same sexual freedom for women that conventional moral standards already gave men. Although sounding similar to the Quaker view that a couple need not have their marriage sanctified by clergy or law, Andrews was not advocating a monogamous union, and unlike the moral reformers who also sought one moral standard for the sexes, he advocated equal license rather than equal restraint. He agreed with reformers like Henry Wright that a wife had a right not to surrender her body if she did not reciprocate the desire, but he added that a wife also had the right to offer it at will to anyone.[10]

In the summer of 1853, a few weeks before the woman's rights convention in New York City, Andrews sent Stone a copy of his book and followed up with a personal visit, asking if there could be any cooperation between their two reforms. Stone turned him out with a "scorching rebuke," saying "neither free love nor its advocates would be tolerated on the platform dedicated to woman's rights." Despite the rebuff, Andrews attended the convention and tried to gain the floor to speak. But the presiding officers, whom Stone had forewarned, recognized him and denied him the floor.[11]

Although not ready to speak publicly on a wife's sexual rights, Stone addressed other aspects of the marriage question in her four-lecture series. As she spoke on marriage throughout the West, the November 1853 issue of *Harper's Monthly Magazine* issued a scathing attack on the woman's rights movement and said its most serious threat was to the marriage institution. "The blindest must see that such a change as is proposed in the relations and life of the sexes cannot leave either marriage or the family in their present state," it said. Giving a wife the right to own property separately from her husband and the right to manage it free from his control would destroy the "oneness" that was essential to marriage and replace it with "the unholy alliance of concubinage." "Was there ever falsehood meaner than that?" fumed Stone. She said the editor saw clearly that their movement would give the wife "more freedom, and her husband less power over her, and he trembles for his throne. Well, he can't keep it."[12]

Taking her marriage lecture to New England in 1854, Stone discussed with other activists the urging of Channing, Davis, and Stanton for her to speak out on a wife's sexual rights. Harriet Ingersoll, a leader in Maine, advised her not to do it: "It is very bold in me to counsel differently from one whom almost more than any other I reverence, William H. Channing, yet I do so counsel. And in answer to your friend Mrs. Stanton, who says, 'Does not the fact that the truth has come to you show that God says the time also has come to utter it,' I would say that particular truth has come to many other minds who can and do utter it. Let Dr. Whiting, and Graham's writing, and many others continue the work begun some years since, for even Lucretia Mott could not do it without loss, great loss to other parts of the great reform." Ingersoll said many more women already thought for themselves on these private matters than on their industrial and political wrongs, and so Stone was needed more in those areas.[13]

Stone discussed the matter with other woman's rights leaders in Philadelphia that fall and found they all had differing opinions. So when Davis pressed her to raise the marriage question at the 1855 convention, Stone said, "It is clear to me that question underlies this whole movement and all our little skirmishing for better laws and the right to vote will yet be swallowed up in the real question, viz., Has woman as wife a right to herself?" She believed the question would someday *"force* itself upon us," but they were not yet ready for it.[14]

Ready or not, the marriage question forced itself upon the woman's rights movement that very summer when Mary Gove Nichols, a pioneer in physiology, female lecturing, and dress reform, published an autobiographical free-love novel, *Mary Lyndon; Or, Revelations of a Life*. After six years of marital separation, Mary Gove had divorced her first husband, married hydrotherapist Thomas Low Nichols, and adopted his more radical philosophies. With him she established a school for training water-cure physicians, edited a monthly magazine that promoted theories of individual sovereignty and free love, and wrote a book called *Marriage: Its History, Character, and Results*. During New York City's 1854 anniversary week, their agents stood at the doors of various conventions and handed out advertisements for their books "worded in the most specious and attractive manner," complained Elizabeth Blackwell, who cited their "doctrines of abortion and prostitution under spiritual and scientific guise" as evidence of the need for responsible sex education.[15]

Because Mary Nichols claimed her novel was an autobiography and not "a work of fiction in autobiographic garb," it was accepted as such. Like Mary Gove, Mary Lyndon found herself in an unhappy marriage, asked herself, "What constitutes true marriage?" and answered, "Marriage without love is adultery." Cured from illness by hydropathy, Lyndon, like Gove, studied and lectured on physiology, left her husband, began public speaking on "marriage as annihilation of woman," and established herself in a medical career. She cohabited with a lover before divorcing her husband, and when divorce was granted, married her lover in a ceremony that mocked fidelity. "In a marriage with you, I resign no right of my soul," Lyndon's marriage vows declared. "I enter into no compact to be faithful to you. I only promise to be faithful to the deepest love of my heart. If that love is yours, it will bear fruit for you and enrich your life—our life. If my love leads me from you, I must go." Sounding very much like Lucy Stone, she asked, "When will woman cease to be an appendage, a parasite of man? Oh, when will woman stand before the universe an individual being," but continued, "faithful to her own life-law, fully sensible of her God-given dower of love and her right to bestow it according to the divine law of her attraction?" So even had Mary Lyndon not called Albert Brisbane "one of the most remarkable men of our age or of any age," the Fourierist doctrine of Passional Attraction was unmistakable as the novel's underlying theme. In reviewing the book, the *New York Times* railed against a moral philosophy that taught "that the passions are the lawgivers for mankind; that the instincts of nature, the impulses and cravings of appetite, should be indulged and obeyed as the highest revelations of divinity—as the true voice of God in the human heart" while "reason and conscience . . . are ignored or divested of all meaning." The object of *Mary Lyndon*, declared the *Times*, was to convince "the world of the advantages of hydropathy, the abominations of Christianity, and the reforming influence of fine art and fornication."[16]

If Stone had wanted a great work of fiction to set forth the principles and aims of the woman's rights movement, to rouse public attention and sympathy in the same way *Uncle Tom's Cabin* had done for the antislavery movement,

Mary Lyndon was not what she had in mind. Nevertheless, this novel became identified in the minds of multitudes as representing the woman's rights position on marriage. Because it came on the heels of the highly publicized Stone-Blackwell "marriage protest," it is not surprising the public was confused. And when Stone refused to adopt the Blackwell name, suspicion that she had entered one of those "unlegalized" free-love relationships was only natural. Nor was it surprising that the public should confuse the author, Mary Gove Nichols, with Vermont woman's rights leader, Clarina I. H. Nichols. The *Times* did not help at all with a long editorial that explained the interconnections of the free-love movement, Fourierism, Spiritualism, and the woman's rights movement. The woman's rights movement, it said, or at least the "extreme" part that claimed "the absolute and indefensible right of woman to equality in all respects with man and to a complete sovereignty over her own person and conduct," led directly to the principles of free love.[17]

Henry Blackwell spent a Sunday in September 1855 reading *Mary Lyndon* and bristling at the exposure of his own sister Anna in a character Nichols did not even rename. He identified for Lucy who the novel's real-life counterparts were but said he had no confidence in the accuracy of the descriptions. He remembered Nichols's "angelic Eva" as one of the "most disagreeable, depraved young girls" he ever knew. Blackwell said the Nicholses, who were relocating to Cincinnati and establishing an office from which to promulgate their views, were trying to thrust their ideas on the public in the guise of woman's rights. "It would be an infinite shame and pity," he said, "to allow the just claims of women to liberty of person, to rights of property, to industrial, social, and political equality to be associated with a conspiracy against . . . the holiest relations of life." But he knew Stone would not allow that to happen.[18]

Although Mary Nichols and her husband later converted to Catholicism and retracted their free-love teachings, in the summer and fall of 1855 the scandal that her novel ignited singed the woman's rights movement. *Free-lover* had for many years been a label thrown in contempt at anyone who criticized marriage, but it became even more so in 1855 as an anti-free-love crusade swept across the country. In August, an investigating committee called a mass meeting in Ripon, Wisconsin, to expose a neighboring free-love community, formed the previous summer after a visit from a Nichols disciple. New York police raided Pearl Andrews's Progressive Union Club on Broadway, accused of being a front for a secret Free Love League, and the *New York Times* targeted other groups across the country, including a free love community at Berlin Heights, Ohio.[19]

The 1855 National Woman's Rights Convention was held in Cincinnati, Ohio, new home not only of Lucy Stone, but also of Mary Gove Nichols. Stone held her breath in fear that Nichols would try to gain a hearing, but she did not. After the convention, however, Nichols claimed she had been prevented from speaking there. "The artful creature knows that if she can make people believe that she is oppressed, it is her best chance of securing sympathy," said

Stone. Believing she could no longer remain silent on the marriage question, Stone used a November lyceum engagement in Chicago to distinguish between the free-love claim for woman's unrestricted sexual freedom and the woman's rights claim for "a wife's right to her own body." "It has got to be done," she said, "and may as well be begun first as last." And she decided to bring the issue to the next national woman's rights convention.[20]

Stone was now also convinced that there must be a special convention to discuss the marriage question. She wanted a forum separate from the woman's rights platform because their movement had been defined as an equal rights movement, and the marriage question included much more than a claim for equal rights. Their meetings might argue that marriage should be an equal partnership—that spouses had equal rights to own and control their earnings and property, that parents had equal rights to their children, that married women had as much right as married men to their birth names, and that marriage partners had equal sexual rights and responsibility. Questions about divorce, about whether the marriage relation required legal sanction, and about whether it was a permanent bond, she believed, did not belong on their platform. "All that pertains intrinsically to marriage is an entirely distinct question from ours," she said, "just as temperance is not part of our distinct movement." And yet responsible women needed to speak out on these issues. So during the next few years, Stone urged those who felt keenly on these issues to call a special convention where woman's voice might be heard on the marriage question.[21]

"The Field Is the World"

By the time Lucy Stone married in May 1855, she had lectured in seventeen states, the District of Columbia, and Canada. Calling her "one of the great Providences of history," Thomas Wentworth Higginson declared that "Lucy is queen of us all . . . and delights the whole country from Maine to Kentucky." During the first year of her marriage, Stone left the East to other capable hands and devoted her energy to the West. Noting her absence from the eastern field, one newspaper commentator observed that the woman's rights movement was "dying out" because its principal advocates had married. But Higginson, who relayed the report to Stone, chuckled, "I am afraid that poor editor will find himself disappointed."[1]

Strangers were not the only ones who thought marriage might end Stone's career. Perhaps it was her absence from the May meetings in New York that planted seeds of doubt in Susan Anthony's mind, for shortly after those meetings she asked Stone to consider what the world would think if she stopped attending reform meetings. Stone repelled the remark with a playful retort, but when Antoinette Brown expressed a similar concern, she became defensive: "What do you and Susan mean by such little sentences as 'the world needs you' etc. etc.? Do you think I am likely to forget that the least service is needed? When you see me listlessly on my oars, heedless of the heavy throbbing of Humanity's tired, sick heart, then it will be time to start with such little insinuations. As yet, I do not deserve them."[2]

Far from diminished activity, Stone's first year of marriage was one of her busiest. The purpose of her summer trip east was not solely to recuperate, but to assist petition campaigns in New York and New England. William Henry Channing had moved to England and left Susan Anthony and Antoinette Brown in charge of the work in New York. They were holding a convention at Saratoga Springs in August and expected assistance from Stone. Stone had discouraged scheduling a convention in a resort town, arguing that the "rich and fashionable" who gathered there, who had reputations and ambitions to protect, would not help advance their ideas. But it was precisely the prominent people who vacationed at Saratoga Springs that Brown and Anthony wanted to reach, and they counted on Stone's reputation to attract them.[3]

Stone attended the second day of the New York State Woman's Rights Convention on August 16, which appointed a committee to organize the state's third woman's rights campaign. As hoped, her name filled the hall for the closing session, and her speech roused interest in the coming work. Speaking on woman's right to the elective franchise, which included the right not only to elect but also to be elected, Stone countered the objection that women could not serve in Congress because they would have to leave their babies. Of all people, she said, a Saratoga audience ought to see the weakness of that objection, for here sat scores of women who found time for extended stays at a spa, but "Wherever are the babies?" she asked in mock consternation. Rounds of applause greeted the home thrust. A reporter to the *New York Tribune* said he had never heard Stone speak with more "wit and sparkle," and that her "self-evident logic" easily vanquished the prejudices of the audience. Indeed, Martha Wright, who from her platform position surveyed the audience as Stone spoke, said she watched interest grow among some who had come to scoff. One woman in particular, whom Wright described as a "perfect marvel of flounces," enthusiastically acknowledged her conversion and bought a large supply of tracts to take home to friends.[4]

A month later, Stone attended the second New England Woman's Rights Convention in Boston, organized by Paulina Wright Davis. Still unhappy with the way national conventions were run, Davis had seized control of this regional meeting and was determined to demonstrate how a convention should be managed. When state committees appointed the previous year had tried to organize the convention for May, she thwarted their efforts, saying there had not been sufficient preparation, then invited a select group to meet with her to lay proper groundwork. In a published account of that meeting, she said the national conventions had too much talking and too little practical action. She objected to their vague appeals for equal rights and, maintaining that petitions should address specific legal injustices, said state legal codes should be carefully examined before activists drafted and circulated petitions. Accordingly, reports on laws affecting women in the New England states were the focus of the convention held on September 19 and 20, 1855.[5]

Two recent transplants had reinforced New England's forces and helped plan the convention—Caroline Dall, who had come from Toronto to coedit the floundering *Una*, and Caroline Severance, who moved from Cleveland. But the convention was in all respects the special project of Davis, who, as convention president, read a history of the laws of New England. This was followed by reports on individual states. Reporting on Massachusetts, Dall noted the progress made the previous spring when the governor signed a married women's property act that was considered the most significant gain for the woman's rights movement to date. Taking the floor after Dall's report, Stone used that advance to appeal for continued suffrage petitioning. She said the rights recently won, as well as any future gains, were precariously held as long as women could not vote, for what one legislature could pass, another could repeal. There were already indications some members of the next legislature might vote to reinstate the husband's right to his wife's earnings, she warned. And Massachusetts women would deserve to forfeit that right if they did not petition for a voice in their government. So persuasive was her appeal that the following day Dall presented a resolution calling the ballot "woman's sword and shield; the means of achieving and protecting all other civil rights," and urging the national convention meeting in Cincinnati the next month to make suffrage petitioning its priority.[6]

Stone and Wendell Phillips were featured speakers on the convention's first evening, but the spot of honor at the closing session was reserved for Ralph Waldo Emerson, who made his only appearance at a woman's rights convention and added his voice to the ranks of those advocating woman suffrage.[7] Davis's rivalry with Stone, obvious from the moment she took control of the convention, was evident also at its close. Elizabeth Oakes Smith, absent from woman's rights meetings since her denial of the convention presidency at Syracuse, had not attended this convention and no notice had been given that she was expected. But after Emerson finished what all thought was the convention's final speech, Davis announced that Smith would close the meeting with a reading of one of her poems. Smith appeared "dressed in a very thin white muslin, . . . low neck and bare arms, a very thin white scarf pinned on the shoulders with gold arrows. Two bracelets on each arm, an immense pin on her bosom, and her hands glittering with rings. Her head rigged in the latest fashion, . . . she seemed like a picture out of an old novel." As she read a poem as inappropriate as her dress, some women "almost wept" at this finale to their serious deliberations.[8]

In accordance with the resolution passed by the New England convention, the primary object of the National Woman's Rights Convention that met in Cincinnati on October 17 and 18 was to initiate suffrage petitioning in as many states as possible.[9] At this time, all suffrage petitioning was directed to state legislatures, which had sole jurisdiction over determining who could vote. Not until post–Civil War congressmen started drafting amendments to the United States Constitution extending federal authority in this area would suffragists think of seeking a federal suffrage amendment. With standing committees in place in New York and the New England states, Stone concentrated on activating the West. The Ohio Woman's Rights Association had conducted an extensive campaign the previous year and obtained a hearing before the legislature, but it had no plans to repeat the effort. Stone drafted a petition for her new home state and recruited Adeline T. Swift to circulate it in northern Ohio. Seeking volunteers to circulate petitions in other states, she lined up Hannah Tracy Cutler to work in Illinois and Euphemia Cochrane in Michigan. The work in Indiana was under the direction of the Indiana Woman's Rights

Association, which would be holding its annual convention the next week. One of its officers, Mary Birdsall, was at the Cincinnati convention to take home the plan. Amelia Bloomer, who had recently moved to Council Bluffs, Iowa, on the Nebraska border, was not at the convention but took up the work in that area.[10]

Urging petition work, Stone delighted the audience with a clever twist on an old taunt leveled at the woman's rights movement. Taking up the previous speaker's reference to opponents' gibe that the movement was comprised of "disappointed women," meaning women disappointed in love, the newly married Stone surprised the audience by confessing that she was, indeed, a disappointed woman. Disappointment, she said, had been with her since the earliest days of her memory. She was disappointed as a child, when she wished for things her brothers received but she was denied because they were not proper for girls. She was disappointed when her brothers went off to college and she was left behind because education was not needed by women. She was disappointed when she came to choose an occupation and found nearly every employment closed to her. Disappointment was women's lot, Stone said, but it should also be men's, for the ties of father and mother, brother and sister, husband and wife were so close that whatever affected one must affect the other. Stone told her listeners that it should be their business, as it was hers, to deepen the disappointment in the hearts of women until they would accept it no longer.[11]

This impromptu appeal introduced Stone's only major speech of the convention. Although she had scheduled herself to give the closing address, Ernestine Rose insisted that she be allowed to give it and raised such a row that Stone acquiesced. Rose was another critic of the national conventions, so perhaps Stone was not surprised by her demanding tone. But she was nonetheless appalled by the hostility Rose exhibited at a postconvention meeting at the Blackwell house. Although the convention had drawn many new faces from western states, few eastern activists had made the long trek to Cincinnati, and there were no big names other than Stone to attract a crowd. Attendance had been disappointingly low and after subtracting expenses from proceeds, there were not enough funds to reimburse traveling expenses of all of the speakers and officers. Rose had lectured on her way to the convention and had lectures pending at Cincinnati and Louisville, which Stone herself had arranged. Because the trip was profiting Rose, Stone asked her to accept one-way reimbursement. Rose haughtily replied that it was none of the convention's business what she did on her own account and insisted she be paid her full expenses. When Stone said she could not conjure up money that did not exist, Rose accused her squandering movement funds. Deciding to ask Phillips for money to pay the others, Stone met Rose's demand. Fortunately, the doorkeeper produced a roll of overlooked coins and it was not necessary to draw on Phillips.[12]

Susan Anthony, in charge of planning the New York campaign, had asked Stone to recruit workers for her at the national convention. But Rose refused to accept Stone as an intermediary and, with a "forced toss of her head," said Anthony herself must ask. Stone was so disgusted by Rose's attitude that she recommended Anthony not ask her. If Rose would work for the cause's sake, taking loss as well as gain, fine; "if not, don't torment yourself with her," Stone advised.[13]

Every organization has internal disagreements, personality conflicts, and rivalries, and the woman's rights movement was no exception. But this confrontation with Rose, coming on the heels of Davis's maneuvers, disheartened Stone so much she began to think of suspending national conventions and letting everyone work independently. Confiding her misgivings to Anthony had therapeutic effect, however, and she concluded that she was not discouraged because so many of their workers proved "small," but grateful there were so many "to whom a principle is more important than a selfish interest."[14]

After winding up postconvention business, Stone placed her suffrage petition in Ohio papers with instructions for return by the middle of January. Then she headed for Wisconsin to get the work started there. She opened what one paper called "the first attempt . . . to inaugurate a movement of this kind in Wisconsin" on November 1, with three lectures in Racine followed by three in Milwaukee. At both towns her audiences were poor. By the time she reached Madison on November 8, she had had no audience larger than two hundred and had found no one willing to circulate petitions. Dismayed, she wrote to Anthony that for the first time in her life, she felt "day after day completely discouraged." At her boarding house table, a gentleman had encouraged a woman to stay another night so she could hear Lucy Stone and learn something of her rights. "I have no desire to hear," was the woman's languishing reply, and this woman, said Stone, "represents the majority of women everywhere. Shall we let them die and be damned? I feel disposed to, but it is my moody week with its periodical headaches, and I shall feel braver and more hopeful when it is past." Stone had large audiences at Madison. She found volunteers to circulate petitions and two members of the legislature to present them and get them referred to select committees. After another three weeks in the state, she had petitions in full circulation. "The ball is set in motion here," she rejoiced, "and earnest men and women will keep it up." On her way back to Cincinnati, she lectured at several towns in northern Illinois and got petitions in "brisk circulation" at Hamilton, Ohio.[15]

During the next few weeks as she lectured close to home so she could spend more time with her husband, another cold blast of criticism came, this time from Gerrit Smith. Declining to help fund the New York campaign, Smith published a letter in *Frederick Douglass' Paper* saying that although he enthusiastically supported the goals of the woman's rights movement, its leaders, by abandoning the reform dress, had proven themselves unable to make the sacrifices necessary to attain those goals. Although his criticism was not directed at Stone alone, she had been the most prominent and visible of the Bloomer wearers. But after adding the ankle-length dress to her otherwise total Bloomer wardrobe, she had begun appearing in it as often as in the short. She still had a number of Bloomers when she moved into the Blackwell home, which she intended to wear until they wore out, but her husband's quip that he hoped they wore out quickly communicated his preference for the longer skirt. Stone and other leaders had abandoned the short dress and were not involved in the movement that would organize a National Dress Reform Association in February 1856. And this was why, in Gerrit Smith's estimation, the woman's rights movement was not "in the proper hands."[16]

Although Stone gave no hint to anyone but her husband that her resiliency was fading, Smith's loss of faith in her, coming on top of Anthony's and Brown's doubts, Davis's criticism, and Rose's overt hostility, undermined Stone's confidence in her leadership and in choices she had made. In addition to the criticism, the expectations of others weighed heavily on her. Although some criticized her management of the national conventions, no one else seemed willing to assume responsibility for them. Even Rose, who had reproached Stone to her face, refused to take charge of the next one, slated for her hometown of New York City. The *Una*'s new publisher, S. C. Hewitt of Boston, looked to Stone to rescue the paper, which was on the verge of folding. In October, he had warned her that the paper would die without an infusion of money or subscribers and insisted that only she could save it. Stone had sold hundreds of subscriptions in western states and Canada and established agents for the paper in several towns. What more could she do? Within a few months, Davis sold the *Una* to Mary Birdsall to merge with the *Lily*, which Birdsall had purchased from Amelia Bloomer. And Davis, considering herself "an aggrieved person," began writing for the *Woman's Advocate* of Philadelphia, whose object was to elevate women through improving employment opportunities, rather than "to clamor for the legal or political rights of woman."[17]

Anthony, too, continued to seek Stone's help. Like Stone, Anthony had been exhausted by her previous winter's labors, but she had not sought rest or recuperation until after the Saratoga convention. Although appointed to head the New York campaign, she was at the Worcester Hydropathic Institute for most of the fall, too ill to conduct the necessary preliminaries. She had asked Stone to recruit workers for her, but Stone got no commitments. She had requested funding from the national convention, but its proceeds had not covered its own costs. To encourage Anthony, Stone said even one petition, such as she could get in Rochester, would be as effective in influencing the legislature as more. When Stone received a letter outlining plans that would require strenuous labor on Anthony's part, she cautioned her to take time to get well before resuming work. A few weeks later Stone reported that Frances Gage was on her way to work for her, but again she urged Anthony not to lecture herself.[18]

Now in early January Stone received another appeal from Anthony. Besides Brown who worked independently, Anthony had only Gage working in New York, and she had no money to pay her or print tracts. Stone said she would try to send something from her lecture proceeds, although they were slim that winter, and suggested Anthony not hold another costly convention at Albany. The very fact that petitions were sent, however few or many, was enough to call public attention to the issue. Stone said she would soon be sending petitions to the Ohio legislature, and petitions were on their way in other states. "And the newspapers will tell of it, and people will talk and think, and that will be this year's gain."[19]

Although Stone's letters to Anthony maintained an air of self-assurance, the barrage of criticism from friends and coworkers shook her confidence as no opponent's attack could. Blackwell tried to counterbalance the criticism with love and appreciation. If she had defects, he said, he was not conscious of them. He admired her fidelity, honor, good sense, cheerfulness, sensitiveness, generosity. To those who would have her be "more womanly" and domestic, he countered that the popular novel character Ruth, who supposedly exemplified ideal womanhood, possessed "too little self assertion" and lived "too exclusively an affectional life." When he contrasted Stone's "broader views and stronger individuality," he could truly say she was "worth a hundred thousand ideal Ruths." Far from discouraging her public work, as one biographer maintained he did, Blackwell tried to provide a home life that would make Stone "younger and more active" and give her "a more elastic spirit and a fresher flow of life." Believing that the soul needed periods of relaxation just as the body needed sleep, he wanted to provide a refuge from "all the weariness and care of [her] public duties" so she could go forth refreshed and strengthened. He tried to help his wife live up to her ideals. When he received a letter from a sister scolding him for pressuring Stone to give up the reform dress, he was surprised to be perceived as the cause of her resumption of longer skirts and immediately sought to undo the damage. "Dearest Lucy, I shall have to go on my knees to you to induce you to resume the short dress. If your judgment still decides that you had better wear it, I would infinitely rather you should do so. I am not so thin skinned as you imagine and am quite willing to help you wear it and indeed to *help* you carry out your own convictions in every way."[20]

Stone did emerge from her few weeks at home with a "more elastic spirit and a fresher flow of life." After an Ohio lyceum engagement on January 22, she opened a tour of Indiana with a nerve-racking but soul-satisfying experience at Fort Wayne. With her train running late and due to arrive only half an hour before her scheduled appearance, she wired ahead for someone to pick her up at the depot and take her directly to the hall. On the way, she was told that the town was in a ferment over her visit. There had been so much opposition to her coming the previous week, when she was originally expected, that two balls had been organized to compete with her lectures. Stone rose to the challenge. "Of course the opposition must be killed," she wrote to Blackwell afterwards, "and the first evening must do it." She went "full of faith and hope" and gave such a lecture that "at times the house rang with cheers, and then again was still as the grave with a deeper feeling." Just half an hour into the lecture, she said, truth had triumphed.[21]

Stone made many converts, said one Fort Wayne editor, even among those who had previously ridiculed the movement, and her appeal for suffrage petitioning met great favor. Another editor, who had opposed her coming, said he had expected to hear ideas "altogether in discordance with reason and circumstances" but was surprised to find Stone "a clear and cogent reasoner" and very persuasive. Although he thought her only forceful point was the unfair disparity between male and female pay, he advised "all to hear her, and then judge like men."[22]

The triumph came as succor to Stone's spirit. Having shared her doubts and misgivings with her husband, she now shared the healing joy of good effect. "It was such an *infinite blessing* to feel again the old inspiration and faith in myself, and to see the audience swayed as the wind [sways] the grain," she told him. Not given to self-praise, she said she would not write this even to him except he knew how she had feared and loved to rejoice with her. She gave three more lectures at Fort Wayne and reported that all "were such as they used to be, and the papers came out quite in Louisville style. I am so glad to find again the old inspiration, and it comes to me more and more."[23]

Stone was lecturing in Ohio when news about the results of the season's work began arriving in March. "The petitions which I set on foot in Wisconsin asking for suffrage have been presented, made a rousing discussion, and then were tabled with three men to defend them!" Stone reported. Legislative action had taken place in both houses. C. Latham Sholes, one of the legislators she recruited in November, had presented the petitions in the senate, which referred them to a committee. He sent her a copy of his minority report along with a letter inviting her to "[c]ommand me whenever I can be of service to yourself and any good work." In the assembly, Hamilton H. Gray introduced a bill to extend suffrage to women under certain conditions. It was referred to the judiciary committee, which recommended against passage and tabled it.[24]

"In Nebraska too," Stone rejoiced, "the bill for suffrage passed the House and was only lost in the Senate because there was not time for a third reading. The world moves!" This was achieved by Amelia Bloomer, who, after lecturing and circulating petitions, addressed the territorial legislature on woman's right to vote. A week after her address, a bill granting suffrage to "all white persons" was introduced, but too near the end of the session for full action in both houses. The day after Stone reported this medley of progress, her petition to the Ohio legislature was referred to a select committee of the senate. In New York, the petitions circulated by Gage and Anthony were assigned to the House Judiciary Committee, which reported against them.[25]

Stone cheered the presentation of another petition, this one in England. In March 1856, a petition seeking revision of property laws affecting women was presented to Parliament, with Anna Blackwell's name heading the list of twenty-six thousand signatories. Anna was part of a circle of British women who were just beginning to organize agitation. Ellen Blackwell, who had met leaders of that group upon her arrival in London the previous fall, had notified Stone that her lectures were wanted there, and she and Henry had begun considering when they might be able to go.[26]

Stone closed her 1855–56 lecture season in mid-April and returned to Cincinnati to spend two weeks with her husband before they again took off in opposite directions. Instead of joining Henry for the combined investment and lecture tour he had proposed, she went east to look for possible home sites and to attend the American Anti-Slavery Society's anniversary on May 7 and 8, where she made the public announcement concerning her name. Henry and Sarah Lawrence were ending their residence in Cincinnati as well, so accompanying Stone were her sister and two nieces, the youngest of whom Stone had helped deliver in December. After her New York activities, Stone went to Coy's Hill to await word from Henry on where to join him for the summer.[27]

Blackwell had not only been inspecting their own properties, but also seeking additional investment opportunities for his Cincinnati partners. That spring the country was caught up in a national "speculation fever." Hundreds of men, their pockets full of land warrants, were crowding into land offices in Iowa, Minnesota, and Wisconsin, grabbing up land, sometimes sight unseen. Two of Blackwell's partners gave him $9,000 to invest for them at his discretion, offering the usual 10 percent commission. He purchased town lots in La Crosse, Wisconsin, which was just then being laid out, and land across the river at the site of a proposed town that would become La Crescent, Minnesota. As the men's agent, he needed to stay in Wisconsin another six to eight weeks to get the lots on the market, so he asked Lucy to meet him in Chicago so they could drive to La Crosse together.[28]

The couple left Chicago by horse and buggy on Sunday, June 8. Driving across the prairie through waist-high fields of clover and wheat, they arrived six days later at Richland Center, where they were persuaded to stay over and lecture. With only an hour's notice, the community filled the school house and adjacent grounds to hear Stone and Blackwell lecture on woman's rights that night, and they returned to hear antislavery the next morning. Amazed at this reception on the remote Wisconsin prairie, Stone was reminded of the *Liberator*'s old motto and wrote to Anthony that "Truly 'the field is the world.'" With such enthusiasm for reform lectures even here, Stone said she was tempted to forgo summer rest and resume lecturing at once. The next day the couple arrived in Bad Ax County, present-day Vernon County, and spent several days in La Crosse while Henry and George subdivided tracts and completed paper work required to put them on the market. Then they went to Viroqua, the county seat, and rented rooms at the North Star Hotel, where they made a summer home overlooking what Stone called "some of the most beautiful prairie land in the world."[29]

Blackwell owned hundreds of acres of this prairie land, which produced no income and required annual payments of interest and taxes. Because he now had no business income, he wanted to liquidate some of his assets and reduce investment expenses. Stone had purchased some "wild lands," too, which they wanted to get on the market. So while completing the work on his partners' La Crosse lots, he surveyed his and Stone's Bad Ax County lands and wrote up descriptions of the location and topography of each forty-acre parcel. To make some of the land income-producing, he hired teams to break the sod for a farm on a quarter section near town. Although he was strong and used to physical labor, Stone said he worked enough to kill two men and she expected to return east with only his skeleton.[30]

Stone found plenty to keep her busy, too. After speaking at the county's Fourth of July celebration before an audience of two thousand, she accepted invitations from across the region and spoke without charge. Sometimes she spoke at one town in the morning and another in the afternoon. On Sundays, Blackwell joined her for antislavery meetings. During the first week of August, they lectured several times in La Crosse and then Stone traveled down the Mississippi to Prairie du Chien.[31]

Like her Fourth of July oration, many of Stone speeches were about the crisis in Kansas, which had been building for more than a year as free-state and proslavery forces struggled for political control of the territory. Emigrant aid societies had sent so many settlers that northerners were in the majority in March 1855 when voters were to elect representatives to a territorial legislature. However, unwilling to cede the territory to an antislavery population, hundreds of Missouri invaders drove voters from the polls, stuffed ballot boxes, and elected a proslavery legislature. Convening at Shawnee Mission, this body adopted the revised statutes of Missouri as the territorial law and denied public office to anyone who opposed slavery. Refusing to be robbed of their political voice, northern settlers organized a Free-State Party and elected representatives to a convention at Topeka to draft a state constitution. Despite increased violence from the Missouri "border ruffians," voters ratified the constitution, elected state legislators, and sent a delegation to Washington to apply for Kansas' admission to the Union as a free state.

Congress sent a special committee to Kansas to investigate the Free State Party's charges of fraud, intimidation, and usurpation of authority. But President Pierce blamed the turmoil on the emigrant aid societies and warned that resistance to the Shawnee Mission legislature would be regarded as insurrection. In May 1856, a federal grand jury indicted members of the free-state government for high treason and, just as eastern papers began publishing the congressional committee's reports confirming its charges, authorities imprisoned many of its leaders. On May 22, guerrillas invaded the free-state center of Lawrence, destroyed its printing press, ransacked and burned buildings, and vowed to hang leaders held at Lecompton. In Washington on the same day, a South Carolina congressman, offended by a speech about Kansas, brutally assaulted Massachusetts Senator Charles Sumner on the floor of Congress.

The North sent money, guns, and emigrants to reinforce the free-staters, while the South sent armed troops to "maintain order." Proslavery forces guarded entry routes, confiscated guns and supplies, and blockaded Topeka and Lawrence. Confrontations between proslavery and free-state settlers escalated, and by the end of June, civil warfare raged that neither the territorial militia nor the U.S. Army could stop. In the summer of 1856, the whole nation watched with consternation the events in "bleeding Kansas."[32]

But although Stone lectured about the violation of free-staters' rights, she told her family she cared "less and less every day which triumphs, freedom or slavery. In either case, all the women of the land are yet subjects, ruled over by the white male population." Her financial dealings during her first year of marriage intensified her hatred of the legal incapacity she now shared with other wives. In March when she sent the Ostrom notes to Bowman, her trustee, and again in July when she wanted money for Henry's farm, she complained about laws that would not let her manage her own affairs. "From my heart deeper and deeper breathes the prayer that slavery may yet crush every white man into the same condition in which the white men have placed women. Then we will struggle up together out of our common wrong; but until the grip pinches them as it does us, they will never know that we are hurt."[33]

Despite irritation with her legal status, Stone shared happy, intimate days with her husband, driving with him over the prairie, visiting immigrant families, gathering berries in the woods, and planning their farm and future life. When she learned that Antoinette was pregnant, she sent a letter of congratulations and confided her despair that she herself might never be a mother. Nevertheless, she would try to "get the honey from each moment" with her husband. Anthony was perturbed by Stone's decision to spend the summer with her husband in the pursuit of "baby-making." "Such a body as I might be spared to rock cradles," she complained to Stanton, "but it is a crime for you and Lucy Stone and Antoinette Brown to be doing it." Anthony was planning a series of summer conventions and told Martha Wright she hated to think of holding them without Lucy or Antoinette, but because they were giving "themselves over to the ineffable joys of maternity, we must either abandon conventions altogether or learn to do without them." Unwilling to do the latter, she canceled the conventions when Stone wrote that she might not return until September.[34]

For four years Anthony had been learning from Stanton how marriage and motherhood kept women from participating in public work, and she could not forgive Lucy and Antoinette for assuming those bonds. She had complained bitterly after Antoinette's marriage, but Lucy said it was absurd for her to think she was left alone. Antoinette, too, told Anthony she had no intention of leaving her work and promised to hold meetings with her. But neither assurances nor actual work allayed Anthony's fears. When she suggested to Stone that Martha Wright and Wendell Phillips were concerned about her abandoning public work, Stone answered, "What bad thing have I done, or in what been remiss, that makes it possible for Mrs. Wright to say, 'it is pleasant to find Lucy's interest undiminished.' Now that I occupy a legal position in which I cannot even draw in my own name the money I have earned, nor give a valid receipt when it is drawn, nor make a contract, but am rated with fools, minors and madmen, does she think that in the grip of such pincers I shall be likely to forget and grow remiss?" To the implication that Phillips thought she was neglecting duty because she was not working in the East, she countered, "Does Phillips not know that 'our country is the world?' And that work done anywhere is done in the common field?"[35]

Stone and Blackwell's stay in Wisconsin extended beyond their expectation. A request from one of Blackwell's partners to buy more land threatened to keep him in Viroqua until the end of August or longer. In an effort to give settlers a chance to preempt speculators, the government ordered western land offices closed, and Blackwell could not register new selections until they reopened. While waiting, he helped Sam Blackwell prepare his holdings for the market. Then, unwilling to stay longer, he arranged for a friend to complete his partner's land entries when the offices reopened, and he and Stone left Viroqua during the third week of August.[36] Although Stone continued to consider the West an important field for labor, she would not return for three years.

Representative Woman

The letter from Susan Anthony awaiting Stone at her parents' home perplexed her. In May she had taken Anthony with her to reserve Broadway Tabernacle for the 1856 National Woman's Rights Convention and during the summer had written from Wisconsin asking her to issue the convention call and begin recruiting speakers. She had reminded Anthony that the call should appear over the names of Paulina Davis and Lucy Stone, as president and secretary of the Central Committee, and now Anthony reported that the call had been sent and that she had made sure Higginson signed their names to it. Higginson? "But why did he have anything to do with the call?" Stone asked. Because, Anthony replied, she had not wanted to take the responsibility. When no call was in circulation by the end of August, members of the Central Committee began to worry that if it were not issued soon, the convention would be a failure. Knowing Stone was in the West but unaware of her instructions to Anthony, Higginson took charge.[1]

When Stone saw the call in the *Tribune* a few days later, she was surprised to see that Higginson had scheduled the convention for October 8–10, instead of the two days, October 1 and 2, for which she had reserved the hall. But when her eyes reached the bottom, and she saw her signature as "Lucy Stone Blackwell," the surprise turned to pain. She had instructed Anthony to sign her as "Lucy Stone (only)," specifically saying "leave off the Blackwell." The sight of the unwanted name and a sense of betrayal made her feel "faint and sick." "O Susan! what did make you do it?" she asked. "At New York last spring, I had announced that I kept my own name. The public understood it. Newspaper criticism was nearly over, the battle more than half fought; and here, apparently by my own act, I seem to be now this and now that with no mind of my own, and the war is all to go over again." If it had been done by an enemy, Stone said, she could bear it. "But from you and Mr. Higginson, when I had so dearly loved you both, when I had trusted and believed fully in your integrity and firmness. Oh! Susan, it seems to me that it has wrought a wrong in me that will take many years to wear out."[2]

Higginson replied to Stone's complaint that although he fully agreed it was unjust for a wife to have to merge her identity with her husband's, still he was one "to submit to what appears inevitable." "Your *legal* name is Blackwell," he told her. "In all legal matters you *have* to sign it; and so I don't see how you can consistently sustain your position and fear that by and by you will entirely give it up." Higginson had been away all spring and summer and missed Stone's announcement at the antislavery convention and the newspaper reaction. When she explained that the question of legality had been resolved, that "Lucy Stone" was her legal name, he apologized: "When I told Susan Anthony to put the obnoxious Blackwell to your name I had not the slightest idea that you had made a public point of it and been criticized for it. . . . Had I known then what I know now, nothing would have induced me to do it. I don't wonder at your indignation."[3]

Name aside, Higginson's intercession exacerbated a problem Stone had already tried to lessen—finding a sufficient number of convention speakers when so many were preoccupied with Kansas and upcoming presidential election. She had directed Anthony to announce only two sessions each day, instead of the usual three, so they would not need as many speakers. Now, with Higginson's three days instead of two, they were back to a minimum of six sessions and Stone did not see how she could fill them. By the second week of September, she had not received one positive reply to her letters and had only Lucretia Mott and herself as speakers. Pouring out her misgivings to Anthony, she said she might cancel the third day. Anthony had no sympathy for one who had chosen to spend the summer in the West. She scolded Stone for putting off the correspondence and said Stone's pessimism made her want to undo all she had done. Stone apologized for having procrastinated and said her only hope for a successful convention lay in Anthony's "great indomitable perseverance and power of work."[4]

Despite Anthony's assistance, a successful convention became increasingly doubtful. Clarina Nichols was organizing relief efforts for the Kansas National Aid Committee. Antoinette Brown Blackwell was now several months pregnant and would not be at the convention. Anthony insisted she was not a public speaker and refused to read her paper on coeducation that Stone thought might be needed. In desperation Stone asked Davis, Garrison, and Phillips what they thought of reducing the convention to one day. After joining the Blackwell clan in New York and consulting with Antoinette, she took Davis's suggestion and postponed the convention until after the November elections.[5]

The seven-week reprieve gave Stone time to attend to personal matters. Henry and Sam were looking for small farms they could obtain in exchange for Wisconsin property, and she joined in the search. But the market for western land was glutted. Unable to raise income through land sales or trade, Henry began looking for a business position and by the end of October had joined a friend, Augustus O. Moore, in a firm that published agricultural books, purchasing his third interest with land and borrowed funds. His job for C. M. Saxton and Company would be similar to his previous work, traveling and selling in the West, but instead of hardware he would be selling books to farmers' libraries. He gave the firm a three-year commitment, and because he would be away from home so much, he and Lucy decided not to buy a house. Instead, they took a cozy attic apartment at Elizabeth's house in New York. "Harry has gone into business which will make him travel about six months of the year," Stone told her mother, "but it promises well, so we must bear the temporary loss of a home and during these three years look out for just such a place as we want."[6]

Meanwhile, the conflict in Kansas had ended. A new governor set the free-state prisoners free and formed a militia of bona fide settlers. The U.S. Army put down an another attempted march on Lawrence and arrested many of the Missouri ruffians. The even-handed justice quelled the five-month civil war, but not before it had claimed two hundred lives and cost two million dollars in destroyed property.[7] With the crisis over by election day, a successful "Save the Union" campaign gave the presidency to the Democrats' James Buchanan.

The seventh National Woman's Rights Convention met at New York City's Broadway Tabernacle on November 25 and 26, with Stone presiding. Early in their preparations, Anthony had suggested that Stone announce herself as president as a way of attracting a larger audience. Stone had rejected the idea, saying she always had too much "side work" to do to make the conventions run smoothly, and recruited Abby Kelley Foster for the post. But Foster's late notification that she could not attend had left Stone no choice but to preside herself, so she had quickly put together an opening address celebrating the progress of the movement. The postponement had given her time to put together a good convention program. She had not set the new date until learning when Wendell Phillips would be available and scheduled him to speak on the first evening. And when Garrison could not prepare resolutions for her, she wrote them herself.[8]

The extra time also allowed her to arrange introduction of the claim for woman's sexual equality in marriage. The free-love uproar of the previous summer and its association with woman's rights had convinced her the time had come to discuss the marriage question, and when Paulina Davis said Elizabeth Stanton was willing to introduce it, Stone wrote asking what she would cover. She knew Stanton was eager to discuss divorce, but her reply identified issues Stone considered not only "legitimate" for their platform, but also essential. Stone said she wanted to "push" the issue of "a wife's right to her own body," told Stanton she was "the one to do it," and urged her to come and "speak it all out." But Stanton could only send a letter.[9]

Stone found someone else to introduce the claim—Mary F. Davis, whose husband had just authored a book on the nature of marriage and the rights of marriage partners. Although the convention received the claim with respectful consideration, Davis's explicit references to sexual relations provoked the ire of those not sympathetic with the demand. The *New York Observer* called her speech "too disgusting to be put in print" and said she deserved to be "tongue-tied to prevent her foul mouth from being opened in public again." Unfortunately, Davis's speech was not supported by the expected letter from Stanton, which did not arrive until after the convention was over.[10]

The convention's primary business was adoption of a strategy devised by Stone and Brown Blackwell to replace the multistate petition campaign of the previous year. It had been difficult to find workers and money for that effort, and now with politics pulling activists into the antislavery field, it would be even more difficult to try again. Even Anthony, the mainstay of New York, said she would take an antislavery agency unless Stone had other work for her. So Stone and Brown Blackwell proposed that the convention, as a national organization, memorialize the state legislatures.[11]

Despite adoption of the memorial plan, Stone continued to urge individuals to petition. Since September she had been charming audiences with novel arguments for suffrage in a new lecture called "Border Ruffianism at Home." Drawing a parallel between the trampling of free-state rights and the trampling of women's rights, she struck a chord with those whose outrage and sympathies had been aroused by "bleeding Kansas." "One need not go to Kansas to find border ruffians or bogus legislation," she said. When future historians explained that Missourians deprived free-state men of the franchise and that New York men deprived women of the same, it would be said "that the border ruffians of Missouri and . . . New York were very much alike. One came with gloved hand and smiled and bowed, saying, 'I can't let you vote,' while the other said, 'If you do, I will blow out your brains.' The result is the same." Stone pointed out that despite all the injustices Kansas settlers had suffered at the hands of Missouri border ruffians, no law denied the free-state man's right to his child or his earnings. No law took away his right to vote or to the custody of his own person. "If his vote has been overruled, his property taken from him, it has been by lawless violence," violence that evoked the outrage and pity of a nation. But, she reminded her audiences, women had suffered those very same atrocities for generations, with no public outrage. What if the rights of the free-state man were successfully denied for fifty or a hundred years, she asked, and the present outrages became settled custom? What if the free-state man, with his spirit crushed into indifference, said, "I have all the rights I want; I do not care to vote; I am content to be as I am." Would not the world pity him? So if women said they had all the rights they wanted, all the more did they need to be taught the value of exercising "a great self-evident truth."[12]

Now at the height of her popularity and fame as an orator, Stone was one of three women included on *Life Illustrated*'s list of fifty-five speakers recommended for the 1856–57 lyceum season. The other women—Elizabeth W. Farnum and Elizabeth Oakes Smith—read literary essays on topics that appealed to sophisticated elites. The fact that three women ranked among the nation's eminent public speakers demonstrated that women had come a long way in the nine years since Stone fought for the right to read a graduation essay at Oberlin College. Stone was also included in a portrait grouping offered for sale to the public in the spring of 1857. Titled "Representative Women," the print alluded to Ralph Waldo Emerson's 1850 essay *Representative Men*, which extolled the influence of exemplary individuals. The print celebrated the accomplishment and influence of Stone, Lucretia Mott, Harriet Beecher Stowe, Abby Kelley Foster, Lydia Maria Child, Antoinette Brown Blackwell, and Maria Weston Chapman.[13]

Popular with the general public, Stone was highly sought by lyceums and offered top pay. But that winter the principles she tried to exemplify as a reformer collided with what was expected of a lyceum practitioner. She had accepted an engagement with the People's Literary Institute in Philadelphia, but not until a week before her scheduled appearance did she realize that the course was being held in Musical Fund Hall, the only hall in Philadelphia that barred blacks and the very place where, nearly three years earlier, she had promised never again to lecture in a segregated hall. Having to withdraw on such short notice was a sticky situation, made more awkward by Stone's having reconfirmed the engagement just two weeks earlier. At that time, she had wanted to cancel for other reasons, but the booking agent had begged her not to renege, saying she was the main attraction of the course and many people had bought season tickets solely because she was in it. "Almost any other lecturer on the list could be spared," he had told her, alluding to a roster that included Henry Ward Beecher, Thomas Starr King, Edwin Hubbell Chapin, and Horace Greeley, "but such is your popularity that I have reason to anticipate very unpopular results if you should fail to come." So Stone had kept the engagement.[14]

Then a member of Philadelphia's black community called her attention to the location of the course, and Stone notified the agent she would not lecture there if blacks were still denied admittance. Henry Blackwell appended a note saying he had been told by legal counsel that unless the restriction against colored people was dictated by state law, which was not the case in Pennsylvania, those who leased a building had the legal right to its unrestricted use and could themselves determine who should be admitted. But James and Lucretia Mott, from whom the agent sought help in resolving the matter, told Blackwell he was mistaken—the literary society could not overrule the hall's policy. It was too late to change location, they said, and if Stone did not lecture, the agent would be held personally accountable for the failure. Urging her not to break the contract, the Motts said they saw no reason why one class should exclude themselves from those things wrongly denied another. They frequently attended lectures at Musical Fund Hall and rode the omnibus, from which blacks were excluded. Lucretia thought it would be "too womanish and capricious" of Stone to break the contract and said she would accomplish more good by going ahead with the lecture and making an oral protest as she had before.[15]

Stone disagreed. She sent the booking agent a letter explaining her refusal to lecture and exonerating him of any blame. But he did not publish it. Instead, he announced that Stone had been forced to cancel her lecture because of the "indisposition" of some of her family.[16]

Meanwhile, the prospect of Stone lecturing in Musical Fund Hall had touched off a heated dispute within the Pennsylvania Anti-Slavery Society. Outraged that she would break her promise, the society's black members vetoed her appointment to speak at its fund-raising fair in mid-December and planned an indignation meeting for the night of Stone's lecture. Equally incensed by Lucretia Mott's defense of Stone, they censured her as well. The lecture's cancellation checked the indignation meeting but did not defuse the controversy, for the incident laid bare a festering sore—black abolitionists' resentment of their white coworkers' insensitivity to the pain of segregation. The feelings of Mary M. Jennings, a black woman who had been among those denied admittance to Stone's 1854 lecture, were shared by many. In the letter that first alerted Stone to the situation, Jennings related how painful it had been to stand at the door enduring the pitiless stares of those who flocked to hear Stone, many of whom belonged to the same antislavery society she did. After the fair committee voted Stone off its program, Jennings wrote again saying that culpability lay not with Stone, who had nobly sustained her principles even against the opinions of respected friends, but with the most prominent members of the Pennsylvania Anti-Slavery Society, who sanctioned Musical Fund Hall's segregationist policy with their patronage.[17]

Rescheduled to speak on December 29 at Philadelphia's National Hall, Stone gave her lecture on "Border Ruffianism at Home" to a racially mixed audience of four thousand. By all measures, it was a resounding success, but she was paid only thirty-five of the contracted fifty dollars. Although she felt certain the lecture was more profitable than it would have been on the original date when a winter storm had kept people homebound, she was in no position to demand that terms of the contract be met.[18]

While Stone lectured in Pennsylvania, Delaware, New York, Rhode Island, Massachusetts, and Maine, Antoinette Brown Blackwell mailed the national convention's suffrage memorial to twenty-five legislatures. Toward the end of February word came that it had been referred to legislative committees in several states and that Massachusetts and Maine had granted hearings. Meanwhile, Stone had learned she was pregnant. Mitigating her joy over this long-desired condition was the fear with which nineteenth-century women faced the uncertainties of childbirth. Afraid that her testimony before these legislatures could be her last work, she wrote to her husband, "Harry, dear, if in that hour that is before me, I should go out of my body or have it left a wreck, *this* work will be worthy work to leave as my *last*—an immortal cause will gain by it."[19]

Stone addressed the Judiciary Committee of the Massachusetts Senate on March 6, 1857, preceded by James Freeman Clarke and Wendell Phillips. She told the committee she appeared before them not only as one of the memorialists, but as the representative of one-half the nation's population, who sought equal legal rights and the right of suffrage as a matter of "simple justice." Women were not asking lawmakers to adopt some new idea that conflicted with established principles of government, but instead wanted them to make the practice of government consistent with the theories upon which it was based. Reminding them that Massachusetts stood in advance of nearly every other state in recognizing the legal equality of the sexes, she said it was because Massachusetts women had these rights that they also needed the vote. "All we ask," Stone said, "is the right to protect ourselves; for, after all, a woman does not want to be protected; all she wants is simple justice." Four days later, Stone and Phillips addressed a select committee of the Maine Legislature. But like Massachusetts' earlier Constitutional Convention, this committee believed that too few women desired the vote to warrant changing the constitution. Both legislatures gave the petitioners "leave to withdraw."[20]

With a baby on the way, Stone wanted a home of her own despite the fact that her husband would be absent half of each year. So Blackwell interrupted his western travels and joined her in another house search. Although nineteenth-century decorum dictated that pregnancy be kept private, he could not keep from dropping subtle hints. Reporting a visit from him, Lucretia Mott told her sister, "They are now looking for a house at South Orange or somewhere near New York, and he thought Lucy would rest and not do much this year. Perhaps some prospects interfere, if so 'he spoke in parables.'" They found their home in Orange, New Jersey, a two-story, nine-room "Gothic cottage" on a one-acre, tree-covered lot. It was not the farm they wanted, but it was the best they could manage at the time. "As soon as we can," Lucy wrote to a friend, "we mean to have a larger domain in the free, open country. But for the present, it is so good to say 'our own' to this little spot!"[21]

They purchased the $5,000 house with Wisconsin land, $500 cash, and a mortgage. Stone took half interest by supplying the cash and surrendering the $2,000 note she held against her husband for money invested in the hardware firm. They moved in on April 1, and then Blackwell resumed his work in the West while Stone got the house in order, supervising carpenters, masons, cleaners, and gardeners and putting in a vegetable garden. They had hardly any furnishings, but she arranged their many books on the floor around the parlor walls and assured her parents that "this snug little place . . . though not at all grand, gives us a good, pleasant home."[22]

Shortly after moving into her new home, Stone made her final public appearance of the season, at the American Anti-Slavery Convention on May 13. Now five months pregnant, she addressed her speech to the nation's mothers and extolled the power of maternal influence.[23] Her first two years of marriage had proved to be as active and influential as her single years, but motherhood, she knew, would change that. What she did not realize was that her having a baby would also change the woman's rights movement. Although she had exulted two years earlier that the movement had grown so large it depended on no one individual, during the summer and fall of 1857 it became apparent that the movement's vitality depended on her.

The Path for My Feet

The 1856 National Woman's Rights Convention was a celebration of the achievements of the woman's rights movement, but it also marked a turning point. The last national convention to be held in the fall and to be managed by Lucy Stone, it was followed by a year's lapse in the annual meetings. For the next decade, the movement would be virtually swallowed up by the sectional conflict over slavery. In 1857, the growing fervor for disunion made it increasingly difficult for Stone to keep woman's rights activists. Thomas Wentworth Higginson, who had emerged as one of the movement's primary leaders, was also a leader of the disunion movement.[1] And Susan Anthony, whom Stone had hoped would take over some of her own duties, turned to antislavery work instead.

When the American Anti-Slavery Society organized a series of conventions to be held across the North in the winter of 1857, it asked Anthony to manage the work in New York. Anthony checked with Stone before accepting the appointment: "Lucy and Nettie, is there any special woman's rights work for me to do this winter that will prevent me from working for the American Anti-Slavery Society? They talk of sending two companies of lecturers into this state, wish me to lay out the route of each and accompany one. They seem to think me possessed of a vast amount of executive ability."[2] Stone could not help but be disappointed. Antoinette Brown had once asked her if she did not grow weary from pushing the woman's rights movement by herself. But Stone had always expected new recruits to join in the work, and Anthony, whom she had been prodding onward for four years, had been her most promising recruit. The previous winter, when Stone had anticipated pregnancy, she had urged Anthony to protect her health, saying she was going to "retire from the field" and if Anthony returned to work too soon and died, "the two 'wheel horses' will be lost and then the chariot will stop." Now Stone was pregnant, and if Anthony did not take over, who would keep the chariot going? None of the figures who had stood out in the first years of the movement as leaders or potential leaders had embraced the cause as their primary work. Most, like Abby Foster, Elizabeth Jones, Lucretia Mott, and now even Clarina Nichols, were dedicated foremost to the antislavery cause. Paulina Davis had retired from active work after the *Una*'s failure. Chronic illness kept Ernestine Rose out of the field. Other ardent supporters—Harriot Hunt, Caroline Dall, Caroline Severance, and Antoinette Brown Blackwell—served the cause through their avocations. Elizabeth Stanton was still yearning to leave the "bondage of babies and children and house chores" so she could "make up for these long years of silence." Frances Gage and Hannah Cutler were also kept from sustained work by family obligations. So Stone told Anthony, "I don't know what to say about your going to lecture and work for the antislavery society. At first, when I thought that all the outdoor work would be done for you, I rather rejoiced and thought you would have an easier winter. But if you are to lay out the work and do all the financiering, it will kill you, and you must not do it."[3] She could not ask her to turn down the agency, however, for she could not compensate Anthony for woman's rights work.

So during the winter of 1857 Anthony organized antislavery meetings. And just as she had expected Stone to assist her temperance and woman's rights efforts, so she expected assistance with her antislavery work. But Stone refused to curtail her woman's rights lectures to help a cause already served by scores of other laborers. Anthony would not take no for an answer and insisted she at least attend the state convention at Albany. When Stone again refused, Anthony pleaded, "Lucy don't say no, I beseech you. . . . Your woman's voice is needed on the side of 'No Union with Slaveholders'." The Albany meeting would be preceded by conventions at Rochester, Buffalo, Syracuse, Utica, Albany. "Now, Lucy, say by return mail which of these, if not all, you will attend. We want you, the Cause needs you, oh! how much. Never was there so much need for the true word to be spoken." Again Stone refused: "Three voices of women are enough for one convention. I know just how you feel, with all the burden of these conventions . . . But Susan, brave, good Susan, I really am not needed with the force you have." But when Stone returned to New York in mid-January, there was another appeal from Anthony, insisting that she was needed and begging her to change her appointments. With a throbbing headache she trudged through a snow storm to see Oliver Johnson and learn what the situation was, and when he assured her that Garrison, Phillips, Pillsbury, Elizabeth Jones, Sarah Remond, and others would be at Albany, Stone again rejected Anthony's pleas. "The gain will be much less than the loss if I have to go and change a whole month's plans," said Stone. "Now Susan, don't fret and think you have no success when the meetings are large. The real success is to get a chance to tell the truth."[4]

Although the conventions ended in February, Anthony continued working with the antislavery society another three months and told Abby Foster. "I can truly say *my spirit has grown in grace,* and that the experience of the last winter is worth more to me than all my temperance and woman's rights work, though the latter were the school necessary to bring me into the antislavery work."[5] Anthony's priority had shifted, and Stone was left to bear the weight of the woman's rights movement alone.

Stone headed into the summer of 1857 with a growing sense of despair over the movement's lack of forces and money. As she began the correspondence for that year's national convention, she knew she must have it well-organized so others could easily assume its management. And Higginson reminded her that the *Woman's Rights Almanac,* a publication he had proposed after the last convention, to be edited by Stone and her husband, should be ready for distribution at the convention in October. But there was no money for the almanac or any other project. Stone's lectures had supplied an income sufficient enough to permit her to finance projects from her own purse—reimbursement of expenses in state campaigns as well as printing of tracts, proceedings, petitions, and memorials. Now, her fund-raising ability was about to be crimped, so she suggested that the almanac be postponed until funds were available.[6]

Also weighing heavily on her mind was what to say to the National Dress Reform Association, which had asked her to speak at its convention in June. Being six months pregnant, she would not go, but she must send a letter answering the continuing criticism of her having abandoned the short skirt. Since January, dress reformers had been accusing her of doing irreparable harm to the cause of woman by caving in to public opinion and compromising her own principles. The attacks were led by Lydia Sayer Hasbrouck, editor of the *Sibyl.* Hasbrouck was a staunch advocate of woman's rights and had been a warm admirer of Lucy Stone—until she abandoned the dress for reasons Hasbrouck considered dishonorable and traitorous. Hasbrouck said the excuse Stone gave a few months after she resumed wearing long hair and long dresses was that she thought the benefits of the short dress did not offset the inconveniences of wearing it. Hasbrouck found the explanation puzzling, for Stone had boldly worn the dress when it was far more difficult to do so. But then Antoinette Brown told her what she believed to be the true reason—that Mr. Blackwell did not like the dress. If this was the reason, Hasbrouck said, then Stone's action was reprehensible. "The great champion of woman's independence and freedom of action, yielding this grand principle, the foundation of her wrongs, for the sake of getting—and pleasing when got—a *husband.*" A person "of such frail powers to sustain principles" was not a reliable leader for the woman's rights movement, said Hasbrouck. Stone's defenders denied that her dress was a betrayal of principle; it was simply a matter of convenience, of trying "to strike a balance between the annoyance of long dresses and the annoyance of constant observation." But Hasbrouck insisted it was indeed a matter of principle, for the long dress was a physical curse that imposed "disease, pain, and death" and prevented women from participating equally with men in political, professional, and business affairs—the very objective for which Stone strove. *Sibyl* readers in Illinois, Michigan, and Iowa denounced Stone's "backsliding," and one went so far as to suggest that if Stone did not stay off the public platform until she resumed the short skirt, she would be an obstacle to those who did have the courage to act on their principles.[7]

In asking Stone to address the National Dress Reform Association's convention, its president, Charlotte Joy, said critics of the dress "presented as a most unanswerable objection" the fact that Stone no longer considered it important. If only Stone and other prominent women would lend their movement the leadership of their example, "the greatest obstacle to rapid progress would be at once removed." A change in woman's dress, Joy believed, was "of the first importance" in preparing women to understand and appreciate the necessity for change in their conditions and position in society.[8]

Responding to the idea that dress reform must precede other advances, Stone told the convention she did not expect widespread change until women, as a body, felt "a deeper discontent with their present entire position." While women "suffer taxation without representation and are placed, politically, lower than thieves, gamblers, and blacklegs, and bear it without a murmur; while as wives they quietly surrender the name their mother gave them and prefer to be called by that of their legal owner and to change it as often as they change husbands; while, as wives in most of the states, they have no right of personal property, or of earnings, and nowhere the right to the baby warm nestling in their bosoms; nor even the right to themselves, and yet with exultant boast iterate and reiterate that they have all the rights they want; believe me, they who can bear all this are not in a condition to quarrel with the length of their skirt." Stone said woman's "miserable style of dress" was a consequence of her "vassalage," not its cause, and once woman clothed herself in the dignity of claiming and exercising her natural human rights, then she would be able, "unquestioned, to dictate the style of her dress."[9]

But just as Stone was replying to those who thought the dress issue was "of the first importance" to the woman's rights cause, Anthony wrote that she thought woman's "social freedom" was the crux, and she wanted the next convention to "strike deeper than any of its predecessors" by discussing divorce. "The world, even the religious part of it," Anthony argued, was "ready to grant to woman her property rights, her industrial, and almost her political." It was time to move on to "personal liberty." She pointed to the struggles of Eliza Eddy and Mary F. Davis as indications of the need.[10]

Eliza Eddy, daughter of Francis Jackson, had left an abusive husband after seven years of marriage and returned to her father's Boston home with two young daughters. Stone had renewed her friendship with Eliza when she stayed in the Jackson home in March while addressing the state legislature. Shortly thereafter, the children's father abducted them and absconded to France. After consulting a lawyer and learning she had no legal recourse, Eliza declined Stone's offer for Blackwell to accompany her to Europe to retrieve the girls. But she urged Stone to tell her story to awaken women to the "necessity of their having a voice and hand in making the laws." Mary Davis had divorced an abusive husband before marrying spiritualist leader Andrew Jackson Davis.

Although Anthony had worked with Davis in the temperance movement years earlier, she had only recently heard her speak on the marriage question and now considered her the "moral hero of this generation." In urging Stone to introduce the divorce question at the next convention, Anthony said, "It seems to me we have played on the surface of things quite long enough. Getting the right to hold property, to vote, to wear what dress we please, etc. etc. are all good; but social freedom, after all, lies at the bottom of all, and until woman gets that, she must continue the slave of man in all other things."[11]

Stone agreed that women and men needed to be able to dissolve unloving marriages. But having just had a complete stranger tell her that she had no right to go before the world as a public reformer until she resumed the short skirt, she was in no mood to have one of her dearest friends belittle her hard labors of the past ten years. "I don't know what you mean by saying that we have played on the surface etc.," Stone responded. "Now if to break down every barrier so that all departments of industry shall be open to women; to compel colleges, theological and law schools to open their doors, and society to give us the motives which urge men to enter these; to change the constitutions of every State in the Union so as to secure the ballot; to sweep away all statutes that make distinctions on account of sex—[if] this seems to you to be 'playing upon the surface,' to me it has been work most terribly in earnest, and laying so deep that it will take years after we are all dead to bring to light."[12]

Stone agreed that the question of woman's self-sovereignty did underlie their demand for equal rights, and that wives should have the right to control their own bodies, but this claim was already part of their agenda. The question of divorce, on the other hand, she considered as distinct from their movement as antislavery or temperance. It was not a question of equal rights between man and woman, she said, for "divorce is free to one as to the other. If man finds it less hard to bear, it is because the things we are struggling to get for woman are his already." Insisting that the question did not belong on the woman's rights platform, she urged Anthony to call a special convention to discuss divorce and said she would attend it and aid that cause all she could.[13]

Another letter piqued Stone's defensiveness. Higginson scolded her for allowing domestic work to put her in the exhausted state in which she had appeared at the May anniversaries. He appealed to her not to "be like dear Mrs. Child, who enslaved herself for some three years to . . . do nothing but keep house." Stone was stung. After six months of lecturing, she had spent three or four weeks getting a new house in order while still working in several engagements. This was cause to suspect her of abandoning reform work for domestic life? Higginson's fear, he said, was generated by two factors: one, her "sigh after 'new laborers,'" and two, her proposal to postpone the almanac for lack of money. "Never before did you give up anything that ought to be done for no better reason than that," he protested. Unaware of the condition that would keep Stone from active fund-raising for several months, Higginson saw her caution as a slacking of commitment.[14]

Higginson was, more than any other man at that time, dedicated to the success of the movement and willing to take on the work needed to sustain it. He and Stone had known each other for more than eight years. He knew her dedication, so she could not understand why he feared she might lay the work aside. Higginson said her note suggesting the almanac's postponement made him think that she must be depressed or tired, that something was wrong. He consulted Anthony and she agreed—Stone did not appear "quite right" in New York.[15]

There was Stone's answer: Susan Anthony. In pleading for Stone to speak at her antislavery meetings, Anthony had said she was "terribly afraid lest what everybody says will be true, that like other wives you will flat out and do nothing." At the time, Stone had been perplexed by the suggestion that people might be saying such things about her, but it had become evident that the "everybody" Anthony talked about was herself. It was she who had complained to Elizabeth Stanton, Martha Wright, and Wendell Phillips about Stone's presumed lack of activity the previous summer—during months Stone normally set aside for rest. And now, hearing from Higginson what she had been hearing from others for two years, Stone's "cup ran over" and she confronted her critic.

"Susan, pray tell me what is the basis of the intimation I hear from so many, viz. 'Susan says Lucy does not seem exactly right,' or 'Susan says Lucy does not work as well as she used to,' or 'Susan says Lucy is not as self-sacrificing as she used to be?'" When Anthony asked who said such things, Stone cited examples and said that when these people repeated, as from Anthony, what Anthony had put in most of the letters written to her since her marriage, she had "every reason to believe them." Stone said Anthony's lack of faith made her feel "wounded, grieved, hurt almost as I never was before." "I felt that whether I hold more or fewer meetings, gave more or less money, went less or more to help you, *you*, next to Nettie of all persons in the world, should not distrust me." But Stone refused to be directed by Anthony's expectations. For ten years she had been setting her own course, planning and executing, as she had earlier told Blackwell, "without counsel and without control." She would continue to "make the path for my own feet," and she owed no explanation to anyone.[16]

Anthony shrugged off Stone's complaint. They had no time for such "personal matters," she said. If Higginson implied she had said anything disparaging of Stone's faithfulness to women, then he misunderstood. "I assure you no such feeling is with me."[17] Despite the disclaimer, the women's warm friendship had cooled.

Nevertheless, Stone still looked to Anthony to take a larger role in the woman's rights movement. Unable to accept lyceum invitations for the fall and winter, she referred the committees to Anthony, hoping they might entice her to pass up antislavery work for woman's rights. Since their acquaintance, Stone had been urging Anthony to become a lecturer despite Anthony's insistence that she could not put ideas "in symmetrical order" or say the "right words in the right place and time" and that people simply would not listen to her. Anthony had concluded that the "good spirits" simply had not made her a "speaking medium." But Stone dismissed these complaints and urged her to have as much faith in her speaking power as in her "acting power." Anthony had been reading essays at teachers conventions and after a meeting in August triumphantly reported that she had spoken extemporaneously to answer an opponent of equal pay for equal work. Although she wished Stone had been there to "dress him down," she said she did the best she could and "never spoke more to my own satisfaction in my life. And my prayer continually is that *somebody's mantle* may fall upon me and I be enabled to speak the needed word wherever I may chance to be."[18]

Stone had hoped that Anthony would, indeed, take up her mantle when motherhood forced her to lay it aside, and now the time was near. With her baby due in September, she would not be able to attend the national convention in October and called on Anthony and Higginson to take charge of it. Urging Anthony to cultivate her "power of expression" so as to overcome her lack of confidence, she asked her to preside, which involved giving the convention's opening address. "The subject is clear to you, and you ought to be able to make it so to others. It is only a few years ago that Mr. Higginson told me he could not speak, he was so much accustomed to writing. But he tried, and now he is only second to Phillips. 'Go thou and do likewise.'" Stone already had convention arrangements well under way. After consulting with other members of the Central Committee, she had decided on Providence, where the novelty of a woman's rights convention would offset the fact that they would have no new speakers. Elizabeth Chace had agreed to superintend local arrangements and Paulina Davis to arrange lodging. She had speaking commitments from Lucretia Mott, Elizabeth Jones, Antoinette Brown Blackwell, and several others, so there would be little for Anthony and Higginson to do but manage the meetings.[19]

But Anthony wanted the convention to meet in Chicago. The Central Committee had talked of holding it there to continue the brief practice of alternating between east and west, but Stone had recommended against it because there was no one in Chicago to take charge of local arrangements and the committee could not afford to send speakers that distance. Early in July, before learning of Stone's pregnancy, Anthony reported to her that temperance activists were planning a world convention in Chicago and suggested they take advantage of that gathering and its attendant publicity by holding their convention in conjunction with it. But Stone pointed out that that convention was scheduled for the summer. Even if they considered it desirable to move the woman's rights convention up from October, there would not be enough time to make new arrangements. And because nearly all their speakers would have to be sent west at great expense, and the aging Lucretia Mott could not be expected to travel so far, Stone thought it best to stay east. But, she concluded, because Anthony and Higginson would have to manage the convention wherever it was held, she would let them decide.[20]

When Anthony saw the call for a National Disunion Convention in Cleveland during the third week of October, she wrote to Stone full of enthusiasm. "To me, it now seems that the great objection to our holding our Woman's Rights Convention in Chicago is removed—viz. that of the great expense of importing speakers from the East. . . . If our convention could follow the Disunion, the distance from Cleveland to Chicago is not great, and I see no reason why we could not get a good force of speakers to stop and go on to Chicago." Saying she would love to have the convention in the West because she had never been there, she volunteered to go to Chicago to take care of the preliminaries herself.[21]

Although Higginson preferred Providence, Stone gave Anthony permission to arrange a western convention. "It would be grand if we *could* have a convention at Chicago," she agreed, "for many would gather from all over the great West who yearn to come to our conventions but cannot come 'away East.' Aunt Fanny, Mrs. [Mary F.] Davis, Elizabeth Jones, S. B. Anthony for certain and two or three of the Disunion speakers, with various letters, would give material enough for workers. I doubt whether Lucretia would go, but maybe she would, and I should dearly love to have you know something of that wonderful West. You must manage it, Susan, and if you can make it work I shall be glad. . . . You have my consent to anything your judgment approves." Saying she would write the call, arrange eastern publicity, and recruit a Chicago friend to help with preliminaries, Stone urged Anthony to do "the whole getting up." "Do just what you think best, and I will say amen. Only be sure of your funds and speakers and [do] not hold more days than you have persons to fill well."[22]

Although Higginson could not go to Chicago, he approved having the convention there if Anthony could get enough commitments from western women. So when Anthony received positive replies from Elizabeth Jones, Frances Dana Gage, Mary F. Davis, and Josephine Griffing, Anthony asked Stone to issue the call for Chicago. But, instead of accepting responsibility, she asked what more Stone wanted her to do. She was going to work as general agent for a corps of antislavery lecturers and wanted to finish all woman's rights assignments before September first.[23]

Stone could not help but be discouraged. For four years she had been prodding Anthony to make woman's rights her primary work. Even before Anthony's appointment to the Central Committee, Stone had included her in its decision-making processes. She had cheered her on in the New York campaigns, secured workers for her, sent drafts of petitions and bills, sent money out of her own pocket, given advice and moral support. The previous year she had involved Anthony in convention planning, grooming her to take over that responsibility. And now Anthony repelled the work just when Stone needed her most.

Stone did not issue the call—not for Chicago, not for Providence. Her hand was stayed not only by Anthony's refusal to take charge but also by indications that the disunion convention might not meet. In August the nation plunged into financial panic, with banks and major business firms failing, stocks and property values tumbling, thousands thrown out of work, and money sources drying up. Across the country, public meetings of all sorts were canceled, and Garrison was trying to get the disunion convention postponed. Stone also learned that Phillips, and perhaps others upon whom Anthony counted, did not intend to go to Cleveland regardless and, therefore, would not go to Chicago.[24]

Although a successful convention in Chicago seemed improbable, there was nothing to prevent one in Providence. But Stone was now eight months pregnant and in no condition to do anything herself. As the weeks passed with no call, others became concerned. "Then the Woman's Rights Convention. When? and where?" Lucretia Mott asked Martha Wright. "Now that Lucy Stone is otherwise occupied, Antoinette, too, not able to attend, S. B. Anthony lecturing on Slavery, Mrs. Rose very poorly . . . , who is there to lead? Wilt thou? I have rather hoped this year would 'slide' but I'm ready to do the little that remains for one, only I don't want to spend any money in traveling."[25] Although Mott shared this willingness to do what remained with Wright, she did not with Stone, and so the convention's success depended on Anthony while Stone awaited the birth of her baby.

The final weeks of Stone's pregnancy were filled with anxiety made sharper by a sense of personal failure. "Why are there so few women workers?" Anthony had asked her. "Why do we not have new women coming onto the stage of public action?"[26] Stone must have wondered if dress reformers were correct, that her example did not inspire followers. Rejecting the argument expressed in Stone's letter to the dress reform convention, a writer to the *Sibyl* said it mattered little if the long dress was cause or consequence of woman's vassalage. What was needed to effect change was for those who recognized the "evil of the present style" to demonstrate a better way. "If the most talented and able advocates for the equal rights of women have decided that it is no use to advocate a reform in her dress until the great body of women rise en masse and fearlessly claim their God-given rights . . . then I fear they will look and hope in vain in this their day and generation."[27] This argument was the very echo of the one Stone had expressed to Anthony three years earlier. Yet, despite her belief in the short skirt's importance to woman's advancement and her personal preference for it, she had resumed a long skirt. Why? Antoinette had said it was because of her husband's preference; and this was probably true. The notice and trouble it gave her, the urging of friends to give it up, the abandonment by others—all these had made it easier, but had she, after all, given it up to please her husband? Had she proven false to her own principles? And had this recreancy to principle caused those who looked to her for inspiration to lose faith in her? Had she made the path of others more difficult?

Stone poured out her fears and self-reproach to her husband. Blackwell blamed himself for his wife's feelings of failure. It had been he, after all, who had turned her from her determined path and persuaded her that she was entitled to the personal happiness of a family life. He had promised she would be able do more with him as a partner than she could alone, but he had been more hindrance than help. Alone in the New York room where he stayed overnight when work kept him late, he pondered his own failures and resolved to do better. "My own love, what can I say to comfort you in your lonely sufferings; what can I do to benefit you! I know of nothing better than to promise to live bravely and honestly and to subject mere material aims to loftier purposes. . . . In any event, my own wife, take courage! God is near you; he will not desert you. No final failure is possible to you."[28]

On Sunday morning, September 14, Stone "ushered into the world a brave, vigorous little girl." The new mother's relief was dulled a few days later when a letter from Anthony asked her to postpone the woman's rights convention until spring. "It seems impossible to array our forces for effective action this autumn," Anthony said. "Nothing looked promising, nobody seemed to feel any personal responsibility," and she felt "utterly incompetent" to proceed without commitments from reliable speakers. Stone had little sympathy. "I am glad you have had to 'groan' for this convention," she told Anthony. "I have had to do it so many years that it seems good to have someone else have the burden of it."[29]

Nevertheless, she did not like the idea of skipping a convention. She had been tempted to cancel the previous year's convention but dismissed the idea when she considered that the annual meetings were the movement's only formal organization. A call could yet be issued for Providence in November, but who would take charge? Even Antoinette Blackwell, despite willingness to speak there, advised postponement. With a heavy heart, Stone acquiesced. "Since I can't do anything to help the convention and so many of you are for letting it slide, I will make the announcement for next May," she told Anthony. "I have no doubt it is best *in the circumstances,* but I have a lingering regret at a departure from our old mode of acting." Sending an announcement to the papers that the convention would meet in New York City during anniversary week in May 1858, Stone authorized the only break in the annual meetings of the National Woman's Rights Convention.[30]

Taxing Times

The financial panic that thwarted the 1857 National Woman's Rights Convention ushered in a depression that frustrated Henry Blackwell's attempts to achieve financial independence and provide the kind of home life that would permit Stone to lecture despite maternal demands. Although he considered land speculation "the only good business in the west," he knew it was growing precarious and tried to get his land on the market and make some of it income-producing before the "Western bubble" burst.[1] Wisconsin land had purchased his and Lucy's home and a rental house next door. Illinois land worth $2,500 had purchased part of his business partnership, while additional acres served as collateral on a $5,000 loan for the remainder. Other land sales and income from his Viroqua farms offset his investment expenses and allowed him to contribute $200 annually toward his mother's upkeep and to pay George for managing his western affairs. As long as investment income continued to cover his investment costs, he and Stone could live quite comfortably on his $1,500 annual salary.[2]

The economic down turn in 1857, however, upset his calculations. Even before the actual collapse in August, money was tight. In June, Stone sold bank stock to pay the $900 balance on her Appleton property and borrowed $500 so Blackwell could pay interest on his business loan. One evening in July, Blackwell returned from New York with Abby Kelley Foster in tow. She had spent the entire day in a fruitless effort to raise funds for an antislavery campaign, and he brought her to Stone for a list of potential donors in their area.[3] As people tightened their hold on money, the economy slowed and businesses stagnated, among them C. M. Saxton and Company. With greater debts than Blackwell had realized when he bought in, the business could not sustain three partners in the current economic climate. He wrestled with the dilemma for two months and finally, unwilling to risk more borrowed capital to buy out Saxton, decided to leave. Saxton returned his land but only half the cash. So in addition to costing him $2,500, the sell-out jeopardized the land he had put up as collateral.[4]

Blackwell expected to rejoin the company within a couple of months, after Moore arranged to buy out Saxton. But meanwhile he took a position as book-keeper and confidential clerk with the Vanderbilt steamship line. Difficult as it was to raise cash in June and July, it was even harder in August when the crash came. When George asked Henry to raise two or three thousand dollars for another La Crosse investment, Henry replied with consternation, "Why, George, there are firms here worth $100,000 who would pay five percent a month for that sum . . . *it cannot be got.*" The West, evidently, had not yet begun to feel the full impact of the crisis, so Henry hastened to inform his brother that "the *worst of times* financially are upon us and will not rally until they have caused a *complete smash* in all Western operations." Some New York banks had closed, he reported, and others were paying in specie rather than paper money. Bank notes were selling at 5 to 10 percent discount, and land warrants were down to half their previous cost. Cash simply was not circulating. Henry was due the proceeds of an Illinois land sale but the agent had not sent him one penny. With western land unmarketable at present, Henry told George the entire family would need all their small cash means to pay taxes and avoid forfeitures.[5]

At the end of August, Moore took over the firm and hired Blackwell to take charge of a new venture. While selling agricultural books the previous winter, Blackwell had put together a new line for the firm—a collection for school libraries. He had consulted with the Illinois superintendent of schools, compiled a list of appropriate books, called on New York and Boston publishers to get special terms, and obtained a contract from the state of Illinois allowing the firm to canvass school districts to sell the collections, or "libraries." Moore was especially attracted to the venture, saw its potential in other states, and put Blackwell in charge of the enterprise. Now free to manage his time, Blackwell went to Illinois to collect the money owed him and attend to other investment concerns. Although he would have to return in the spring to organize sales and distribution of the school libraries, for now he had more time at home.[6]

Over the summer of 1857, as her husband juggled credits and debits, Stone coped with shifting plans for the national convention and helped Higginson compile the *Woman's Rights Almanac.* Intended as the first in an annual series, the book combined data collected for the reports on the status of women with new material such as C. Latham Sholes's minority report to the Wisconsin legislature and Stone's address to the 1856 convention on the "Results of the Woman's Rights Agitation." When the almanac was printed in October, she placed it in area bookstores, sent bundles to activists in various states, and, because Higginson did not want it "known as written by a man," arranged publicity.[7]

On December 22, Stone made her first public appearance since the birth of her baby, speaking at an antislavery meeting arranged by Susan Anthony in

Orange. Although she intended to continue lecturing in nearby towns, she spent the following weeks nursing her husband through recurrent cases of boils instead. Already instigated, however, was a bold demonstration that carried her voice across the nation that winter. When the tax bill on their home arrived earlier that month, she acted as she had long urged women property owners and returned the bill unpaid. Although she paid land taxes in Iowa and Wisconsin, as a nonresident she could not vote in those states even if they had permitted women to vote. Now taxed in the state of her residence, she took the opportunity to protest the violation of American principles: "Sir—Enclosed I return my tax bill without paying it. My reason for doing so is that women suffer taxation and yet have no representation, which is not only unjust to one half the adult population, but is contrary to our theory of government." Stone said that although some women had been paying taxes under protest for several years, they had had no effect. By refusing to pay her tax, she wanted to call men's attention to "the wide difference between their theory of government and its practice" and believed their sense of justice would them induce them end taxation without representation.[8]

The township collector called to make sure Stone understood the consequences of her action. A justice of the peace, he informed her, would have to authorize the sale of some of her personal property to pay the tax and related court costs. Sympathetic to her cause, he showed her a similar protest, written eighty years earlier by a sister of Richard Henry Lee, one of the signers of the Declaration of Independence, and let her copy it to use in her lectures. He had her protest published in the *Orange Journal*, along with the relevant provisions of state law concerning tax delinquency, and shortly thereafter, public notice was posted that on January 22, 1858, at two o'clock in the afternoon, at Stone's home, a constable would sell "to the highest bidder, for cash, the following goods, to wit:—Two tables, four chairs, one stand and two pictures," to make the tax assessed against her.[9]

At the appointed hour, the constable carried the attached items onto her porch. As Stone stood holding her four-month-old daughter, he sold a marble table worth $12 for $7.50 and photographs of Gerrit Smith and Salmon P. Chase together for $3. The proceeds from these items exceeded the $10 needed, so he closed the sale and paid Stone the balance.[10]

Stone's protest attracted much notice. Even before the sale, it inspired a scholarly paper presented to the New Jersey Historical Society by one of its prominent members. Noting the similarity between Stone's letter and that written in 1778, he pointed out that Richard Henry Lee had dismissed his sister's demand as unreasonable. He related the history of New Jersey's brief experiment with woman suffrage, including problems that prompted the legislature to rescind it in 1807, and predicted that now as then, consideration for the "good order and dignity of the State" would keep legislators from adopting woman suffrage. Newspapers across the nation reported the auction under such headlines as "Revival of the Spirit of Seventy-Six," "Lucy Stone and the Col-

lector," and "Sale of Gerrit Smith and Gov. Chase for Taxes." The event supplied ample meat for Stone's critics, who raged over her defiance of law, her
impertinent show of independence from her husband, and her continual thrust-
ing herself before the public. One critic suggested that the affair was a sham.
The valuable articles Stone wanted to keep, he said, were bought by friends
and returned to her, while worthless things she no longer wanted were disposed
of without the expense of an auctioneer. But others praised Stone's "exhibition
of pluck," "good grit," and constancy to principle. Lydia Sayer Hasbrouck
lauded Stone's action, announced to *Sibyl* readers that she, too, would refuse
to pay taxes, and issued a call to action: "Let every taxpaying woman in the
United States refuse to meet these unjust demands."[11]

Two weeks after the auction Stone and Blackwell lectured on "Taxation without Representation" in Orange. Reflecting his interest in politics, Blackwell
argued that no matter what a party's interests and goals, woman suffrage was
politically expedient. Enfranchising women would allow Democrats to uphold
the Jeffersonian doctrine of giving votes to labor, the American Party to double
the number of native-born voters, and Republicans to more than double their
influence toward abolishing slavery and the liquor traffic. Stone focused on
America's political ideals, which, she reminded the audience, decreed that political power was vested in "the people." But by limiting suffrage to "male
citizens," New Jersey and other states created an "aristocracy of sex" and placed
women with paupers, criminals, insane persons, and other incompetents not
considered part of "the people." She urged the women in her audience not to
take the insult as a compliment, but to sign her petition asking the legislature
to grant them the right to vote.[12]

The conclusion reached by a Stone biographer that Blackwell was "furious"
about Stone's tax protest is based on the misreading of a letter Stone wrote
two nights after the lecture, delivered in a hall that newspaper accounts reported as "filled to overflowing long before the speaking commenced." Telling
her mother of her refusal to pay her taxes, Stone said, "Harry and I had an
overflowing meeting about it night before last." Unaware of the couple's lecture
on February 8, this biographer interpreted "overflowing meeting" to mean an
argument. But Blackwell fully supported his wife's protest, just as he supported
and tried to facilitate her lecturing. After a second lecture in Orange a week
later, he made preliminary contacts for her to lecture at Jersey City and Brooklyn, even as he prepared to leave for Chicago. When Stone worried that caring
for the baby would prevent her from preparing adequately, he advised her to
postpone the lectures until she could spend a week at Elizabeth's. With a nursemaid watching the baby there under his mother's supervision, she would be
free to "make well planned arrangements." Later, when Stone reported that
she had agreed to speak in a prestigious course in New York City, he urged her
to take sufficient time to prepare and offered suggestions for her text.[13]

Illness had kept Blackwell homebound for much of December and January,
and another outbreak of boils in February delayed his departure for the West.

But a couple of matters requiring his immediate attention sent him packing despite a swollen knee that hampered his walking. He received word that money expressed to Viroqua for taxes had not arrived and, not wanting to risk sending more money astray, he decided to pay in person those due in Madison. Just as he was leaving, George notified him that land warrants he had deposited in La Crosse were missing, and four hundred dollars would be needed to buy replacements and complete pending land entries for one of Henry's investment partners.

This second matter occupied much of the correspondence between Blackwell and Stone over the next few weeks, and a misreading of those letters has resulted in the erroneous conclusion that Blackwell mishandled investment funds and took some of Stone's land and savings to extricate himself from resultant legal difficulties. The problem stemmed from the government's closing of western land offices in the summer of 1856. Unable to finish registering tracts selected for Lewis Worthington, Blackwell deposited the land warrants and registration fees with a La Crosse firm and arranged for a friend to complete the entries when the offices reopened. However, the offices remained closed through the rest of 1856 and all of 1857, during which settlers moved in and established themselves on tracts Blackwell had chosen for Worthington. This was precisely the effect the government intended—allowing settlers to preempt speculators—but it required Blackwell to repeatedly make new selections. Now, with land offices expected to open in April, he wanted to get his selections registered promptly to avoid further preemptions. When Henry learned that some of the deposited warrants were missing, he immediately thought George was to blame. The previous year as the price of warrants dropped, George authorized the holding firm to sell some of the idle warrants and replace them with lower priced ones. Henry scolded George for using assets without the owner's permission and directed him to seal the packet before a notary and deposit it with a different firm. Because warrants were now missing, Henry assumed George had again authorized their sale and resented the new demand on his own finances.[14]

Henry could ill afford four hundred dollars for new warrants. C. M. Saxton had failed to make payments on his notes to Henry, and L. A. Ostrom, purchaser of the Blackwell brothers' shares of the hardware firm, had also defaulted on his payments. One of the matters Henry had to attend to in Illinois was inspecting the farm Ostrom had put up as security before beginning foreclosure proceedings. Despite these losses, Henry had scraped together enough money to repay his business loan, but he now had no cash reserves. A six-month salary advance gave him the means to pay his western costs, pay the hall rental for Stone's lectures, and leave her a small fund for incidental expenses. He now had only one means of raising additional cash. Although he had wanted to hold the grain from one of his Viroqua farms until spring when it would bring a higher price, he directed George to sell it at once and purchase warrants from the proceeds.[15]

For the first weeks after his arrival in the West, Blackwell thought he had his finances under control. He had arranged for Stone to draw money from his account with Moore for a visit to Massachusetts and any other needs. Just before leaving, he traded more land for another house, which Stone put on the market together with his rental property. Hoping to purchase the farm of their dreams that summer, she listed their residence as well. The money sent to Viroqua had been located, and he had taken care of matters in Madison. Turning his attention to the library enterprise, he negotiated a partnership with an existing book firm in Chicago, set up an office there, sent letters to school commissioners in the state's one hundred counties, and began hiring agents to canvass the state. He traveled downstate to get written endorsements from the state superintendent of schools at Springfield and the principal of the normal school at Bloomington, and recruited a professor at Illinois College in Jacksonville to endorse the libraries in an article for the *Prairie Farmer* magazine. During trips to Wisconsin he made initial contacts for introducing the libraries there. With great enthusiasm he reported to Stone that it looked like the enterprise would give him "a field of usefulness for several years to come."[16]

But his careful arrangements soon unraveled. Stone had planned to pay her investment costs with proceeds from the Jersey City and Brooklyn lectures, but successive bouts of headache and boils forced her to cancel those engagements. Blackwell had to come up with money for her taxes as well as for unexpected rate increases. Next, Stone received a request for two hundred dollars from Ellen Blackwell whom, in persuading to reinvest proceeds from a land sale three years earlier, she had promised to supply with cash when needed. Having no money herself, she forwarded the request to her husband. Then, the seller of his second house waffled on the trade, and he had to try to save that deal from afar. And Marian Blackwell, whom he had authorized to trade some of his land for a house for their mother, wanted him to accept a deal that greatly undervalued the land. Finally, George could find no buyer for the farm produce, and Henry had no other means for purchasing new land warrants. "It seems as though, do what I will," he lamented to Stone, "I cannot extricate myself from these unexpected complications."[17]

Stone sold some of her remaining bank stock so he could complete the land entries. Blackwell had adamantly rejected her suggestion that she do so. "I feel that this little sum of yours, the only *available cash* reliance in case of my death or other accident, should be held *sacred* for you and baby—not to be touched. . . . No! Lucy, dear, don't sell the stock, please don't!" But Stone sold it. "I hope the only feeling you will have about the use of my bank stock will be one of gladness that I had it for you to use. If you knew how freely I part with it, I am sure you would accept it cheerfully," she wrote. Blackwell accepted the money and sent her a bill of sale for the grain, which was worth more than the advance. But Stone insisted he give it to George for what they owed him. By now Henry had learned that the company who had held the investment packets had not only sold the warrants without George's authorization but had also taken cash intended for entry fees. Now having a stake in the investment, Stone joined her husband and brother-in-law in a claim to recover the embezzled funds. This was the only lawsuit involved in the matter. None of Stone's land was involved, and Blackwell repaid her advance a few months later when he sold one of his houses.[18]

Through all her husband's difficulties Stone offered sympathetic encouragement. "Dearest Harry, take care of yourself. Don't get discouraged. We shall live on and through all." "We are not poor with our baby, our love, and our friends," she reminded him. When he learned of her illness he wanted to return home, knowing she would not cancel lectures for a minor complaint. But Stone assured him she was well cared for and urged him to stay and give the library venture "a full and fair trial." Blackwell hated being away from Stone in her time of need, not being able to nurse her as she had him. Their domestic life had not developed as he had planned, and again he apologized for being a "drag instead of a helpmate." "Poor Lucy, I have kept you ever since our marriage in so *unsatisfied* a condition. I have carried you off to Cincinnati and Chicago and Wisconsin and New York and New Jersey; have given you no rest or permanent home; have separated you from your mother and brothers and sisters and friends; have fettered you in your public career of usefulness and fame; have given you anxiety, pain, sickness, privations manifold." Although he would fulfill this commitment to Moore, he said he would never again "violate the order of nature and the dictates of common sense" by separating himself from his loved ones.[19]

Stone's reassurances belied a growing anxiety. An outbreak of arson had prompted her to use most of the cash Blackwell had left to buy insurance on their three houses. Determined not to increase his debt by taking money from Moore, she decided to economize instead. She dismissed the housekeeper, canceled her trip to Massachusetts, ignored her husband's pleas to hire help with the garden and his suggestion, made after learning she had concocted a defense of cayenne pepper and chloroform against burglars, that she stay with a neighbor who took boarders.[20]

Stone found the physical labor and stress of caring for an infant while keeping house alone more difficult than anything she had ever done. In addition to "making, mending, washing, ironing, etc." for both of them, the constant feeding, diapering, and comfort of the baby took all her energy. When Anthony complained of exhaustion after completing an antislavery tour, Stone replied unsympathetically, "You are tired with four months work. If you had had measles and whooping cough added to all you have done, it would not be half as hard as the taking care of a child day and night is, I *know*." When Stone went into the city to lecture on April 22, friends were shocked by her haggard and worn-out state.[21]

The lecture in New York was the one Stone had told her husband about shortly after his departure. Although illness had forced her to cancel other engagements, she was determined to keep this one, for besides paying fifty dollars, it took her before a class of women not inclined to attend woman's rights lectures. Hers was the final lecture in a benefit course organized to raise funds for thousands of seamstresses hurt by the depression. In her audience were moderate and conservative women who advocated improved property rights and educational and employment opportunities for women but rejected claims for equal legal rights, coeducation, and suffrage. Some were actively involved in the work of the American Female Guardian Society with houses of refuge, women's prisons, training schools, and workshops, but were careful not to associate themselves with the "radical" woman's rights movement. But Stone's lecture so impressed the society's officers that they printed it almost in its entirety in their journal, along with a very favorable report.[22]

Although an immense success, the lecture cost Stone hours of anxiety. She had stayed with the Moores during the week preceding the engagement so they could care for the baby while she prepared. But the baby had caught a severe cold and, no doubt haunted by the recent loss of babies by both her brother Frank and a cousin, Stone was racked with guilt and worry as she lay awake at Elizabeth's after the lecture. Despite her husband's urging that she accept an invitation to repeat the lecture in Brooklyn, she did not lecture again that spring.[23]

Declining opportunities for more lecture income, Stone sought other ways to ease their financial straits. She considered taking in boarders or, when it became apparent Blackwell would have to stay west until July, renting their house and staying with family in Massachusetts until his return. She decided to sell her Appleton property, at cost if necessary, and wrote to friends seeking a buyer. Already frustrated by his wife's "short-sighted" frugality in refusing to hire help, Blackwell was exasperated by her decision to "force off" investment property. He appreciated her desire to help him, but their investment costs were paid for the coming year and the library enterprise was going to pay well. There was no need, he assured her, to sacrifice good investments or take other drastic measures. He vetoed the idea of taking in boarders, and although he preferred not to complicate prospects for selling their home by turning it over to renters, he deferred to her wishes. Regardless of what she decided, he urged her to go to Massachusetts for much-needed rest and recuperation. Finally persuaded that her frugality was not needed, Stone hired a woman to help with the house and garden and made arrangements to go to Massachusetts after the National Woman's Rights Convention, where she would await her husband's return.[24]

Sometime in the winter, probably in late December when Anthony was in Orange, Stone, Anthony, and Antoinette Brown Blackwell had met to discuss arrangements for the 1858 convention and divide up the preliminary correspondence. Now as they lined up speakers, Stone said she herself would "make no set speech" this year. Disappointed with her performance in the benefit lecture, she concluded that she could not speak well while nursing the baby.

Overwhelmed by maternal duties, she also told Anthony she would not manage another convention while she had young children. Henry Blackwell had addressed the two previous conventions and had intended to speak at this one, too, but when it became apparent he would not be back in time, he promised to send a letter to be read there and asked Stone to have him appointed a vice president, an honorary post that did not require presence. Because he was not able to arrange advertising for her, she asked Anthony to do that, too. The program Anthony sent to the papers listed Stone as a speaker, despite her instruction to the contrary, and omitted Antoinette, who had said she would speak. When Antoinette complained of her omission, Anthony pointedly replied that the mistake would not have been made had either she or Lucy prepared the list.[25]

Anthony resented the effect of motherhood on Lucy's and Antoinette's careers. Upon the birth of Antoinette's second child she scolded, "Now Nette, not another baby, is my peremptory command—two will solve the problem, whether a woman can be anything more than a wife and mother." Instead of rejoicing that illness had not prevented Stone from lecturing in the benefit course, Anthony criticized her for exhausting herself before the engagement. "Just to think that she will attempt to speak in a course with such intellects as Brady, Curtis, and Chapin," Anthony complained to Antoinette, "and then as her special preparation take upon herself in addition to baby cares—quite too absorbing for careful, close and continued intellectual effort—the entire work of her house. A woman who is and must of necessity continue for the present, at least, the representative woman, has no right to thus disqualify herself for such a representative occasion."[26]

Despite Anthony's criticism, Stone remained resolved to put her child first. As the convention neared and she could not find child care, she considered not going. Having lined up a full slate of speakers, Anthony to preside, and Higginson to write resolutions and manage, she was certain it would progress smoothly without her. "I shall not be needed, thank God, so it is no matter whether I go or not," she told Henry.[27]

But she could not stay away. On the morning of May 13 she boarded the train with the baby and went into the city. Leaving the child with Hannah Blackwell at Elizabeth's, she went to the convention accompanied by Elizabeth, Antoinette, and Sam. The morning session was ready to adjourn when they arrived, but Higginson noticed her entrance and asked the audience if they were willing to prolong the session to hear from Lucy Stone. Amid much applause, she ascended the speakers' platform and offered brief remarks. After the session adjourned, she learned that Stephen Pearl Andrews, whose ideology she had so emphatically repelled five years earlier, had tried again, perhaps emboldened by the introduction of the claim for a married woman's right to her body at the last convention. Arguing that women's "very first right" was their right to "maternity under the best physiological circumstances," and that women should be able "to change and experiment" to determine the best relations "under which the human race can be sired and generated," he asked if this question was welcome on their platform. Anthony ruled it in order, but delegates adeptly steered discussion in other directions. Stone's timely arrival gave Higginson the opportunity to end the session on a completely different note.[28]

Newspaper editors were not as easily diverted. Identifying Andrews as the "apostle of free love," they exploited his brief remarks and the convention's failure to disclaim him. Some charged that the convention had considered whether to cooperate with "free loverism" and "received with much favor" the claim for woman's right "to be unchaste." Not wanting to reinforce that perception on the convention's second day, activists cut short Henry C. Wright when he introduced resolutions concerning a wife's right to control her body. Wright, who had just published another book, *The Unwelcome Child*, was no free-lover, but his claim that wives should be able to decide for themselves how often and under what conditions they would risk pregnancy sounded to some much like Andrews's demand for sexual license. His resolutions were sent to committee without discussion.[29]

Stone reported the results of the 1856–57 memorial campaign, and the convention decided to expand the effort by recruiting someone from each state to memorialize his or her legislature as the convention's representative. It also voted to meet thereafter in New York during anniversary week and to reorganize the Central Committee. Garrison and Phillips had suggested making the convention part of the New York anniversaries after Stone had to reschedule the 1856 meeting, and Anthony seconded the idea when she had trouble trying to organize the 1857 convention in Chicago. Although Stone preferred moving the convention to different states as a means of attracting attention and rousing interest, she had to agree it would be easier to organize with a fixed time and place. The second measure was just as practical. Although the Central Committee was the movement's only organizational form, its primary function of arranging the national conventions had devolved to just a few individuals. Higginson proposed that the committee shed its roster of state representatives and reconstitute as a smaller, more functional group. Nine individuals were appointed to the new committee: Stone, Anthony, Higginson, Rose, Stanton, Samuel J. May, Frances Dana Gage, Caroline Dall, and Caroline Severance. Paulina Davis, who except for one term had been president of the committee since its inception, was not reappointed. Her position had been nominal for several years, and she had told Stone she did not like to give the appearance of being active when she was not. So the presidency was given to Stanton, who was eager for an active role now that her youngest child was two years old. And Stone, wanting a less active role, passed the secretarial post to Anthony.[30]

After the convention, Stone went to Massachusetts to introduce her family to her eight-month-old daughter, who at long last had been given a name— Sarah (soon changed to Alice) Stone Blackwell. Lucy settled in with her sister at Gardner, but her own recurring outbreaks of boils and the baby's continual colds made rest and recuperation difficult. Convinced she need not pinch pennies, she hired a woman to help her sister with children and housework.[31]

Lucy regretted that Henry was missing the "miracle of the unfolding child" and, as countless mothers have done for countless absent fathers, described the baby's growth, her babbling and smiles, her first attempts at sitting and crawling, and the appearance of her first tooth. Henry's letters were filled with longing and remorse. "I am terribly weary of this prolonged absence from all I hold dear. . . . I feel pained at the thought that while every Irish laborer who earns 75 cents a day is rich enough to stay with wife and child, I should go rambling over this desolate world month after month with a perpetual hunger gnawing at my heart." He often sat up late with the photograph of wife and child that Lucy had slipped into his bags as a surprise. "My own love, I long for you and baby. I have no hope, no ambition, but to rejoin you. . . . [A]s the thought of you and baby comes over me, I am seized with a perfect despair at being separated from you and feel like cursing library, business, my own folly, and western lands the root of all evil." Lucy, too, grieved that their lives were so "severed." But although she wished Henry could be with them, she praised his perseverance, which, she said, was better than yielding "to the feeling of heart hunger that would send one rushing home."[32]

Despite a discouragingly slow start, library orders were pouring in by the middle of June, and Blackwell exulted: "I am greatly gratified at the result as it *justifies* me to [Augustus Moore] and, what is better, to myself." It was apparent, he said, that with proper management the school line would be very profitable. However, he had decided not to claim the third of that profit Moore had promised him. Unwilling ever again to abandon his family for such a long time, he resigned his management of the enterprise. It would need a man in Illinois for eight to nine months of the year, he told Moore, but he would not be that man. Having developed the line with no mercenary expectation, he asked nothing but a salary and to be permitted to live east.[33]

As the time for his return neared, Henry wondered how he had borne the separation. "Alas," he concluded, "on the same principle that a man endures amputation or submits to be hanged." But he had the satisfaction of knowing that he had performed "a very great and almost inestimable service," and that he had not been found lacking in his "hour of trial." Lucy was relieved, too. "Now that your exile is so nearly over, dear Harry, I want to tell you that in no other absence have I ever felt your loss so much, never so longed for you, never needed you, as I have during these four weary months."[34]

At the end of June, Henry made a quick trip to Des Moines to see the superintendent of schools about placing the school libraries in Iowa. On his way back east, he stopped in Columbus to make initial contacts for placing them in Ohio. Then, without stopping in New York, he hurried to Massachusetts to rejoin his family. While relaxing together he and Lucy inspected a farm for sale in nearby Warren and made an offer on it. But upon returning to New Jersey, they found one more to their liking in an area where several of their friends lived and where they had originally looked. Cancelling the Warren offer, they traded Stone's house and one acre as down payment on a twenty-acre farm in the area of Orange that would later be called Montclair.[35]

In September, Moore offered Blackwell a salary of three thousand dollars—more than double his previous salary—if he would stay with the library enterprise another year. Until then, Blackwell did not want to go west again even though Stone had offered to accompany him. But Moore's proposal was too good to refuse. Already arranging to vacate their house, the couple postponed the move to their new farm.[36]

Even before she knew for sure she would be going west, Stone declined invitations for fall and winter work. Turning down Anthony's request that she lecture in upstate New York, she said she would not go anywhere that required an overnight stay. Mindful of Anthony's vexation with the restrictions motherhood imposed on her public work, she begged Anthony to accept her decision. Raising a child, she said, was much more important than the work of merchants or manufacturers, and no one thought it strange that *they* did not take on additional labors. She would resume traveling when her daughter was old enough to be left; until then, Anthony need not ask her.[37]

Stone declined another important invitation. Wanting to "proclaim the equality of woman in the lecture room" by becoming the first Boston lyceum to put a woman in a course of popular lectures, the Fraternity of the Twenty-Eighth Congregational Society, Theodore Parker's church, asked Stone to fill the "apex" position in the middle of a series with twelve of the nation's top male orators. Sending her regrets, Stone suggested they ask Elizabeth Stanton instead. After speaking with good effect at a Meeting of Progressive Friends in June, Stanton wanted to start lecturing and Anthony had asked Stone to see if she could get Greeley to recommend her in the *Tribune*.[38]

Stanton accepted the Boston engagement but canceled two weeks before her scheduled appearance. She was pregnant again, and although she had hoped to work until January she became too ill to carry on. Caroline Severance stepped in to fill the void, but the fact that maternity had prevented first Stone, then Stanton, from capitalizing on this opportunity angered Anthony, who sent an "outpouring of wrath" to Antoinette Blackwell. "My vision finds no mountain in the way, but the *individual women*. Nette, institutions, among them marriage, are justly chargeable with social and individual ills, but after all, the *whole man* or *woman* can and *will* rise above them. Woman must take to her soul a purpose, and then *make* circumstances to meet that purpose, instead of this *lackadaisical* way of doing and going *if* and *if* and *if*."[39]

Anthony's ideas about women creating their own circumstances and rising above societal constraints echoed those Blackwell had expounded to Stone during their courtship. But Stone found she could not order her circumstances to permit even a fraction of her previous public work. It was impossible, she said, for anyone who cared for a baby to find time even to rest. But having wanted to demonstrate by personal example that marriage need not restrict women to domesticity, she curtailed her public speaking only with great guilt and self-doubt. Although she told herself it was necessary to neglect one holy calling to attend to another, her waning "impulse and power to lecture" troubled her. She told Anthony she could not speak well because of nursing; she told her husband it was because of illness. She assured him that she still possessed the good he saw in her when they first met, and although it was dimmed by her inability to adapt to new circumstances, it would reappear when she was well.[40]

Another round of illnesses struck that fall. First, Lucy nursed the baby through dysentery exacerbated by teething. In the last weeks of September, a carbuncle swelled Henry's face so much he could not open his eyes for five days and it was feared he would lose his sight. Then in October, dysentery confined Lucy to bed for two weeks.[41] But the couple managed to vacate their home in November. Stone visited her parents in West Brookfield while Blackwell attended to last-minute library arrangements in New York. Then they left for Chicago, where Stone would continue her struggle with conflicting aspirations and diminishing self-confidence.

Passing the Mantle

When Lucy Stone and Henry Blackwell arrived in Chicago at the beginning of December 1858, Lucy was pregnant. She had had several miscarriages, and her mother worried about care available to her in the West. But after they settled into a comfortable boarding house on the north side of the city, Henry sent Hannah Stone reassurances. Several acquaintances had already called on Lucy and she had formed warm friendships with all the boarders, so there would be many hands to assist her when her time came.[1]

As Blackwell set up the "Chicago Agency of A. O. Moore & Co., Illinois School District Library," Stone drew up two petitions, gathered several signatures, and sent them to the Illinois legislature. Introduced in the senate on February 1, 1859, the petition for a woman suffrage amendment was tabled while the one for a married women's property act was referred to the Committee on the Judiciary. Stone spoke in several towns around Chicago but not in the city itself, for she no longer felt capable of delivering the grand scale of oratory expected there. "I wish I felt the old impulse and power to lecture, both for the sake of cherished principles and to help Harry with the heavy burden he has to bear," she wrote to Antoinette Brown Blackwell, "but I am afraid, and dare not trust Lucy Stone." While listening to an inspiring lecture on Joan of Arc, she felt she could do anything. But at home, looking into Alice's sleeping face, she thought of all that could happen while her maternal eye was turned away. Alice had been very ill soon after their arrival and required round-the-clock care. Stone's fear for her health, no doubt punctuated by the death of Antoinette's baby in August, made her shrink "like a snail into its shell" and resolve that for the time being, she could be "only a mother."[2]

But Stone's commitment to motherhood conflicted with her desire to maintain financial independence. Although she told her mother she lectured because "*somebody* has got to earn some money," her husband's salary of $250 a month amply covered their $70 monthly charge for room and board. The "heavy burden" she wanted to share was the cost of holding their western lands. Still determined to pay her own investment costs if not half their joint expenses, she continued lecturing even after telling Antoinette she would not. But when she returned from an engagement to find that the nursemaid had taken Alice outdoors without sufficient bundling against the cold, she suspended public work altogether to stay home with her child.[3]

Antoinette, on the other hand, was trying to reestablish her career as a minister. In the fall she had arranged a series of weekly sermons and lectures in Newark, and in January had made a lecture tour of New York State. Although she made good money, she did not consider lecturing her true calling. Wanting to establish an independent ministry in New York, she asked Stone if a newly established woman's rights fund could advance half the hall rental for a six-month trial, which she would repay from proceeds. The fund was five thousand dollars given to the movement with Stone, Wendell Phillips, and Susan Anthony designated as trustees, to spend as they deemed best calculated to obtain equal civil and social rights for women. Although the donor wished to remain anonymous, Stone may have guessed it was her good friend Francis Jackson, one of the movement's most consistent benefactors. Stone thought Antoinette's ministry an appropriate use of the fund but Anthony did not, and Phillips deferred decision until Stone's expected return in the spring.[4]

Stone wrote to Francis Jackson about Antoinette's difficulties and asked if she might be engaged to preach in Theodore Parker's pulpit, which guest ministers were filling during his absence in Europe. Jackson immediately arranged Antoinette's appointment and congratulated Stone on the "executive power" she exerted from afar. While she sat in Chicago tending her babe with one hand, said Jackson, with the other she "pulled a wire" that brought Antoinette and the "gospel of Woman's Rights" to two or three thousand people in Boston.[5]

Indeed, even as Stone withdrew from public speaking, her influence continued to be felt. Her tax protest had inspired a mini tax resistance movement among women in several states. Sarah Elizabeth Wall, a longtime Worcester friend who had paid taxes under protest for several years, returned her tax bill in October 1858, saying she would not pay again until the word *male* was removed from the state constitution. A New Hampshire woman refused to pay her tax and lost furniture as a consequence. After losing a sewing machine in 1858, Lydia Sayer Hasbrouck stopped cooperating with the collector and locked her doors against him on auction day in 1859. Publishing accounts of her own rebellion and that of others, Hasbrouck kept the issue alive in her *Sibyl* for the next five years. While some women refused to pay taxes, others took the opposite tact and, following a suggestion made at the national convention, went to the polls and demanded their right as taxpayers to vote. Learning from one of her readers that Wisconsin's state constitution specified that "every word importing the masculine gender only may be applied to female as well," Hasbrouck urged Wisconsin women to go to the polls, too, and claim their right to vote.[6]

Stone believed that taxing women while denying them the vote was unconstitutional, at least in those states whose constitutions contained a clause similar to one in Massachusetts' Bill of Rights that said a person's property could
not be taken from him and applied to public uses "without his own consent,
or that of the representative body of the people." For years she had been urging
women not to pay their taxes, to take their cases to court and, acting as their
own lawyers, to plead that taxation and representation are inseparable. With a
fund now at their disposal, she wanted to underwrite a lawsuit challenging
state laws that taxed women. She got her court case in 1862. Instead of raising
Sarah Wall's tax at auction, Worcester's collector paid the tax for four years
and then sued for repayment. Wall argued her own case in court, basing her
defense on the Massachusetts Bill of Rights and the premise that, because
women were barred from voting, she was not represented in the state's "representative body of the people." But the court ruled in the collector's favor and
ordered Wall to repay him. She appealed to the Massachusetts Supreme Court,
which in 1863 upheld the lower court's ruling and quenched Stone's hope of
winning suffrage in the courts.[7]

Michigan felt Stone's influence in another way. After her lectures there in
1855, a meeting of the State Teachers' Association endorsed coeducation and
urged its trial at the state university at Ann Arbor. Two years later Euphemia
Cochrane, one of the teachers at that meeting and a woman's rights activist,
saw that the legislature was considering endowing a women's college at Lan-
sing, drafted a remonstrance against a separate college, and circulated a petition
asking the legislature to remove any legal barriers against women attending
the existing university. The Committee on Public Instruction discovered no
statutory basis for women's exclusion and urged the board of regents to admit
them. Support and enthusiasm were so widespread, Cochrane told Stone, that
there was little doubt women applicants would be accepted.[8]

It was not until 1858, however, that a group of young women applied. Sarah
Burger, the schoolgirl who credited Stone's 1853 address in Cleveland for persuading her to press for admission, recruited eleven young women to join her.
Despite support among half the faculty and nearly the entire student body, the
university's president opposed educating men and women together and persuaded the regents not to make a precedent-setting decision without consulting
other educators. The committee solicited advice from eminent educators, ministers, and public officials, and published the results in the fall.[9] Although Horace Mann of Antioch College and Charles Finney of Oberlin recommended
admitting women, the presidents of Harvard, Yale, Williams, Union, Columbia,
Dartmouth, and numerous other institutions advised against "disturbing the
present system" and impairing "that line of distinction between the sexes
which keeps alive a refined and retiring delicacy in woman." Summarizing this
majority view, the Michigan committee noted that although the university's
founding statute did, indeed, open the institution to "all persons" resident in
the state, it also authorized the regents to deny admission to any class of

persons whose presence might disrupt or detract. The board reduced the question to economics, however, declaring that admitting women to the state university would be a "misappropriation of funds." Cochrane drafted another petition, Sarah Burger and three companions resubmitted applications, but the regents again denied admission.[10]

As newspaper accounts of these proceedings roused national interest in the claims of the woman's rights movement, Stone turned her attention to the 1859 national convention. Saying nothing of her pregnancy, she told Anthony she did not expect to be at the May meeting and did not think she should keep the "old responsibility in regard to it." But although Anthony was willing to carry out Stone's directives, she did not want to take charge. Her wish that Stone's mantle would fall on her referred only to speaking ability, not to responsibility for the annual meetings. So Stone outlined some basic plans, suggesting that they limit the convention to one day and schedule three individuals to speak at each of three sessions. Many of their activists were preoccupied with the escalating crisis over slavery, but she thought they could get nine speakers and sent suggestions of whom to invite. Under the circumstances, however, Anthony thought one public session and a private meeting of the Central Committee would suffice and asked Oliver Johnson to book a hall for one evening. When Stone insisted there be at least two public sessions and Johnson could not find an adequate hall, Anthony protested that she should have to "shoulder the sole responsibility of settling all these matters," and asked Antoinette Blackwell to go to New York, consult with Johnson, decide on the hall and number of sessions, issue the call, and recruit more speakers if necessary. Antoinette went with Anthony's plan for a one-session convention.[11]

This was the first National Woman's Rights Convention that Stone did not attend. By the middle of May she was living in Evanston, a country village twelve miles from Chicago, which she and Henry considered a healthier setting for her expected confinement. Around the first of June, her seven-month pregnancy terminated with the birth of a premature baby boy, who died either at birth or shortly thereafter. Although Henry notified their mothers immediately, the news filtered slowly to the rest of the family, for pregnancies were kept private, any reference to them a polite allusion to "illness." Unaware of the loss, Sam and Antoinette sent Henry and Lucy congratulations on their "parental prospects" toward the end of June. It was another two months before Antoinette sent condolences: "You must know I have heard of the poor premature little baby and that I sympathize with you deeply . . . I know how it has made your heart ache to lose so many new hopes." Antoinette asked permission to tell friends, some of whom had heard rumors of Stone's pregnancy and were surprised not to learn of a new baby. Especially did she want to tell Anthony, who was "anxious" about Stone's inactivity. Antoinette said Susan did not "blame" her for not lecturing, but could not understand why she did not.[12]

Stone's absence in the West not only kept her from attending the May convention but also complicated planning for the coming year's work. Memorializing state legislatures instead of attempting another costly petition drive, the 1856 convention had gained hearings in Massachusetts and Maine while the memorial was referred to select committees in Pennsylvania and Indiana. The 1858 convention had appointed a committee to send another memorial, but disagreement on form and procedure resulted in no action. Now the Central Committee had decided to try again, and a committee headed by Susan Anthony was preparing another memorial. But the Jackson fund made petition campaigns possible again, too. Stone had suggested that the trustees consult with other longtime activists to decide how to use the fund, and when it became apparent she would not be able to travel east in May, offered to appoint someone to act in her place. Whether such a meeting took place or plans were agreed upon through correspondence, allocations began in June.[13]

The first appropriation went to Kansas, where activists were petitioning against sex-based classifications in a state constitution being drafted that summer. The constitution drafted three years earlier by the free-state convention at Topeka had directed the first state legislature to enact a law "securing to the wife the separate property . . . and equal right with the husband to the custody of the children during their minority." Samuel N. Wood, a member of that convention and candidate for the legislature, had asked Stone for a draft of such a law in time to be presented to the legislature, expected to meet in March 1856. She secured a copy of the 1855 Massachusetts act, added a provision on parental guardianship and other measures to make it a comprehensive bill, and sent it to Wood. Invalidation of the free-state movement and subsequent civil warfare halted action until 1858, when voters returned a free-state majority to the territorial legislature and Wood presented the draft. On February 11, 1858, the acting governor signed into law a married women's property act very similar to the Massachusetts act, with no provision for equal guardianship rights.[14] Now, a new constitutional convention was meeting in July, and in asking framers to reject "constitutional distinctions based on difference of sex," woman's rights activists hoped to win complete legal and political equality. The effort was led by John O. Wattles and his sister-in-law, transplanted antislavery and woman's rights activists from Indiana, who had organized a county woman's rights association the previous year. They asked Clarina Nichols, now also of Kansas, to draft the petition and requested money from the Jackson fund to enable her to circulate it across the settled part of the territory. Despite strong support among the reform-minded population, woman suffrage was in danger because eastern advisors had warned Kansas Republicans not to jeopardize Congressional approval of their constitution, and thereby statehood, by including either Negro or woman suffrage. In the end, the convention went as far as it felt safe to go, providing for married women's property rights, securing mothers' guardianship rights, and even granting women the right to vote in school board elections—but sticking to "white male" in general voting provisions.[15]

Agitation had proceeded in other states, too. In January 1859 the Indiana

Woman's Rights Association had culminated a petition drive with a hearing before a joint session of the legislature. In Massachusetts, where the legislature had already granted most demands for women's legal equality, activists focused on winning suffrage. They had just concluded one petition campaign and were planning another. In Illinois, Stone had recruited a group of women to disseminate woman's rights tracts, requisitioned the last of the old tracts for that work, and had five hundred copies of a new series sent there, too. But she, Phillips, and Anthony had decided to use the Jackson fund for campaigns in Ohio and New York, where prospects for legislative success seemed most promising. Anthony and Brown Blackwell began the New York work in July, and Stone contacted Frances Gage, Hannah Tracy Cutler, and Elizabeth Jones about working in Ohio in the fall.[16]

But by the time Stone arrived in the East in mid-September, the New York campaign had come to a halt. Anthony and Brown Blackwell had made a preliminary tour of the state's resort towns and then opened the official campaign with a series of county conventions. But neither woman had intended to stay with the campaign. Anthony wanted to resume antislavery work and Brown Blackwell wanted to begin her ministry in October. Notifying Stone at the end of August that she would leave the campaign in a couple of weeks, Brown Blackwell said Phillips had "thrown the whole responsibility" for New York on Anthony, authorizing her to spend up to one thousand dollars, but Anthony did not want it. And other than Anthony, said Brown Blackwell, there was no one to take charge.[17]

The women held their last county convention on September 16 and Brown Blackwell went home to prepare for her ministry. Anthony agreed to serve as general agent through December and, wanting to hold conventions in every county before then and having only one New Yorker to help, asked that the western recruits be assigned to New York instead of Ohio. Agreeing, Stone suggested that, to get the fullest use of the small force, the women hold meetings individually along the rail lines instead of pairing off for county conventions. But Anthony had already advertised county meetings. Cutler and Jones opened the second phase of the campaign on November 11, and Gage and Lucy M. Coleman, a friend of Anthony's from Rochester, joined them shortly thereafter. They held afternoon and evening meetings in sixteen counties before December 27, when Anthony left the campaign, then split up according to Stone's plan and visited thirty-eight more.[18]

Stone capped the campaign with a grand meeting at Cooper Institute in New York City on February 2, 1860. A bill modeled on Massachusetts' married women's property act was moving through the legislature and activists were trying to get legislators to add guardianship rights and other provisions. So Stone focused on issues related to this bill and left the topic of suffrage to a second speaker, Henry Ward Beecher. Son of Lyman Beecher, brother of Harriet Beecher Stowe, and probably the most popular and influential American minister of his time, Beecher was an important new ally for the woman's rights movement, and the address he gave that night on "Woman's Influence in Politics" became one of the movement's most popular tracts.[19]

Optimism ran high as the campaign ended with a state convention at Albany on February 3 and 4. The *New York Times* said there was so little opposition to the property bill that, as far as this aspect of her work was concerned, Stone could expect an easy victory. Passing the senate on February 27 and the assembly on March 15, the act gave married women the right to their own earnings, the rights to own property, conduct business in their own names, enter into contracts, sue and be sued, and the right to joint legal guardianship of their children. "We don't well see what more than this Mrs. Lucy Stone can ask the state of New York," the *Times* said. "The legislature has done all it can do, and we fear that if she wishes to remove any other hardships or grievances from which women suffer, she will have to wage war upon human nature itself, and the ordinances of high Heaven." But of course Stone and her colleagues did have more to ask. A few days after assembly action secured women's property rights, Elizabeth Cady Stanton appeared before a joint committee of the two houses to plead for woman suffrage.[20]

Stanton's appearance before the New York legislature marked her emergence from long years of what she considered domestic and maternal "bondage." After attending two of Anthony's antislavery meetings in January, she attended the Albany convention, her first woman's rights meeting in six years.[21] And although she had never attended a National Woman's Rights Convention, she willingly accepted responsibility for arranging the 1860 meeting.

Upon their return from Chicago in September, Stone and Blackwell had moved into one of his rental houses in Orange until they could renovate the farmhouse on their new property. After taking a couple of months to wrap up the library enterprise for Moore, Blackwell set up a real estate business and, in addition to selling and renting for others on commission, traded western land for eastern properties. Before the year's end he had traded his Viroqua farm for a sixteen-acre tract adjoining their Montclair farm, and with another five hundred acres he paid off the mortgage on the house in which they were living. He soon had a string of rental properties, including the house on their new tract, and to supply cash for taxes, he took a sales position with fellow abolitionist Cornelius Bramhall, manufacturer of kitchen stoves. From this arrangement Stone got a new stove which, she boasted to her mother, was not only more efficient than their old cooking range but also provided heat through the night.[22] Stone did what she could for the New York campaign, but her domestic activities were hard on her. While moving a trunk from storage, she suffered a knee injury that crippled her for several weeks before her Cooper Institute address. Around the same time, Alice nearly severed her tongue in a fall, and the slow healing required Stone's constant attention. Absorbed by domestic cares, Stone placed the program for the 1860 National Woman's Rights Convention in Stanton's hands and said not to announce her as a speaker. And after being its only continuous member since 1850, she also resigned from the Central Committee.[23]

With Stanton eager for active work, Stone suggested she organize the marriage convention they had often talked about. Current events indicated the time was ripe. A bill extending grounds for divorce and securing the right of remarriage was moving through the New York legislature, and a protracted newspaper debate between Horace Greeley and Robert Dale Owen, sponsor of a similar bill recently passed in Indiana, heightened interest. The question of marriage as a legitimate social institution continued to be stirred by the free love movement, and confusion was rampant over its alleged link with woman's rights. At a "Free Convention" in Vermont a month after Stephen Pearl Andrews stirred the controversy at the 1858 woman's rights convention, Ernestine Rose adamantly rejected his philosophy, but the *New York Times* reported that she went "for free love on principle." Other papers repeated the charge, and movement leaders found themselves fighting off the "free love" label anew.[24] New York and New Jersey papers were reporting several cases of abandoned babies and infanticide, the result of unwanted pregnancies. A wife's right to decline sexual intercourse had received no hearing on their platform since its introduction four years earlier. After the 1858 convention refused to consider resolutions on the issue for fear of bolstering charges of "free loverism," no one attempted the topic at the 1859 meeting. It had received attention on other platforms, however. The Vermont Free Convention discussed it in 1858. Meetings of Progressive Friends, the liberal reform wing of the Quakers, discussed it in 1857 and again in 1859, unanimously adopting a resolution by Higginson that claimed for the wife "the supreme control of her own person" and denied her husband's right to force upon her "the sacred duties of maternity against her will." So now, wanting a broad, inclusive examination of all aspects of the marriage question but believing them beyond the parameters of an equal rights agenda, Stone urged Stanton to call a convention "to discuss divorce, marriage, infanticide, and their kindred subjects."[25]

But Stanton believed the divorce question was a legitimate issue for the woman's rights platform, said she would raise it at the upcoming woman's rights convention, and asked Stone to second her in any debate that resulted. Stone did not discourage her: "I am glad you will speak on the divorce question, provided you are yourself clear on the subject. It is a grave topic that one shudders to grapple, but its hour is coming—and will have fully come when we are ready." Repeating that she herself would not make *any* speech, she nevertheless gave Stanton her blessing: "God touch your lips if you speak on it."[26]

Stone was absent from the May anniversaries and missed the debate Stanton's resolutions and speech sparked. Objecting to Stanton's proposal that marriage be a simple civil contract, easily dissolved when the partners willed, Antoinette Brown Blackwell countered with resolutions saying that although marriage was a voluntary alliance, the relation of parent and child could not be undone and therefore marital obligations must be lifelong. Phillips objected to both sets of resolutions as extraneous to the convention and moved that they be omitted from the record. Garrison also believed the subject extraneous but thought its discussion helped highlight the need for measures they did advocate. Brown Blackwell and Anthony defended the propriety of the marriage question on the woman's rights platform, but the assembly, while refusing to expunge them from the record, tabled both sets of resolutions.[27]

Stanton's speech incited a fresh round of criticism from newspaper editors, who charged her with advocating an "exceedingly loose view" of marriage or wanting to abolish it altogether. The speech so offended some members of the convention that they publicly disavowed her ideas, while others quietly withdrew from a movement that permitted such "erratic" people on its platform. Because Stone was absent, scholars have suggested that she, too, objected to Stanton's raising the divorce issue and stayed away in protest. But there was nothing in Stanton's address with which Stone did not agree. When movement activists criticized Stanton for bringing the issue to the convention, she pleaded sanction from Stone. "I wrote to Lucy Stone at least six weeks before the convention met, telling her that I should speak on divorce," Stanton told Martha Wright. "Not a word of disapproval, or the least hint that divorce was not a proper subject for our platform."[28]

There was no enmity between Stone and Stanton. In the same letter blessing her speech, Stone invited Stanton to stay at her home during the convention. It was most likely illness that prevented Stone's attendance, for in the nearly three years since Alice's birth there had been few periods when all members of her family were simultaneously well. For the third year Stone also missed the American Anti-Slavery Society Anniversary that preceded the woman's rights meeting. The previous year the executive committee had begged her to come, saying they could not do without her: "As the contest waxes closer, no one must be missing from his post." This year, however, Garrison asked Stanton to fill Stone's post and urged her with the same lines he had used with Stone: "When woman's heart is bleeding, Shall woman's voice be hushed?" Picking up Stone's mantle, Stanton made her debut on the antislavery platform.[29]

The transfer was complete. Stone passed to Stanton not only the reins of the National Woman's Rights Convention but also her place at the public rostrum. Her own voice would, indeed, be hushed for several years.

Expectancy

In her last public appearance before the Civil War, Lucy Stone addressed a convention at Worcester on September 19, 1860, called by Stephen Foster to form a new political party. John Brown's raid, trial, and execution at the end of 1859, along with the differing reactions of North and South, created a political tension that divided the Democratic Party into northern and southern factions and made it vulnerable to defeat. Republicans nominated Abraham Lincoln, a moderate candidate whose public record would not repel voters with abolitionist "extremism," and although most political abolitionists accepted him, those wanting a true antislavery candidate again put forth Gerrit Smith. The intoxicating prospect of a Democratic defeat enticed Foster to renounce his nonpolitical action principles and join the political excitement. He wanted a party whose only object would be the abolition of slavery.[1]

In the days leading up to Foster's convention, Stone was in Massachusetts nursing her seriously ill mother. When Hannah Stone died on September 14, Lucy felt like rushing home. "I long for you when my heart is so bruised," she wrote to her husband. But her father needed comfort, too, so she stayed and attended the Worcester convention three days after her mother's funeral. The meeting was an embarrassing failure for Foster. Only four of his eight announced speakers showed up, and only one of those supported his proposal for a new party. Thomas Wentworth Higginson urged support of Lincoln while Frederick Douglass asked the convention to ratify Smith's nomination. Sticking to Garrisonian principles, Stone urged abolitionists to stay out of the political fray altogether. That position struck a chord with those attending the meeting, which adjourned without forming a party or endorsing candidates.[2]

Stone held fast to her nonresistance principles throughout the Civil War. While even Garrison and Phillips decided to "seize the thunderbolt" forged for annihilating slavery and supported the war, Stone remained true to the pledge she had made in her college days never to sanction war "by whomever, for whatever purpose." Believing reformers could better influence public affairs as

independent moral critics than as political partisans, she regretted Garrison's
and Phillips's involvement in Republican politics and was less than enthusiastic
about joining the loyalty movement that emerged during the war's second year.
To counteract a Democratic antiwar, anti-emancipation campaign, Republicans
organized clubs to promote loyalty to their war aims and to press for an Emancipation Act that would go beyond Lincoln's Emancipation Proclamation and
abolish slavery throughout the entire nation. They hired a rising young oratorical sensation, Anna E. Dickinson, to stump several states, and during the
winter of 1863 they formed hundreds of county, town, and even professional
loyal leagues across the North. After a National Loyal League was formed in
March, Elizabeth Cady Stanton called a convention to form a Women's Loyal
National League.[3]

Although Stone could not endorse the war effort, she heartily approved the
plan to organize petitioning for the Emancipation Act and agreed to preside at
Stanton's convention. Shortly into the proceedings, debate erupted over a resolution linking the war effort to the demand for civil and political equality of
all citizens, including blacks and women. Opponents thought the phrase *and
all women* should be stricken because woman's rights had nothing to do with
the war. Several speakers defended the resolution, but the audience would not
be swayed. Finally, in a move to end the impasse, a delegate called for a plan
of action on which all could unite. Unwilling to let the resolution die, Stone
vacated the president's chair and addressed the assembly. If this war was to
bring a lasting peace, she said, then it must advance the principles contained
in the Declaration of Independence. It was because those principles were ignored by the founding fathers, who wanted union at all cost and let slavery
stand, that the nation was now at war. To again ignore those principles for the
sake of unity, she said, would be to take the "same backward step." As women
loyal to their country and to the Republican war aim, they must assert those
high truths—that all human beings have equal rights, and that governments
derive their just powers from the consent of the governed. Again, Stone's words
acted like "oil upon the troubled water." The resolution passed, and the convention moved ahead.[4]

Stone's participation in the loyal league's founding convention in May 1863
and in the American Anti-Slavery Society's Third Decade celebration at Philadelphia seven months later were her only public appearances during the war.
Although she managed the league's office for two weeks to give Anthony a
much-needed break and helped compile petitions for presentation to Congress,
she refused to join a proposed corps of lecturing agents for the league.[5] Several
factors contributed to her silence.

Although Alice Stone Blackwell was six years old in 1863, certainly old
enough to be left in the care of others, she was a sickly child whose recurring
maladies required constant attention. During their 1861 vacation in Massachusetts, she became so ill that Lucy summoned Henry from New York to help
manage the crisis. It was not until her fifth year that Lucy and Henry passed

the summer with no "special dread" on their daughter's account. Alice's illness-prone childhood convinced Stone that the job of raising children did not permit outside work.[6]

But even if she had been willing to leave Alice, there was no formal woman's rights agitation in which she could participate. Agreeing with Martha Wright and Lucretia Mott that it was futile to press women's claims during the war, Stanton did not call another National Woman's Rights Convention. Stone could have agitated on her own or spoken at Progressive Friends meetings or the National Dress Reform Conventions, both of which met throughout the war. Lydia Sayer Hasbrouck criticized national leaders for abandoning woman's rights agitation and through her *Sibyl,* kept up a steady call for tax resistance and petitioning.[7] But Stone took a furlough from public work and poured all of her energy into developing a farm that would provide the independence she and her husband would need to work as free agents when the war was over.

Stone and Blackwell had moved into the renovated house on their Montclair farm in 1861. Although they hired the cultivation and harvest of their fields, Stone did much work herself—landscaping, grafting fruit trees, and planting and tending vegetable gardens. Blackwell was away much of the time, at first with his real estate business and job for Bramhall. Then in 1862, he joined Dennis Harris, his father's foreman and the man under whom he himself had learned refining in the forties, as bookkeeper and salesman for the Congress Steam Sugar Refinery. Having absorbed his father's interest in producing an alternative to slave-grown cane sugar, Henry had experimented with crystallizing sorghum in 1858. Now, with the war pushing the price of cane sugar up, he persuaded Harris to try producing beet sugar, recruited farmers to grow beets for them, and by the summer of 1864 was making a profit with the new product. But his job was demanding. Needed at the refinery six days a week, he at first hired an agent to manage his real estate business but finally transferred it to George. And he left Stone in charge of farm and tenants.[8]

The couple worked so hard that when they attended the antislavery reunion in December 1863, friends remarked how run-down they both appeared. By then, Lucy had become disillusioned with the farm. Henry's long hours at the refinery and her heavy workload did not permit them to "study more, think more, talk more." "Disgusted" with the work and convinced there was no such thing as "housekeeping made easy," she rented out their house—"furniture and all"—and in January 1864 they moved into an apartment in New York City. The move cut out the three hours Henry had spent commuting each day, and for the first time since Chicago the family spent long, leisurely evenings together. Lucy rejoiced that she had neither hired hands nor housekeeper to worry about, nor candlelight breakfasts before her husband's cold ride to the station. But city life was not to her liking, either, and when she and Alice made their annual trek to Massachusetts, she decided to stay the summer.[9]

Henry sought a way to join them there. He hoped to sell one of his larger properties, clear enough money to leave business, and then begin an intellectual career. Early in their relationship, Lucy had been impressed with his writing ability and suggested that his true calling might be as an editor. In recent years, the *Atlantic Monthly* had published some of his poetry and the *New York Tribune* had published his articles urging Lincoln to commission black soldiers and to extend emancipation to the border states. Still thinking newspaper work might be her husband's niche, Lucy suggested he write a few things for the *Independent*, which might serve as "a stepping stone to a permanent engagement." Henry thought he might start by lecturing that fall for Lincoln's re-election. Despite her aversion to reformers becoming partisans, Lucy fully accepted her husband's political leanings and encouraged him to leave the refinery, go west to take charge of a pending land sale, and then join her to prepare campaign speeches. She was certain he could be paid as a campaign worker, but if not, they could live comfortably on their rental income. Or, she said, if they must be "pinched," they knew how to do it and would be amply paid by the knowledge that they were aiding a noble cause.[10]

When Lucy and Alice left New York in June, Henry moved in with his mother and sister in Roseville so he could supervise work on the farm while commuting into the city. His job at the refinery had taken a toll on his health, and Lucy urged him to take time off for rest and relaxation. So before going west to see about land sales, he spent a long Fourth of July holiday with her and Alice in West Brookfield. Although Stone used the word *separation* in referring to their summer living arrangement, it was not a marital separation and did not indicate a troubled relationship, as one biographer concluded. With their house rented out for two years, they had no permanent home and she did not want to live in the city or with Blackwell's mother in Roseville. She needed the quiet hills of her childhood farm, she said, to regain her lost "soul & spirit" so she could resume public work after the war.[11]

Here was the primary reason for Stone's wartime silence—a lingering sense of lost eloquence and power. Anthony wished Stone could just "forget the *old Lucy Stone* and her *oratorical powers*, so beyond match" and devote whatever power she did possess to the loyal league's campaign. "I know the old fires are in her," she told Stanton, "or if not the *old ones*, still brighter and grander ones." Feeling guilty for not lecturing, Stone was relieved to learn that when Nathaniel Hawthorne experienced a similar loss of drive, "no trying or coaxing" could summon it back. She hoped the solitude and peace of her father's farm, where she had "fewer cares and nothing to vex" her, would give her back the "state of soul & spirit" that had carried her forward before.[12]

Stone's recuperation was stymied, however, by a physically draining and mentally disorienting menopause. "I escaped the last month, with only one day's headache, and none of the mental confusion that has so tormented me before," she told Anthony. "And if I can only survive the inevitable change of constitution and be right side up at the end of it, I shall pray again for the return of that great impulse that drove me into the world, with words that *must* be spoken." In June when she urged Blackwell to lecture in the fall, she said she might join him, for she felt she was improving. But a month later when he suggested a joint lecture tour, she said she needed to remain "in some quiet corner, free from criticism, or scrutiny, where I shall be able *perhaps,* to find that better self of me, which during all the years of my poverty-stricken girlhood, steadily aspired to a life of worthy use . . . I must keep in some quiet 'Cleft of the Rock' till the Angels of healing make me whole again."[13]

This need of healing outweighed Stone's desire to be with her husband. "I would *rather* live with you, Harry dear, *a great deal.* But I *need* to be hidden, and shielded, and comforted by the large silence of the country. And if all our future is made rich by this separation we shall be glad, when it is past, that we braved it through, or if not, we shall at least feel, that we tried to get over a bridge that, after all broke. . . . I wish we could live together. I want you all the time, for speech, for silence, for rest, and sympathy, and all good things Harry dear." But she had to stay in the country to "gain strength, and courage, and patience, and hope, and all graces and virtues for future use."[14]

The land sale Stone wanted her husband to take charge of was that of the Illinois farm they had obtained when L. A. Ostrom defaulted on his debt to the Blackwells. Henry had since sold the farm, but the buyer had also defaulted and it was back in the brothers' hands. Stone had traded her Ostrom notes and no longer had any ownership interest in the Illinois farm. Nevertheless, she had to surrender her right to inherit it, and after doing so before a notary she informed her husband, "I have just come back from Warren where I relinquished my dower (free from your compulsion)." The parenthetical comment was mocking reference to a legal requirement that irritated her. She had earlier complained to Anthony, "If I sign any transfer of his property, I am insulted by being 'examined separately and apart from my husband' to know if it is by my own free will."[15]

Although Henry was unable to clinch the Illinois deal, he sold half of their Montclair farm, retaining their residence and eighteen acres. Lucy received his "astonishing dispatch" informing her of the sale just as she was making arrangements to move into the vacant half of her sister's house in Gardner, where she and Henry were to winter together. The sale brought them thousands of dollars, and Henry proposed that, instead of buying the farm in West Brookfield they had been considering as a "summer resort," they invest some of the proceeds in property on Martha's Vineyard. After visiting the coast to check out the proposed vacation property, Lucy returned to Gardner to find a large barrel of provisions from Henry to help her "set up house." Overwhelmed with their sudden change in circumstances she wrote ecstatically that now she could "write a treatise on 'Housekeeping Made Easy' for the benefit of young wives. The beginning and the end should be this: 'Choose a provident and thoughtful husband, who voluntarily will take the burden on himself.'"[16]

Income from the sale also eased Stone's concern about an upcoming draft. Blackwell had already made it through three militia calls. In 1862, he and Sam had contributed one hundred dollars apiece to a community fund to pay volunteers, which allowed New Jersey's Essex County to meet its quota without holding a draft. The chances of his being conscripted under the Enrollment Act of 1863 were slim. As a married man over thirty-five, he was not liable unless the pool of single men and married men between twenty and thirty-five in his district was exhausted. Nevertheless, Lucy worried. Before the spring 1864 call she urged Henry, if drafted, to "buy a substitute at any price—Draw on my credit if necessary!!!!!" Hiring a substitute was a practice with longstanding precedent in America and Europe and carried no ignominy. Now that money was no concern, she faced the autumn call with the certainty that if drafted, he would be able to get a substitute with no difficulty.[17]

Although Blackwell remained connected with the sugar refinery for another four years, he left it in September to stump for Lincoln. Stone sent him into the campaign with enthusiastic cheers. "Success to you darling! I have no doubt this fall's work will do you good in every way. . . . I expect to see you when the campaign is over, fresher, fairer, fitter, stronger, and looking ten years younger than now. So swinging my hat and shouting hurrah! again I say 'Success to you, my own darling Harry!'" Blackwell canvassed New Jersey for five weeks and earned praise for being as good a speaker as many men with a national reputation. Then, after voting in Essex County on November 8, he caught an afternoon train to join his wife and daughter in Gardner.[18]

The joy of their reunion was dampened only by Lucy's still-fresh grief from the death of her father on September 30. In the last months of his life, Francis Stone's sight had failed and he had suffered periods of total blindness. "He was glad to die," Lucy had written to Henry, "and we felt that it was best." But now, she said, her childhood home no longer felt like home, and she seemed "to stand on another round in life's ladder, and to feel that those below were broken."[19]

With the war drawing to an end and the sale of the farm bringing their long-sought financial independence, Stone and Blackwell did stand on a new rung in their life. Lucy rejoiced that her husband was at last free from "all business treadmills, with the means and time to rest." They invested the proceeds in government bonds, and Henry went west again to sell the Ostrom farm, sell timber off some of their lands, and negotiate release from contracts with his Cincinnati partners. He repaid his longstanding debt to cousin Kenyon Blackwell and, with George, paid off the mortgage on their mother's house and gave her the deed as a New Year's gift.[20] Lucy kept her Montclair farmhouse as rental property for the rest of her life. Although she and Henry had intended to keep their assets separate to ensure her independence, their joint ownership of the farm and other properties had made that impossible. Now, with these investments liquidated, Lucy reminded Henry to purchase her bonds in her own name, saying it was more important to her than he had ever realized that she receive the income of her property. Having achieved their financial independence, the couple were free to devote their lives to reform.[21]

Six years earlier, Blackwell had suggested that once he was free from business they should settle in Massachusetts. "To get *Woman the right of suffrage in Massachusetts!* that must be our aim. There, . . . where human rights are household words and where the revolutionary spirit burns most brightly, there we will *win for woman absolute equality before God and the Law.*" But Stone thought a home near New York City would better suit his entrepreneurial interests. "It is my opinion, Harry, that you will never be satisfied to discontinue for any length of time, the business to which you have all your life been accustomed, and it is perhaps not wise that you should, and we must shape our lives accordingly."[22] Relinquishing once and for all their dream of a small farm that would supply their needs and be a refuge from public work, they bought a house in Roseville, from which they could easily commute into New York.

If the war years had been a period of reduced activity for Stone and the woman's rights movement, they had also been a time of heightened expectancy. Across the nation, women had moved into positions vacated by men, and as they proved themselves competent, public attitudes changed. Even the *New York Times,* once a staunch defender of woman's sphere, became convinced that, if trained and educated in the same manner as men, women could be as "useful to the world" as men. Although the *Times* still believed marriage was woman's "highest destiny," it now thought "every woman should be prepared for a profession." The war led many women to expect a change in their legal and political status, as well. Years earlier, Stone had said the country needed a "revolution" to "shake [the Constitution] in pieces" and produce another in its place that would be unmistakably "in favor of righteousness that knows no sex, color, or condition." She was not alone in seeing the Civil War as that revolution. A *Sibyl* reader expressed the hope of many when she wished the war might "cause an upturning of things in general" so that when order was restored, women would be "recognized in the Constitution." As the war drew to a close and the nation's leaders began proposing various measures to extend the right of suffrage to the freedmen, Stone bristled at the assumption that this alone would create a true democracy. "Such wide-seeing good men . . . *hunting for justice,* forget that every man's wife, mother, and daughter has no political existence," she protested. There was much work to be done, and she looked forward to resuming her public work in partnership with her husband. They would work together, she said, to make the country a true democracy, one that recognized "the equal political rights of *all* the people."[23]

Agitation resumed in 1865. Reminding her audiences that the root cause of the conflict between North and South had been disagreement over the question of equal rights, Antoinette Brown Blackwell called on a reunited nation to reject oligarchical notions and give women a voice in their government. At several events that summer, Henry C. Wright appealed for suffrage "without regard to color or to sex," and Pennsylvania's Progressive Friends put two petitions in circulation: for an amendment to the state constitution extending suffrage to both women and blacks, and for a federal amendment guaranteeing them equal civil and political rights. Voter qualification had always been a matter of state jurisdiction, so seeking suffrage through an amendment to the national Constitution was a new and controversial approach. As Republicans debated how far to go in trying to secure Negro suffrage, Stone, Anthony, and Stanton, acting on behalf of the National Woman's Rights Committee, issued a petition for a federal amendment prohibiting states from disfranchising citizens "on the ground of sex."[24]

As woman's rights forces reactivated in January 1866, Stone accompanied Susan Anthony to Boston to try to forge a merger with abolitionists. With slavery soon to be abolished by the Thirteenth Amendment, antislavery societies were redirecting their efforts to securing the Negro's civil rights, and Anthony hoped to consolidate the two causes into one broad equal rights movement. Stone appealed to meetings of the American and Massachusetts antislavery societies to include women in their demand for "universal suffrage."[25] But unbridled violence against blacks in the postwar South made many abolitionists consider Negro suffrage more urgent, while opposition to Negro suffrage in both North and South made securing it an uphill battle. Unwilling to jeopardize the measure by attaching another controversial issue, most abolitionists insisted on keeping appeals for Negro and woman suffrage separate. Nevertheless, the women forged ahead with a one-sided merger. Meeting in May 1866 for the first time since before the war, the National Woman's Rights Convention voted itself into an American Equal Rights Association to work for the rights of both women and blacks. Stone became chair of the executive committee and Henry Blackwell, a recording secretary.

Stone resumed public work despite lingering doubts about her ability, and soon she was speaking "with all her old force and fire." In vain, she and Blackwell lobbied against use of the word *male* in the Fourteenth Amendment, which implied constitutional sanction for states to withhold suffrage from women. They spoke at equal rights meetings from Massachusetts to Pennsylvania; organized a state Equal Rights Association in New Jersey and numerous local auxiliaries; and spent two months campaigning in far-off Kansas. Granted hearings before the New Jersey and Connecticut legislatures and New York's constitutional convention, Stone appealed to lawmakers to use the time of national reconstruction to at last conform American government with the theories upon which it was based.[26]

For nearly two years, Stone worked for equal rights regardless of race or sex. But finally, the way opponents pitted Negro and woman suffrage against each other convinced her that the measures must be won separately. In November 1867 she founded the New Jersey Woman Suffrage Association, and the following spring, as sponsors stepped up efforts for a Fifteenth Amendment prohibiting states from withholding the vote on account of race, she issued two woman suffrage petitions at the annual meeting of the American Equal Rights Association: one for suffrage in the District of Columbia and territories, which

Congress alone could enact, and one for a Sixteenth Amendment to the United States Constitution.[27]

Stanton and Anthony, however, insisted that black men should not be enfranchised before women and advocated "educated suffrage," or basing suffrage on literacy. Refusing to endorse the strategy of separate amendments, they countered with a petition asking Congress to include women in any suffrage measure they passed—in effect, asking Congress not to pass *any* suffrage amendment that did not include women.[28] Interpreted as *the Negro with women or not at all*, this position was soundly rejected by the Equal Rights Association. The disagreement over separate amendments led to a schism among suffragists that resulted in the formation of rival national associations in 1869. With the founding of these organizations, the antebellum woman's rights movement formally became the postwar woman suffrage movement. Believing the goal was just a few years off, the leaders could not have imagined that the struggle would last another fifty years.

Stone and Blackwell returned to Massachusetts in late 1869 to establish the American Woman Suffrage Association's headquarters in Boston. As scores of women surged onto the postwar lyceum circuit and earned lucrative incomes in a profession that Stone had done so much to open for them, she herself quit lecturing to take charge of a new woman's rights paper, the *Woman's Journal*. Nevertheless, she continued to be a forceful speaker and addressed countless suffrage meetings and state legislatures. As both orator and editor, Lucy Stone remained until her death in 1893 one of the nation's strongest and most consistent voices for woman's rights.

Abbreviations Used in Citations

AAS: American Antiquarian Society, Worcester, Mass.

AGW: Angelina Grimké Weld

AKF: Abby Kelley/Abby Kelley Foster

ALB: Antoinette L. Brown/Antoinette Brown Blackwell

ALB Rem.: "Aunt Nettie's Reminiscences," recorded by Alice Stone Blackwell, pp. 29–30 of LS Rem.

ALSL: Alma Lutz Collection, SL

ASB: Alice Stone Blackwell

Barnes and Dumond: Gilbert H. Barnes and Dwight L. Dumond, eds., *Letters of Theodore Dwight Weld Angelina Grimké Weld and Sarah Grimké.* 1822–44. 2 vols. 1934; reprint, Gloucester, Mass., 1965

BLC: Blackwell Family Papers, Library of Congress

BPL: Boston Public Library

BSL: Blackwell Family Papers, Schlesinger Library

Bugle: *Anti-Slavery Bugle* (Salem, Ohio)

CCB: Charles Calistus Burleigh

CHD: Caroline Healy Dall

ECS: Elizabeth Cady Stanton

EzB: Elizabeth Blackwell

FDG: Frances Dana Gage

FS: Francis Stone, father of Lucy Stone

FS Jr.: Francis Stone Jr., (Frank), brother of Lucy Stone

GFP: Garrison Family Papers, Sophia Smith Collection, Smith College, Northampton, Mass.

Gilson: Mrs. Claude U. (Sarah) Gilson, "Antoinette Brown Blackwell, The First Woman Minister," unpublished manuscript, BSL

Gordon: Ann D. Gordon, ed. *The Selected Papers of Elizabeth Cady Stanton and Susan B. Anthony. Vol 1: In the School of Anti-Slavery, 1840–1866.* New Brunswick, N.J.: Rutgers University Press, 1997

GWB: George Washington Blackwell

HBB: Henry Browne Blackwell

HBB Rem.: Henry Browne Blackwell, "Reminiscences of Lucy Stone," ctr. 86, BLC

HCW: Henry Clarke Wright

HS: Hannah Stone

HWS: Elizabeth Cady Stanton, Susan B. Anthony, Matilda Joslyn Gage, et al., *History of Woman Suffrage,* 6 vols. Vols. 1–3, New York, 1881–85; vol. 4, Rochester, 1902; vols. 5–6, New York, 1922

Lasser and Merrill: Carol Lasser and Marlene Merrill, eds. *Friends and Sisters: Letters between Lucy Stone and Antoinette Brown Blackwell, 1846–1893.* Urbana: University of Illinois Press, 1987

LC: Library of Congress, Manuscript Division, Washington, D.C.

LCM: Lucretia Coffin Mott

LS: Lucy Stone

LS Rem.: "Reminiscences of Lucy Stone," recorded by Alice Stone Blackwell, ctr. 86, BLC

MCW: Martha Coffin Wright

MHS: Massachusetts Historical Society, Boston, Mass.

NASS: *National Anti-Slavery Standard* (New York)

NAWSAR: National American Woman Suffrage Association Records, LC

NES: *New England Spectator* (Boston, Mass.)

NWRC 1850: *Proceedings of the Woman's Rights Convention, Held at Worcester, October 23rd and 24th, 1850.* Boston: Prentiss and Sawyer, 1851

NWRC 1851: *Proceedings of the Woman's Rights Convention, Held at Worcester, October 15th and 16th, 1851.* New York: Fowlers and Wells, 1852

NWRC 1852: *Proceedings of the Woman's Rights Convention, Held at Syracuse, September 8th, 9th, and 10th, 1852.* Syracuse: J. E. Masters, 1852

NWRC 1853: *Proceedings of the Woman's Rights Convention Held at the Broadway Tabernacle in the City of New York Tuesday and Wednesday, Sept. 6th and 7th, 1853.* New York: Fowlers and Wells, 1853

NWRC 1856: *Proceedings of the Seventh National Woman's Rights Convention, Held in New York City at the Broadway Tabernacle, on Tuesday and Wednesday, Nov. 25 & 26, 1856.* New York: Edward O. Jenkins, 1856

NWRC 1860: *Proceedings of the Tenth National Woman's Rights Convention, Held at the Cooper Institute, New York City, May 10th and 11th, 1860.* Boston: Yerrinton and Garrison, 1860

NYWRC 1853: *Proceedings of the Woman's Rights Convention Held at the Broadway*

Tabernacle in the City of New York, Tuesday and Wednesday, Sept. 6th and 7th, 1853. New York: Fowlers and Wells, 1853

OCA: Oberlin College Archives, Oberlin, Ohio

PWD: Paulina Wright Davis

SBA: Susan Brownell Anthony

SCB: Samuel Charles Blackwell

SEB: (Sarah) Ellen Blackwell

SG: Sarah Grimké

SJM: Samuel Joseph May, of New York

SL: Schlesinger Library, Radcliffe Institute, Harvard University

SM Jr.: Samuel May Jr., of Massachusetts

SSF: Stephen Symonds Foster

SSL: Sarah Stone Lawrence

SSL Rem.: "Aunt Sarah's [Sarah Stone Lawrence] Reminiscences of Lucy Stone," recorded by Alice Stone Blackwell, pp. 23–28 of LS Rem.

Stanton and Blatch: Theodore Stanton and Harriot Stanton Blatch, eds., *Elizabeth Cady Stanton as Revealed in Her Letters, Diary, and Reminiscences,* 2 vols. New York: Harper, 1922

TWH: Thomas Wentworth Higginson

VCHS: Vernon County Historical Society, Viroqua, Wisc.

WBS: (William) Bowman Stone

WHC: William Henry Channing

Wheeler: Leslie Wheeler, *Loving Warriors: Selected Letters of Lucy Stone and Henry B. Blackwell, 1853–1893.* New York: The Dial Press, 1981

WJ: *Woman's Journal* (Boston, Mass.)

WLG: William Lloyd Garrison

WLG Letters: Walter M. Merrill and Louis Ruchames, eds. *The Letters of William Lloyd Garrison,* 6 vols. Cambridge, Mass.: Belknap Press of Harvard University Press, 1971–81

WLG Life: Wendell Phillips Garrison and Francis Jackson Garrison, *William Lloyd Garrison: The Story of His Life As Told by His Children,* 4 vols. New York: Century Co., 1885–89

WP: Wendell Phillips

Notes

CHAPTER 1

1. SBA to LS, 16 Feb 1854, BLC, Gordon, 260.

2. *New York Daily Times,* 8 May 1856; *Liberator,* 14 Jul 1832. The lines are from abolitionist poet Elizabeth Margaret Chandler, published in *Elizabeth Margaret Chandler: Poetical Works, with a Memoir of Her Life and Character by Benjamin Lundy* (Philadelphia: L. Howell, 1836), 64.

CHAPTER 2

1. J. Gardner Bartlett, *Gregory Stone Genealogy: Ancestry and Descendants of Dea. Gregory Stone of Cambridge, Mass., 1320–1917* (Boston: Stone Family Association, 1918).

2. William Warren Sweet, *Religion in the Development of American Culture, 1765–1840* (New York: Charles Scribner's Sons, 1952), 53, 93–94, 146; John Kobler, *Ardent Spirits: The Rise and Fall of Prohibition* (New York: G. P. Putnam's Sons, 1973), 30–31.

3. Bartlett, 237–39; John Howard Temple, *History of North Brookfield, Massachusetts* (Boston: Rand, Avery, 1887), 746–47.

4. LS Rem., 22, 1, 9, 20; Emma Lawrence Blackwell to ASB, 29 Mar 1901, BLC.

5. LS Rem., 1.

6. LS Rem., 2, 7.

7. Nancy Woloch, *Women and the American Experience* (New York: Alfred A. Knopf, 1984), 120–21.

8. Sweet, 53, 190–200; Ronald G. Walters, *American Reformers, 1815–1860* (New York: Hill & Wang, 1978), 31–32.

9. LS Rem., 7; Sweet, 11–17; Chard Powers Smith, *Yankees and God* (New York: Hermitage House, 1954), 48, 70.

10. LS Rem., 12.

11. LS Rem., 19.

12. LS Rem., 8.

13. Andrea Moore Kerr, *Lucy Stone: Speaking Out for Equality* (New Brunswick, N.J.: Rutgers University Press, 1992), 15; SSL Rem., 27; LS Rem., 3. Based on a letter from Stone to her brother Frank, Elinor Rice Hays also concluded that Stone had been ill-treated as a child (*Morning Star: A Biography of Stone, 1818–1893* [New York: Harcourt, Brace and World, 1961], 15; LS to FS Jr., 15 Feb 1846, BLC). In the letter, Lucy urged Frank to look for opportunities to praise "Willy,"

saying she knew from "experience and from observation . . . that one word of approval will do more to make a child good than all the scoldings and whippings in the world put together." Hays concluded that Lucy advised her brother on raising a son and alluded to treatment she received from their father. But Lucy advised Frank in his dealings with a young black boy he was teaching to read, and she referred to her experience both as a student and as a teacher. She had just finished teaching a term in which, she said, her use of kind words and praise had transformed a particularly unresponsive student (LS to SSL, 13 Mar 1846, BLC).

14. LS biographical note recorded by ASB, 15 Nov 1881, ctr. 86, BLC; LS Rem., 22–23.

15. LS Rem., 9.

16. LS Rem., 8, 10.

17. LS Rem., 7; BLC. Kerr's suggestion that Stone may have been sexually abused by one of her father's friends is speculation based solely upon attitudes assigned to Stone that can characterize victims of abuse—"need to feel in control, her rejection of sexuality, low self-esteem, rigid behavior patterns, and her later expressions of disgust at men and their vices" (Kerr, 15, 251 n. 18). I find no evidence that Stone possessed such attitudes and no indication in any family records that she was abused.

18. LS Rem., 11.

19. LS to SSL, 14 Sep 1845, BLC. When Stone told her daughter of instances of her father's "ugliness" with money, she also said not to use them in any biography she might write. "I will not have my father blamed. It is enough to say that he had the Puritan idea that women were to be governed, and that he had a right to hold the purse and to rule his own home" (LS Rem., 11).

20. LS Rem., 14.

21. Bartlett, 239; LS biographical note recorded by ASB, ctr. 90, BLC.

22. LS Rem., 20.

23. LS Rem., 20; LS, Luther Stone, and WBS to FS Jr., 31 Aug 1838, BLC. The decision to remain single was not uncommon among women of Stone's day. Nancy Cott describes a definite "marriage trauma" among New England women of this period, which stemmed from the prevalent view of marriage as, for women, voluntary self-abnegation. *The Bonds of Womanhood: "Woman's Sphere" in New England, 1780–1835* (New Haven: Yale University Press, 1970), 80.

CHAPTER 3

1. B. A. Hinsdale, *Horace Mann and the Common School Revival in the United States* (New York: Charles Scribner's Sons, 1911), 3–5, 18, 29–30.

2. Alice Stone Blackwell, *Lucy Stone: Pioneer of Woman's Rights* (Boston: Little, Brown and Co.), 19; Nancy Woloch, *Women and the American Experience* (New York: Alfred A. Knopf, 1984), 294.

3. Educator Hannah Adams in 1831, quoted in Louise Schutz Boas, *Woman's Education Begins: The Rise of the Women's Colleges* (Norton, Mass.: Wheaton College Press, 1935), 22–23.

4. LS Rem., 10.

5. Boas, 52–57. Dating of encounter is based on Lyon's fund-raising tour, mentioned in Arthur C. Cole, *A Hundred Years of Mount Holyoke College: The Evolution of an Educational Ideal* (New Haven: Yale University Press, 1940), 24.

6. Nancy F. Cott, *The Bonds of Womanhood: "Woman's Sphere"' in New England, 1780–1835* (New Haven, Conn.: Yale University Press, 1977).

7. Woloch, 122.

8. Boas, 38; Cott, *Bonds*, 68.

9. Woloch, 126–28.

10. Edward Hitchcock, *The Power of Christian Benevolence, Illustrated in the Life and Labors of Mary Lyon* (Northampton, Mass.: Hopkins, Bridgeman, 1852), 212.

11. LS Rem., 4; *WJ*, 6 Feb 1892; LS biographical note recorded by ASB, ctr. 90, BLC.

12. Blackwell, 16; LS to HS, 29 Jan 1847, BLC.

13. LS Rem., 4, 18; LS to FS Jr., 26 Jul, [Aug], 20 Sep 1836, BLC; LS to HBB, 26 Apr 1854, BLC, Wheeler, 82; *Una*, Jul 1854.

14. Woloch, 129.

CHAPTER 4

1. LS to FS Jr., 28 Feb 1836, BLC; Merle Eugene Curti, *The American Peace Crusade, 1815–1860* (New York: Octagon Books, 1965), 23.

2. *Journal of Humanity*, 16 Aug 1832, quoted in Keith Melder, *Beginnings of Sisterhood: The American Woman's Rights Movement, 1800–1850* (New York: Schocken Books, 1977), 54.

3. Timothy L. Smith, *Revivalism and Social Reform: American Protestantism on the Eve of the Civil War* (New York: Harper & Row, 1957), 36–37.

4. Robert William Fogel, *Without Consent or Contract: The Rise and Fall of American Slavery* (New York: W. W. Norton, 1989), 244–54; John R. McKivigan, *The War against Proslavery Religion: Abolitionism and the Northern Churches, 1830–1865* (Ithaca, N.Y.: Cornell University Press, 1984), 24–29.

5. WLG Life, 1:294–95; *Liberator*, 13 Aug 1831; Fogel, 266; Aileen Kraditor, *Means and Ends in American Abolitionism: Garrison and His Critics on Strategy and Tactics, 1834–1850* (New York: Pantheon Books, 1969), 26–29, 79.

6. Henry Mayer, *All on Fire: William Lloyd Garrison and the Abolition of Slavery* (New York: St. Martin's Press, 1998), 120–23.

7. *Liberator*, 5 May, 18 Feb 1832.

8. Fogel, 271–72; Mayer, 196–210.

9. Quoted in WLG Life, 1:156–57.

10. *Liberator*, 17 Dec 1831, 7, 14 Jan, 18 Feb, 14 Jul 1832.

11. *Liberator*, 14 Jul, 17 Nov, 1, 17 Dec 1832; WLG Life, 1: 305; Deborah Bingham Van Broekhoven, "'A Determination to Labor . . .': Female Antislavery Activity in Rhode Island," *Rhode Island History* 44 (May 1985): 35–38.

12. Mayer, 145–48, 134, 170–73; Dorothy Sterling, *We Are Your Sisters: Black Women in the Nineteenth Century* (New York: W. W. Norton, 1984), 153–54.

13. Nancy Woloch, *Women and the American Experience* (New York: Alfred A. Knopf, 1984), 163; Celia Morris Eckhardt, *Fanny Wright: Rebel in America* (Cambridge, Mass.: Harvard University Press, 1984), 172–87, 191–95, 205; Lillian O'Connor, *Pioneer Woman Orators* (New York: Columbia, 1954), 53–54.

14. Carolyn Williams, "The Female Antislavery Movement: Fighting against Racial Prejudice and Promoting Women's Rights in Antebellum America," in *The Abolitionist Sisterhood: Women's Political Culture in Antebellum America*, ed. Jean Fagan Yellin and John C. Van Horne (Ithaca, N.Y.: Cornell University Press, 1994), 161–62; *Liberator*, 21, 28 Dec 1833; NES, 19 Nov 1834.

15. Carroll Smith-Rosenberg, *Religion and the Rise of the American City: The New York City Mission Movement, 1812–1870* (Ithaca, N.Y.: Cornell University Press, 1971), 101, 110–19; Melder, 50–55; *Advocate of Moral Reform*, 15 Oct 1846.

16. *NES*, 19 Nov 1834, 10 Sep, 14, 21, 26 Oct, 25 Nov 1835.

17. *NES*, 21 Jan 1835, 13 Jun, 16 Nov 1836.

18. Gerda Lerner, *The Majority Finds Its Past: Placing Women in History* (New York: Oxford University Press, 1979), 117; Catharine E. Beecher, *An Essay on Slavery and Abolitionism, with Reference to the Duty of American Females, Addressed to Miss A. E. Grimke* (Philadelphia, 1837), 97–105; James Thome, *Address to the Females of Ohio, Delivered at the Anti-Slavery Anniversary, April 1836, Cincinnati, Ohio* (Cincinnati: Ohio Anti-Slavery Society, 1836); John Quincy Adams, *Speech . . . upon the Rights of the People, Men and Women, to Petition* (Washington, 1838), quoted in Eleanor Flexner, *Century of Struggle: The Woman's Rights Movement in the United States* (1959; reprint, New York: Atheneum, 1968), 344; Abraham Lincoln to Editor of the *San-*

gamon Journal, 13 Jun 1836, in *The Life and Writings of Abraham Lincoln,* ed. Phillip Stern (New York: Modern Library, 1942), 225.

19. *Liberator,* 13 Aug 1836; Clifford S. Griffin, *Their Brothers' Keepers: Moral Stewardship in the United States, 1800–1865* (New Brunswick, N.J.: Rutgers University Press, 1960), 125–26.

20. Melder, 80; Dorothy Sterling, ed., *Turning the World Upside Down: The Anti-Slavery Convention of American Women Held in New York City, May 9–12, 1837* (New York: The Feminist Press, 1987), 12–13.

21. *Liberator,* 9 Jun 1837.

22. Gerda Lerner, *The Grimké Sisters of South Carolina: Pioneers for Woman's Rights* (New York: Schocken, 1967), 119–21; *NES,* 19 Nov 1834; Theodore Weld to SG and AG, 22 May 1837, Barnes and Dumond, 1:389–91.

23. AGW to Jane Smith, 29 May 1837, quoted in Melder, 80; *Liberator,* 9 Jun 1837; SG to Theodore Weld, 11 Jun 1837, and SG to Gerrit Smith, 28 Jun 1837, Barnes and Dumond, 1:402, 410. The explanation that the Grimkés spoke to mixed audiences because men insisted on attending was first advanced in an article in the *NES,* 6 Sep 1837. The author was Henry C. Wright (SG and AGW to HCW, 12 Aug, 27 Aug 1837, Barnes and Dumond, 1:419–23, 436–41).

24. WLG Life, 1:477–81, 2:130–35; *NES,* 3 Jul 1837; *Liberator,* 11 Aug 1837.

25. LS Rem., 18; *WJ,* 14 Apr 1888.

26. *Liberator,* 21 Jul 1837.

27. *Liberator,* 11 Aug 1837; SG and AGW to HCW, 12 Aug 1837, Barnes and Dumond, 1:419–23.

28. *NES,* 19 Jul, 1, 29 Nov 1837; *Liberator,* 13 Oct 1837.

29. *NES,* reprinted in *Liberator,* 6 Oct 1837; LS to SSL, 4 Jan 1847, BLC.

CHAPTER 5

1. Theodore Weld to SG and AG, 26 Aug 1837, Barnes and Dumond, 1:436.

2. *Liberator,* 11 Aug 1837; *NES,* 16 Aug 1837; WLG Life, 2:141–60.

3. *Liberator,* 1 Sep, 6 Oct 1837; *NES,* 11 Oct, 1837; Merle Eugene Curti, *The American Peace Crusade, 1815–1860* (New York: Octagon Books, 1965), 7–11, 21–33, 64–80; Deborah Weston to "Aunt Mary," 15 Jun 1837, Weston Sisters Collection, BPL.

4. *Liberator,* 15 Dec 1837.

5. WLG Life, 157; *NES,* 29 Nov 1837.

6. *NES,* 23 Feb 1838; *Liberator,* 4 May 1838.

7. *Liberator,* 5 Jan–16 Feb 1838.

8. LS, Luther Stone, and WBS to FS Jr., 31 Aug 1838, BLC.

9. *Liberator,* 2 Mar 1838; *WJ,* 21 Aug 1875; Angelina Grimké, *Letters to Catherine E. Beecher, in Reply to an Essay on Slavery and Abolitionism, Addressed to A. E. Grimke* (Boston: Isaac Knapp, 1838), 113. In her reference to the injustice of taxation without representation, Sarah Grimké said she thought it better to bear that injustice than participate in the political affairs of a nation that supported slavery. When a fellow abolitionist told Lydia Maria Child he wished women could vote, Child replied that though she believed women had as much right to vote as men did, she thought "politics rested on such a thoroughly bad foundation" that she felt "no inclination to use the right." To which her friend replied, "Then you are *fit* to be a slave" (Child to Caroline Weston, 7 Mar 1839, Weston Sisters Collection, BPL).

10. Carroll Smith-Rosenberg, *Religion and the Rise of the American City: The New York City Mission Movement, 1812–1870* (Ithaca, N.Y.: Cornell University Press, 1971), 119–20; *Advocate of Moral Reform,* 1 Jan, 1 Feb, 1 Jun 1848; Amy Swerdlow, "Abolition's Conservative Sisters: The Ladies' New York City Anti-Slavery Societies, 1834–1840" in *The Abolitionist Sisterhood: Women's Political Culture in Antebellum America,* ed. Jean Fagan Yellin and John C. Horne (Ithaca, N.Y.: Cornell University Press, 1994), 31–44.

11. Lucia Weston to Deborah Weston, 28 Apr 1839, Weston Sisters Collection, BPL; Alma Lutz,

Crusade for Freedom: Women of the Antislavery Movement (Boston: Beacon Press, 1968), 121–43; WLG Life, 2:220–21, 227, 276; *Liberator,* 8 Jun 1838, 25 Jan 1839; Curti, 81.

12. LS, Luther Stone, and WBS to FS Jr., 31 Aug 1838, BLC; LS Rem., 20, 14; SSL Rem., 26; Sarah Grimké, *Letters on the Equality of the Sexes, and the Condition of Woman, Addressed to Mary S. Parker, President of the Boston Female Anti-Slavery Society* (Boston: Isaac Knapp, 1838); LS to FS Jr., 29 Nov 1838, BLC; *A Catalogue of the Members of the Congregational Church in West Brookfield, From 1758 to 1861* (West Brookfield, Mass.: Thomas Morey, 1861), 38–39.

13. LS to FS Jr., 29 Nov 1838, BLC; LS, Luther Stone, and WBS to FS Jr., 31 Aug 1838, BLC; LS Rem., 5; SSL to LS, 28 Mar 1847, BLC.

14. LS Rem., 4; Arthur C. Cole, *A Hundred Years of Mount Holyoke College: The Evolution of an Educational Ideal* (New Haven: Yale University Press, 1940), 36, 39; *Second Annual Catalog of the Officers and Members of the Mount Holyoke Female Seminary, South Hadley, Mass., 1838–1839,* 8–9; *Godey's Lady's Book,* quoted in Norma Basch, *In the Eyes of the Law: Women, Marriage, and Property in Nineteenth-Century New York* (Ithaca, N.Y.: Cornell University Press, 1982), 143. The *General Catalog of Mount Holyoke Seminary, South Hadley, Mass., 1837–1887* lists Stone as a nongraduate of 1839, but no college records indicate her exact dates of attendance. Stone said she attended for less than one year (LS Rem., 21), and because correspondence and other records reveal that she did not attend either of the first two terms, I conclude she attended only the last, 18 Apr–24 Jul 1839.

15. LS speech, NWRC 1851, 28; LS to Charles Franklin Thwing, 2 Feb 1893, Robert Samuel Fletcher Papers, OCA.

16. Cole, 53; LS Rem., 21.

17. Merton L. Dillon, *The Abolitionists: The Growth of a Dissenting Minority* (DeKalb, Ill.: Northern Illinois University Press, 1974), 44–45.

18. WLG Life, 2: 260–71; Aileen Kraditor, *Means and Ends in American Abolitionism: Garrison and His Critics on Strategy and Tactics, 1834–1850* (New York: Pantheon Books, 1969), 96, 100, 120–23.

19. *Liberator,* 14 Jun 1839; *Liberator Extra* [Apr 1840]; Debra Gold Hansen, *Strained Sisterhood: Gender and Class in the Boston Female Anti-Slavery Society* (Amherst: University of Massachusetts Press, 1993), 21–27.

20. *Liberator,* 17 May 1839.

21. WLG Life, 2:307; Elizur Wright Jr. to Henry B. Stanton, 12 Oct 1839, *Liberator,* 13 Dec 1839. See also *Bugle,* 17 Apr 1846.

22. Theodore Weld to Gerrit Smith, 23 Oct 1839, Barnes and Dumond, 2:810–11.

23. LS Rem., 21.

24. Cole, 46–47; NWRC 1852, 88; LS to WBS, 18 Jun 1840, BLC.

CHAPTER 6

1. *Catalogue of the Officers and Students of the Wesleyan Academy for the Year 1839–40* (Hartford, 1840); Reminiscences of Maria Barlow, ctr. 86, BLC; LS to WBS, 18 Jun 1840, BLC.

2. LS to WBS, 18 Jun 1840, BLC; WBS to WLG, 21 Feb 1840, *Liberator,* 10 Apr 1840.

3. Stephen Nissenbaum, *Sex, Diet, and Debility in Jacksonian America: Sylvester Graham and Health Reform* (Westport, Conn.: Greenwood Press, 1980), 20, 115, 126.

4. Nissenbaum discusses Graham's theories as a departure from seventeenth- and eighteenth-century sexual attitudes and the beginning of Victorian sexual attitudes (3, 26–30, 111–116).

5. LS to WBS, 18 Jun 1840, BLC.

6. *Water-Cure Journal,* Mar 1849.

7. *Liberator,* 9 Aug, 15 Nov, 6, 27 Dec 1839; WLG Life, 2:319–20.

8. *Liberator,* 21 Jun, 5, 26 Jul 1839, 22, 29 May 1840; HCW to George W. Benson, 20 Feb 1840, and HCW to WLG, [May] 1840, both quoted in WLG Life, 2:339–44.

9. Debra Gold Hansen, *Strained Sisterhood: Gender and Class in the Boston Female Anti-Slavery Society* (Amherst: University of Massachusetts Press, 1993), 28, 93–94.

10. LS to WBS, 18 Jun 1840, BLC.

11. *Liberator,* 29 May 1840.

12. LS to WBS, 18 Jun 1840, BLC.

13. *Liberator,* 29 May 1840.

14. WLG Life, 2:353; Lewis Tappan to Theodore Weld, 4 May 1840, Barnes and Dumond, 2:834; Gerda Lerner, *The Grimké Sisters of South Carolina: Pioneers for Woman's Rights* (New York: Schocken, 1967), 296–97; Frederick B. Tolles, ed., *Slavery and the Woman Question: Lucretia Mott's Diary of Her Visit to Great Britain to Attend the World's Anti-Slavery Convention of 1840* (Haverford, Penn.: Friends' Historical Association, 1952), 7–9.

15. WLG Life, 2: 367–373; The Massachusetts society had also appointed Maria Weston Chapman, Lydia Maria Child, and Abby Kelley, but they considered their work too important to leave for uncertain participation in the conference. Harriet Martineau, an English reformer who held a lifetime membership in the Massachusetts society, was also delegated, but she did not attend because of illness.

16. *Liberator,* 24 Jul, 4 Dec 1840. Elizabeth Griffith, *In Her Own Right: The Life of Elizabeth Cady Stanton* (New York: Oxford University Press, 1984), 36; Dorothy Sterling, ed., *Turning the World Upside Down: The Anti-Slavery Convention of American Women Held in New York City, May 9–12, 1837* (New York: The Feminist Press, 1987), 24; John Bowring to WLG, *Liberator,* 25 Dec 1840.

17. Frederick B. Tolles, ed., *Slavery and the Woman Question: Lucretia Mott's Diary of Her Visit to Great Britain to Attend the World's Anti-Slavery Convention of 1840* (Haverford, Penn.: Friends' Historical Association, 1952), 22–29; Anna Davis Hallowell, ed., *James and Lucretia Mott: Life and Letters* (Boston: Houghton, Mifflin, 1884), 50; LCM speech, *NASS,* 26 Dec 1863; LCM to AKF, 18 Mar 1839, AKF and SSF Papers, AAS; Alma Lutz, *Crusade for Freedom: Women of the Antislavery Movement* (Boston: Beacon Press, 1968), 172–73; LM to Grimkés in ECS to AGW and SG, 25 Jun 1840, Barnes and Dumond, 2:847. Elizabeth Cady Stanton, who attended the convention as an observer accompanying her husband, Henry B. Stanton, was also affected by the controversy, but her initial reaction is not clear. Before sailing for London she and Henry had visited the Weld-Grimkés, who, despite their role in inciting the woman question, regretted its effect on the antislavery movement, and Sarah, at least, had hoped it would not invade the London convention. After the convention's close, Stanton wrote to them that it had "passed off more smoothly than any of us anticipated. The woman's rights question, besides monopolizing one whole day, . . . created some little discord, for on this point we find a difference of opinion among the men and women here as well as with us in America." The letter reflects only disdain for Garrison, whom, Stanton said, "tempted Christ" when he tried to speak on "woman's rights, poor laws, temperance, etc." at a postconvention event. Despite this apparent lack of sympathy, Garrison wrote a few days later that "Mrs. Stanton . . . goes for woman's rights with all her soul." It appears that Stanton's enthusiasm developed from her association with Lucretia Mott, whom she found "an entire new revelation of womanhood." Although she later said the women's treatment at the London convention made her and Mott decide to call a woman's rights convention, Mott recalled that the idea of a convention did not arise until a year later when the two met again in Boston. ECS to AGW and SG, 25 Jun 1840, Barnes and Dumond, 2:846; Lerner, *Grimké Sisters,* 295–98; WLG to Helen Garrison, 29 Jun 1840, WLG Life, 2:383; LM to ECS, 16 Mar 1855, ECS Papers, LC.

18. *Catalog of the Officers and Students of the Monson Academy 1840–1841* (Springfield, Mass., 1841).

19. Wesleyan College in Macon, Georgia, chartered as Georgia Female College in 1836, bestowed degrees upon eleven women in 1840, a year before Oberlin. However, its curriculum did not include classical studies, at that time the core of other college curricula, and having begun classes only in 1839, its 1840 graduates had completed most of their studies at academies or other such schools.

20. William Warren Sweet, *Religion in the Development of American Culture, 1765–1840* (New York: Charles Scribner's Sons, 1952), 228–29; SSL to LS, 9 Aug 1845, BLC; SSL Rem., 28.

21. Alice W. Cowles to Henry Cowles, 19 Jul 1840, Robert Samuel Fletcher Papers, OCA; AKF to SG, 14 Jan 1839, Barnes and Dumond, 2:744–48.

22. LS Rem., 13.

23. *Catalogue of the Theological Seminary, Bangor Maine* (Bangor, 1838–39, 1839–40, 1841, 1842, 1843); *Historical Catalogue of the Bangor Theological Seminary, 1820–1916* [Bangor], 1928.

24. "But it is my moody week with its periodical headaches, and I shall feel braver and more hopeful when it is past" (LS to SBA, 8 Nov 1855, BLC). Stone's headaches were such a constant, normal part of her life that their occasional absence was worth noting: "I get along well, have very little of the headache" (LS to FS Jr., 20 May 1844, BSL).

25. *Quaboag Seminary Catalogue of the Corporation, Trustees, Instructors, and Students for the Autumn Term Ending Nov. 16, 1842* (West Brookfield, Mass., 1842); "Order of Exercises at the Exhibition of the Male and Female Departments [of the Quaboag Seminary], Wednesday, Nov. 16, 1842," AAS; SSL Rem., 23.

26. *Liberator*, 19, 26 Apr 1839; LS speech, *NASS*, 26 Dec 1863; George Bradburn, Chairman, "Report of the Special Committee to whom were referred the petition . . . as concerns especially the intermarriage of persons differing in complexion or belonging to different races," 19 Jan 1841, and *Act Relating to Marriages between Individuals of Certain Races, Approved Feb. 25, 1843*, Massachusetts State Archives, Boston, Mass.

27. *Liberator*, 11 Jul 1845; *WJ*, 4 Nov 1893; LS Rem., 18.

CHAPTER 7

1. LS to Family, 30 Aug 1843, BLC. Borrowed funds: LS to Family, 28 Sep 1845, BLC; LS to SSL, 14 Sep 1845, 13 Mar 1846, BLC; Luther Stone to LS, 3 Aug 1846, BLC; LS editorial, *WJ*, 17 May 1884. College costs: J. A. Thome to Theodore Weld, 12 Sep 1843, Barnes and Dumon, 2:982–83; Robert Samuel Fletcher, *A History of Oberlin College*, vol. 1 (1943; reprint, New York: Arno Press, 1971), 615–16.

2. LS biographical note recorded by ASB, 13 May 1893, ctr. 86, BLC.

3. LS Rem., 3–4; LS to Family, 30 Aug 1843, BLC.

4. LS to HS, 11 Sep 1843, BLC; LS Rem., 4.

5. Fletcher, 617–19, 626; LS to HS, 11 Sep 1843, BLC.

6. LS to Family, 30 Aug 1843, BLC; LS to HS, 11 Sep 1843, BLC; Fletcher, 248–49.

7. LS to Family, 30 Aug 1843, BLC; LS to HS, 11 Sep 1843, BLC.

8. LS to FS Jr., 4 Jul 1845, 15 Feb 1846, BLC.

9. LS to Family, 12 Apr [1844], BLC; LS to FS Jr., 4 Jul 1845, BLC; HBB to LS, 15 Jan 1856, BLC.

10. LS to FS Jr., 4 Jul 1845, BLC.

11. LS to SSL, 4 Jan 1847, BLC; Merle Eugene Curti, *The American Peace Crusade, 1815–1860* (New York: Octagon Books, 1965), 145.

12. *Advocate of Moral Reform*, 15 Jul 1845.

13. Fletcher, 377.

14. Fletcher, 299–300, 302, 682, 671.

15. Elinor Rice Hays, *Morning Star: A Biography of Lucy Stone, 1818–1893* (New York: Harcourt, Brace and World, 1961), 46.

16. Fletcher, 318; LS to Family, 30 Aug 1843, BLC.

17. LS to FS Jr., 11 Jul, 15 Feb 1846, BLC; LS to WBS and SSL, 4 Jul 1847, BLC; LS Rem., 4.

18. Fletcher, 233–35.

19. *Advocate of Moral Reform*, 1 Jan 1844, 15 Jul 1845.

20. *Catalog of the Officers and Students of the Oberlin Collegiate Institute, 1845–46*; FS to LS,

11 Jan 1845, BLC; Marianne Finch, *An Englishwoman's Experience in America* (London: Richard Bentley, 1853), 358.

21. LS to SSL, 14 Sep 1845, 13 Mar 1846, 31 Mar 1845, BLC; LS to FS Jr., 12 May 1845, BLC.

22. Finch, 356–58; LS to SSL, 31 Mar, 14 Sep 1845, BLC; LS to FS Jr., 6 Jul 1845, BLC.

23. Finch, 358; Board of Trustees Records, 1833–48 (126–1/3/1, Box 1, Ledger January 1, 1844–December 31, 1846, #5 p. 223; 1 Jan 1847–31 Dec 1850, #6 p. 141), OCA; Series of Teacher Pay Reports, 1841–52, OCA.

24. FS to LS, 11 Jan 1845, BLC.

25. LS to FS Jr., 6 Jul 1845, BLC.

26. LS to FS Jr., 12 May, 4–15 Jul 1845, BLC; LS to SSL, 14 Sep 1845, BLC.

27. LS to SSL, 14 Sep 1845, BLC; Untitled essay addressed to Mr. Sturge, NAWSAR; Adolphus Sturge to LS, 19 Jul 1845, NAWSAR.

28. Edward Henry to LS, [Feb 1847], BLC; Mary A. Barnes to LS, 13 Dec 1845, NAWSAR; Camilla Stephens to LS, 29 Jul 1846, BLC; Oberlin Moral Reform Society, Minute Book 1835–1857, entry for 12 Aug 1845, OCA; Oberlin [College] Young Ladies' Association, Minute Book 1846–1850, entry for 9 Sep 1846, OCA.

29. William Platt to LS, 11 Dec [1845], NAWSAR; LS to SSL, 14 Sep, 1845, 13 Mar 1846, BLC.

30. LS to Family, 3 Feb 1846, BLC; LS to Parents, [fall 1845], 16 Sep 1846, BLC.

31. LS to Family, 3 Feb 1846, BLC; WBS to LS, 17 Feb 1846, BLC.

CHAPTER 8

1. William Warren Sweet, *Religion in the Development of American Culture, 1765–1840* (New York: Charles Scribner's Sons, 1952), 336; LS to SSL and Henry Lawrence, 13 Mar 1846, BLC; LS to Parents, 12 Feb 1846, BLC.

2. LS to FS Jr., 12 May 1845, BLC; Cicero, *De oratore*, 1.8.

3. *Liberator*, 24 Jan 1839.

4. Russell Errett to Salmon P. Chase, 9 May 1846, quoted in Merton L. Dillon, *The Abolitionists: The Growth of a Dissenting Minority* (DeKalb, Ill.: Northern Illinois University Press, 1974), 171.

5. LS to SSL and Henry Lawrence, 13 Mar 1846, BLC; LS to Parents, 12 Feb 1846, BLC.

6. LS to SSF and AKF, 25 Mar 1846, AKF and SSF Papers, AAS; *Oberlin Evangelist*, 4 Mar 1846.

7. LS to SSF and AKF, 25 Mar 1846, and LS to AKF, 3 Jul 1846, AKF and SSF Papers, AAS.

8. AKF to LS, 20 Apr 1846, NAWSAR; Robert Samuel Fletcher, *A History of Oberlin College*, vol. 1 (1943; reprint, New York: Arno Press and The New York Times, 1971), 292.

9. Oberlin [College] Young Ladies' Association, Minute Book 1846–50, entry dated 6 May 1846, OCA; LS to AKF, 3 Jul 1846, AKF and SSF Papers, AAS; [Oberlin College] Union Society, Minute Book 1841–50, entry dated 20 May 1846, OCA.

10. AKF to LS, 20 Apr, 17 Jul 1846, NAWSAR; LS to AKF, 3 Jul 1846, AFP; AKF to LS, 15 Aug [1846], Woman's Rights Collection, SL.

11. LS, "The Province of Woman," BLC.

12. LS biographical note recorded by ASB, 5 Apr 1885, ctr. 86, BLC.

13. LS, "Why Do We Rejoice Today," Woman's Rights Collection, SL; LS to HBB, [31 Dec 1853], BLC.

14. Article excerpted in LS to Parents, 16 Aug 1846, BLC.

15. LS biographical note recorded by ASB, 5 Apr 1885, ctr. 86, BLC; NYWRC 1853, 18; LS to Parents, 16 Aug 1846, BLC.

16. LS to SSL, 31 Mar 1845, BLC; LS to FS Jr., 4 Jul 1845, BLC; LS to Parents, 12 Feb 1846, BLC; LS to FS Jr. and Harriet Stone, 15 Feb 1846, BLC; LS biographical note recorded by ASB, 5 Apr 1885, ctr. 86, BLC; Transcript of Oberlin College Alumni Questionnaire completed by LS in 1883, NAWSAR.

17. ALB, "Lucy Stone at Oberlin College," *WJ*, 10 Feb 1894.

18. Mercy Lloyd to LS, 10 Mar 1847, NAWSAR; LS to ALB, 9 Jun 1850, [Aug 1849], BLC, Lasser and Merrill, 72–74; 53–60; LS to SSL, 4 Jan 1847, BLC.

19. LS Rem., 4; Gilson, 59.

20. LS to SSL, 4 Jan 1847, BLC; Norma Basch, *In the Eyes of the Law: Women, Marriage, and Property in Nineteenth-Century New York* (Ithaca, N.Y.: Cornell University Press, 1982), 27–28, 50–53, 65; Peggy A. Rabkin, *Fathers to Daughters: The Legal Foundations of Female Emancipation* (Westport, Conn.: Greenwood Press, 1980), 19–21, 113; *Sibyl*, 15 Jun 1861; *Liberator*, 3 Jul 1846.

21. *Brother Johnathan* 5 (Jun 1843); *Liberator*, 29 May 1840, 5, 19 Nov 1857; NASS, 6 Aug 1846; Elisha P. Hurlbut, *Essays on Human Rights* (New York: 1845); Samuel J. May, *The Rights and Condition of Women: A Sermon Preached in Syracuse, November, 1845* (Boston, 1846), 3, 6, 14.

22. Carl J. Guarneri, *The Utopian Alternative: Fourierism in Nineteenth-Century America* (Ithaca, N.Y.: Cornell University Press, 1991); Parke Godwin, *A Popular View of the Doctrines of Charles Fourier* (New York: J. S. Redfield, Clinton Hall, 1844).

23. Albert Brisbane, *Association, or a Concise Exposition of the Practical Part of Fourier's Social Science* (New York, 1844); *The Present*, 15 Dec 1843; Guarneri, 407–8.

24. Charles Fourier, *Theorie des quatres mouvements et des destinees generales* (1808), republished as *The Utopian Vision of Charles Fourier: Selected Texts on Work, Love, and Passionate Attraction*, trans. and ed. Jonathan Beecher and Richard Bienvenu (Boston: Beacon Press, 1971), 194–96; *Path-Finder*, 3 Jun, 29 Apr 1843; Godwin, 89.

25. Samuel J. May, *Rights and Condition*, 13.

26. FS Jr. and Harriet Stone to LS, 30 Jan 1847, BLC; SSL and WBS to LS, 28 Nov 1846, BLC; LS to Parents, 29 Jan 1847, BLC; FS to LS, 10 Jan 1847, BLC.

27. LS to Parents, 29 Jan 1847, BLC.

28. SSL and WBS to LS, 28 Nov 1846, BLC.

29. LS to SSL, 4 Jan 1847, BLC. Stone probably picked up the idea of marriage as "legalized adultery" from Harriet Martineau's article "Marriage," which called marriage as established by law "legalized prostitution." Arguing for a "true love" marriage over a marriage for connections, money, estates, or convenience, Martineau said: "Marriage, which was designed to protect the sanctity of the love of one man for one woman, has become the very means of obstructing such love, and destroying the sanctity of it." Her article was republished shortly before Stone wrote this letter, in the December 1846 issue of the *Harbinger*.

30. FS Jr. and Harriet Stone to LS, 30 Jan 1847, BLC.

31. LS to HS, 14 Mar 1847, BLC.

CHAPTER 9

1. Although Stone told her sister that she had "corresponded freely" with several individuals about woman's rights, she named only May and Tracy (LS to SSL, 4 Jan 1847, BLC). Hannah Tracy to LS, 26 Oct 1846, NAWSAR; Obituary of Hannah Tracy Cutler, *WJ*, 7 Mar 1896.

2. LS to SSL, 4 Jan 1847, BLC; Edward Deering Mansfield, *Legal Rights, Liabilities and Duties of Women* (Salem, Mass., 1845).

3. Louise Schutz Boas, *Woman's Education Begins: The Rise of the Women's Colleges* (Norton, Mass.; Wheaton College Press, 1935), 74; Pat Creech Scholten, "A Public 'Jollification': The 1859 Women's Rights Petition before the Indiana Legislature," *Indiana Magazine of History* 72, no. 4 (1976), 348–49.

4. LS to SSL, 31 Mar 1845, BLC; Orson S. Fowler, *Matrimony, or Phrenology and Physiology Applied to the Selection of Congenial Companions for Life* (New York, 1847); Mercy Lloyd to LS, 10 Mar 1847, NAWSAR. Stone's views are gleaned from her and Brown's reminiscences, the responses of her brothers and sister, her correspondence with Lloyd, and a letter from Henry C. Wright, all cited below. Another source that is helpful in understanding her views is Wright's

Marriage and Parentage; Or, The Reproductive Element in Man, as a Means to His Elevation and Happiness, first published in 1854 (Reprinted as *Sex, Marriage and Society,* ed. Charles Rosenberg and Carroll Smith-Rosenberg, New York: Arno Press, 1974). Stone discussed this topic with Wright in the fall of 1847 (HCW to LS, 3 Jan 1848, NAWSAR), and when he published his book, she cited his ideas as the ideal relationship between husband and wife (LS to HCW, 23 Apr [1854], Yale University Library; LS to HBB, 23 Apr [1854], BLC, Wheeler, 78–79).

5. Harriet Martineau, "Marriage," *The Harbinger,* Dec 1846; Parke Godwin, *A Popular View of the Doctrines of Charles Fourier,* 2nd ed. (New York: J. S. Redfield, Clinton Hall, 1844), 89; Wright, *Marriage and Parentage.*

6. SSL and WBS to LS, 28 Nov 1846, BLC; Luther Stone to LS, 1 Jun 1847, BLC.

7. FS Jr. to LS, 6 Jun 1847, BLC.

8. SSL and WBS to LS, 28 Nov 1846, BLC.

9. WBS to LS, 13 Jun 1847, BLC; LS biographical note recorded by ASB, 5 Apr 1885, ctr. 86, BLC; LS to HBB, 26 Apr 1854, BLC, Wheeler, 81–82. Stone wrote of her reprimand in a letter to Maria [Weston Chapman?], to be delivered by Henry C. Wright, who read it himself and told Stone that he, too, often talked with men and women "on their responsibilities in giving existence to human beings" and that he "mourned that such things can be tolerated in the instruction to the females at Oberlin" (HCW to LS, 3 Jan 1848, NAWSAR).

10. Oberlin College Library records; LS to SSL, 13 Mar 1846, BLC.

11. ALB to LS 5 Oct 1846, BLC, [winter 1847], BSL, Lasser and Merrill, 15–22.

12. Oberlin [College] Young Ladies' Association, Minute Book 1846–50, entry for 12 Feb 1847, OCA; Hannah Tracy Cutler Reminiscences, *WJ,* 26 Sep 1896; LS to Parents, [May 1847], BLC; LS to ALB, 5 May 1892, BLC, Lasser and Merrill, 263; ALB, "Reminiscences of Early Oberlin," BSL; Gilson, 64–65.

13. ALB speech, *Report of the International Council of Women* (Washington, D.C.: National Woman Suffrage Association, 1888), 340; ALB Rem., ctr. 92, BLC; Gilson, 64–65.

14. LS to HS, 14 Mar 1847, BLC; ALB Rem., 29, BLC.

15. Elizabeth Cazden, *Antoinette Brown Blackwell: A Biography* (Old Westbury, N.Y.: Feminist Press, 1983), 30; 274n. 36.

16. Carroll Smith-Rosenberg, *Disorderly Conduct: Visions of Gender in Victorian America* (New York: Alfred A. Knopf, 1985), 53, 69, 68; LS to ALB, [Aug 1849], BLC, Lasser and Merrill, 53–60. Expressions of love and intimacy similar to those contained in the Stone-Brown correspondence are found, too, in the two women's correspondence with their sisters and other friends. Stone wrote to her sister Sarah on the eve of her marriage: "I cannot repress the bitter tears that come brimming to my eyes as I think that the last one of all our family, who was left entire to me, must also go away . . . The deep love that burns in my bosom towards you can never go out" (LS to SSL, 31 Mar 1845, BLC). Sarah wrote to Lucy: "Once I thought I loved you better than I could if I had five or six other sisters, but it is not so. The more we love, the more we are capable of loving" (SSL to LS, 9 Aug 1845, BLC). Stone later developed another relationship she considered comparable to her relationship with Brown—an intimate but platonic friendship with fellow antislavery agent Charles Burleigh, a married man. She told Henry Blackwell when he was courting her: "It would be as foolish as it would be untrue for me to pretend that I feel an ordinary friendship for you. Indeed Harry, I have made no pretenses to you. When I loved you less than Charles and Nette, I told you so, and when I loved you more than them, I told you as frankly" (LS to HBB, 30 Dec [1853], BLC, Wheeler, 66–67). Elizabeth Cazden, who interpreted a passage in one of Brown's letter as longing to recapture lost sexual intimacy with Stone, ignored the circumstances surrounding that passage. Stone had asked Brown to come to Massachusetts to help with a speaking and petition campaign, but Brown remained in New York to work with Susan Anthony. After months of working alone, Stone nearly collapsed from physical exhaustion and wrote to Anthony: "I am tired of the hard labor of stirring this state to do something before the Constitutional Convention. If Nettie only could see how important it is that much should be done right now, she would come. But I can't get her." Compelled to continue alone, Stone said: "I am tired and nervous,

and half sick, too, and just this minute can't help wishing that my body was safely at rest" (LS to SBA, 22 Mar 1853, BLC). Anthony showed the letter to Brown, who responded: "Lucy Darling . . . If you were only here so I could put my arm close around you and feel your heart beating against mine as in lang syne" (ALB to LS, 29 Mar 1853, BLC, Lasser and Merrill, 130). This response, which Cazden viewed as evidence of a lesbian relationship (75), expressed sympathy and concern for a friend's fainting spirit, not longing for lost sexual intimacy.

17. LS to HS, 14 Mar 1847, BLC; LS to Family, [Apr 1847], 4 Jul 1847, BLC. Stone's family commended her action (FS Jr. to LS, 6 Jun 1847, BLC; WBS to LS, 13 Jun 1847, BLC).

18. *Liberator,* 5 Nov 1847; James P. McKinney to the Editors, *WJ,* 14 Jun 1902.

19. Oberlin [College] Young Ladies' Association, Minute Book 1846–1850, entries for 9, 16, 23 Jun 1847; ALB to LS, [Jul 1847], BSL, Lasser and Merrill, 22–25.

20. LS to SSL, 13 Mar 1846, 4 Jan 1847, BLC; Luther Stone to LS, 3 Aug 1846, BLC; LS to Parents, 16 Aug 1846, BLC; WBS to LS, 13 Jun 1847, BLC.

21. AKF to LS, 28 Mar 1847, NAWSAR.

22. LS to Family, [Apr 1847], BLC.

23. Elizabeth Hitchcock Jones to LS, 1 Jul 1847, BLC.

24. FS Jr. to LS, 6 Jun 1847, BLC; SSL and WBS to LS, 28 Nov 1846, BLC.

25. *Alumni Catalogue: Officers and Graduates of Oberlin College, 1833–1936,* vol. 1 (Oberlin, 1837); Robert Samuel Fletcher, *A History of Oberlin College,* vol. 1 (1943; reprint, New York: Arno Press and The New York Times, 1971), 294–95.

26. Frederick Douglass speech, *WJ,* 24 Mar 1894; WLG to Helen Garrison, 28 Aug 1847, WLG Letters, 3:523- 24.

27. ALB to LS, 22 Sep 1847, [June 1848], BSL, Lasser and Merrill, 30–33, 40–45; Fletcher, 294–95. Sarah Pellet, a friend of Stone's who entered Oberlin upon her urging, refused to be graduated in 1852 unless permitted her to read her own essay, and did not receive her degree until 1858 (ALB to LS, 4 Aug 1852, BSL, Lasser and Merrill, 29, 121).

28. Frank married Harriet Amelia Ann Blake in the spring of 1844, and they lived at the Coy's Hill farm until the spring of 1851, when he bought a farm. Only one of the three children born to them while Lucy was at Oberlin is recorded in Bartlett's Genealogy—their second child, Harriet (1 Jul 1846–27 Jan 1847). Their first child, who was born and died in 1845, is mentioned in LS to Harriet Stone, 8 Jul 1845. Rhoda (b. 7 May 1847) and a son (b. shortly before 9 Jun 1848) died in September 1851 (FS Jr. to LS, 6 Jun 1847, and LS to Harriet Stone, 9 Jun, 1848, BLC; LS to SM Jr., 23 Sep 1851, ALSL).

29. SSL and WBS to LS, 13 Jun 1847, BLC; WBS to LS, 3 Feb 1848, BLC.

30. Reminiscence of the former Anna Watkins, ctr. 87, BLC. This account does not indicate when the Warren lecture took place, but internal evidence places it in the fall of 1847 (Mercy Lloyd to LS, 12 Dec 1847, NAWSAR).

31. Reminiscence of the former Anna Watkins, ctr. 87, BLC.

CHAPTER 10

1. WBS to LS, 3 Feb 1848, BLC; SSL and WBS to LS, 13 Jun 1847, BLC; AKF to LS, 1 Jan, 29 Mar 1848, NAWSAR.

2. LS to WBS, 9 Jun 1848, BLC; *Liberator,* 9 Jun 1848.

3. LS to WBS, 9 Jun 1848, BLC.

4. *Liberator,* 9 Jun, 7 Jul 1848.

5. *Liberator,* 23, 30 Jun, 14 Jul 1848.

6. Mary Ashton Livermore, *The Story of My Life* (Hartford: A. D. Worthington, 1899), 77; *Liberator,* 30 Jun, 7, 14 Jul 1848.

7. *Pennsylvania Freeman,* 10 Aug 1848.

8. *Blackstone Chronicle,* reprinted in *Liberator,* 25 Aug 1848.

9. William Edward Farrison, *William Wells Brown: Author and Reformer* (Chicago: University of Chicago Press, 1969), 120–21.

10. *Liberator,* 14 Jul 1848.

11. Robert William Fogel, *Without Consent or Contract: The Rise and Fall of American Slavery* (New York: W. W. Norton, 1989), 334–37.

12. Merton L. Dillon, *The Abolitionists: The Growth of a Dissenting Minority* (DeKalb, Ill.: Northern Illinois University Press, 1974), 135; Fogel, 346–47.

13. "T. W. Higginson on Lucy Stone," *WJ,* 28 Oct 1893; Parker Pillsbury, *Acts of the Anti-Slavery Apostles* (Concord, N.H., 1883), 353-61; *Liberator,* 15 Sep 1848. As secretary of the convention, Stone helped write the report that appeared in the *Liberator* but made no mention of the speech she made after the mob broke up the meeting. However, she told others, among them Thomas Wentworth Higginson, whom she met two weeks after the incident, and it became an oft repeated story in antislavery circles, though the details became confused. Higginson, *Contemporaries* (Boston: Houghton, Mifflin Co., 1899), 336–37; TWH to ASB, 8 Nov 1899, NAWSAR.

14. Ralph Korngold, *Two Friends of Man: William Lloyd Garrison and Wendell Phillips* (Boston: Little, Brown, 1950), 182–83; LS to HBB, 27 Jul 1853, BLC, Wheeler, 48–52.

15. Mary Thacher Higginson, *Thomas Wentworth Higginson: The Story of His Life* (Boston: Houghton Mifflin, 1914), 97; Caroline Severance to ASB, 19 Feb 1894, NAWSAR.

16. LS Rem., 13.

17. William Norwood Brigance, ed., *A History and Criticism of American Public Address* (New York: McGraw-Hill Book Co., 1943), 166.

18. LS to WBS, 9 June 1848, BLC.

19. Marianne Dwight to Anna Q. T. Parsons, 30 Aug [1844], in *Letters from Brook Farm, 1844–1847,* ed. Amy L. Reed (Poughkeepsie, N.Y.: Vassar College, 1928), 29–34.

20. *Harbinger,* April 1847.

21. *Liberator,* 2 Jun, 3 Mar 1848, 5, 19 Nov 1847; ALB to LS, [late winter 1848], Lasser and Merrill, 33–35; *Rochester Daily Democrat,* 3 Aug 1848, in Scrapbook of 1848 Woman's Rights Conventions, ECS Papers, LC; *Pennsylvania Freeman,* 22 Jun 1848. The names of most of the organizers of the two conventions can be found in the list of signatories to an "Address of Antislavery Women of Western New York," published in the *North Star,* 9 Jun 1848.

22. Elizabeth Cady Stanton proposed asking Stone to lecture in New York (ECS to Amy Post, 24 Sep 1848, Vassar College Library), and the invitation came from Hathaway, as reported to Stanton: "I send thee another letter which I received from Lucy Stone by last mail. Thou wilt be glad to hear she can come to this state so much sooner than she expected. Perhaps thou hast written her before this, and told her something definite relative to the plans of the society. I have written her but once, and then little more than to ask her if she would be willing to enter this field, and if so, upon what terms. I suppose she wishes to know definitely what her work is to be, and as nearly as possible where . . . " (Phoebe Hathaway to ECS, 11 Nov 1848, ECS Scrapbook, vol. 1, Vassar College Library). Stone wrote of her acceptance to Helen Cook at Oberlin (ALB to LS, [Dec 1848], Lasser and Merrill, 46–47).

23. Harriet H. Robinson, *Massachusetts in the Woman Suffrage Movement: A General Political, Legal and Legislative History from 1774 to 1881,* 2nd ed. (Boston: Roberts Brothers, 1883), 96–97; *Liberator,* 20 Apr 1849. The petition does not survive in state archives.

24. *Philadelphia Public Ledger and Transcript,* 20 Jul 1848.

25. *Philadelphia Public Ledger and Transcript,* 18, 20, 23, 24, 25, 26, 27 Apr, 2, 3 May 1849; *Pennsylvania Freeman,* 26 Apr 1849, 7 Feb, 1850.

26. LCM to ECS, 3 Oct 1848, ECS Papers, LC; *Philadelphia Public Ledger and Transcript,* 3 May 1849; *NASS,* 10 May 1849; LM speech, *Liberator,* 8 Oct 1852.

CHAPTER 11

1. Edward Deering Mansfield, *Legal Rights, Liabilities and Duties of Women* (Salem, Mass.: 1845), quoted in Elinor Rice Hays, *Morning Star: A Biography of Lucy Stone, 1818–1893* (New York: Harcourt, Brace and World, 1961), 8.

2. LS to ALB, [Aug 1849], 9 Jun 1850, BLC; ALB to LS, 22 Sep 1847, BSL, [Dec 1848], BLC, all in Lasser and Merrill, 56, 73, 31, 46.

3. LS to ALB, [Aug 1849]; CCB speech, *NASS*, 31 Oct 1850. Two "true marriages," HBB to LS, 13 Jun 1853, Wheeler, 37.

4. ALB to LS, [Jun 1848], 23 Mar [1852], BSL, Lasser and Merrill, 41, 112.

5. LS to ALB, [Aug 1849]; ALB to LS, 25 Mar 1849, BLC, Lasser and Merrill, 49–51.

6. "To the Senate and House of Representatives of the Commonwealth of Massachusetts: The undersigned citizens of _____, respectfully request that, since the women of the State are made to pay taxes, and are held amenable to its criminal laws, they may be allowed a voice in the imposition and use of the first, and in the enactment of the second; and hence that they be permitted to vote, and to be eligible to office" (Woman's Rights Petitions, House Unenacted Documents 2577, Massachusetts State Library, Boston); *Liberator*, 14 Dec 1849, 1 Feb 1850. Fourteen petitions bearing four hundred signatures survive in the state archives, eight of them from towns where Stone lectured between December 1 and February 10. "Report of the Committee on the petition of Charles Brigham. . . . praying that women be made voters and access to off[ice]," House Unenacted Document 2972, Massachusetts State Library.

7. LS to Sarah Pellet, 12 Mar 1850, BSL; *Liberator*, 25 Jan, 8 Mar, 20 Feb 1850.

8. LCM to ECS, 25 Oct, 27 Nov 1849, GFP; LS to LCM, [spring 1850], ALSL; LS to ALB, 9 Jun 1850, BLC, Lasser and Merrill, 73; *Liberator*, 15 Feb 1850; *Lily*, Mar 1850.

9. *Bugle*, 30 Mar 1850; LS to "Dear Friends," *Bugle*, 27 Apr 1850.

10. *NASS*, 9 May 1850; *Bugle*, 1 Jun 1850; LS to Sallie B. Gove and Others, in *Bugle*, 22 Jun 1850.

11. LS speech, *WJ*, 14 Feb 1891; Dorothy Sterling, *Ahead of Her Time, Abby Kelley and the Politics of Antislavery* (New York: W. W. Norton, 1991), 159–61, 202; *Liberator*, May 18, 1849.

12. LS report in *Liberator*, 7 Jun 1850.

13. Ibid.

14. LS to ALB, 9 Jun 1850, BLC, Lasser and Merrill, 72–73. Stone identified William Elder as author of the call in her speech at the Fortieth Anniversary of the First National Woman's Rights Convention (*WJ*, 14 Feb 1891), and Davis seems to confirm this in referring to a letter she received "from W. Elder giving me a most tremendous blowing up for altering the heading of the Call" (PWD to Anna Parsons, 15 [Sep 1850], NAWSAR).

15. LS to SM Jr., 23 Jun 1850, BPL; LS to ALB, 9 Jun 1850; ALB Rem., 16 Aug 1896, ctr. 92, BLC. Henry Blackwell said he first met Stone in the summer of 1850 when she came to his Cincinnati hardware store to cash a draft drawn by Samuel Brooke on the Western Anti-Slavery Society (HBB Rem., 109).

16. PWD to Anna Q. T. Parsons, [Aug 1850], NAWSAR; LS to SM Jr., 25 Jul, 13 Oct 1850, BLC.

17. LS to SM Jr., 13 Oct 1850, BLC.

18. Ibid.; *Liberator*, 6 Sep 1850; LS speech, *NASS*, 31 Oct 1850.

19. SG to LS, 9 Sep 1851, NAWSAR.

20. NWRC 1850, 6–13.

21. *NASS*, 31 Oct 1850.

22. Ibid.

23. NWRC 1850, 14.

24. NWRC 1850, 5–17.

25. ALB Rem., BSL; *NASS*, 31 Oct 1850.

26. NWRC 1850, 18. Central Committee 1850: Paulina W. Davis, chair; Sarah H. Earle, secretary; Wendell Phillips, treasurer; Mary A. W. Johnson, William Henry Channing, Gerrit Smith, John H. Forman, Martha H. Mowry, Lucy Stone, Joseph C. Hathaway, Abby Kelley Foster, Pliny Sexton, J. Elizabeth Jones, William Elder, William Stedman, Emily Robinson, Abby H. Price, and William Lloyd Garrison.

27. *NASS*, 31 Oct 1850.

28. "Enfranchisement of Women," reprinted from the *Westminster and Foreign Quarterly Re-*

view, Jul 1851, in *Woman's Rights Commensurate with Her Capabilities and Obligations* (Syracuse: J. E. Masters, 1853); ECS, Call to the Twentieth Anniversary Celebration of the Woman's Rights Movement, in PWD, *A History of the National Woman's Rights Movement for Twenty Years . . . From 1850 to 1870* (1871; reprint, New York: Source Book Press, 1970), 5.

CHAPTER 12

1. LS to WBS, 7 Feb 1850, BSL; LS Rem., 6, 14; LS to SM Jr., 14 Apr, 13 Oct 1850, BLC.

2. *Lily,* Feb 1851; *Liberator,* 24 Jan 1851; ECS to Amy Post, 4 Dec 1850, Stanton and Blatch, 2:24–25; Petitions and Report of the Committee on the Judiciary, 23 May 1851, Massachusetts Archives at Columbia Point.

3. ALB to LS, 19, 30 Dec 1850, 30 Jan 1851, BLC, Lasser and Merrill, 96–102; ALB Rem., ctr. 92, BLC.

4. LS to SM Jr., 13 Oct 1850, BLC.

5. *Liberator,* 2 May 1851; Alice Stone Blackwell, *Lucy Stone: Pioneer of Woman's Rights* (Boston: Little, Brown and Co., 1930), 87–88.

6. LS biographical note recorded by ASB, 17 Jan 1882, ctr. 86, BLC; Sylvia E. Crane, *White Silence: Greenough, Powers, and Crawford; American Sculptors in Nineteenth-Century Italy* (Coral Gables, Fla.: University of Miami Press, 1972), 203–5, 214. See also "Hiram Powers's *The Greek Slave,*" in Jean Fagan Yellin, *Women and Sisters: The Antislavery Feminists in American Culture* (New Haven: Yale University Press, 1989), 99–124.

7. LS speech, *Report of the International Council of Women* (Washington, D.C.: National Woman Suffrage Association, 1888), 333–34.

8. LS to AKF, 3 Aug 1851, AKF and SSF Papers, Worcester Historical Museum, Worcester, Mass.; LS to SM Jr., 5, 14 Aug 1851, BPL.

9. LS to SM Jr., 9, 23 Sep 1851, ALSL; Francis Jackson to LS, 16 Sep 1851, NAWSAR; Record of Woman's Rights Lectures, ctr. 90, BLC; *Liberator,* 3, 17 Oct 1851; Clipping from *Lynn Democrat,* BLC.

10. Carl J. Guarneri, *The Utopian Alternative: Fourierism in Nineteenth-Century America* (Ithaca, N.Y.: Cornell University Press, 1991), 210–11; Clipping from *Boston Chronotype,* Aug 1848, Scrapbook of 1848 Woman's Rights Conventions, ECS Papers, LC; *Saturday Evening Post,* excerpted in *Pennsylvania Freeman,* 1 Sep 1848; *Water-Cure Journal,* reprinted in *Lily,* Mar 1851.

11. *Water-Cure Journal,* Oct, Dec 1849, Jan, Feb, Jun 1850; *Pittsburgh Saturday Visiter,* reprinted in *Water-Cure Journal,* Feb 1850; NWRC 1850, 76–77; LS biographical note, ctr. 90, BLC.

12. See *Lily,* Mar, May, Jun 1851. Louise R. Noun, *Strong-Minded Women: The Emergence of the Woman Suffrage Movement in Iowa* (Ames: Iowa State University Press, 1986), 16–17. To reports that she was the new style's originator, Amelia Bloomer said in June 1851 that women in Massachusetts and Wisconsin had been wearing it for more than a year. "The first we heard of it, it was worn as an exercise dress at the Water Cures; the first article we saw advocating it was an editorial in the *Seneca County Courier,* which article we transferred to our columns [*Lily,* Jan 1851]; the first person we saw wearing such a dress was Mrs. Charles D. [Elizabeth Smith] Miller of Peterboro, daughter of Gerrit Smith, who has worn it for the last five or six months" (*Lily,* Jun 1851). Miller introduced Bloomer and her cousin Elizabeth Cady Stanton to the dress during her visit to Seneca Falls in February 1851, but she was not its originator.

13. *Liberator,* 1 Aug 1851; *Lowell Courier* and *Toledo Republican,* reprinted in *Lily,* Jul, Aug 1851; *Water-Cure Journal,* Aug, Oct 1851; William H. Fish to ASB, 15 Nov 1893, NAWSAR.

14. *Cleveland Daily True Democrat,* 6 Aug, 3 Nov 1851; *New York Daily Tribune,* 8 Jul 1851; Noun, 15.

15. *Bugle,* 21 Dec 1851; *Lily,* Sep 1851.

16. *New York Daily Tribune,* 19 Sep 1851; William H. Fish to ASB, 15 Nov 1893, NAWSAR; *Lynn Democrat* clipping in BLC; *Salem Observer,* reprinted in *Liberator,* 17 Oct 1851; *Boston Transcript* interview with Mary A. Livermore, reprinted in *WJ,* 28 Oct 1893.

17. *New York Daily Tribune*, 17, 21 Aug, 17 Oct 1851; LS to Sarah Pellet, 12 Mar 1850, BSL; A. W. Plumstead, et al., eds., *The Journals and Miscellaneous Notebooks of Ralph Waldo Emerson*, vol. 11 (Cambridge, Mass.: Belknap Press of Harvard University Press, 1975), 443–44.

18. *New York Daily Tribune*, 21 Oct 1851; PWD to ECS, 1 Sep [1851], ECS Papers, LC (The edited transcript dates the letter 1852, but reference to the upcoming Worcester convention places it in 1851); NWRC 1851, 28.

19. NWRC 1851, 10–13, 47–58; *Liberator*, 3 Jul 1846; *New York Daily Tribune*, 20 Oct 1851.

20. NWRC 1851, 79–89; NWRC 1852, 88. For Hale's opposition to coeducation and support for the Female Medical College of Philadelphia, see Frances D. Gage's letter to the *Lily*, Aug 1852.

21. NWRC 1851, 18–29.

22. NWRC 1851, 99–102.

23. LS speech, *WJ*, 14 Feb 1891.

24. *Christian Inquirer*, reprinted in *NASS*, 6 Nov 1851; *Liberator*, 7 Nov 1851.

25. "Woman's Rights Expenses . . . Collections," LS notebook, ctr. 90, BLC; LS to ALB, 3 Nov 1851, BSL, Lasser and Merrill, 111.

CHAPTER 13

1. Although not mentioned in convention reports, the incident became known among abolitionists and was referred to four years later in a sermon by Theodore Parker (*Liberator*, 4 Jan 1856). Stone identified the second national convention as its occasion (LS speech, *WJ*, 14 Feb 1891).

2. Dorothy Sterling, *Ahead of Her Time: Abby Kelley and the Politics of Antislavery* (New York: W. W. Norton, 1991), 301.

3. *New York Daily Tribune*, 17 Oct 1851; PWD to ECS, 1 Sep [1851], ECS Papers, LC.

4. PWD to ECS, [July 1851], 1 Sep [1851], 9 Feb [1852], ECS Papers, LC.

5. LCM to LS, 16 Aug 1852, BLC; WP to LS, 20 Aug 1852, BLC; ALB to LS, 14 Apr 1852, BSL, Lasser and Merrill, 114; *Liberator*, 6 Aug 1852.

6. PWD to CHD, 23 Aug 1852, CHD Papers, MHS.

7. Caroline Putnam to AKF, 24 Sep 1855, quoted in Sterling, 301n; LS to HBB, 26 Nov 1853, BLC.

8. PWD to CHD, *Liberator*, 29 Oct 1852.

9. Francis Jackson to LS, 7 Dec 1851, NAWSAR; NWRC 1852, 34.

10. *Syracuse Standard*, 10 Sep 1852; PWD to CHD, *Liberator*, 29 Oct 1852.

11. NWRC 1852, 78–89, 92–93; *Syracuse Standard*, 10 Sep 1852; *Liberator*, 1, 8 Oct 1852.

12. *Syracuse Standard*, 11, 13, 16 Sep 1852.

13. WP to LS, 20 Aug 1852, BLC.

14. *Lily*, Oct 1852; *Frederick Douglass' Paper*, 17 Sep 1852.

15. PWD to CHD, *Liberator*, 29 Oct 1852.

16. LS to ALB, 24 Nov 1852, BLC, Lasser and Merrill, 124.

17. CHD to PWD, *Liberator*, 15 Oct 1852; PWD to CHD, 2 Jan, 23 Aug 1853, CHD Papers, MHS. Davis attended Stone's independent New York convention in September 1853 but not the national convention in Cleveland the following month. She did not attend the 1855 national convention in Cleveland but was elected a vice president in absentia. Some newspaper reports of the 1856 national convention misidentified Martha C. Wright as Davis, but Davis was not there.

18. ALB to LS, 16 Dec 1852, BSL, Lasser and Merrill, 127; PWD to LS, 18 [19 Dec 1852] NAWSAR.

CHAPTER 14

1. *Liberator*, 10 Jun 1853.

2. *Syracuse League*, excerpted in *Liberator*, 24 Sep 1852; *Syracuse Standard*, 13 Sep 1852;

NASS, 7 Oct 1852; *Bugle,* 30 Oct 1852; William G. Allen to *Pennsylvania Freeman,* 6 Oct 1852, quoted in Benjamin Quarles, *Black Abolitionists* (New York: Oxford University Press, 1969), 209–11.

   3. *Lily,* December 1852; X.Y.Z. to *Banner of the Times,* DeRuyter, 11 Oct 1852, clipping in BLC; Expenses in New York, LS notebook, ctr. 90, BLC; A. V. Bentley to Gerrit Smith, 8 Nov 1852, Gerrit Smith Papers, Syracuse University Libraries; *Bugle,* 18 Dec 1852.

   4. Alfred Charles True, *A History of Agricultural Education in the United States, 1785–1925* (New York: Arno Press and the New York Times, 1969), 54–55; *Lily,* Sep, Nov, Dec 1852.

   5. *Lily,* Jun, Jul, Nov 1852; *Liberator* 17 Jun 1853.

   6. *Bugle,* 18 Dec 1852, 8 Mar 1851; Expenses in New York, LS notebook, ctr. 90, BLC; SBA to LS, 12 Nov 1852, BLC; LS to ALB, 24 Nov 1852; LS biographical note recorded by ASB, 17 Jan 1882, ctr. 86, BLC; Benjamin Jones to LS, 21 Jan 1853 and Mary Ann Earle to LS, 19 Aug 1852, NAWSAR.

   7. LS to ALB, 24 Nov 1852; *Beverly Courier* and *Fitchburg News,* reprinted in *Liberator,* 31 Dec 1852.

   8. LS biographical note recorded by ASB, 17 Jan 1882, ctr. 86, BLC.

   9. SBA to LS, 12 Nov, 19 Dec 1852, 18 Jul 1853, BLC. Anthony said she was converted to woman suffrage by reading Stone's speech at the 1850 National Woman's Rights Convention (*Report of the International Council of Women* [Washington, D.C.: National Woman Suffrage Association, 1888], 47). But Anthony's authorized biographer said that when Anthony read newspaper reports of the 1850 convention, she sympathized with its demands but was "not yet quite convinced that these included suffrage." It was at the Syracuse Convention that Anthony became "thoroughly convinced that the right which woman needed above every other . . . was the right of suffrage." Ida Husted Harper, *The Life and Work of Susan B. Anthony* (Indianapolis: Bobbs, 1889), 1:61, 81.

   10. Some accounts cite twenty-eight thousand signatures (e.g., Louise R. Noun, "Amelia Bloomer: A Biography. Part I: The Lily of Seneca Falls," *Annals of Iowa* 47, no. 7 [Winter1985]: 607), but Emily Clark reported that the women's society gathered one hundred thousand signatures total, twenty-eight thousand of them women's (*New York Daily Tribune,* 14 May 1853, clipping in BLC).

   11. SBA to LS, 19 Dec 1852, BLC; LS to SBA, 7, 8, Jan, 1853, BLC; ALB to SBA, 14 Jan 1853, BSL.

   12. SBA to LS, 19 Dec 1852, 8, 24 Jan 1853, BLC; ALB to SBA, 14 Jan 1853, BSL; *Albany Argus,* 20 Jan 1853; *Rochester Daily Advertiser,* 22, 24 Jan 1853; *Lily,* 1 Feb 1853.

   13. True, 57.

   14. *Liberator,* 18 Feb, 4 Mar 1853; *Windham County (Brattleboro) Democrat,* reprinted in *Liberator,* 25 Feb 1853; Mary Thatcher Higginson, *Thomas Wentworth Higginson: The Story of His Life* (1914. Reprint, Port Washington, N.Y.: Kennikat Press, 1971), 136; Thomas Wentworth Higginson, *American Orators and Oratory* (Cleveland: Imperial Press, 1901), 86.

   15. "The Constitutional Convention and Equal Political Rights," printed circular, BLC; Printed appeal signed by Thomas S. Stone, BLC; Charles K. Whipple to LS, 26 Jan 1853, NAWSAR; *Liberator,* 4 Feb, 4 Mar 1853; *Una,* 11 Apr 1853. Stone identified Phillips as author of the documents in *Liberator,* 15 Apr 1853. In addition to Stone, the signatories were Abby Kelley Foster, Thomas W. Higginson, Ann Green Phillips, Wendell Phillips, Theodore Parker, William I. Bowditch, Samuel E. Sewall, Ellis Gray Loring, Abby H. Price, John Pierpont, A. Bronson Alcott, Abby May Alcott, Josiah F. Flagg, Mary Flagg, Thomas S. Stone, Francis Jackson, Wm. Lloyd Garrison, Anna Q. T. Parsons, Harriet K. Hunt, Elizabeth Smith, Eliza Barney, John W. Browne, William C. Nell, Robert Morris, Samuel May Jr., Robert F. Wallcut, Charles K. Whipple.

   16. SJM to LS, 20, 29 Sep 1852, 14 Mar 1853, NAWSAR; SM Jr. to LS, 22 Sep 1852, NAWSAR; *Lily,* Mar 1853; *Bugle,* 26 Mar, 4 Jun 1853; *Woman's Rights Commensurate with Her Capabilities and Obligations: A Series of Tracts* (Syracuse: J. E. Masters, 1853).

   17. LS to SBA, 22 Mar 1853, BLC; SBA to LS, 24 Jan 1853, BLC; ALB to LS, [24 Jan 1853], 29 Mar, 1 Apr 1853, BLC, Lasser and Merrill, BLC, 128–31.

18. LS to SBA, 22 Mar 1853, BLC; "A Sermon on the Public Function of Woman, by Theodore Parker, delivered March 27, 1853 in Music Hall in Boston," *Liberator*, 15 Apr 1853; "The Public Function of Woman, a Sermon Preached at the Music Hall, March 27, 1853. By Theodore Parker, Minister of the Twenty-Eighth Congregational Society," (Boston: Robert F. Wallcut, 1853); ALB to LS, 1 Apr 1853, BLC, Lasser and Merrill, 131.

19. *Illustrated News*, 28 May 1853; *New York Daily Tribune*, undated clipping in BLC; *New York Daily Tribune*, 28 Apr 1853.

20. *New York Daily Tribune*, reprinted in *Liberator*, 10 Jun 1853; SBA to LS, 1 May 1853, BLC.

21. *New York Daily Times*, 26 Apr 1853; Unidentified clipping in BLC.

22. Phineas T. Barnum to Russell T. Trall, 27 Apr [1853], NAWSAR; *Illustrated News*, 28 May 1853.

23. *Journal of the Constitutional Convention of the Commonwealth of Massachusetts, Begun and Held in Boston, on the Fourth Day of May, 1853* (Boston: White and Potter, 1853), 35, 44, 61, 78, 98, 124, 125, 142, 156; *Official Report of the Debates and Proceedings in the State Convention, Assembled May 4th, 1853, to Revise and Amend the Convention of the Commonwealth of Massachusetts*, (Boston: White and Potter, 1853), 1:216–18; SBA to LS, 25 May 1853, BSL.

24. *NASS*, 19 May 1853; *Liberator*, 1 Jul 1853; *New York Daily Tribune*, 12 May 1853; Douglass speech, *WJ*, 24 Mar 1894. Although the signatures on the petitions recorded in convention proceedings totaled under three thousand, Stone later gave the total as five thousand, two thousand of which belonged to women ("The Right of Suffrage for Women. Speech of Mrs. Lucy Stone Before the Judiciary Committee of the Massachusetts Senate, on the Memorial of a Committee of the National Woman's Rights Convention, . . . , March 6, 1857," ctr. 85, BLC).

25. ECS speech, *WJ*, 24 Mar 1894; Unidentified Hamilton, Ontario, newspaper clipping in BLC; *Una*, April 1855; *Liberator*, 2 Sep 1853, 8 Dec 1854; *NASS*, 20 Aug 1853; Thomas Lothrop to HBB, 23 Oct 1893, BLC; Caroline Severance to ASB, 19 Feb 1894, NAWSAR.

26. Amasa Walker to LS, 25 May 1853, NAWSAR; *New York Daily Tribune*, 6 Jun 1853; *Liberator*, 3, 10 Jun 1853; CCB to the *Pennsylvania Freeman*, reprinted in *Liberator*, 1 Jul 1853; Francis Jackson to LS, 28 May 1853, NAWSAR; Thomas Wentworth Higginson, "Woman and Her Wishes," and "Remarks of Rev. T. W. Higginson Before the Committee of the Constitutional Convention on the Qualification of Voters, June 3, 1853," *Woman's Rights Tracts* (Boston: Robert F. Wallcut, 1854).

27. *Official Report*, 2: 434–35.

28. Ibid., 2: 726–52.

29. LS to ECS, 14 Aug 1853, ECS Papers, LC, Gordon, 223–25.

CHAPTER 15

1. *Lily*, Feb 1852; *Liberator*, 18 Mar 1852; Tilden G. Edelstein, *Strange Enthusiasm: A Life of Thomas Wentworth Higginson* (New Haven: Yale University Press, 1968), 145–46.

2. *Pennsylvania Freeman*, 6 Sep, 25 Oct 1849, 31 Jan 1850; *Lily*, Feb, Mar, May 1852; *Bugle*, 8 Jan 1853; *Liberator*, 30 Apr 1852.

3. SBA to LS, 29 Mar, 1 May 1853, BLC.

4. Ibid.

5. *Lily*, May 1852; *Bugle*, 10 Jul 1852; ALB to LS, 14 Apr 1852, BSL, Lasser and Merrill, 114.

6. NWRC 1852, 77, 78, 96; *Syracuse Standard*, 13 Sep 1852; *Lily*, Oct 1852.

7. NWRC 1852, 78, 94–96; *Syracuse Standard*, 13 Sep 1852; SBA to LS, 1 May 1853, BLC.

8. Clarina Nichols speech, *New York Daily Tribune*, 6 Jun 1853; *Lily*, November 1852; LS to SBA, 22 Mar 1853, BLC; LS to Anna Q. T. Parsons, 8 Jul [1853], BLC; SBA to LS, 1 May 1853, Gordon, 219–21.

9. Mary Thacher Higginson, ed., *Letters and Journal of Thomas Wentworth Higginson* (Boston: Houghton Mifflin, 1921), 55; *New York Daily Tribune*, 13 May 1853; *Liberator*, 27 May 1853.

10. *New York Daily Tribune*, 13 May 1853; *Liberator*, 27 May 1853. Although not listed among

committee appointees in newspaper accounts, subsequent correspondence shows that Anthony served on the correspondence committee (SBA to Neal Dow, 7 Jun 1853, SBA Papers, SL).

11. *New York Daily Tribune*, [May 1853], clipping in BLC; *Bugle*, 21 May 1853; Quotations from *Commercial Advertiser*, 16 May 1853, clipping in BLC.

12. LS to CHD, 17 May 1853, CHD Papers, MHS; FDG to LS, 30 May [1853], NAWSAR; SBA to LS, 25 May 1853, BSL.

13. *Lily*, Nov, Dec 1849, Feb 1850, Jul 1851; Amelia Bloomer to "Home Journal," reprinted in *Sibyl*, 15 Sep 1856.

14. *Liberator*, 15 Sep 1848; Press clippings in Scrapbook, ECS Papers, LC; LM to ECS, 16 Mar 1855, ECS Papers, LC; ECS to SBA, 2 Apr 1852, Stanton and Blatch, 2:38–42; HBB to LS, 24 Aug 1853, Wheeler, 52–57.

15. LS to SBA, 7, 8 Jan 1853, BLC; *New York Daily Tribune*, 6 Jun 1853; *Rochester Daily Democrat*, 3 Jun 1853.

16. *Rochester Daily Democrat*, 3, 4, 9 Jun 1853; *Rochester Daily Union*, 4, 7 Jun 1853; Laura Smith to "Children," 13 Jun 1853, Sidney Smith Collection, Michigan Historical Collection, Bentley Historical Library, University of Michigan; ECS to SBA, 20 Jun 1853, Stanton and Blatch, 2:50–52.

17. *New York Daily Tribune*, 6 Jun 1853.

18. *Rochester Daily Democrat*, 2, 3, 4 Jun 1853; *Rochester Daily Union*, 2 Jun 1853; *New York Daily Times*, 2 Jun 1853; *New York Daily Tribune*, 2, 3, 6, 7 Jun 1853; *Rochester Daily Advertiser*, 2 Jun 1853.

19. *Rochester Daily Democrat*, 4 Jun 1853.

20. ECS to SBA, 20 Jun 1853, Stanton and Blatch, 2:50–52; *HWS*, 1:493, 495, 498.

21. ECS to SBA, 20 Jun 1853, Stanton and Blatch, 2:50–52; LS to SBA, 4 Jul 1853, BLC.

22. *Una*, 1 Jun 1853; WP to LS, [Jun 1853], BLC.

23. TWH to LS, 10 Jun 1853, NAWSAR; WP to LS, [Jun 1853], BLC; LS to SBA, 4 Jul 1853, BLC; SBA to LS, 12 Jul 1853, BLC.

24. SBA to LS, 18 Jul 1853, BLC.

25. WP to LS, [Jun 1853], BLC; ALB to LS, 8 [Jul] 1853, BSL, Lasser and Merrill, 134; LS to Anna Q. T. Parsons, 8 Jul 1853, BLC; LS to WHC, 8 Jul 1853, NAWSAR; SBA to LS, 18 July 1853, BLC; PWD to LS, [early Aug 1853], NAWSAR; Oliver Johnson to LS, 13 Aug 1853, NAWSAR; *Bugle*, 6 Aug 1853.

26. *NASS*, 20, 27 Aug, 3 Sep 1853; *Liberator*, 12 Aug, 2 Sep 1853; LS to SM Jr., 23 Jul [1853], ALSL; *Liberator*, 2 Sep 1853; PWD to LS, [Jul/Aug 1853], NAWSAR; ALB to LS, 16 Aug 1853, BSL, Lasser and Merrill, 136–37; LS to SBA, 14 Jul 1853, BLC; SBA to LS, 18 Jul 1853, BLC; ECS to SBA, 20 Jun 1853, Stanton and Blatch, 2:50–52; LS to ECS, 14 Aug 1853, ECS Papers, LC.

27. LS to ECS, 14 Aug 1853, ECS Papers, LC; *NASS*, 10 Sep 1853; *Bugle*, 17 Sep 1853.

28. *NASS*, 3 Sep 1853; Lloyd C. M. Hare, *Lucretia Mott: The Greatest American Woman* (1937; reprint, New York: Negro Universities Press, 1970), 219–20.

29. *NASS*, 10 Sep 1853; WLG to Helen Garrison, [5] Sep 1853, BPL; *New York Daily Tribune*, 6 Sep 1853.

30. *New York Evangelist* and *New York Herald*, reprinted in *NASS*, 17 Sep 1853. Rose and Garrison had been speakers at the Hartford Bible Convention on June 1 and 2, 1853, called by reformers "for the purpose of freely and fully canvassing the authority and influence of the Jewish and Christian Scriptures" (*New York Daily Times*, 4 Jun 1853).

31. *New York Daily Tribune*, 9 Sep 1853; NYWRC 1853, 36; *Liberator*, 30 Sep 1853.

32. *Liberator*, 16 Sep 1853.

33. Ibid.; *New York Daily Tribune*, 9 Sep 1853; NYWRC 1853, 91–94; *Una*, Sep 1853.

34. *Bugle*, 17 Sep 1853.

35. *NASS*, 10 Sep 1853; "From the New York Courier & Enquirer of Sept. 8," reprinted in *Liberator*, 16 Sep 1853.

36. Reprinted in *Liberator*, 14 Oct 1853.

37. *New York Daily Tribune*, 9 Sep 1853; *Bugle*, 17 Sep 1853.

CHAPTER 16

1. HBB to LS, 18 Mar 1855, 13, 21 Jun 1853, Wheeler, 127, 35–41; HBB to SSL, 21 Apr 1854, BLC; *NASS*, 4, 11 Jun 1853.

2. HBB to SCB, 2 Jun 1853, BLC; HBB Rem., 111–13.

3. HBB to LS, 13 Jun, 2 Jul, 24 Aug 1853, and LS to HBB, 21 Jun, 27 Jul 1853, BLC, Wheeler, 35–57.

4. HBB to LS, 13 Jun, 24, 26 Aug 1853, BLC, Wheeler 36–37, 54–57.

5. *NASS*, 20, 27 Aug, 3 Sep 1853; *Liberator*, 12 Aug, 2, 30 Sep, 14 Oct 1853; *Bugle*, 8 Oct 1853; *Albany Evening Journal*, 16 Sep 1853; ALB to LS, 16 Aug 1853, BSL, Lasser and Merrill, 136–37; *Rochester Daily Advertiser*, 26 Sep 1853; HBB to LS, 20 [Sep, misdated Aug] 1853, BLC; SCB Diary, entries for 2, 9 Oct 1853, BLC.

6. *Bugle*, 7 Jun 1851, 5 Jun 1852, 4 Jun 1853; *Cleveland Daily Plain Dealer*, 6 Oct 1853.

7. *Cleveland Daily Plain Dealer*, 5–8 Oct 1853; "Caroline Severance," *Eminent Women of the Age: Being Narratives of the Lives and Deeds of the Most Prominent Women of the Present Generation* (Hartford, Conn.: S. M. Betts, 1868), 380–82.

8. LS to HS, 10 Oct 1853, BLC; *Cleveland Daily Plain Dealer*, 5–8 Oct 1853; NWRC 1853, 23, 69–70.

9. NWRC 1853, 95–97, 100–101; *Cleveland Daily Plain Dealer*, 6 Oct 1853; Unidentified Cleveland newspaper clipping, BLC; LS to Anna Q. T. Parsons, 7 [Oct, misdated as Sep] 1853, BLC; *Lily*, 15 Apr 1854. Thinking it would require too long to complete, the lawyer recruited for the legal study laid the project aside after a couple of years (CHD, "Report Concerning the Laws of Massachusetts in Relation to Women," *Una*, 15 Oct 1855).

10. NWRC 1853, 68, 70, 73–74, 80–81; *Cleveland Daily Plain Dealer*, 6 Oct 1853.

11. NWRC 1853, 75–77, 80–81, 87–88, 94–96; *Cleveland Daily Plain Dealer*, 6 Oct 1853.

12. *Cleveland Daily Plain Dealer*, 8 Oct 1853; *Cincinnati Daily Enquirer*, 18 Oct 1855; *Cincinnati Daily Commercial*, reprinted in *Lily*, 15 Nov 1855.

13. *Cleveland Daily Plain Dealer*, 8 Oct 1853; Sarah Burger Stearns to ASB, 30 Oct [ca. 1895–97?], BLC; Dorothy Gies McGuigan, *A Dangerous Experiment: 100 Years of Women at the University of Michigan* (Ann Arbor: Center for Continuing Education of Women, 1970), 17–19, 23–24; "Sarah Burger Stearns," *National Cyclopedia of American Biography* (New York: Charles Scribner's Sons, 1928), 10:230.

14. HBB to LS, 7 Oct 1853, BLC.

15. *Bugle*, 22 Apr 1854.

16. *Cincinnati Dollar Weekly*, 20 Oct 1853; *Cincinnati Daily Enquirer*, 15, 16 Oct 1853; LCM to Children, 27 Oct 1853, LCM Papers, Friends Historical Library, Swarthmore College, Swarthmore, Pa.

17. *Cincinnati Daily Enquirer*, 16 Oct 1853; *NASS*, 5 Nov, 31 Dec 1853.

18. HBB to LS, 9 Sep 1853, BLC; Dorothy Sterling, ed., *Turning the World Upside Down: The Anti-Slavery Convention of American Women Held in New York City, May 9–12, 1837* (New York: The Feminist Press, 1987), 10, 24; Anna Blackwell to John Quincy Adams, *NES*, 21 Jun 1837.

19. SCB Diary, entry for 30 Oct 1853, BLC.

20. *Cincinnati Daily Enquirer*, 18, 19 Oct 1853; *Cincinnati Dollar Weekly*, 27 Oct 1853.

21. Letter to the *Columbian*, 27 Oct 1853, clipping in BLC; *Columbus (Ohio) Statesman*, reprinted in *NASS*, 17 Dec 1853.

22. Letter to the *Columbian*, 27 Oct 1853, clipping in BLC; SCB Diary, entry for 23 Oct 1853, BLC; *Cincinnati Daily Enquirer*, 27 Oct 1853; *Cincinnati Daily Times*, 28 Oct 1853, clipping in BLC.

23. Unidentified Louisville newspaper clipping, BLC; Louisville newspapers reprinted in *NASS*, 12 Nov 1853.

24. LS to HBB, 7, 11, 12 Nov 1853, BLC, Wheeler, 64.

25. LS Rem., 17; LS to SSL, 6 Nov 1853, BLC.

26. LS to HBB, 26 Nov 1853, BLC; LS speech, *NASS*, 4 Feb 1854; LS speech, *Bugle*, 22 Apr 1854.

27. LS to HBB, 26, 27 Nov [1853], 1 Dec 1853, BLC; Undated clippings from Indianapolis papers in BLC; *Indianapolis Star* magazine section, 16 Nov 1917, BLC; Unidentified Evansville newspaper clipping, BLC; HBB to LS, 7 Dec 1853, BLC.

28. *St. Louis Republican*, reprinted in *NASS*, 31 Dec 1853; FDG to *New York Daily Tribune*, clipping, BLC.

29. *St. Louis Republican*, reprinted in *NASS*, 31 Dec 1853; FDG to Editor, *Bugle*, 7 Jan 1854.

30. Unidentified St. Louis newspaper clipping, BLC; *St. Louis Intelligencer*, reprinted in *NASS*, 31 Dec 1853.

31. LS to HBB, 26 Nov 1853, BLC; LS Rem., 16.

32. Unidentified Chicago newspaper clipping, BLC.

33. LS to HBB, 30 Dec [1853], [31 Dec 1853, misdated Jan 1854], 22 Jan 1854, BLC, Wheeler, 66–71; LS to SBA, 10 Jan 1854, BLC; *Chicago Free West*, 5 Jan 1854; Undated *Chicago Journal* clipping, BLC; Record book of "Young Men's Debating Club of Muscatine, 1853–54," cited in Louise Noun, *Strong-Minded Women* (Ames: Iowa State University Press, 1986), 307.

34. *Eminent Women*, 392; Reminiscences of Dr. Caroline B. Winslow, ctr. 87, BLC; *WJ*, 24 Mar 1894.

35. LS to Anna Q. T. Parsons, 12 Jan 1854, BLC.

CHAPTER 17

1. *Pittsburgh Dispatch*, reprinted in *Bugle*, 21 Jan 1854; LS to SBA, 10 Jan 1854, BLC; LS to Anna Q. T. Parsons, 12 Jan 1854, BLC; LS to Gerrit Smith, [9, misdated 8] Jan 1854, Gerrit Smith Papers, Syracuse University Libraries; *Daily National Intelligencer*, 19 Jan 1854; *National Era*, reprinted in *NASS*, 18 Feb 1854.

2. *Philadelphia Daily Register*, 20 Jan 1854, clipping in BLC; LS to Lydia Mott, 5 Mar 1854, BLC.

3. LS to Lydia Mott, March 5, 1854, BLC; Notice to *Daily Register* reprinted in *Bugle*, 4 Feb 1854.

4. *Bugle*, 17 Dec 1853; *NASS*, 28 Jan, 4 Feb 1854; LCM to MCW, 30 Jan 1854, LCM Papers, Friends Historical Library, Swarthmore College, Swarthmore, Pa.; James Mott to LS, 30 Jan 1854, BLC; LS to SBA, 2 Feb 1854, BLC.

5. *Frederick Douglass' Paper*, 10 Feb 1854; *Frederick Douglass' Paper*, 17 Feb 1854, in *Frederick Douglass on Women's Rights*, ed. Philip S. Foner (Westport, Conn.: Greenwood Press, 1976), 67–70.

6. Dorothy Sterling, *Ahead of Her Time: Abby Kelley and the Politics of Antislavery* (New York: W. W. Norton, 1991), 273–75; Henry Mayer, *All on Fire: William Lloyd Garrison and the Abolition of Slavery* (New York: St. Martin's Press, 1998), 431–33.

7. James Mott to LS, 18 Feb 1854, Lydia Mott to LS, 19 Feb 1854, LS to Lydia Mott, 5 Mar 1854, all in BLC.

8. *Frederick Douglass' Monthly*, Oct 1859, Foner, 74–77; LS to WLG, *Liberator*, 21 Oct 1859.

9. *Rochester Daily Democrat*, 1, 2, 3, 10 Dec 1853; *NASS*, 24 Dec 1853; *Lily*, 1 Feb 1854; SBA to LS, 13 Dec 1853, 31 Jan 1854, BLC; LS to SBA, 10, 25 Jan 1854, BLC; ALB to Unidentified friend, 13 Jan 1854, BSL; LCM to MCW, 30 Jan 1854, LCM Papers, Friends Historical Library, Swarthmore College, Swarthmore, Pa.; SBA to WP, 22 Feb 1854, WP Papers, BPL.

10. SBA to LS, 13 Dec 1853, Gordon, 232–33; SBA to LS, 31 Jan 1854, and LS to SBA, 2 Feb 1854, BLC.

11. SBA to LS, 7 Mar 1854, Gordon, 261–62; *Albany Evening Journal*, 21 Feb, 2 Mar 1854; *Albany Argus*, 20, 21, 22 Feb, 3 Mar 1854; *Una*, Jan 1855.

12. SBA to LS, 25 May 1853, BSL; SBA to LS, 9 Feb 1854, Gordon, 239–40.

13. LS to SBA, 13 Feb 1854, BLC.

14. SBA and ECS to LS, 16 Feb 1854, Gordon, 260–61; ALB to LS, 18 Feb 1854, BSL, Lasser and Merrill, 138.

15. LS to SBA, 3 Mar 1854, BLC; SBA to LS, 7 Mar 1854, Gordon, 261–62.

16. *Una*, Mar 1854; Henrietta Ingersoll to LS, 15 Mar [1854], NAWSAR; Unidentified Bangor newspaper clippings in BLC; Eliza Spaulding to LS, 15 Jul 1854, NAWSAR.

17. LS to SBA, 3 Mar 1854, BLC; Howard Griswold to LS, 30 Dec 1853, NAWSAR; Phineas T. Barnum to Russell T. Trall, 11 Feb 1854, NAWSAR; LS to Anna Q. T. Parsons, 9 Apr 1854, NAWSAR; Call to New England Woman's Rights Convention, NAWSAR.

18. *Bugle*, 22 Apr 1854; *NASS*, 29 Apr 1854; *Sibyl*, 15 Jan 1857; Elizabeth B. Chace to LS, 30 May 1854, NAWSAR.

19. LS to HBB, [15 Apr], BLC; LS to HBB, 23 Apr [1854], BLC, Wheeler, 78–79; Lorle Anne Porter, "Amelia Bloomer: An Early Iowa Feminist's Sojourn on the Way West," *Annals of Iowa* 41, no. 8 (Spring 1973): 1251–54.

20. Robert William Fogel, *Without Consent or Contract: The Rise and Fall of American Slavery* (New York: W. W. Norton, 1989), 355–58; *Bugle*, 24 Sep, 1 Oct, 24 Dec 1853; LS to HBB, 23 Apr [1854], BLC, Wheeler, 78–79.

21. Clipping from unidentified Columbus paper, BLC; *Lily*, 1 May 1854; Amelia Bloomer to PWD, 14 Nov 1854, CHD Papers, MHS.

22. Howard N. Meyer, *Colonel of the Black Regiment: The Life of Thomas Wentworth Higginson* (New York: W. W. Norton, 1967), 82–92; *Bugle*, 3, 17 Jun 1854; TWH to LS, 1 Jun 1854, NAWSAR; *Una*, Jul 1854.

23. SBA to LS, 22, 23 May 1854, BLC; *Bugle*, 10 Nov 1855.

24. ALB to LS, 21 May 1854, BSL, Lasser and Merrill, 139; EzB to LS, 1 Jun 1854, and LS to Elizabeth Blackwell, 10 Jun 1854, BLC.

25. James Mott to LS, 15 Mar, 6 Sep 1854, BLC; LS to TWH, 15 Jul 1854, TWH papers, BPL; WP to LS, 29 Aug 1854, BLC; ALB to LS, 16 Aug, 14 [Sep] 1854, BSL, Lasser and Merrill, 141; W. C. Crosby to LS, 23 Mar 1854, NAWSAR; LS to Anna Q. T. Parsons, 25 Aug 1854, BLC; LS to HBB, [2], 6 Apr 1854, BLC, 22 Oct [1854], BLC, Wheeler, 103–4; *Woman's Rights Tracts* (Boston: Robert F. Wallcut, 1854).

26. Proceedings of the Fifth Annual National Woman's Rights Convention," *Liberator*, 12 Jan 1855; TWH to Maria Weston Chapman, 15 Dec 1854, TWH Papers, BPL.

27. MCW to Ellen Wright Garrison, 18 Oct, 4 Nov 1854, GFP.

28. LS to Anna Q. T. Parsons, 20 Oct [1854], BLC; LS to HBB, 22 Oct [1854], BLC, Wheeler, 103–4; ALB to SBA, 5 Nov 1854, Gordon, 282; "The Woman's Rights Convention, Correspondence of the N.Y. *Tribune*, . . . Oct. 20, 1854," reprint in unidentified newspaper clipping, BLC.

29. TWH to Maria Weston Chapman, 15 Dec 1854, TWH papers, BPL; Undated *Chicago Tribune* clipping, BLC; Reprint from *Richmond (Kentucky) Examiner, Bugle*, 3 Dec 1853; Unidentified Hamilton, Ontario, newspaper clipping in BLC; *Una*, Apr 1855, Jul 1854; *Lily*, 15 Aug 1854; Reprint from *Statesman* in unidentified newspaper clipping, BLC; "To Miss Lucy Stone," 1853 *Indianapolis Locomotive* clipping, BLC; "To Lucy Stone," *Fitchburg News*, 5 Jan 1853, clipping at Quaboag Historical Society Museum, West Brookfield, Mass.; Handwritten copy of *Boston Post* parody, BLC.

CHAPTER 18

1. HBB to Theodore Parker, 16 Apr 1853, BSL.

2. HBB "Autobiography," ctr. 67, BLC HBB to GWB, 18 Nov 1854, BSL.

3. HBB to Theodore Parker, 16 Apr 1853, BSL.

4. HBB Rem., 112–14; HBB to LS, 2 May 1854, BLC, Wheeler, 83.

5. HBB to LS, 13 Jun, 2 Jul, 24 Aug 1853, and LS to HBB, 21 Jun, 27 Jul 1853, BLC, Wheeler, 35–57.

6. HBB to LS, 26 Aug, 13 Jun 1853, and LS to HBB, 21 Jun, 27 Jul 1853, BLC, Wheeler, 38–

41, 48–52; LS speech, *The Whole World Temperance Convention held at Metropolitan Hall in the city of New York on Thursday and Friday, Sept. 1st and 2d, 1853* (New York: Fowlers and Wells, 1853), 62.

7. HBB to LS, 2 Jul, 24 Aug 1853, and LS to HBB, 27 Jul 1853, BLC, Wheeler, 41–57.

8. HBB to LS, 2 Jul, 9 Sep 1853, BLC, Wheeler, 42–44, 59.

9. LS to HBB, 27 Jul 1853, BLC, Wheeler, 49.

10. LS to HBB, [31 Dec 1853, misdated Jan 1854 in Wheeler], BLC, Wheeler, 67–68.

11. HBB to LS, 9 Sep, 2 Jul 1853, BLC, Wheeler, 59, 43–44; LS to HBB, 27 Jul 1853, BLC, Wheeler, 49.

12. NYWRC 1853, 74–75; HBB to LS, 9 Sep 1853, BLC, Wheeler, 61; LS to HBB, 24 Sep 1853, BLC, Wheeler, 62.

13. SCB Diary, entries dated 2, 9 Oct 1853, BLC; HBB to LS, 2 May 1854, 7 Oct 1853, BLC, Wheeler, 83–84; HBB Rem., 120; LS copy of EzB letter, LS to SSL, 6 Nov 1853, BLC.

14. LS to HS, 10 Oct 1853, BLC; SCB Diary, entry dated 30 Oct 1853, BLC; LS to HBB, 7, 10, 12, 26, 27 Nov, 1, 4 Dec 1853, BLC; LS to HBB, 11 Nov 1853, BLC, Wheeler, 64–65; LS to HBB, 17, 22 Nov 1853, telegraphs, BSL; John Woolley to HBB, 21 Nov 1853, with note appended, HBB to LS, 22 Nov 1853, NAWSAR; HBB to LS, 7 Dec 1853, BLC; LS to Hannah Blackwell, 28 Dec 1853, BLC.

15. LS to HBB, 30 Dec [1853], BLC, Wheeler, 66–67.

16. HBB to LS, 22 Jan 1854, BLC, Wheeler, 69–71.

17. HBB to LS, 12 Feb 1854, BLC, Wheeler, 75–76.

18. LS to ALB, [Aug 1849], BLC, Lasser and Merrill, 56; HBB to SSL, 21 Apr 1854, BLC.

19. HBB to SSL, 21 Apr 1854, BLC.

20. LS to HBB, [25 Apr 1854], BLC; LS to HBB 23 Apr 1854, [2 May 1854, misdated 25 Apr in Wheeler], BLC, Wheeler, 79, 80–81.

21. HBB to LS, [6, misdated 5 in Wheeler] May 1854, BLC, Wheeler, 85.

22. LS to EzB, 10 Jun 1854, BLC; LS to HBB, 23 Jul, 3 Sep 1854, BLC, Wheeler, 91, 96–97.

23. LS to HBB, 3 Sep 1854, BLC, Wheeler, 96–97.

24. *NASS*, 17, 24 Jun 1854.

25. *Liberator*, 7 Jul 1854; LS to HBB, 10 Sep 1854, BLC, Wheeler, 98.

26. LS to HBB, [2 May, misdated 25 Apr in Wheeler], 17 Mar, 26 Oct 1854, BLC, Wheeler, 81, 78, 104.

27. HBB Rem., 122–23; *Bugle*, 9, 16 Sep 1853; *NASS*, 4 Nov 1854.

28. LS to HBB, 3, 10 Sep 1854, BLC, Wheeler, 97, 98.

29. LS to HBB, 8 Oct [1854], BLC, Wheeler, 100–101.

30. LS to HBB, 10 Sep, 18 Oct 1854, BLC, Wheeler, 99.

31. LS to HBB, 10 Sep, 19, 22, 26 Oct 1854, BLC, Wheeler, 99, 104.

32. LS to HBB, 8, 10 Oct 1854, [2, 10 Nov 1854], BLC, Wheeler, 99–100, 103; HBB to LS, 22 Dec 1854, BLC; HBB to Emily Blackwell, 3 Mar 1855, BSL. There is no record of the actual points they discussed at this meeting, but preceding and subsequent correspondence suggest these.

33. LS to HBB, [25 Dec 1854], 25 Dec [1854], BLC, Wheeler, 112–13 (Stone wrote two letters to Blackwell on this date).

34. MCW to LCM, 29 Jan 1855, GFP; ALB to SBA, 9 Jan 1855, BLC.

35. LS to Motts, 14 Jan 1855, BLC; LS to HBB, 25 Dec [1854], BLC.

CHAPTER 19

1. *Delaware State Journal*, 27, 31 Oct 1854; *Bugle*, 11 Nov, 2 Dec 1854; *Liberator*, 24 Nov, 1, 8 Dec 1854; *NASS*, 3 Mar 1855; LS to SSL, 12 Jan [1855], BLC; LS to HS, 30 Jan, 19 Feb 1855, BLC; SCB Diary, entry for 28 Jan 1855, BLC; *Adrian (Michigan) Expositor*, 10 Feb 1855; *Ann Arbor (Michigan) Argus*, 23 Feb, 2 Mar 1855; Unidentified Hamilton, Ontario, newspaper clipping in BLC; *Una*, Apr 1855; SJM to LS, 19 Mar 1855, NAWSAR.

2. HBB to LS, 22 Dec 1854, BLC, Wheeler, 109–11.

3. HBB to LS, 12 Feb, 22 Dec 1854, BLC, Wheeler, 75, 110.

4. HBB to Emily Blackwell, 3 Mar 1855, BSL; HBB to GWB, 11, 16, Feb, 24 Dec 1853, 20 Jan, 6 Jul, 18, 30 Nov 1854, BSL; HBB to LS, 22 Jan 1854, 3 Jan [1855], BLC, Wheeler, 69, 116; HBB to C. V. Porter, 18 Feb [1894], VCHS.

5. LS to HBB, 18 Jan 1855, BLC, Wheeler, 118; NWRC 1853, 100–101; *Cincinnati Daily Times,* 28 Oct, 1853, clipping in BLC; HBB to LS, 12 Feb, 22 Dec 1854, 3 Jan, 18 Mar 1855, BLC, Wheeler, 74, 111,115.

6. HBB to LS, 22 Dec 1854, BLC, Wheeler, 109–10.

7. LS to ALB, 11 Jul [1855], BLC, Lasser and Merrill, 144; LS to HBB, 23 Apr [1854], BLC, Wheeler, 79; Wright, *Marriage and Parentage; Or, The Reproductive Element in Man, as a Means to His Elevation and Happiness* (2d ed., 1855; reprint as *Sex, Marriage and Society,* ed. Charles Rosenberg and Carroll Smith-Rosenberg, New York: Arno Press, 1974), 138.

8. HBB to LS, 12 Feb, 5 May, 22 Dec 1854, 18 Mar, 2 Apr 1855, BLC, Wheeler, 74, 85, 109, 125, 130; LS to HBB, 23 Apr [1854], [25 Apr 1854], 10 Oct 1854, [early Jan 1855], BLC, Wheeler, 79. Female governance of sexual relations was advocated by a variety of nineteenth-century reformers, from those like H. C. Wright and O. S. Fowler, who taught exclusive love, to Albert Brisbane, Stephen Pearl Andrews, and Mary Gove Nichols, who advocated "free love."

9. HBB to LS, 22 Dec 1854; 3 Jan [1855, misdated 1854], BLC, Wheeler, 108, 115–16.

10. HBB to WBS, 21 Mar 1855, BLC; HBB to LS, 20 Apr 1855, BLC, Wheeler, 134; TWH to LS, 23 Apr 1855, NAWSAR.

11. "Protest. Published by Lucy Stone and Henry B. Blackwell, on their Marriage, May 1st, 1855," copy in BLC.

12. Mary Thacher Higginson, ed., *Letters and Journal of Thomas Wentworth Higginson* (Boston: Houghton Mifflin, 1921), 60–61; HBB to Emily Blackwell, 9 May 1855, BSL.

13. *New York Daily Times,* 4 May 1855; *Cincinnati Daily Enquirer,* 6 May 1855; *Weekly Chicago Democrat,* 12 May 1855; *Worcester Palladium,* quoted in 1946 newspaper article on file at Quaboag Historical Society Museum, West Brookfield, Mass.; *Washington Union,* clipping in BLC.

14. *Pittsburgh Saturday Visiter* article reprinted in *Liberator,* 8 Dec 1854; Undated clipping in BLC.

15. *Lily,* 1 Jun 1855; *Sibyl,* 1 Oct 1856, 15 Dec 1859, Oct 1862.

16. LS to SBA, 30 May 1855, BLC; ALB Rem., BLC; Lydia Maria Child, *History of the Condition of Women in Various Ages and Nations* (Boston: J. Allen, 1835); LS notebook, ctr. 90, BLC.

17. Rochester newspaper clipping in ECS Scrapbook on 1848 conventions, ECS Papers, LC; *Bugle,* 27 Apr 1850.

18. Alice Stone Blackwell, *Lucy Stone: Pioneer of Woman's Rights* (Boston: Little, Brown and Co., 1930), 171; HBB to GWB, 19, 29, 31 Oct 1855, BSL; LS to Horace Greeley, 2 Oct 1855, Greeley Papers, New York Public Library; *Lily,* 15 Sep 1855; *Journal of the Senate of the State of Ohio, 1856,* 308.

19. LS to SBA, 30 May 1855, BLC.

20. HBB to LS, [28 Aug 1855], BLC, Wheeler, 144.

21. LS to HBB, 7 Nov 1855, BLC; LS to SBA, 2 Nov 1855, BLC; LS to HS, 6, 28 Dec 1855, 26 Mar [1856], BLC.

22. HBB Rem., 132; HBB to GWB, 19 Oct 1855, BSL; HBB to LS, 26 Jan, 27, 31 Mar, 1 Apr 1856, BLC; LS to HBB, 24, 30 Jan, 1856, BLC, Wheeler, 151.

23. LS to ALB, 20 Jan [1856], BLC, Lasser and Merrill, 146–47; ALB to SBA, 12 Mar [1856], BSL.

24. HBB to LS, 29 Aug 1855, 7 Feb 1856, BLC, Wheeler, 155–56

25. HBB to LS, [28 Aug 1855], BLC, Wheeler, 144.

26. HBB to LS, 22 Dec 1854, [28 Aug 1855], BLC; SEB to Emily Blackwell, 10 May [1855], BSL; HBB to GWB, 6 Aug 1854, 19, 29, 31 Oct 1855, BSL.

27. SEB to HBB, 5 Sep [1855], BSL; HBB to GWB, 19 Oct 1855, 14 Mar, 9 May, 8 Jun, 17 Aug 1857, BSL.

28. HBB to GWB, 19, 31 Oct, 12, 22 Nov 1855, BSL; LS to GWB, 12, 21, 24, 30 Nov [1855], BSL; LS to HBB, 9 Aug 1864, Wheeler, 198.

29. Andrea Moore Kerr, *Lucy Stone: Speaking Out for Equality* (New Brunswick, N.J.: Rutgers University Press, 1992), 74–75; HBB to Emily Blackwell, 3 Mar 1855, BSL; LS to HS, 25 Mar [1856] BLC; HBB to GWB, 5 Apr 1858, BSL. The assertion that Stone had her brother send $750 of her money "to meet an overdue loan of Harry's" and a week later another $2,000 "taking notes secured by Blackwell's property in Illinois" (Kerr, 94) is inaccurate. The $750 Blackwell said Stone might have to send (HBB to LS, 19 Mar 1856) was the amount he hoped to get the $900 balance on her Lyons farm discounted to for paying cash. He got it reduced only to $850, and this is what Stone withdrew—for her own investment, not his (HBB to GWB, 23 Mar 1856). The $2,000 was not a withdrawal at all. Having sent Bowman the Ostrom notes, secured by a farm in Illinois, she asked Bowman to send her $2,000 worth of the Coombs, Ryland, and Blackwells notes that were canceled by the Ostrom notes (LS to HS 25 Mar [1856]).

30. HBB to LS, 22 Dec 1854, BLC, Wheeler, 110.

31. HBB to LS, 3 Apr 1856, BLC.

32. EzB to HBB, 22 Feb [1855], BSL; SEB to Emily Blackwell, 13 Dec [1855], BSL; HBB to LS, 10 Jan 1855, BLC.

33. LS to HBB, 18 Jan 1855, 8 Oct 1854, BLC, Wheeler, 118, 99.

34. LS to HBB, 30 Jan [1856], BLC; HBB to Emily Blackwell, 3 Mar, 9 May 1855, BSL; HBB to LS, 1 Apr 1856, BLC.

35. HBB to GWB, 19 Oct, 12 Nov 1855, BSL; HBB to LS, 6 Mar 1855, 12 Apr 1856, BLC.

36. LS to FS, 12 Nov 1855, BLC; LS to WBS, 21 Nov 1855, BLC; LS to HBB, [22 Apr], 26 Apr 1856, BLC, Wheeler, 159; HBB to GWB, 12 Apr 1856, BSL.

37. LS to SBA, 7 Sep 1856, BLC; TWH to LS, 26 Oct 1856, NAWSAR. Although there is no record of what, exactly, Chase told Stone, two years later she was reported to have explained that it was "a mistaken idea that woman is obliged to give up her name and take that of her husband," and that "no law" could compel her to (Julia Branch speech, *Proceedings of the Free Convention held at Rutland, VT., June 25th, 26th, 27th, 1858* [New York: S. T. Munson, 1858], 52–53).

38. LCM to LS, 31 Oct 1856, BLC; ECS to LS, 8 May [1856], NAWSAR; Unpublished autobiography of Olympia Brown, 33, Olympia Brown Papers, SL; LS to M. H. Cobb, 21 Oct 1856, BLC.

39. MCW to Ellen Wright Garrison, 7 Jan 1857, GFP; LS to HBB, 25 Jan 1856, BLC, Wheeler, 150.

CHAPTER 20

1. *Rochester Daily Advertiser*, 1 Jun 1853. Other books on marriage included Alexander Walker, *Woman Physiologically Considered, as to Mind, Morals, Marriage, Matrimonial Slavery, Infidelity, and Divorce* (New York, 1840); Orson S. Fowler, *Love and Parentage, . . . [with] Suggestions to Lovers and the Married concerning the Strongest Ties and the Most Momentous Relations of Life* (New York, 1843); Lorenzo Fowler, *Marriage: Its History and Ceremonies, with a Phrenological and Physiological Exposition of the Functions and Qualifications for Happy Marriages* (New York, 1847); Nelson Sizer, *Thoughts on Domestic Life; Or Marriage Vindicated and Free Love Exposed* (New York, 1848); M. Edgeworth Lazarus, *Love vs. Marriage* (New York, 1852); Karl Heinzen, *The Rights of Women and the Sexual Relation* (Boston, 1852); Thomas L. Nichols, *Esoteric Anthropology* (New York, 1853); Andrew Jackson Davis, *The Great Harmonia* (Boston, 1855); William A. Alcott, *Moral Philosophy of Courtship and Marriage* (Boston and Cleveland, 1857); Austin Kent, *Free Love: Or, A Philosophical Demonstration of the Nonexclusive Nature of Connubial Love* (Hopkinton, N.Y.: 1857).

2. LS to HBB, 3 Sep 1854, BLC, Wheeler, 96; LS to Anna Q. T. Parsons, 8 Jul [1853], BLC; HBB to LS, 22 Dec 1854, 6 Jan 1855, BLC. Stone called Blackwell "my dear husband" months before their actual marriage (LS to HBB, 18 Jan 1855, BLC).

3. *Liberator*, 12 Jan 1838.

4. Hal D. Sears, *The Sex Radicals: Free Love in High Victorian America* (Lawrence: The Regents Press of Kansas, 1977), 25.

5. Edith Roelker Curtis, *A Season in Utopia: The Story of Brook Farm* (New York: Thomas Nelson & Sons, 1961), 187, 210–12, 300–301.

6. EzB to Marian Blackwell, 22 Jun [1845], BLC; Nancy Ann Sahli, *Elizabeth Blackwell, M.D., 1821–1910: A Biography* (New York: Arno Press, 1982), 77.

7. LS to ECS, 14 Aug 1853, ECS Papers, LC, Gordon, 223–25; *Liberator,* 29 Oct 1852.

8. ECS to SBA, 1 Mar [1853], ECS Papers, LC.

9. SBA to LS, 18 Jul 1853, BLC; ECS to SBA, 20 Jun 1853, Stanton and Blatch, 2:50–52; SBA to LS, 18 Jul 1853, BLC; ECS to LS quoted in Harriet Ingersoll to LS, 15 Mar [1854], NAWSAR; LS to ECS, 14 Aug 1853, ECS Papers, LC, Gordon, 223–25.

10. Sears, 6; *New York Daily Tribune,* 17 May 1853.

11. Clarina I. H. Nichols to editor of the *Western Home Journal,* 18 Jun 1867, reprinted in Joseph G. Gambone, ed., "The Forgotten Feminist of Kansas: The Papers of Clarina I. H. Nichols, 1854–1885," *Kansas Historical Quarterly* 39, no. 4 (Winter 1973), 522–23; Nichols to SBA, [ca. 1880–85], SBA Papers, SL.

12. LS to HBB, 11 Nov [1853], BLC, Wheeler, 65.

13. Harriet Ingersoll to LS, 15 Mar [1854], NAWSAR.

14. LS to ALB, 11 Jul [1855], BLC, Lasser and Merrill, 143–45.

15. EzB to Emily Blackwell, 12 May 1854, quoted in Sahli, 174.

16. *New York Daily Times,* 17 Aug 1855. See, Joel Myerson, "Mary Gove Nichols' *Mary Lyndon:* A Forgotten Reform Novel," *American Literature* 58, no. 4 (December 1986): 523–39.

17. Sears, 9; Sarah Grimké essay "Marriage" refuting the *Times* charges, in Gerda Lerner, *The Female Experience: An American Documentary* (Indianapolis: Bobbs-Merrill Educational Publishing, 1977), 89. As late as 1867 Stone was still refuting accusations that she and Blackwell were involved in a free-love relationship (LS to Editor of the *Atchison* [Kansas] *Daily Champion,* 10 May 1867, Gambone, "Part Four," 523n). Confusion over Nichols's identity, Gambone, "Part Two," 233.

18. HBB to LS, 17 Sep 1855, BLC, Wheeler, 146–47.

19. Sears, 9–10.

20. LS to SBA, 2, 25 Nov [1855], BLC; LS to ECS, 22 Oct [1856], ECS Papers, LC.

21. LS to SBA, 2 Nov [1855], BLC; LS to ECS, 17 Sep [1856], 16 Mar [1860], ECS Papers, LC.

CHAPTER 21

1. TWH to Maria Weston Chapman, 15 Dec 1854, TWH Papers, BPL; TWH to LS, 9 Jul 1856, BSL.

2. LS to SBA, 30 May 1855, BLC; LS to ALB, 11 Jul [1855], BLC, Lasser and Merrill, 143–45.

3. LS to ALB, 11 Jul [1855], BLC, Lasser and Merrill, 143–45; LS to SBA, 30 May 1855, BLC.

4. *Lily,* 15 Sep 1855; *New York Daily Tribune,* 20, 22 Aug 1855; *Liberator,* 14 Sep 1855; MCW to W. R. G. Mellen, Sep 1855, GFP.

5. *Una,* Jun 1855; *Lily,* 1 Aug 1855; LS to SBA, 2 Nov 1855, BLC.

6. *Lily,* 1 Aug 1855; *Una,* 15 Oct 1855; *Reports on the Laws of New England, Presented to the New England Meeting, Convened at the Meionaon, Sept. 19 & 20, 1855* [Boston, 1855]; *Liberator,* 21, 28 Sep 1855; *Boston Herald,* 19 Sep 1855.

7. *Liberator,* 28 Sep 1855.

8. Reminiscence of Sally Holley, Gilson; MCW to LCM, 29 Jan 1856, GFP.

9. *Bugle,* 12 Jan 1856.

10. *Cincinnati Daily Enquirer,* 18 Oct 1855; LS to HS, 23 Oct 1855, BLC; *Liberator,* 30 Nov 1855; LS to SBA, 2 Nov 1855, BLC; Amelia Bloomer to Anne McDowell, 12 Mar 1856, *Woman's Advocate,* 5 Apr 1856.

11. While several sketches of Stone's "disappointment speech" exist, none is an exact record of

her words. This description combines accounts from the *Cincinnati Daily Commercial,* reprinted in *Lily,* 15 Nov 1855; the *Cincinnati Daily Enquirer,* 18 Oct 1855; and *HWS,* 1:165–66.

12. LS to SBA, 2 Nov 1855, BLC.

13. Ibid.

14. Ibid.

15. *Bugle,* 10 Nov, 1 Dec 1855, 12 Jan 1856; *Wisconsin State Journal,* 13 Nov 1855; LS to HBB, 4 Nov 1855, BLC; *Weekly Chicago Democrat,* 18 Nov 1855; LS to SBA, 8, 25 Nov 1855, BLC; LS to GWB, 30 Nov 1855, BSL; LS to CCB, 10 Mar 1856, BLC.

16. LS to SBA, 11 Jan 1856, BLC; Gerrit Smith to ECS, 1 Dec 1855, published in *Frederick Douglass' Paper, HWS,* 1:836–39; SEB to EzB, 6 May [1855], BSL; *Water-Cure Journal,* Apr 1856.

17. LS to SBA, 10 Jan 1854, 2 Nov 1855, BLC; *Una,* Apr 1855; *Lily,* 14 Apr 1856; Mary Birdsall to CHD, 2 Jun 1856, CHD Papers, MHS; *Lily* 1 Mar 1855.

18. LS to SBA, 8, 25 Nov 1855, BLC.

19. LS to SBA, 11 Jan 1856, BLC.

20. Andrea Moore Kerr, *Lucy Stone: Speaking Out for Equality* (New Brunswick, N.J.: Rutgers University Press, 1992), 93–94; HBB to LS, 12 Sep, 13 Oct, [28 Aug] 1855, 7 Feb 1856, BLC, Wheeler, 146, 148, 156.

21. LS to HBB, 25 Jan 1856, BLC, Wheeler, 149–50.

22. *Fort Wayne Weekly Sentinel,* 26 Jan 1856; *Lily,* 15 Feb 1856; *Fort Wayne Times,* 31 Jan 1856.

23. LS to HBB, 25, 30 Jan 1856, BLC, Wheeler, 149–51.

24. LS to SBA, 25 Mar 1856, BLC; C. Latham Sholes to LS, 28 Mar 1856, NAWSAR; Theodora W. Youmans, "How Wisconsin Women Won the Ballot," *Wisconsin Magazine of History* 5 (1921–22): 6.

25. LS to SBA, 25 Mar 1856, BLC; Amelia Bloomer to Anne McDowell, 12 Mar 1856, *Woman's Advocate,* 5 Apr 1856; *Journal of the Senate of the State of Ohio, 1856,* 308; *HWS,* 1:629–31.

26. LS to Anna Q. T. Parsons, 11 Mar 1856, NAWSAR; *Liberator,* 28 Mar 1856; LS speech, *Lily,* 15 Dec 1856; SEB to LS, 20 Dec [1855], BSL; HBB to LS, 26 Mar, 1 Apr 1856, BLC.

27. *New York Daily Tribune,* 3, 4 Jun 1858; HBB to GWB, 17 Dec 1855, 12, 16, 20 Apr, [18], 22 May 1856, BSL; LS to HBB, [22 Apr 1856], BLC; HBB to LS, 22 May 1856, BLC.

28. HBB to LS, 6, 12, 22 May 1856, BLC; HBB to GWB, 16, [18] May 1856, BSL.

29. HBB to SCB, 20 Jun 1856, BLC; LS to SBA, 25 Jun 1855, BLC; LS to HS, 1 Jul 1856, BLC.

30. HBB Reminiscences, VCHS; LS to SBA, 22 Jul 1856, BLC, Gordon, 327–29; LS to HS, 1 Jul 1856, BLC.

31. LS to SBA, 1, 22 Jul 1856, BLC, Gordon, 327–29; *Western Times,* 28 Jun, 5, 19 Jul 1856, clippings in BLC; Typescript copy of *Western Times* articles, VCHS; C. V. Porter to HBB, 15 Mar 1894, NAWSAR; LS to Family, 29 Jul 1856, BLC; LS to GWB, 7 Aug 1856, BSL; HBB to GWB, 7 Aug 1856, BSL.

32. James A. Rawley, *Race and Politics: "Bleeding Kansas" and the Coming of the Civil War* (New York: J. B. Lippencott, 1969), 87–96, 125–33.

33. LS to HS, 25 Mar 1856, BLC; LS to Family, 29 Jul 1856, BLC.

34. HBB to C. V. Porter, 18 Feb 1894, newspaper clipping at VCHS; LS to ALB, [summer 1856], BSL, Lasser and Merrill, 147; SBA to ECS, 5 Jun [1856], ECS Papers, LC, Gordon, 321–23; SBA to MCW, 6 Jul 1856, GFP.

35. LS to SBA, 25 Mar, 30 Jul 1856, BLC; ALB to SBA, 14 Feb, BLC; ALB to SBA, 12 Mar 1856, BSL, Gordon, 317–18.

36. HBB to GWB, 17 Aug 1856, BSL; LS to SBA, 23 Aug, 11 Sep 1856, BLC.

CHAPTER 22

1. LS to SBA, 22 Jul 1856, BLC, Gordon, 328; SBA to MCW, 6 Jul 1856, GFP; MCW to SBA, 30 Aug 1856, GFP; LS to SBA, 1 Jul, 4, 7 Sep 1856, BLC.

2. LS to SBA, 7 Sep 1856, BLC.

3. TWH to LS, 26 Oct, 28 Nov 1856, NAWSAR.

4. LS to SBA, 4, 11, 17, 21 Sep 1856, BLC.

5. LS to SBA, 22 Jul, 4, 7, 11, 17, 21, 30 Sep 1856, BLC.

6. LS to HS, 13 Oct [1856], 1 Dec 1856, BLC; HBB to GWB, 11, 29 Sep, 27 Oct, 5, 15 Dec 1856, BSL.

7. James A. Rawley, *Race and Politics: "Bleeding Kansas" and the Coming of the Civil War* (New York: J. B. Lippencott, 1969), 160.

8. LS to SBA, 22 Jul, 4 Sep, 14, 22 Oct 1856, BLC; SBA to LS, 19, 22, 27 Oct, 11 Nov 1856, BLC; NWRC 1856, 4–6.

9. LS to ECS, 22 Oct 1856, ECS Papers, LC.

10. Andrew Jackson Davis, *The Great Harmonia* (Boston, 1855). *New York Observer*, 11 Dec 1856, clipping in BLC; ECS to LS, 24 Nov 1856, NWRC 1856, 88–90; LS to SBA, 4 Jul 1857, BLC. By request, Jackson's speech was not published in the convention proceedings, but a good sketch appears in *Woman's Advocate*, 29 Nov 1856.

11. LS to SBA, 22 Oct 1856, BLC (The page discussing the memorial plan is separated from the first part of the letter and can be found in ctr. 81); SBA to LS, 19 Oct 1856, BLC; NWRC 1856, 48–49.

12. NWRC 1856, 84, 86–87; *NASS*, 28 Feb, 14 Mar 1857; "The Right of Suffrage for Women. Speech of Mrs. Lucy Stone Before Judiciary Committee of the Massachusetts Senate, on the Memorial of a Committee of the National Woman's Rights Convention, asking that the Right of Suffrage may be granted to Woman. In the Representatives Hall, March 6, 1857," ctr. 85, BLC.

13. *Lily*, 1 Dec 1856; *Bugle*, 9 May 1857; *NASS*, 16 May 1857.

14. LS to William H. Richardson, 10 Dec 1856, BLC; William H. Richardson to LS, 13 Oct, 13 Nov 1856, NAWSAR; "People's Literary Institute, Second Annual Series of Lectures," BLC.

15. Mary M. Jennings to LS, 26 Nov 1856, NAWSAR; LS to William H. Richardson, 7 Dec 1856, BLC; James Mott and LCM to LS, 9 Dec 1856, BLC.

16. LS to William H. Richardson, 10 Dec 1856, BLC; LS to HBB, 31 Dec 1856, BLC.

17. MCW to David Wright, 12 Dec 1856, GFP; Mary M. Jennings to LS, 12 Dec 1856, NAWSAR.

18. LS to HBB, 31 Dec 1856, BLC; MCW to David Wright, 2 Jan 1857, GFP.

19. *House Journal of the Commonwealth of Pennsylvania for 1857*, 177, 200, 252; *Bugle*, 28 Feb 1857; *Boston Traveller*, reprinted in *NASS*, 28 Feb 1857; *Maine Journal of the House for 1857*, 168–69, 434; *Maine Journal of the Senate for 1857*, 152, 166, 372; LS to HBB, 4 Mar 1857, BLC.

20. *Liberator*, 15 Mar 1857; "The Right of Suffrage for Women. Speech of Mrs. Lucy Stone Before Judiciary Committee of the Massachusetts Senate, . . . March 6, 1857," BLC; *Maine Journal of the House for 1857*, 434; "Report of the Committee on the Memorial of Antoinette L. Brown Blackwell," Maine State Archives.

21. HBB to GWB, 27 Mar 1857, 5 Apr 1858, BSL; LCM to MCW, 17 Mar 1857, GFP; LS to friend, quoted in Alice Stone Blackwell, *Lucy Stone: Pioneer of Woman's Rights* (Boston: Little, Brown and Co., 1930), 193.

22. LS to HBB, 19 Apr 1857, BLC; LS to Parents, 11 Jun 1857, BLC.

23. *Liberator*, 23 May 1857; *NASS*, 23 May 1857.

CHAPTER 23

1. *Bugle*, 27 Dec 1856.

2. *Bugle*, 5 Jul 1856; SBA to LS, 19 Oct 1856, BLC.

3. LS to SBA, 8 Nov 1855, BLC; SBA to LS, 18 Jul 1857, BLC; LS to SBA, 22 Oct 1856, BLC.

4. SBA to LS, 11 Nov, 10 Dec 1856, 12 Jan 1857, BLC; LS to SBA, 15, 17 Jan 1857, BLC.

5. SBA to SSF and AKF, 20 Apr 1857, AKF and SSF Papers, AAS.

6. TWH to LS, 28 Nov 1856, 20 May, 8 Jun 1857, NAWSAR.

7. *Sibyl*, 1, 15 Jan, 1 Mar, 1 Apr, 15 Jun 1857.

8. Charlotte A. Joy to LS, 8 May 1857, NAWSAR,

9. LS to Charlotte Joy, 16 Jun 1857, *Sibyl*, 1 Jul 1857.

10. SBA to LS, 16 Jun 1857, BLC, Gordon, 345.

11. Eliza Jackson Eddy to LS, 20 Jul 1857, NAWSAR; LS to SBA, 20 Jul 1857, BLC; SBA to LS, 16 Jun 1857, BLC, Gordon, 345.

12. LS to SBA, 4 Jul 1857, BLC.

13. Ibid.

14. TWH to LS, 8 Jun 1857, NAWSAR.

15. Ibid.

16. LS to SBA, 20 Jul 1857, BLC; LS to HBB, [2 May 1854], BLC.

17. LS to SBA, 24 Jul 1857, BLC; SBA to LS, 11 Aug 1857, BLC.

18. SBA to MCW, 6 July 1856, GFP; LS to SBA, 22 Jul, Aug 2 1856, BSL, Gordon, 327–29, 347–48.

19. LS to SBA, 11 Jun, 4, 18, 20 Jul 1857, BLC; SBA to LS, 16 Jun, 18 Jul 1857, BLC, Gordon, 345; LS to LCM, 23 Jun 1857, ALSL; LS to Elizabeth Buffum Chace, 23 [Jun, misdated Jan] 1857, Lillie B. C. and Arthur Wyman, *Elizabeth Buffum Chace, 1806–1899; Her Life and Environment* (Boston: W. B. Clarke Co., 1914), 1:160; LCM to LS, 1 Jul 1857, BLC; PWD to LS, [ca. 1] Jul 1857, NAWSAR; Elizabeth Buffum Chace to LS, 17 Jul 1857, NAWSAR.

20. LS to SBA, 4, 20 Jul 1857, BLC; SBA to LS, 18 Jul 1857, BLC.

21. LS to SBS, 11 Jun 1857, BLC; SBA to LS, 18, 21 Jul 1857, BLC.

22. LS to SBA, 24 Jul 1857, BLC.

23. SBA to LS, 2 Aug 1857, BSL, Gordon, 346–49; SBA to LS, 11, 18 Aug 1857, BLC.

24. *Bugle*, 24 Oct 1857; Merton L. Dillon, *The Abolitionists: The Growth of a Dissenting Minority* (DeKalb, Ill.: Northern Illinois University Press, 1974), 232–33; WP to LS, 11 Aug 1857, BLC.

25. LCM to MCW, 7 Sep 1857, GFP.

26. SBA to LS, 2 Aug 1857, BSL, Gordon, 349.

27. *Sibyl*, 1 Sep 1857.

28. HBB to LS, 8 Sep 1857, BLC, Wheeler, 171–72.

29. HBB to GWB, 16 Sep 1857, BSL; SBA to ECS, 29 Sep 1857, ECS Papers, LC, Gordon, 352–56; LS to SBA, 29 Sep 1857, BLC.

30. ALB to SBA, 28 Sep 1857, BSL; LS to SBA, 29 Sep 1857, BLC; *Bugle*, 17 Oct 1857.

CHAPTER 24

1. HBB to GWB, 9 Mar 1856, 15 May, 3 Jun, 13 Apr 1857, BSL.

2. HBB to GWB, 23 Jun, 9 Jul, 1857, 15 Dec, 11 Sep 1856, 3 Mar, 8 Jun 1857, BSL.

3. HBB to GWB, 9 May, 17 Aug, 8 Jun 1857, BSL; AKF to SSF, 16 Jul [1857], AKF and SSF Papers, Worcester Historical Museum, Worcester, Mass.; Dorothy Sterling, *Ahead of Her Time: Abby Kelley and the Politics of Antislavery* (New York: W. W. Norton, 1991), 307–10.

4. HBB to GWB, 15 May, 13 Jun, 27, 28 Jul 1857, BSL.

5. HBB to GWB, 27 Jul, 23 Aug 1857, BSL.

6. HBB to C. E. Hovey, 27 Feb 1857, BSL; HBB to GWB, 3, 14 Mar, 13 Apr, 3 Sep [two letters of same date], 15 Oct 1857, BSL.

7. TWH to LS, 28 Nov 1856, 12 Aug [two notes of same date], 15 Sep, 22 Oct 1857, 3 Oct 1858, NAWSAR; LS to WLG, 27 Nov 1857, in *Liberator*, 11 Dec 1857; *Sibyl*, 1 Dec 1857.

8. *NASS*, 9 Jan 1858; LS to Abraham Mandeville, 18 Dec 1857, in *Orange Journal*, 16 Jan 1858.

9. LS to Mrs. Hussey, 23 Mar 1876, BLC; *Liberator*, 29 Jan 1858.

10. *Liberator*, 29 Jan 1858.

11. "A Brief Statement Read before the [New Jersey Historical] Society, January 21, 1858, by William A. Whitehead," in Gerda Lerner, *The Female Experience: An American Documentary*

(Indianapolis: Bobbs-Merrill Educational Publishing, 1977), 324–29; Newspaper clippings in BLC; *Sibyl*, 1 Feb 1858.

12. *Newark Daily Advertiser*, 9 Feb 1858.

13. Andrea Moore Kerr, *Lucy Stone: Speaking Out for Equality* (New Brunswick, N.J.: Rutgers University Press, 1992), 104; *Liberator*, 19 Feb 1858; LS to HS, 10 Feb [1858], BLC; HBB to LS, 3 Mar 1858, BLC, Wheeler, 174–75; HBB to LS, 13 Apr 1858, BLC.

14. Kerr, 97–98, 105; HBB to GWB, 17 Aug 1856, 9, 13, 21 Jul 1857, 28 Feb, 7, 8, 24 Mar, 1858, BSL; HBB to LS, 7, 19, 24 Mar 1858, BLC.

15. HBB to LS, 10 Apr, 1, 9 May, 7, 20 Mar 1858, BLC; HBB to GWB, 13 Dec 1857, 28 Feb, 7, 8 Mar 1858, BSL.

16. HBB to LS, 7, 12, 16, 20, 24, 25, 30, [31] Mar, [ca. 11 Apr] 1858, BLC.

17. HBB to GWB, 24 Mar 1858, BSL; HBB to LS, [15], 16, 19, 20, 24, 25, 30, [31] Mar 1858, BLC; LS to HBB, 7 Mar, 4 Apr 1858, BLC.

18. HBB to LS, 3, 5, 13 Apr 1858, BLC; LS to HBB, 1, 4 Apr, 11 May 1858, BLC; HBB to GWB, 5, 13 Apr, 17 May 1858, 11 Jan 1859, BSL.

19. LS to HBB, 4, 25 Apr 1858, BLC, Wheeler, 178, BLC; HBB to LS, 16, 19, 20, 25 Mar 1858, BLC, Wheeler, 176–78.

20. HBB to LS, 3, 30 Mar, [ca. 11], 13, [25] Apr, 1 May 1858, BLC; LS to HBB, 4, 25 Apr, 7 Mar 1858, BLC.

21. LS to HBB, 20 [misdated 2 in Wheeler] Jun 1858, BLC, Wheeler, 184; SBA to LS, 22 Mar 1858, BLC; LS to SBA, 1 Apr 1858, BLC.

22. *NASS*, 20 Mar 1858; *Sibyl*, 15 Apr, 1 May 1858; *New York Daily Times*, 23 Apr 1858; *Advocate and Family Guardian*, quoted in Barbara J. Berg, *The Remembered Gate: Origins of American Feminism* (New York: Oxford University Press, 1978), 254, 260–61.

23. LS to HBB, 25 Apr 1858, BLC, Wheeler, 178–79; LS to HS, 16 Mar 1858, BLC; LS to Cousin J., [Nov 1857], BLC; HBB to LS, 1 May 1858, BLC, Wheeler, 180.

24. HBB to LS, [6, misdated 7], 9 May 1858, BLC; LS to HBB, 11 May 1858 BLC.

25. HBB to LS, 1 May 1858, BLC, Wheeler, 180; LS to HBB, 9 May, 1858, BLC, Wheeler, 181; LS to CHD, 18 Mar 1858, CHD Papers, MHS; SBA to LS, 22 Mar 1858, BLC; LS to SBA, 1 Apr 1858, BLC; SBA to ALB, 22 Apr, 2 May 1858, BSL, Gordon, 360.

26. SBA to ALB, 22 Apr 1858, BSL, Gordon, 360. Other orators in the course included New York jurist James Topham Brady, *Harper's Weekly* editor George William Curtis, and noted Universalist minister Edwin Hubbell Chapin.

27. SBA to ALB, 22 Apr 1858, BSL, Gordon, 360; LS to HBB, 9 May 1858, BLC, Wheeler, 181–82.

28. *New York Daily Times*, 14 May 1858; *New York Daily Tribune*, 18 May 1858.

29. *New York Daily Times*, 14, 15 May 1858; *Newark Daily Advertiser*, 14 May 1858; *Boston Courier*, reprinted in *Liberator*, 4 Jun 1858.

30. *New York Daily Times*, 15 May 1858; *Sibyl*, 1 Jun 1858; LS to SBA, 22 Oct 1856, BLC; PWD to LS, Jul 1857, NAWSAR. There was some confusion over the presidency of the Central Committee in 1854. When James Mott notified Davis of dates so she could issue the convention call, she replied that it should be issued by Lucretia Mott and Antoinette Brown because they were president and secretary. Surprised that she was president, Mott asked Stone if this was so. Stone confirmed that the Cleveland convention had so appointed her, but Mott evidently refused to accept the office, for the 1854 call appeared over the names of Davis and Brown (LS to TWH, 15 Jul 1854, TWH Papers, BPL; James Mott to LS, 6 Sep 1854, BLC; *Una*, August 1854). When Anthony and Higginson issued the 1856 call without contacting Davis, Stone chided Anthony for the failure, saying that even though it made no difference in the end, Davis still had an *"official* position" (Stone's emphasis) and should have been notified (LS to SBA, 1 Jul, 17 Sep 1856, BLC).

31. LS to HBB, 7, 13, 24, Jun 1858, BLC.

32. LS to HBB, 25 Apr 1858, BLC, Wheeler, 179; LS to HBB, 4, 25 Apr, 7, 9, 26 May 1858, BLC; HBB to LS, 10, [ca. 11], [25 Apr], [31 Mar], 1, 9 May 1858, BLC; HBB to LS, 1 May 1858, BLC, Wheeler, 180.

33. HBB to LS, 10, 17, 23 Jun 1858, BLC.

34. HBB to LS, 8 Jul 1858, BLC; LS to HBB, 20 June 1858, BLC, Wheeler, 184.

35. HBB to LS, 28 Jun, 2 Sep 1858, BLC; HBB to GWB, 27 Jun, 8 Jul, 11 Aug, 1 Oct 1858, BSL; LS to FS, 27 Aug 1858, BLC.

36. HBB to GWB, 11 Aug, 1 Oct, 1858, BSL; LS to HS, 26 Sep 185[8], BLC.

37. SBA to LS and ALB, 22 Aug 1858, BSL; LS to SBA, 26 Aug 1858, ECS Papers, LC.

38. Charles W. Slack to LS, 16 Aug 1858, NAWSAR; SBA to LS and ALB, 22 Aug 1858, BSL; LS to SBA, 26 Aug 1858, ECS Papers, LC; Charles Slack to ECS, 2 Sep 1858, ECS Scrapbook, vol. 1, Vassar College Library.

39. Caroline Severance to ECS, 24 Oct 1858, ECS Papers, LC; Charles Slack to ECS, 9 Nov 1858, ECS Papers, LC; "Caroline Severance," *Eminent Women of the Age: Being Narratives of the Lives and Deeds of the Most Prominent Women of the Present Generation* (Hartford, Conn.: S. M. Betts, 1868), 380–82; ECS to Elizabeth Smith Miller, 4 Jul 1858, ECS Papers, LC, Gordon, 383; SBA to ALB, [late Nov 1858], BSL.

40. LS to HBB, 13 Jun 1858, BLC.

41. HBB to GWB, 11 Aug, 8 Sep, 1, 8, 20, 29 Oct, 24 Nov 1858, BSL; LS to HS, 26 Sep 1858, BLC; LS to CCB, 12 Feb 1859, BLC.

CHAPTER 25

1. HBB to HS, 5, 18 Dec 1858, BLC.

2. LS to CCB, 12 Feb 1859, BLC; LS to SBA, 24 Feb 1859, BLC; *Illinois State Journal*, 2 Feb 1859; "Petition of L. C. Higginson and others . . . ," Illinois State Archives (Among the signatures on the petition are those of friends and boarders named in HBB to HS, 5, 18 Dec 1858, BLC); *Journal of the Senate of the Twenty-First General Assembly of the State of Illinois . . . 1859*, 167–68; *Aurora (Illinois) Weekly Beacon*, 24 Mar 1859; *Sibyl*, 15 Apr 1859; LS to ALB, 20 Feb 1859, BSL, Lasser and Merrill, 150.

3. HBB to HS with note from LS, 5 Dec 1858, BLC; HBB "Autobiography," ctr. 67, BLC.

4. LS to ALB, 20 Feb 1859, BSL, Lasser and Merrill, 150; WP to LS, 6 Nov 1858, *HWS*, 1: 667; LS to SBA, 24 Feb, 24 Mar 1859, BLC; ALB to LS, 12 Mar, 14 Apr 1859, BLC, Lasser and Merrill, 151–53, 153–54; SBA to ALB, 6 Apr 1859, BSL. The fund was referred to as the "Phillips fund" until Jackson's identity as donor was revealed at his death in November 1861. Records of the fund were kept first by Wendell Phillips and then by William I. Bowditch and are in NAWSAR.

5. Francis Jackson to LS, 9 Apr 1859, NAWSAR; ALB to LS, 14 Apr [1859], BLC, Lasser and Merrill, 153–54; *NASS*, 30 Apr 1859.

6. *Liberator*, 15 Oct 1858; *HWS*, 3:373–74; *Sibyl*, 15 Feb, 15 Dec 1858, 15 Feb, 1, 15 Mar 1859; Nov, Dec 1862, Apr, Sep 1863; Robert Samuel Fletcher, *A History of Oberlin College* (1943; reprint, New York: Arno Press, 1971), 290–91.

7. LS to SBA, 24 Feb 1859, BLC; LS speech, NWRC 1852, 34; *NASS*, 6 Dec 1862; "Wheeler vs. Wall," Charles Allen, *Reports of Cases Argued and Determined in the Supreme Judicial Court of Massachusetts* (Boston: Little, Brown, 1864), 6:558–59.

8. *Michigan Journal of Education* (May 1855), cited in Dorothy Gies McGuigan, *A Dangerous Experiment: 100 Years of Women at the University of Michigan* (Ann Arbor: Center for Continuing Education for Women, 1970), 15–17; *Michigan Senate Journal*, 1857, 445–49; Euphemia Cochrane to LS, 25 Feb 1857, 9 May 1858, NAWSAR.

9. Euphemia Cochrane to LS, 9 May 1858, NAWSAR; Sarah Burger Sterns to ASB, 30 Oct [1895?], BLC; McGuigan, 17–19; *NASS*, 1 May 1858.

10. *Bugle*, 30 Oct 1858; McGuigan, 19–22.

11. LS to CCB, 12 Feb 1859, BLC; LS to SBA, 24 Feb, 24 Mar 1859, BLC; SBA to LS, 2 Aug 1857, BSL, Gordon, 346–49; SBA to ALB, 6 Apr 1859, BSL; *NASS*, 16 Apr 1859.

12. ALB to LS, 14 Apr [1859], BLC, Lasser and Merrill, 153–54; HBB to GWB, 21 Apr, 3 May

1859, BSL; Hannah Blackwell to LS, 20 Jul 1859, BLC; SCB to HBB, 22 Jun 1859, BSL; ALB to LS, 29 Aug 1959, BLC, Lasser and Merrill, 156–59.

13. *House Journal of the Commonwealth of Pennsylvania . . . 1857,* 177, 200, 252; *Bugle,* 28 Feb 1857; SBA to LS, 8 Jun 1858, BLC; SBA to LS and ALB, 22 Aug 1858, BLC; LS to SBA, 26 Aug 1858, ECS Papers, LC; SBA to ALB, 4 Sep 1858, Gordon, 378–80, 397n; ALB to CHD, 3 Jun 1859, CHD Papers, MHS; LS to SBA, 24 Feb, 24 Mar 1859, BLC.

14. Samuel N. Wood to LS, 24 Nov 1855, NAWSAR; Samantha Robinson to LS, 5 Jan 1856, NAWSAR; Mrs. S. N. Wood to *Lawrence, (Kansas) Tribune,* May 1867, reprinted in *HWS,* 2:929 (This letter tells of the exchange between Wood and Stone but misdates it as having occurred in 1858 and the Kansas Act as signed in 1859); Kansas Territorial Act in *Sibyl,* 15 Sep 1858.

15. James G. Gambone, ed. "The Papers of Clarina I. H. Nichols, 1854–1884," *Kansas Historical Quarterly* 39, no. 1 (Spring 1973): 21–24, no. 2 (Summer 1873): 240, and no. 3 (Autumn 1873): 413–16; Gordon, 392–96, esp. nn. 2, 3, 4.

16. Pat Creech Scholten, "A Public 'Jollification': The 1859 Women's Rights Petition Before the Indiana Legislature," *Indiana Magazine of History* 72, no. 4 (1976): 347–59; *Sibyl,* 1 Mar 1859; *Liberator,* 10, 14 Jun 1859; *Report of the Woman's Rights Meeting at Mercantile Hall, May 27, 1859* (Boston: S. Urbino, 1859); HBB and LS to SBA, 8 Jun 1859, BLC; SBA to HBB, 14 Jun 1859, BLC; SBA to LS, 30 Aug 1859, BLC; ALB to LS, 29 Aug 1859, BLC, Lasser and Merrill, 156–59; LS to Lydia Mott, 4 Sep 1859, BLC.

17. *Sibyl,* 1, 15 Apr, 1 Aug 1859; ALB to LS, 22 Jul, 29 Aug 1859, BLC, Lasser and Merrill, 156–59; SBA to LS, 30 Aug 1859, BLC; *Sibyl,* 15 Jul 1859; *NASS,* 16 Jul, 6 Aug, 3, 10 Sep 1859; *Liberator,* 12 Aug 1859.

18. ALB to SBA, 25 Oct 1859, BSL; LS to SBA, 22 Sep 1859, BLC; ALB to LS, 29 Aug 1859, BLC; SBA to LS, 30 Aug 1859, BLC; *NASS,* 3, 10 Sep, 12 Nov, 3, 10 Dec 1859; *Liberator,* 9, 16 Dec 1859; *Sibyl,* 15 Jan 1860.

19. *New York Daily Times,* 6, 10 Feb 1860.

20. *New York Daily Times,* 6, 10 Feb 1860; *Journal of the New York Senate,* 1860, 458; *Journal of the New York Assembly,* 1860, 663; *NASS,* 24, 31 Mar 1860.

21. Elizabeth Griffith, *In Her Own Right: The Life of Elizabeth Cady Stanton* (New York: Oxford University Press, 1984), 97–98.

22. LS to HS, 8 Jan 1860, BLC; HBB Rem., 161–65.

23. LS to HS, 8 Jan 1860, BLC; LS to ECS, 16 Mar [1860], ECS Papers, LC. Central Committee members appointed at the 1860 convention were Stanton, president; Anthony, secretary; Phillips, treasurer; Martha Wright, Samuel J. May, and Mary H. Hallowell (NWRC 1860, 93).

24. *New York Daily Tribune,* 1, 5, 6, 12, 17, 28 Mar, 7, 21 Apr, 1 May 1860; *Proceedings of the Free Convention Held at Rutland, Vt., June 25th, 26th, 27th, 1858* (New York: S. T. Munson, 1858), 60–61; Yuri Suhl, *Ernestine L. Rose and the Battle for Human Rights* (New York: Reynal, 1959), 195–96. Rose rebutted Julia Branch, who criticized Stone for keeping the marriage question off the woman's rights platform. Pointing out that Stone's and her husband's different last names would prevent them from sharing a hotel room unless they revealed their marriage, Branch turned a wife's right to keep her name into a demand for a woman's right "to love, when she will, where she will, and how she will" (*Proceedings of the Free Convention,* 52–54).

25. *Newark Daily Advertiser,* 30 Mar 1860; *Proceedings of the Free Convention,* 52–66; *Liberator,* 19 Jun 1857, 17 Jun 1859; LS to ECS, March 16, [1860], ECS Papers, LC.

26. LS to ECS, 16 Apr [1860], ECS Papers, LC; ECS to SBA, 24 Apr 1860, Stanton and Blatch, 2:76–77.

27. NWRC 1860, 73–90.

28. Griffith, 101–2; Kerr, 111–12; ECS to MCW, 2 Jun 1860, Stanton and Blatch, 80–81. For newspaper debate on Stanton's resolutions, see Editorial note, Gordon, 431.

29. SM Jr. to LS, 15 Mar 1859, NAWSAR; WLG to ECS, 23 Mar 1860, ECS Papers, Rutgers University Libraries.

CHAPTER 26

1. *Liberator*, 15 Jun, 14 Sep 1860; Dorothy Sterling, *Ahead of Her Time: Abby Kelley and the Politics of Antislavery* (New York: W. W. Norton, 1991), 327.

2. LS to HBB, 14, 20 Sep 1860, BLC, Wheeler, 190; *Liberator*, 28 Sep 1860; Sterling, 326–28.

3. LS to SBA, 12 Jul 1864, BLC, Wheeler, 195; James M. McPherson, *The Struggle for Equality: Abolitionists and the Negro in the Civil War and Reconstruction* (Princeton: Princeton University Press, 1964), 50, 123; *Liberator*, 14 Jun 1861; *NASS*, 21 Mar, 18 Apr 1863.

4. *Proceedings of the Meeting of the Loyal Women of the Republic, Held in New York, May 14, 1863* (New York, 1863), 15–19; *Sibyl*, Jun 1863.

5. *Proceedings of the American Anti-Slavery Society Third Decade Meeting, December 3 and 4, 1863* (New York, 1864), 83; LS to Gerrit Smith, 26 Jan 1864, Gerrit Smith Collection, George Arents Research Library, Syracuse University; SBA to ECS, October 10, 1863, ECS Papers, LC, Gordon, 502.

6. HBB to GWB, 29 Jul 1861, 18 Jul 1862, BSL; TWH to ECS, 2 May 1866, ECS Scrapbook, vol. 1, Vassar College Library, Gordon, 578.

7. MCW to SBA, 31 Mar 1862, GFP, Gordon, 473–74; *Sibyl*, Jan, Feb, Apr, May 1862, Feb, Apr, Sep 1863.

8. LS to CCB, with note appended by HBB, 12 Feb 1859, BLC; LS to FS, 31 Dec 1862, BLC; LS to HBB, 22 Jun 1864, BLC; HBB to GWB, 22, 29 May, 2 Jun, 23 Jul, 14 Oct 1862, BSL; HBB Rem., 161, 163, 182.

9. Ellen Wright Garrison to William Lloyd Garrison II, 28 Feb 1864, GFP; HBB Rem, 176; LS to CCB, 12 Dec 1864, BLC; LS to HBB, [10 Dec 1864], BLC.

10. LS to HBB, 8 Oct [1854], Wheeler, 99; Elinor Rice Hays, *Those Extraordinary Blackwells* (New York: Harcourt, Brace and World, 1967), 151; LS to HBB, [9, misdated 10], 14 Jun, 20 Sep 1864, BLC, Wheeler, 191–92, 201.

11. LS to HBB, 9, 14 Jun, 21 [Jun], 22 Jul 1864, BLC. Andrea Moore Kerr, *Lucy Stone: Speaking Out for Equality* (New Brunswick, N.J.: Rutgers University Press, 1992), 113–17.

12. SBA to ECS, 10 Oct, 1863, ECS Papers, LC, Gordon, 502–3; LS to HBB, 8 Jun, 22 Jul 1864, BLC.

13. LS to SBA, July 12, 1864, BLC, Wheeler, 194; LS to HBB, 22 Jul [1864], BLC, Wheeler, 196.

14. LS to HBB, 22, 31 Jul 1864, BLC.

15. HBB to GWB, 17 Aug 1862, BSL; LS to HBB, 8, [9, misdated 10] Jun 1864, BLC; LS to SBA, 20 Jul 1857, BLC. Ostrom/Barklow farm: HBB to LS, 1, 9 May 1858, BLC; HBB to GWB, 29 Oct 1858, 30 Jun, 7 Jul 1860, 9 Jan, 23 Jul 1862, BSL.

16. HBB Rem., 161; LS to HBB, 4, 9 Aug, [9, misdated 10] Jun, 1864, BLC; LS to HBB, 4 Sep 1864, BLC, Wheeler, 199.

17. HBB to GWB, 18 Jul, 25 Aug, 11 Sep 1862, BSL; EzB to GWB, 10 Sep [1862], BSL; LS to HBB, 14 Jun, 4, 20 Sep 1864, BLC, Wheeler, 191–92, 198–99, 200–201; James M. McPherson, *Battle Cry of Freedom: The Civil War Era* (New York: Ballantine Books, 1988), 492, 600–3. Hiring a substitute exempted a man from subsequent drafts, so if Blackwell paid a substitute as he later said (HBB Rem., 175), it had to have been after the September 1864 call.

18. LS to HBB, 20 Sep 1864, BLC, Wheeler, 200–201; HBB to GWB, 16, 25 Oct 1864, BSL; LS to CCB, 12 Dec 1864, BLC.

19. LS to HBB, 4 Oct 1864, BLC, Wheeler, 202.

20. LS to HBB, 4 Oct [1864], BLC; LS to HBB, 9 Aug 1864, BLC, Wheeler, 198; LS to Hannah Blackwell, 23 Oct 1864, BLC, Wheeler, 203; HBB to GWB, 6, 7, 12, 19 Dec, [late Dec] 1864, BSL.

21. HBB Rem., 161; LS to HBB, 9 Aug 1864, BLC, Wheeler, 198. Soliciting funds for the *Woman's Journal* a few years later, Stone said she and Blackwell could live on their income and would "cheerfully give" their time and effort to the paper (LS to Francis J. Garrison, [ca. 1870], BLC).

22. HBB to LS, 1 May 1858, BLC, Wheeler, 181; LS to HBB, 31 Jul 1864, BLC, Wheeler, 197.

23. *New York Daily Times,* reprinted in, *Sibyl,* Mar 1864; LS speech, *Bugle,* 2 Dec 1854; *Sibyl,* Jun 1861; LS to HBB, 4 Dec 1864, BLC, Wheeler, 205–6.

24. *NASS,* 28 Jan 1865; *Liberator,* 16, 30 Jun, 14 Jul, 11, 18 Aug 1865; *NASS,* 30 Dec 1865.

25. Margaret Hope Bacon, *I Speak for My Slave Sister: The Life of Abby Kelley Foster* (New York: Crowell, 1974), 199; Ida Husted Harper, *The Life and Work of Susan B. Anthony* (Indianapolis: Hobbs, 1889), 1:256.

26. HBB to ECS, 21 Apr 1867, BLC; E. D. and Anna T. Draper to LS, 15 Nov. 1866, NAWSAR; Lillie B. C. and Arthur C. Wyman, *Elizabeth Buffum Chace, 1806–1899: Her Life and Environment* (Boston: W. B. Clarke, 1914), 1:288–9, 291–2; Broadside announcing Dec. 4, 1866, meeting to form New Jersey Equal Rights Association, BLC; "Cornelius Bowman Campbell," *Vineland Historical Magazine* [n.d.]: 247–8, copy in NAWSAR; *Newark Daily Journal,* 16, 19, 20, 21 Mar 1867; *HWS,* 2:284, 3:334; Unidentified newspaper clippings, BLC; *Woman Suffrage in New Jersey: An Address Delivered by Lucy Stone at a Hearing Before the New Jersey Legislature, March 6th, 1867* (Boston: C. H. Simonds, n.d.), pamphlet in BLC.

27. HBB Rem., 189–91; "Cornelius Bowman Campbell," *Vineland Historical Magazine;* Unidentified newspaper clippings, BLC; *HWS,* 2:310.

28. *Revolution,* 8 Jan, 4 Jun, 26 Nov 1868. The *Revolution* did not carry the petition for a Sixteenth Amendment until May 1869.

Selected Bibliography

Bacon, Margaret Hope. *I Speak for My Slave Sister: The Life of Abby Kelley Foster.* New York: Thomas Y. Crowell, 1974.

———. *Valiant Friend: The Life of Lucretia Mott.* New York: Walker, 1980.

Barnes, Gilbert H., and Dwight L. Dumond, eds. *Letters of Theodore Dwight Weld, Angelina Grimké Weld, and Sarah Grimké, 1822–1844.* 1934. Reprint, Gloucester, Mass.: Peter Smith, 1965.

Bartlett, J. Gardner. *Gregory Stone Genealogy: Ancestry and Descendants of Dea. Gregory Stone of Cambridge, Mass., 1320–1917.* Boston: Stone Family Association, 1918.

Basch, Norma. *In the Eyes of the Law: Women, Marriage, and Property in Nineteenth-Century New York.* Ithaca, N.Y.: Cornell University Press, 1982.

Beecher, Catharine E. *An Essay on Slavery and Abolitionism, with Reference to the Duty of American Females, Addressed to Miss A. E. Grimké.* Philadelphia, 1837.

Beecher, Jonathan, and Richard Bienvenu, eds. *The Utopian Vision of Charles Fourier: Selected Texts on Work, Love, and Passionate Attraction.* Boston: Beacon Press, 1971.

Berg, Barbara J. *The Remembered Gate: Origins of American Feminism.* New York: Oxford University Press, 1978.

Blackwell, Alice Stone. *Lucy Stone: Pioneer of Woman's Rights.* Boston: Little, Brown, 1930.

———. *What I Owe to My Father.* 1931. Reprint ed. Peter C. Engelman, Shelburne, Mass.: Bassett Printing, 1999.

Boas, Louise Schutz. *Woman's Education Begins: The Rise of the Women's Colleges.* Norton, Mass.: Wheaton College Press, 1935.

Bode, Carl. *The American Lyceum.* New York: Oxford [University Press], 1956.

Brigance, William Norwood, ed. *A History and Criticism of American Public Address.* New York: McGraw-Hill Book Co., 1943.

Cayleff, Susan E. *Wash and Be Healed: The Water-Cure Movement and Women's Health.* Philadelphia: Temple University Press, 1987.

Cazden, Elizabeth. *Antoinette Brown Blackwell: A Biography.* Old Westbury, N.Y.: The Feminist Press, 1983.

Cole, Arthur C. *A Hundred Years of Mount Holyoke College: The Evolution of an Educational Ideal.* New Haven: Yale University Press, 1940.

Cott, Nancy F. *The Bonds of Womanhood: "Woman's Sphere" in New England, 1780–1835.* New Haven: Yale University Press, 1977.

————, ed. *Root of Bitterness: Documents of the Social History of American Women.* New York: E. P. Dutton, 1972.

Cromwell, Otelia. *Lucretia Mott.* Cambridge: Harvard University Press, 1958.

Curti, Merle Eugene. *The American Peace Crusade, 1815–1860.* New York: Octagon Books, 1965.

Davis, Paulina Wright. *A History of the National Woman's Rights Movement for Twenty Years with the Proceedings of the Decade Meeting Held at Apollo Hall, October 20, 1870, From 1850 to 1870.* Reprint, New York: Source Book Press, 1970.

Dillon, Merton L. *The Abolitionists: The Growth of a Dissenting Minority.* DeKalb, Ill.: Northern Illinois University Press, 1974.

Eckhardt, Celia Morris. *Fanny Wright: Rebel in America.* Cambridge, Mass.: Harvard University Press, 1984.

Edelstein, Tilden G. *Strange Enthusiasm: A Life of Thomas Wentworth Higginson.* New Haven: Yale University Press, 1968.

Eminent Women of the Age: Being Narratives of the Lives and Deeds of the Most Prominent Women of the Present Generation. Hartford, Conn.: S. M. Betts, 1868.

Finch, Marianne. *An Englishwoman's Experience in America.* London: Richard Bentley, 1853.

Fletcher, Robert Samuel. *A History of Oberlin College.* Vol. 1. 1943. Reprint, New York: Arno Press, 1971.

Flexner, Eleanor. *Century of Struggle: The Woman's Rights Movement in the United States.* 1959. Reprint, New York: Atheneum, 1968.

Fogel, Robert William. *Without Consent or Contract: The Rise and Fall of American Slavery.* New York: W. W. Norton, 1989.

Foner, Philip S., ed. *Frederick Douglass on Women's Rights.* Westport, Conn.: Greenwood Press, 1976.

Gambone, James G., ed. "The Forgotten Feminist of Kansas: The Papers of Clarina I. H. Nichols, 1854–1884." *Kansas Historical Quarterly* 39, no. 1 (Spring 1973): 12–57; "Part Two, April 21, 1855–1856," 39, no. 2 (Summer 1973): 220–61; "Part Three, 1857–1863," 39, no. 3 (Autumn 1973): 392–444; "Part Four, 1867–1868," 39, no. 4 (Winter 1973): 515–63.

Garrison, Wendell P. and Francis J. *William Lloyd Garrison: The Story of His Life as Told by His Children, 1805–1879.* 4 vols. New York: The Century Co., 1885–89.

Ginzberg, Lori D. *Women and the Work of Benevolence: Morality, Politics, and Class in the Nineteenth-Century United States.* New Haven: Yale University Press, 1990.

Godwin, Parke. *A Popular View of the Doctrines of Charles Fourier.* 2nd ed. New York: J. S. Redfield, Clinton Hall, 1844.

Gordon, Ann D., ed. *The Selected Papers of Elizabeth Cady Stanton and Susan B. Anthony. Vol 1: In the School of Anti-Slavery, 1840–1866.* New Brunswick, N.J.: Rutgers University Press, 1997.

Green, Elizabeth Alden. *Mary Lyon and Mount Holyoke: Opening the Gates.* Hanover, N.H.: University Press of New England, 1979.

Griffith, Elizabeth. *In Her Own Right: The Life of Elizabeth Cady Stanton.* New York: Oxford University Press, 1984.

Grimké, Angelina. *Letters to Catherine E. Beecher, in Reply to an Essay on Slavery and Abolitionism, Addressed to A. E. Grimke.* Boston: Isaac Knapp, 1838.

Grimké, Sarah. *Letters on the Equality of the Sexes, and the Condition of Woman, Addressed to Mary S. Parker.* Boston: Isaac Knapp, 1838.

Guarneri, Carl J. *The Utopian Alternative: Fourierism in Nineteenth-Century America.* Ithaca, N.Y.: Cornell University Press, 1991.

Hale, William Harlan. *Horace Greeley: Voice of the People.* New York: Harper & Brothers, 1950.

Hallowell, Anna Davis, ed. *James and Lucretia Mott: Life and Letters.* Boston: Houghton, Mifflin and Co., 1884.

Hansen, Debra Gold. *Strained Sisterhood: Gender and Class in the Boston Female Anti-Slavery Society.* Amherst: University of Massachusetts Press, 1993.

Harper, Ida Husted. *The Life and Work of Susan B. Anthony.* Vols. 1–2. Indianapolis: Bobbs, 1889.

Hays, Elinor Rice. *Morning Star: A Biography of Lucy Stone, 1818–1893.* New York: Harcourt, Brace and World, 1961.

———. *Those Extraordinary Blackwells.* New York: Harcourt, Brace and World, 1967.

Hersh, Blanche Glassman. *The Slavery of Sex: Feminist Abolitionists in America.* Urbana: University of Illinois Press, 1978.

Higginson, Mary Thacher. *Thomas Wentworth Higginson: The Story of His Life.* Boston: Houghton Mifflin, 1914.

———, ed. *Letters and Journal of Thomas Wentworth Higginson.* Boston: Houghton Mifflin, 1921.

Higginson, Thomas Wentworth. *American Orators and Oratory.* Cleveland: Imperial Press, 1901.

———. *Contemporaries.* Boston: Houghton, Mifflin Co., 1899.

Hinsdale, B. A. *Horace Mann and the Common School Revival in the United States.* New York: Charles Scribner's Sons, 1911.

Hitchcock, Edward. *The Power of Christian Benevolence, Illustrated in the Life and Labors of Mary Lyon.* Northampton, Mass.: Hopkins, Bridgman, 1852.

Hoffert, Sylvia D. *When Hens Crow: The Woman's Rights Movement in Antebellum America.* Bloomington: Indiana University Press, 1995.

Hurlbut, Elisha P. *Essays on Human Rights.* New York, 1845.

Isenberg, Nancy. *Sex and Citizenship in Antebellum America.* Chapel Hill, N.C.: University of North Carolina Press, 1998.

Kerr, Andrea Moore. *Lucy Stone: Speaking Out for Equality.* New Brunswick, N.J.: Rutgers University Press, 1992.

Kobler, John. *Ardent Spirits: The Rise and Fall of Prohibition.* New York: G. P. Putnam's Sons, 1973.

Kraditor, Aileen. *Means and Ends in American Abolitionism: Garrison and His Critics on Strategy and Tactics, 1834–1850*. New York: Pantheon Books, 1969.

Lasser, Carol, and Marlene Merrill, eds. *Friends and Sisters: Letters between Lucy Stone and Antoinette Brown Blackwell, 1846–1893*. Urbana: University of Illinois Press, 1987.

Lerner, Gerda. *The Female Experience: An American Documentary*. Indianapolis: Bobbs-Merrill Educational Publishing, 1977.

———. *The Grimké Sisters of South Carolina: Pioneers for Woman's Rights*. New York: Schocken, 1967.

———. *The Majority Finds Its Past: Placing Women in History*. New York: Oxford University Press, 1979.

Lutz, Alma. *Crusade for Freedom: Women of the Antislavery Movement*. Boston: Beacon Press, 1968.

May, Samuel J. *The Rights and Condition of Women: A Sermon preached in Syracuse, November, 1845*. Boston, 1846.

Mayer, Henry. *All on Fire: William Lloyd Garrison and the Abolition of Slavery*. New York: St. Martin's Press, 1998.

McClymer, John F. *This High and Holy Moment: The First National Woman's Rights Convention, Worcester, 1850*. New York: Harcourt Brace, 1999.

McGuigan, Dorothy Gies. *A Dangerous Experiment: 100 Years of Women at the University of Michigan*. Ann Arbor: Center for Continuing Education of Women, 1970.

McKivigan, John R. *The War against Proslavery Religion: Abolitionism and the Northern Churches, 1830–1865*. Ithaca, N.Y.: Cornell University Press, 1984.

McPherson, James M. *Battle Cry of Freedom: The Civil War Era*. New York: Ballantine Books, 1988.

———. *The Struggle for Equality: Abolitionists and the Negro in the Civil War and Reconstruction*. Princeton: Princeton University Press, 1964.

Melder, Keith. *Beginnings of Sisterhood: The American Woman's Rights Movement, 1800–1850*. New York: Schocken Books, 1977.

Meltzer, Milton, and Patricia G. Holland, eds. *Lydia Maria Child: Selected Letters, 1817–1880*. Amherst: University of Massachusetts Press, 1982.

Merrill, Walter M. *Against Wind and Tide: A Biography of William Lloyd Garrison*. Cambridge: Harvard University Press, 1963.

———, ed. *The Letters of William Lloyd Garrison, 1841–49*. 5 vols. Cambridge: Belknap Press, 1973.

Meyer, Howard N. *Colonel of the Black Regiment: The Life of Thomas Wentworth Higginson*. New York: W. W. Norton, 1967.

———, ed. *The Magnificent Activist: The Writings of Thomas Wentworth Higginson, 1823–1911*. Cambridge, Mass.: DaCapo Press, 2000.

Myerson, Joel. "Mary Gove Nichols' *Mary Lyndon*: A Forgotten Reform Novel." *American Literature* 58, no. 4 (December 1986): 523–39.

Nissenbaum, Stephen. *Sex, Diet, and Debility in Jacksonian America: Sylvester Graham and Health Reform*. Westport, Conn.: Greenwood Press, 1980.

Noun, Louise R. "Amelia Bloomer, A Biography: Part I, The Lily of Seneca Falls." *Annals of Iowa* 47, no. 7 (Winter 1985): 575–617; "Part II, The Suffragist of Council Bluffs." 47, no. 8 (Spring 1985): 575–621.

————. *Strong-Minded Women: The Emergence of the Woman Suffrage Movement in Iowa.* Ames: Iowa State University Press, 1986.

O'Connor, Lillian. *Pioneer Woman Orators.* New York: Columbia, 1954.

Oliver, Robert T. *History of Public Speaking in America.* Boston: Allyn & Bacon, 1965.

Pillsbury, Parker. *The Acts of the Anti-Slavery Apostles.* Concord, N.H., 1883.

Porter, Lorle Anne. "Amelia Bloomer: An Early Iowa Feminist's Sojourn on the Way West." *Annals of Iowa* 41, no. 8 (Spring 1973): 1242–57.

Quarles, Benjamin. *Black Abolitionists.* New York: Oxford University Press, 1969.

Rabkin, Peggy A. *Fathers to Daughters: The Legal Foundations of Female Emancipation.* Westport, Conn.: Greenwood Press, 1980.

Rawley, James A. *Race and Politics: "Bleeding Kansas" and the Coming of the Civil War.* New York: J. B. Lippencott, 1969.

Robinson, Harriet H. *Massachusetts in the Woman Suffrage Movement: A General Political, Legal and Legislative History from 1774 to 1881.* 2nd ed. Boston: Roberts Brothers, 1883.

Sahli, Nancy Ann. *Elizabeth Blackwell, M.D., 1821–1910: A Biography.* New York: Arno Press, 1982.

Scholten, Pat Creech. "A Public 'Jollification': The 1859 Women's Rights Petition Before the Indiana Legislature." *Indiana Magazine of History* 72, no. 4 (1976): 347–59.

Sears, Hal D. *The Sex Radicals: Free Love in High Victorian America.* Lawrence: The Regents Press of Kansas, 1977.

Sherwin, Oscar. *Prophet of Liberty: The Life and Times of Wendell Phillips.* New York: Bookman Associates, 1958.

Shiels, Richard D. "The Feminization of American Congregationalism, 1730–1835." *American Quarterly* 33, no.1 (June 1981): 46–62.

Smith, Chard Powers. *Yankees and God.* New York: Hermitage House, 1954.

Smith, Timothy L. *Revivalism and Social Reform: American Protestantism on the Eve of the Civil War.* New York: Harper & Row, 1957.

Smith-Rosenberg, Carroll. *Religion and the Rise of the American City: The New York City Mission Movement, 1812–1870.* Ithaca, N.Y.: Cornell University Press, 1971.

————. *Disorderly Conduct: Visions of Gender in Victorian America.* New York: Alfred A. Knopf, 1985.

Stanton, Elizabeth Cady. *Eighty Years and More: Reminiscences 1815–1897.* 1898. Reprint, New York: Schocken Books, 1971.

Stanton, Elizabeth Cady, Susan B. Anthony, and Matilda Joslyn Gage. *History of Woman Suffrage.* Vol. 1, New York: Fowler & Wells, 1881; Vol. 2, Rochester: Susan B. Anthony, 1881.

Stanton, Theodore, and Harriot Stanton Blatch, eds. *Elizabeth Cady Stanton as Revealed in Her Letters, Diary, and Reminiscences.* 2 vols. New York: Harper, 1922.

Sterling, Dorothy. *Ahead of Her Time: Abby Kelley and the Politics of Antislavery.* New York: W. W. Norton, 1991.

————. *We Are Your Sisters: Black Women in the Nineteenth Century.* New York: W. W. Norton, 1984.

————, ed. *Turning the World Upside Down: The Anti-Slavery Convention of American Women Held in New York City, May 9–12, 1837.* Reprint, New York: The Feminist Press, 1987.

[Stone, Lucy, and Thomas Wentworth Higginson, eds.]. *The Woman's Rights Almanac for 1858*. Worcester. Mass.: Z. Baker, [1858].

Suhl, Yuri. *Ernestine L. Rose and the Battle for Human Rights*. New York: Reynal, 1959.

Sweet, William Warren. *Religion in the Development of American Culture, 1765–1840*. New York: Charles Scribner's Sons, 1952.

Tolles, Frederick B., ed. *Slavery and the Woman Question: Lucretia Mott's Diary of Her Visit to Great Britain to Attend the World's Anti-Slavery Convention of 1840*. Haverford, Penn.: Friends' Historical Association, 1952.

Tyrrell, Ian R. "Women and Temperance in Antebellum America, 1830–1860." *Civil War History* 28, no. 2 (June 1982): 28–52.

Van Broekhoven, Deborah Bingham. "'A Determination to Labor . . . ': Female Anti-slavery Activity in Rhode Island." *Rhode Island History* 44, no. 2 (May 1985): 35–46.

VanDeusen, Glendon G. *Horace Greeley: Nineteenth-Century Crusader*. Philadelphia: University of Pennsylvania Press, 1953.

Walters, Ronald G. *American Reformers, 1815–1860*. New York: Hill & Wang, 1978.

Weiss, Harry B., and Howard R. Kemble. *The Great American Water-Cure Craze: A History of Hydropathy in the United States*. Trenton, N.J.: Past Times Press, 1967.

Wells, Anna Mary. *Dear Preceptor: The Life and Times of Thomas Wentworth Higginson*. Boston: Houghton Mifflin Co., 1963.

Wheeler, Leslie. *Loving Warriors: Selected Letters of Lucy Stone and Henry B. Blackwell, 1853–1893*. New York: Dial Press, 1981.

———. "Lucy Stone, Wife of Henry Blackwell." *American History Illustrated* 16, no. 8 (December 1981): 38–45.

Woloch, Nancy. *Women and the American Experience*. New York: Alfred A. Knopf, 1984.

Wright, Henry C. *Marriage and Parentage; Or, The Reproductive Element in Man, as a Means to His Elevation and Happiness*. 2nd ed. Boston: Bela Marsh, 1855. Reprinted as *Sex, Marriage and Society*, ed. Charles Rosenberg and Carroll Smith-Rosenberg, New York: Arno Press, 1974.

Yellin, Jean Fagan. *Women and Sisters: The Antislavery Feminists in American Culture*. New Haven: Yale University Press, 1989.

Yellin, Jean Fagan, and John C. Van Horne, eds. *The Abolitionist Sisterhood: Women's Political Culture in Antebellum America*. Ithaca, N.Y.: Cornell University Press, 1994.

Youmans, Theodora W. "How Wisconsin Women Won the Ballot," *Wisconsin Magazine of History* 5 (1921–22): 3–32.

Index

abolition movement. *See* antislavery movement

abolitionists: and Bloomer dress, 115; support woman's rights, 27, 29, 33, 35, 47; violence experienced by, 24, 94, 95–96, 97; women, 25, 26, 28–31, 37, 40–41, 46, 50–51 (*see also under individual names*). *See also* clerical abolitionists; political abolitionists

Adams, John Quincy, 27, 159

Adams, Mary Ann, 61

Advocate of Moral Reform, 57, 61

Albany Female College (New Albany, Ind.), 161

Albany, N.Y.: antislavery meetings at, 45, 234; LS speaks at, 154; temperance meetings at, 132, 133, 140, 141; woman's rights meetings at, 167–68, 263

Albro, H. Attilia, 132, 133

American and Foreign Anti-Slavery Society, 45, 48, 55

American Anti-Slavery Society: agents, 29, 30, 34, 36, 40, 50, 223; banned from New York City, 112; debates woman's rights, 40, 45; founding, 24, 48; Frederick Douglass and, 166–67; LS at conventions of, 1, 100, 104, 129, 136, 140, 202, 221, 231, 268; LS on, 55; schism in, 45, 55, 166–67; sends women to London convention, 47;

thirtieth anniversary, 268; women join, 37, 48

American Colonization Society, 22, 23, 95

American Equal Rights Association, 274, 275

American Female Guardian Society, 112, 250

American Party, 185, 246

American Woman Suffrage Association, 275

Andover Theological Seminary, 7, 43

Andrews, Stephen Pearl: club of, 210; free love theories, 207, 251, 303n. 8; LS, calls on, 207–8; at NWRC, 251

Anneke, Mathilde Francesca, 150

Anthony, Susan B.: abolitionists, seeks merger with, 274; addresses New York legislature, 168; as antislavery agent, 228, 233, 234–35, 244, 249; and Bloomer dress, 132, 168–69; and Central Committee, 252, 274; converted by LS, 132, 296n. 9; criticizes LS, 238, 251, 254; divorce and marriage as woman's rights issue, views on, 236, 237, 265; and educated suffrage, 275; and equal rights in temperance society, 140, 144–45; and Jackson fund, 258, 262; and loyal league, 268, 270; on LS, 1, 135; LS encourages woman's rights work, 146,

About the Author

JOELLE MILLION is an independent scholar and historian. She has taught history at Minnesota State University at Mankato.